Corporate Responsibility and Legitimacy

Recent Titles in
Contributions in Philosophy

CORPORATE RESPONSIBILITY AND LEGITIMACY

An Interdisciplinary Analysis

JAMES J. BRUMMER

Contributions in Philosophy, Number 47

GREENWOOD PRESS
New York • Westport, Connecticut • London

Library of Congress Cataloging-in-Publication Data

Brummer, James J.
   Corporate responsibility and legitimacy : an interdisciplinary
analysis / James J. Brummer.
      p.   cm. — (Contributions in philosophy, ISSN 0084–926X ; no.
47)
   Includes bibliographical references and index.
   ISBN 0–313–24726–9 (alk. paper)
   1. Industry—Social aspects. I. Title. II. Series.
HD60.B78   1991
302.3′5—dc20   90–25223

British Library Cataloguing in Publication Data is available.

Library of Congress Catalog Card Number: 90–25223
ISBN: 0–313–24726–9
ISSN: 0084–926X

First published in 1991

Greenwood Press, 88 Post Road West, Westport, CT 06881
An imprint of Greenwood Publishing Group, Inc.

Printed in the United States of America

The paper used in this book complies with the
Permanent Paper Standard issued by the National
Information Standards Organization (Z39.48–1984).

10 9 8 7 6 5 4 3 2 1

CONTENTS

PREFACE

In the present work I propose to analyze a topic around which there has been much controversy, unclarity, and complexity. It is a topic that has a direct bearing upon the question of the effectiveness and legitimacy of our corporate institutions. The controversy, whether carried on in journals or in clubs, has been going on now for several decades without resolution. In fact, it seems to have followed a noticeably cyclical pattern. This can be seen in the works written in the last two decades as well as in surveys of public opinion taken in the United States during this time. Thus, for example, when the question of the effectiveness of corporations in meeting their responsibilities has been raised (however this might be specifically worded in a particular essay or survey), both scholars and the public, when looked upon in general, have shown a vacillating or ambivalent set of attitudes. At times they have expressed considerable respect toward corporations and their leaders; at other times they have shown deep disappointment and criticism. Of course, these periods of pro- and anti-corporate attitudes are not always crystal clear in their demarcations. There are periods in this time frame for which overlaps occur, just as there are certain periods when the attitudes expressed in the journals differ from those expressed by the public at that time. But a general pattern does nevertheless seem to exist.

Thus, for example, a higher level of confidence was exhibited in and by the private sector during the 1980s than was observable in the previous decade. This pattern began to emerge somewhere around 1984. There are exceptions to this, of course. Business scandals broke out in this period, especially in the later years of the Reagan administration. And some very critical works were written in this time period. But the overall attitude was generally upbeat, especially with regard to corporations meeting their economic responsibilities. Noting the resurgence of the private sector in many of the industrial nations, particularly in the United

States and Great Britain, a growing number of works in management theory in the middle and late 1980s praised the skills, decision making, and even the values of executives. By this time the more negative and reform-minded works written in the later 1970s and early 1980s were largely things of the past.

The change in attitude that occurred during this period was rather abrupt, though, for even as late as 1983, the public was expressing largely negative attitudes toward corporations and the handling of their responsibilities. But it seems that we were nearing the end of the critical cycle at this time. A survey of the American public conducted in that year revealed that 49 percent of those polled believed that ethical standards in business had declined in the previous decade, while only 9 percent thought they had risen (*Wall Street Journal*, October 31, 1983, p. 1). Polls conducted in the 1970s point in the same direction. For example, in a Harris Poll conducted in 1976, only 16 percent of those interviewed expressed confidence in the individuals running major American corporations. A decade and cycle earlier, however, figures from a similar poll revealed that 55 percent of those questioned expressed such confidence (*U.S. News and World Report*, September 6, 1982, p. 29). In a related study, Harris found that 82 percent of those polled believed that, if left to itself, business would make profits at the expense of the public. And, finally, Yankelovich reported in 1976 that most people felt while they had worked hard and lived by the rules, those with political or economic power had not done the same and were flourishing at the expense of the law abiders.

In contrast to the ideas and attitudes expressed in the seventies and early eighties, more recent works on corporate responsibility have typically been less negative in their general view of corporations. When they do criticize, they characteristically restrict their attention to specific areas of corporate responsibility such as advertising, the environment, or product safety. They are usually careful to point out that behind their critical remarks there lies few, if any, of the more activist assumptions of the seventies—assumptions that led many theorists of that decade to call for more radical corporate internal reforms and to demand more expanded vigilant and effective government regulation.

Behind these changing attitudes, then, there lie very different theories or views of the nature of corporate responsibility and of the effectiveness of management in meeting these responsibilities. Each of these views sees itself, of course, as the correct one. But how can we tell?

This is not an easy question to answer for we have first to isolate the appropriate theories before we can judge them. And even after having done this, we shall see that the strength of one position on corporate responsibility has typically been checked or counterbalanced by the strength of opposing views. Thus far, no one theory has won the day. Of course, the arguments have become more refined and the positions somewhat more diverse (in fact, a new position has been added), but the basic balance of power or authority among these positions has not been significantly altered.

There is, however, less hint of a cyclical quality to the public's attitude toward government agencies and public officials in the last two or three decades. With the exception of the persistent popularity of former President Reagan throughout his administration, polls have otherwise shown that many Americans typically do not give high marks to elected officials or government agencies. They do not display great confidence in the public sector or in its ability to regulate the private sector.

We are faced then with something of a dilemma. No clear direction in the theoretical, scholarly, or everyday discussions of corporate responsibility has emerged at a time when one of the traditional mechanisms used to correct the real or alleged abuses in the private sector is itself increasingly looked upon with considerable suspicion. This situation demands that one examine with new vigor the discussions of corporate responsibility and organizational self-regulation to understand better the precise nature of the dispute. Even if such a review should prove useless in isolating a dominant position, it can at a minimum help to explain why no such dominating view has yet emerged. It is my belief that one reason why the process of vindication of a single theory has thus far been stalled is that some of the important underlying concepts and assumptions grounding the various theories of corporate responsibility have not been fully or systematically explored. The present volume is devoted to partially addressing this problem—at least as regards the question of the nature of corporate responsibility. The questions of corporate effectiveness in this area and the appropriateness of the public attitudes expressed toward corporations will not be specifically discussed in this work, though their answers clearly depend upon the nature and truth of the theories discussed here.

As we shall see, certain assumptions involved in this debate continually accompany certain substantive views of corporate responsibility. There are some exceptions to this rule, of course—exceptions that will be noted later in the book—but this fact does not alter the basic picture to be presented here. It will be further seen that these assumptions escort their associates rather like chaperons who are introduced or appealed to when the virtue of the substantive view is itself in need of defense. This naturally suggests the appropriateness of a more normative direction for future discussions of this topic, but for now clarifying the substantive issues and theories requires that we clarify the basic concepts and relevant presuppositions upon which the former are said to be based.

One point made in this work is that the inconclusiveness of the debate about corporate responsibility has itself become one of the leading issues in this discussion (and, in fact, in the discussion of corporate legitimacy as well). The uncertainty on this topic has affected the context of these disputes and has influenced the nature of some of the recent arguments raised about these issues. This uncertainty indicates that new methods of inquiry and argument may be necessary, a conclusion developed in the final chapter.

It should also be noted that the research behind this work is taken from a variety of disciplines: management theory, philosophy, organizational theory, administrative science, economics, psychology, and several other related fields.

At a time when there is concern about the precise role and relevance of the humanities to other somewhat more specialized academic disciplines, the present work is proposed as an example of how the humanities might be found useful in helping to comprehend the important public problems of the day. Its specific topic is the responsibility and legitimacy of corporations, but much of what is said here can also apply, with appropriate adjustment, to other types of social institutions, including government.

In reviewing the arguments and assumptions involved in the present debate, I have shied away from endorsing specific theories found in the various disciplines included. Thus, for example, I believe that two of the most prominent theories in recent management thinking—the strategic management and the corporate culture theories—are relatively neutral toward the four positions on corporate responsibility considered in this volume. Important versions of these theories have been developed by thinkers who support one or other of the four positions, of course, but the theories themselves do not entail only one of these views.

A word of clarification is in order with respect to chapters 5 and 6. In these chapters I seek to unearth assumptions that concern the nature of the corporation as a social institution, which involves a discussion of eight paradigms, models, or metaphors of the corporation. The metaphor approach is somewhat common in the philosophical work in this area. Illustrations of this approach can be found in the works of Thomas Donaldson and Patricia Werhane, among others, but no one had yet discussed or developed eight such models. Quite independently, however, Gareth Morgan has recently advanced eight models of organizations in general, and there is clear overlap between some of his models and those discussed here. Where this occurs, I have sought to integrate some of his insights into my discussion. What Morgan's and this work point out is that numerous metaphors may be suggested for the corporation. I have settled upon eight models in large part both because these eight seem to pinpoint the most important features of corporations and developing more paradigms would make the present analysis more cumbersome and unwieldy for me to execute, and it would likely be more tedious for the reader to follow. I have, however, sought to advance a broad picture of these models so that the present treatment would not be judged to be too narrow or stingy in its vision of the corporation.

Finally, it should be noted that the present work is meant to be multi-level and multi-dimensional in its approach to the topic. There are five layers or levels of issues considered in the book; thus there are five objectives to be reached. At the first level, the book can be considered a reference work. It is meant to inform the reader about much of the literature on corporate or organizational responsibility. At the second level, it can be viewed as a work of analysis in which I attempt to unearth and isolate some of the key assumptions in the present debate. At the third level a substantive theory of institutional responsibility and its relation to legitimacy is suggested or proposed. At this level, the question of the feasibility of viewing the concept of responsibility as a (or the) key notion in ethics and social theory is addressed. At the fourth level, it can be seen as a methodological work that is meant to propose a (partial) method of inquiry or justification in the area of collective or applied ethics. Finally, it can be seen as an extended illustration of the use of traditional logic to help comprehend the controversial issues of the day. The reader will note that we first examine general concepts and principles; next we consider the major premises and their supporting evidence, and then, in later chapters we consider certain issues of application that require that we focus our attention upon features found in the minor premises of arguments on this topic. By approaching the topic in this manner, I wish to explore the logic of the concepts and arguments involved.

ACKNOWLEDGMENTS

I am indebted to certain individuals and institutions for their role in bringing this work to fruition. I would like to thank Mary Sive, Cynthia Harris, and Mark Kane at the Greenwood Publishing Group—Mary for first contacting me about writing a book on this topic, and Cynthia and Mark for their editorial work after this initial contact. I owe thanks to my colleagues in the Philosophy and Religious Studies Department; to Ronald Koshoshek for his helpful suggestions early in the work and particularly to Bruce Jannusch who was department chair at the time of my initial research—it was Bruce who helped find the funds that were invaluable in these early stages. I would like to thank the University of Wisconsin Office of Graduate Studies and Research and its dean, Ronald Satz, for authorizing a grant that partially paid for typing this work. I should mention as well three students who helped locate books and articles for me in the library—William Budzinski, Corey Keyes and Jennifer DeBower. I would like to thank my former student Michael Tvaruska for his helpful editorial work, and both Michael and Jennifer for helping to compile the index. I should like to thank Joyce Hageness for her patient work in typing the manuscript throughout its many revisions, the two anonymous reviewers who offered several helpful suggestions for the initial draft of this work, and the copy editor Jeanne Lesinski who helped save the work from many clumsy expressions. I would like to thank Professor Donald Cushman for giving me as a young college student the confidence to believe that I could make an intellectual contribution, and Dr. Phillip Griffin for the support and guidance he gave to me as an undergraduate student. Finally, I want to thank my former wife, Diana Theos, and my stepdaughter, Heather Wickstrom, for the role they played in helping this work become a reality. It is to them that I dedicate this book.

PART I

THE ASSUMPTIONS OF CORPORATE RESPONSIBILITY

1

THE CORPORATE RESPONSIBILITY DEBATE

INTRODUCTION

Unlike persons, social institutions must be legitimated. Because they are human inventions or creations, and thus in some general sense the products of human choice, they cannot completely escape the instrumentalist context of their birth. As can be seen from the events in Eastern Europe, social institutions can be challenged from time to time to prove themselves. Various critics have put them on the defensive, either singly or as a group. Their advocates have sought to fend off these questions or attacks in various ways. One approach, the one that we shall follow in this work, is to argue that their legitimacy is based upon their meeting the responsibilities assigned to them. Institutions that do so, most of the time at least, are typically viewed as legitimate. Those that do not are usually questioned, criticized, weakened, rejected, or abolished. We can see then the importance of determining what responsibilities institutions or their members have. In fact, it is no exaggeration to say that this has become one of the most urgent, if not most controversial, issues of our time. We have been pressed to ask this question of many types of institutions: governments, when they come into power by fraud, deceit, or intimidation, or continue in power by force alone; unions, when they are viewed as corrupt or when they are perceived to be failing to represent adequately the interests of most of their members; professional groups, when they seem to work harder to protect their own members than they do to serve the public; churches or ministries, when they are riddled with charges of greed, fraud, or vice. And so it is with other institutions as well.

Naturally one type of institution that has not escaped the notice of social observers, whether critical or supportive, is the business corporation. When they have focused their attention upon this type of organization, such observers have typically asked four general questions about the nature of its institutional responsibility: (1) Do corporations themselves have responsibilities, or do only some or all of their members have such responsibilities? (2) To whom are corporations or their members responsible in their conduct? (3) What determinate responsibilities do they have? (4) Why do they have these responsibilities?

Addressing these and other questions are four broad theories of corporate responsibility. This book is about these theories and the way in which they confront the four questions just mentioned. It is about their source, meaning and application to certain concrete decision-making situations. And it also deals with the conflicts and controversies that attend these views. This last topic is necessary because no one of these positions has yet emerged as the clearly superior theory. Thus, the debate between them continues.

What we shall see is that the most pointed area of disagreement among these theories actually occurs at a level of argument typically not reached in the more concrete discussions of corporate responsibility found in the literature. The correct definition of key terms accounts for some of the conflict of opinion, but more important are the disputes that concern the most appropriate assumptions upon which to ground these various theories. Four areas of controversy at the assumptional level stand out and will be examined in separate chapters later in the book. There are differences of opinion over the precise nature of the accountability relations that apply to corporations, disputes over the nature of the corporation itself, disagreements over the appropriate method of justification by which one shows that corporations or their actions are legitimate, and, finally, there is controversy over the proper relation of collective to individual responsibility. The focus of this work is thus upon isolating these assumptions, showing their application to the four theories, and indicating the role they have played in extending the duration and complexity of this debate.

It should be mentioned that my purpose in writing this book is not to arbitrate between the four theories or their supporting arguments. The question of the truth or compellingness of a position is bracketed, so to speak, or put on hold. I shall not try to pick a winning theory. The intricacy of these positions and the assumptions that support them precludes my trying to assess their validity at this juncture. What I can do here, however, is to show the complexity of the issues and indicate some of the implications of this complexity for the method of argument and analysis used in the corporate responsibility debate. The method of analysis used here will be clear to those familiar with the Anglo-American analytic tradition.

The fact that the four theories are discussed in a certain order should not be taken as an indication of my favoring one theory over another. Nor should the fact that there are fewer objections mentioned to the final theory discussed than to the first one examined be interpreted to mean that I think this last theory the strongest of the four positions. Fewer objections are considered to it simply because it is the last one examined. By the time we discuss it, the reader will quite easily be able to discern how the other theorists would object to this view, given their commitments and assumptions. In any case, by not arguing for a specific theory, I can more effectively keep the focus of the investigation upon the positions themselves and their supporting assumptions rather than upon what I think or believe about a specific view.

Finally, I should say something about the definition of key terms. There are extended discussions of three key concepts in the corporate responsibility debate. These are the terms or phrases *corporation responsibility*, *social responsibility*, and *whistleblowing*. I also have briefer discussions of the definitions of several other concepts. Part of the reason for these extended discussions lies in the significance of the concepts to be defined; part also lies in the extent of the controversy that attends their proper definition. A third reason is the direct relation that often exists between a theorist's definition of these concepts and his or her views on the four theories. As I examine the various definitions that have been offered for some of these concepts, I shall try to suggest a meaning that is broad enough to include as many of the proposed uses as I can consistently include. For those that I exclude, I will usually indicate briefly why this has been done.

I end the book with some methodological suggestions. If the view that emerges in this work is well founded conceptually and inferentially, it suggests a method of organizing and assessing arguments in this area, which I briefly develop in the last chapter.

THE FOUR THEORIES

Before beginning our investigation of the concepts and assumptions that play an important role in the corporate responsibility debate, we should first briefly outline the four theories themselves. This will help the reader both to follow and to anticipate the examination of concepts and presuppositions that will begin in the next chapter. The four positions are the classical, stakeholder, social demandingness, and social activist theories.

The classical theory is the oldest of the positions, owing its existence to classical economic theory. This theory has two versions. In the first, business executives are said to be solely or primarily responsible to the shareholders of the corporation to promote efficiency and secure effective economic performance. They are responsible to protect and augment the stockholder's investment in the firm. In the second, managers are said to be responsible to respond to the shareholders' wants and demands. These versions are often viewed as coinciding with each other because it is usually assumed that the main demand of the shareholders is for effective economic performance. But there are occasions when conflict is possible. If the majority of shareholders vote to pursue a corporate policy that it thinks is sound or right, even though it may jeopardize the firm's investment-enhancing capacity, this version urges that executive officers should follow the course of conduct endorsed by the majority. Both versions agree, however, that managers are to perform their corporate function according to the laws of the land. They are thus to avoid such things as fraud and deceit.

Beyond this, corporate managers are usually said to have no distinct or additional responsibilities.

Like the classical theory, the stakeholder theory grants that corporate executives are responsible to shareholders. But it also insists that there are other groups of individuals who are directly affected by the conduct of the firm. Because workers, consumers, creditors, suppliers, professional organizations, and the like are constituents who have a stake in corporate decision making, it is said that corporate executives have a direct responsibility to promote the interests of these groups in the areas of decision making that affect them. There is disagreement among stakeholder theorists over whether the stakeholder interests of these groups take precedence over the financial interests of stockholders, just as there is disagreement over which of the stakeholder interests are the overriding ones. But all stakeholder theorists agree that respect for such interests must be included in any list of the responsibilities that corporations or their executives are said to have.

Unlike the first version of the classical theory, which assumes that the financial interests of stockholders for higher dividends and stock values is relatively inelastic, the stakeholder theory maintains that the interests and expectations of various stakeholder groups may vary over time. Thus, no list of the specific responsibilities of corporate executives will be stable or complete; it must change to meet these new expectations.

Some stakeholder theorists broaden the concept of stakeholder so that it includes the general public. For such theorists, there is no essential difference between the stakeholder theory and the third position that we shall discuss in this work. But since not all theorists agree with this broader definition, there is need to discuss a related, yet distinct, view that I shall call the social demandingness theory. The social demandingness theory argues that corporations have a responsibility to protect and promote certain interests of the general public. They agree with stakeholder theorists that the interests of stakeholder groups are important, but they believe that these interests do not always override nonstakeholders' interests or demands for such things as safety, health, freedom, and prosperity. As with the stakeholder theory, this theory rejects the idea that there is some stable or permanent list of concrete responsibilities that corporate executives always have toward the public. The list varies as the nature and ranking of the interests or demands of the public change.

Finally, we have the social activist model, which is typically the most socially or morally demanding of the four theories to be discussed. While agreeing with the stakeholder and social demandingness theories that executives have responsibilities toward stakeholder groups and the general public, social activist theorists contend that corporate managers should sometimes pursue projects that promote the interests of the public even when these projects are neither expected nor demanded by them. Social activist theorists maintain that such projects should for the most part be in an area of corporate expertise, but they sometimes urge that executives voluntarily take on social projects for which they have no special training or expertise. It is also expected by such theorists that these projects will often have no direct relation to the firm's ability to maximize profit. In fact, they may compromise or impair the firm's economic performance. But since the justification of these projects is not primarily an economic one, social activists defend their implementation nevertheless and argue that they can at times supercede the fulfillment or discharge of the corporation's other responsibilities. In arguing in this way, they typically base their position upon notions that they interpret to have universal or objective authority. Such notions as "the basic rights of third parties," "the intrinsic value of an experience or activity," or "the duty to prevent or minimize harm" are used by them to refer to some of the ultimate normative concepts employed in arguments to defend their position. Because they do not base their theory upon what society currently demands from corporations, the list of responsibilities for specific corporations is said to be rather stable. Additions and subtractions occur only if the factual context of corporate decision making notably changes.

These then are the four theories. To better understand the differences between them, we must turn our attention to an examination of the main concepts and assumptions involved in these positions.

2

THE CORPORATION AND RESPONSIBILITY

INTRODUCTION

Some of the key terms employed in the corporate responsibility debate have given rise to considerable controversy, while others have posed no great definitional problem. In this chapter we shall discuss the meaning of two terms—one from each category—beginning with *corporation*.

Initially, the term *corporation* may seem to be lacking a generally agreed upon definition. It is as equally applicable to hospitals and some government agencies as it is to profit-making organizations found in the private sector. Some of this ambiguity can be removed (somewhat artificially by me) by simply indicating that this book concerns only the latter kind of corporation. My use of the term in this work is thus meant to exclude public or governmental corporations as well as nonprofit-making, nongovernmental associations or corporations. Much of what will be said in the coming chapters may refer to these other types of corporation, as well as to the other kinds of business enterprise, but we shall not stop to consider such applications. Much of the remaining ambiguity can be removed by narrowing the definition to that found in our legal tradition for this is the discipline that thus far has provided us the broadest and most firm consensus on the definition of this concept. Most accounts agree that corporations differ from the other two forms of business enterprise in primarily three respects. The discussions of Donaldson and Stone are somewhat typical of this literature, but it can be found in almost any introductory business law or corporate management text (Donaldson, 1982, p. 2; Stone, 1975, pp. 24, 28).

THE LEGAL CONCEPT OF BUSINESS CORPORATIONS

First, corporations are business units that have entity status under the law. They are treated as entities that are distinct from the single members who make them up. This means that for legal purposes corporations have jural standing in their own names. They are not identified with the class of persons who constitute their owners or shareholders. This makes business transactions more simple and convenient for them since they need not put the name of every shareholder on the contracts or other legal documents of which they make use in the course of doing business. It also means that they are involved in collective ownership, thus they cannot characteristically be broken up and distributed to individual shareholders. Shareholders cannot trade in their shares for bits of the company— some of its land, perhaps, or its physical equipment, at least not while the corporation is a solvent and going concern. Stock ownership does not then automatically translate into a distributed or atomistic ownership of the company's physical or social assets. In extreme cases, however, something like this form of disbursement does actually occur. Of course, a firm can go bankrupt and have its assets liquidated, though in such a case the shareholders are typically the last to be paid. But it is also doubtful whether at this stage the firm has much of anything left that could be called, or be called upon to sustain, a collective nature. And certainly, an entire company can be bought out, though it is doubtful that it ever sheds its collective nature in the manner of the types of transaction just pictured.

In the American legal tradition corporations are more than mere entities, however. They have the status of legal persons and have consequently many of the same legal rights, privileges, and obligations that humans do. Thus, they have such legal rights as the right to free association, to hold property, and to receive due process from government. They also have rights against self-incrimination and unreasonable searches and seizures. They have such privileges as the privilege of expanding their business manifold in a single year or of securing a prized contract over their competitors. And finally, they have such legal obligations as the duty to pay taxes, to comply with the courts when summoned or subpoenaed, and to carry out the sentences, decisions, or judgments rendered by the courts or other administrative agencies of government.

The possession of entity status leads us to a second characteristic of corporations in our legal tradition—virtual perpetual duration. Once in existence, the corporation has a life of its own. It will continue to exist despite what happens to its initial owners, managers, or employees. As just said, in the extreme case it can go bankrupt or have its assets liquidated. It can also be acquired by another business enterprise and lose its autonomous status. But its existence is not in general dependent upon the existence of the specific members who make it up. In fact, even the state cannot revoke a corporate charter once it is duly recognized and registered as punishment for corporate malfeasance or nonfeasance (*Trustees of Dartmouth v. Woodward*, 17 U.S. (4 Wheat.) 518 (1819)).

Last, corporations have limited liability for both debts and torts. When sued or going bankrupt, the shareholders of the corporation are liable for payment only to the extent of their personal financial investment in the firm. The other two forms of business enterprise, partnerships and sole proprietorships, on the other hand, usually involve owners in full liability for debts and torts. In non-limited partnerships, for example, any partner may be held liable for the total amount of the unsatisfied partnership's debts. Berle and Means have suggested that the limited liability feature of corporations may be viewed as a result of an implied contract between a firm and its creditors whereby the latter agree to limit their right of recovery to funds possessed by the corporation should it fail to pay its debts (Berle and Means, 1968, p. 120). Thus, the difference between corporations and certain partnerships is simply a matter of degree. But however closely associated corporations are with partnerships, it should be noted that this property, whatever its legal grounding, automatically applies to corporations when they are formed.

For tort liability, only those who play an active role in managing the corporation are additionally liable for damages when sued. Inactive members or shareholders have only limited liability. Subordinate workers or shareholders of the firm may be penalized in the form of lower wages, dividends, or stock values when the corporation is ordered to pay damages, but they are not required to pay these from their personal or noninvested assets.

These three features suggest certain unique problems of responsibility that arise for corporations that do not, or at least not in the same way, apply to the other forms of business enterprise. The feature of entity status has led to the question of whether corporations are mere creatures of the state. If so, it is alleged that they have a set of special obligations directly aimed at the welfare of the public whose permission has, in effect, brought them into existence. Holders of an opposing view suggest that the state merely recognizes their prior and separate existence and duly records this when registering the corporate charter. It is then alleged that corporations have no special obligations to the state beyond what is expected of any legally autonomous citizen. In fact, the multinational character of many corporations is claimed to further temper their legal duty to be loyal members of any single nation-state.

The feature of virtual perpetual existence has led some theorists to wonder if firms have a sufficiently strong motive to act in a socially or morally acceptable way. Serber, for example, has suggested that since corporations are virtually immune from capital punishment, they or their members are likely to have a somewhat muted incentive to fulfill a broad array of their corporate legal, social, or moral obligations (Serber, 1983, p. 84).

The feature of limited liability has reinforced this concern and has raised the question of the incentive of corporate subordinates and stockholders to take on greater responsibility for the decisions of top executives. In addition, the separation of ownership and management control that applies to most modern corporations raises the question of the ultimate responsibilities and loyalties of top management. Is their highest priority to act as competent fiduciaries for the shareholders and protect and augment the latter's investment in the firm, or do they have certain nonfinancial responsibilities that at times supercede their role as effective agents of the stockholders? These are some of the issues that we shall discuss in the coming chapters.

THE CONCEPT OF RESPONSIBILITY

We have purposely simplified our definition of the term *corporation*, but we cannot do this for the term *responsibility*. As with so many abstract terms, it is more frequently used than understood. When we examine its various uses closely, we seem to find it difficult to determine a common theme or idea behind it. Worse yet, some of its uses seem to be inconsistent. Still we must come up with some workable definition of the term if we are to determine when a corporation is said to have a responsibility.

Downie believes that the concept of responsibility has several distinct meanings (Downie, 1964, p. 29). It is used first in a descriptive sense to mean simple *role application*, as, for example, when one is described as acting in the role of a teacher or a police officer. It thus comes to refer to the specific professional or domestic assignments or commitments a party has in these roles. These commitments are understood by Downie to be connected with certain patterns of rights and duties that are wholly or largely spelled out within the institutional framework of the role itself. He believes that many actions can be analyzed in terms of the structure of the social role or roles of which they form a part. Thus, for instance, the conduct of a physician can be described in terms of his or her acting in accordance with the duty of confidentiality or with the Hippocratic oath. Since this use is descriptive in nature, there is no evaluation made or implied about how well one is meeting the commitments of one's roles. One can, for example, recognize the responsibilities that Doctor Jones has without thereby implying that he or she performs these duties or commitments well. It is for this reason that the antonym of this sense of the concept is the term *nonresponsible* rather than the term *irresponsible*. To deny that one is responsible in this sense of the term is simply to deny the application of the allegedly appropriate role.

The second and third senses of the term are more evaluative or prescriptive in nature. This implies that their meaning includes the possibility of a subpar performance by the agent. The antonym of these two senses of the term is thus the term *irresponsible*.

The second sense concerns *role enactment* for Downie (Downie, 1964, p. 31). Here the focus is upon the way in which individuals perform their institutional roles. Persons who perform their roles conscientiously and dependably we call responsible. The term is thus used to praise and its opposite is used to blame. Within this meaning of the term, Downie tells us that one's sense of responsibility or commitment to the social or institutional role springs more from personal initiative and inclination than it does merely from the pressure to respond to social forces or expectations.

Downie's third sense of the term also arises from personal decision making and inclination. It concerns *role acceptance*. In this sense of the term, we would normally call responsible, persons who actively, willingly, or self-consciously accept the institutionally established roles typically applicable to them, such as those found in one's family life, career, and religious or educational activity. It also refers to the choice to assume certain commitments or social roles not typically required of individuals but that nevertheless have a positive impact on others (such as becoming a foster parent or Girl Scout leader, or joining the Peace Corps). In praising persons for being responsible in this way, we are evaluating their willingness to create certain positive social commitments for themselves. Subpar performance here typically involves such things as the failure of an individual to take on those social roles usually assigned to one in his or her situation, as well as the assuming of roles that prove to be more disruptive than helpful to society.

Ellin provides a definition of the term *responsibility* that builds upon Downie's role application sense. He equates the term with the word *duty*. Thus generally one's responsibilities are his or her *duties* or *obligations*. This includes both one's professional or role duties, as Downie mentions, and any other obligations that one has (Ellin, 1981–1982, p. 18). Although, like Downie, many theorists view this as primarily a descriptive use of the term, it can also carry evaluative overtones. These overtones stem from the prescriptive force often associated with the term *duty*, as well as from the fact that most people accept the meta-principle that agents should otherwise carry out their role- and nonrole-related duties.

Other theorists largely agree with the connection Downie makes between the concept of responsibility and role-related activity. Goodpaster, for example, offers a definition of the term that accords in essential respects with the role enactment and acceptance meanings recognized by Downie. Like Ellin, however, he broadens the latter sense of the term to include initiatives outside the context of social roles or their acceptance (Goodpaster, 1984, p. 297). For Goodpaster, any type of decision arising from independent thought processes that encourages an attitude of trust on the part of others can be said to be responsible (at least in the prima facie sense of this term). It does not matter whether the decision concerns the acceptance of a social role. Thus, for example, we can be said to be responsible (vs. irresponsible) whenever we fulfill our promises and carry out our nonsocial role agreements in a dependable and trustworthy manner. Goodpaster recognizes that this is a largely prescriptive or evaluative sense of the term, while the role application or rule-following sense is, for him, largely descriptive in nature (Goodpaster, 1984, p. 297).

In addition to these senses, however, he mentions another descriptive meaning of the term that has had a long history in tort law. This is the purely causal sense that forms the basis of the concept of strict (or faultless) liability. In this sense, "X is responsible for Y" means only "X caused or brought about Y." Such a sense may have legal, normative, or moral significance, but this need not be the case. In fact, the purely causal sense of the term can apply to non-thinking beings and even inanimate objects when, for example, it is alleged that the wind is responsible for slamming a door.

Hart discusses four senses of the term (Hart, 1968, pp. 211ff.). In addition to the purely causal sense of responsibility that we have just considered in which no praise or blame is involved, Hart also describes what he calls the capacity sense of responsibility. In this sense, to refer to persons as responsible means merely that they have the capacity to be legally or morally praised or blamed. Third, Hart advances a sense of the term, which he calls *virtue responsibility*, that is principally evaluative in nature and is used to make favorable or unfavorable assessments of persons or their conduct. This is the key sense of the term for Hart and is analyzed by him in terms of taking seriously our roles and role commitments. It is this concept that Downie analyzes in terms of the twin notions of role acceptance and role enactment, though for Hart the emphasis is upon the latter notion.

The fourth and final sense of the term for Hart is also discussed by Feinberg— the liability sense. As Feinberg analyzes it, the characteristic use of this sense of the term is negative in nature. It is used to show one's disapproval of an action or its agent. We do not typically say that a person is to be held liable (responsible) for positive outcomes. This sense of the term is used when the outcome is injurious or otherwise unfortunate. He tells us then that three conditions apply when it is used in this way (Feinberg, 1970, p. 222). First, the disapproved action is assigned to an agent, that is, the agent's action or omission contributes significantly to the negative outcome. Second, the contribution is faulty and third, there is a direct connection between the agent's conduct (or omission) and the outcome. Feinberg further tells us that there are liability uses of the term that do not imply fault, but these occur in specific classes of cases, the most common of which involve strict and vicarious liability. The latter type of liability is often found in superior-subordinate and parent-child relationships. It implies that the superior (or parent) is to be held responsible or liable for certain actions of the subordinate (or child), even when the former is not, strictly speaking, at fault.

We see this same concept of responsibility developed in agency law. It is also put forth by Werhane and Copp in their discussions of secondary actions (Werhane, 1985, p. 53; Copp, 1979, p. 177). Secondary actions are those that occur through the conduct of other persons, called agents. A person who authorizes another to act in his or her behalf (the principal) is held liable for the authorized actions of the agent. If the agent is malicious or negligent to others in these actions, the principal may be held responsible, even if he or she is not personally at fault. Finally, Feinberg tells us that when the liability sense of the term does involve fault, it implies that an agent is open to blame, guilt, censure, or perhaps even punishment.

The last account of the term to be examined here is offered by Haydon. Like Downie and Goodpaster, Haydon believes, unlike Hart, that the notion of virtue responsibility cannot be analyzed solely in terms of taking seriously one's roles.

Haydon contends, for example, that the role interpretation of responsibility does not explain how one can conscientiously reject otherwise accepted social roles (Haydon, 1978, p. 49). For Haydon, the key aspect of the present concept involves "being accountable." It thus consists of the capacity, willingness, need, or requirement to render an account of one's actions or inactions (Haydon, 1978, p. 55). Haydon maintains that accountability in this sense may be based upon a number of factors. In addition to the having of social roles, it can be based upon such considerations as one's voluntary agreements, one's determination to consider and weigh the consequences of his or her actions, and one's willingness to pursue self-chosen projects. In chapter four we shall further discuss these considerations under the category of the *relations of accountability*.

A SUMMARY OF THE DEFINITIONS

From these accounts, we derive this general picture of the concept. The term *responsible* (or *responsibility*) has both descriptive and evaluative uses. Descriptively, it can be used in four relatively distinct ways.

1. It can be used to mean *simple causal agency*, when, for example, it is said that a fallen timber is responsible for setting off the alarm. Here neither the possibility of fault, nor the need for a rendering of outcome or conduct, is applicable. In fact, the causal agent need not even be human (Goodpaster, Hart, and Feinberg).

2. It can also be used to refer to the *capacity to act in a responsible or irresponsible manner*. Thus, for example, individuals are typically treated as responsible persons when they have reached the age of reason (Hart).

3. It can be used in the *role application* sense to refer to the set of performances or duties usually associated with the social or institutional roles assigned to an individual (Downie).

4. A final and derivative, descriptive sense of the term is when it is equated generally with an agent's *duties*, however these might arise, whether within or outside an institutional or social role context (Ellin).

Because these four senses of the term do not involve or imply an evaluation, there is no possibility of a subpar performance by an agent being built into their meaning. The antonym of these meanings of the term is thus the word *nonresponsible* (or *nonresponsibility*).

When looked at evaluatively, the term has these added senses. The first three are largely role related in nature.

5. There is the sense of the term that means *role acceptance*, when, for example, in calling people responsible, we mean to commend them for willingly taking on the duties and roles appropriate to their station in life. Thus, we applaud as responsible the once wild teenager for "settling down" and accepting the role of parent or professional later in life (Downie).

6. *Role enactment* is another role-related meaning of the term. Here the concern is with the quality of one's role performance. To call persons responsible is to

praise them for acting dependably and conscientiously in their roles or for taking their roles seriously (Downie, Goodpaster, and Hart).

7. Closely associated with the last two senses is another. Here the focus is upon *independent decision making* in taking on roles neither initially assigned to nor expected of one. It can also be used to praise individuals who have found new ways to be effective in their already prescribed social roles. This differs in focus from the last two evaluative senses of the term because it emphasizes the self-imposed nature of the commitment behind the role-related activity. It is based upon personal conviction and initiative rather than social convention or expectation. This sense has a more existential flavor to it (Downie).

8. The next sense of the term broadens the existential component to include reference to acts outside of the context of roles. Thus, to call persons responsible is to commend them for any independent decision making that has, on balance, a positive effect on society (Goodpaster). Some theorists might wish to view these as acts done within the role of being a human being, but clearly as the role gets more general, it seems less appropriate.

9. The role acceptance sense of the term can be expanded in such a way that one's responsibilities can be equated with *one's duties*, but unlike the descriptive version of this definition, the present meaning carries evaluative force. We thus call irresponsible persons who knowingly fail to recognize or discharge their duties.

10. The last evaluative sense of the term carries the general meaning of *being held accountable*. In this sense of this term, the focus is upon the general expectation or requirement to give a rendering or defense of one's conduct. Actions for which one is to be held accountable are not then purely discretionary in nature for the agent. The defense called for may mention factors that we have just considered, or it may include references to added considerations that we shall discuss in chapter 4. A more specific application of this sense of the term implies fault. To be held accountable in this sense involves not only the need for a defense of one's conduct, it implies that the action in question involves a subpar performance. Finally, another type of specific application implies liability (either with or without fault). To be faultlessly or strictly liable means that one may still be held accountable to pay damages or compensate victims for the negative outcomes of one's conduct or the conduct of those who in some way have come to act in one's behalf or in one's name. To be held liable and at fault implies both that one's conduct can be justifiably blamed or censured and that the one may be justifiably punished or asked to provide compensation. We see this last application of the term in the legal context of negligent and criminal liability (Haydon, Feinberg, Hart). The moral dimension of this concept is associated with serious infractions to the moral order or with violations of moral duty.

THE DEFINITION IN THIS WORK

In the present work we shall organize our discussion around the last definition of the concept of responsibility—*being held accountable*. To speak of corporate responsibility (or responsibilities) is to discuss those areas of corporate conduct that require some kind of rendering or explanation from executives. Corporate responsibilities are thus not purely discretionary acts for corporations or their members. They place some kind of authoritative constraint upon corporate managers in the latter's business decision making, constraints that demand that executives explain, excuse, or vindicate themselves relative to these matters.

The concept of being accountable has itself four facets or areas of focus: (1) being accountable *to*, (2) being accountable *for*, (3) the *basis* of the accountability claim, and (4) the *degree of strictness* of the accountability claim. The focus in the first facet is upon the class of persons or institutions toward whom corporations are said to be responsible. In later chapters we shall review various works in which the authors seek to determine the individuals or groups who belong to this class—whether these be stockholders, specific stakeholders, or the public in general. In the second area, the focus is upon the type and quality of the performance or enactment of one's responsibilities. The concern is for both *what* should be done and *how* it should be done to discharge sufficiently and effectively one's corporate commitments or obligations. It is here that evaluations such as being dependable, being trustworthy, and taking seriously one's occupational or professional roles apply. The focus of the third facet is upon the *basis* of the accountability claim or the reasons for which one is said to be responsible. This third facet can itself be defined either descriptively or prescriptively. Descriptively, it can refer to the *expectation* that agents give a rendering or justification for their actions (and omissions of action) or it can refer to their ability and/or *willingness* to provide such a rendering. From a prescriptive point of view, it refers to the *normative need or demand* that such an accounting or justification of one's conduct (or omission of conduct) is given. The evaluative sense of the concept stresses the point that the onus is upon individual or institutional agents to explain why they have acted (or have failed to act) as they did, or to explain why they ignored or poorly performed a certain task or commitment. It is this evaluative facet of the concept that we shall primarily rely upon in this work.

An important question that arises over this aspect of the concept concerns the types of consideration that satisfy the demand for a rendering of one's conduct for when these relations of accountability are isolated, they come to define the boundaries of a corporation's specific domain of responsibility. Outside of this domain, the institutional actions are either purely discretionary (i.e., nonresponsibilities), illegitimate (*ultra vires*, an action may initially be beyond a corporation's domain of responsibility, but the demand to explain why it was done is not), or impossible. It is in addressing the question of the nature of these relations that the integrative nature of the concept I am proposing here can be seen. A number of the definitions of responsibility considered earlier can offer us possible responses to this question. One is expected or required to give a rendering of one's conduct if, among other things, it has a causal effect upon others, it involves professional or role duties (the grounds of which must be further explored), it concerns the acceptance of an institutional role, or it concerns the quality of one's role

enactment. Viewed in this way, the various features involved in the earlier definitions are closely related and may be components of an ostensive definition, but
they are not otherwise analytically tied to the concept of responsibility. We shall
explore additional relations of this kind in chapter 4.

The final facet of the concept concerns the degree of strictness involved in
the accountability claim. Certain areas of institutional action are nondiscretionary, but they (or their omissions) neither involve strict censure or blame, nor do
they typically involve punishment. Other persons may be disappointed and show
their disapproval of certain companies or their executives without endorsing legal
censure or casting moral blame upon them. When third parties would censure,
blame, or punish a corporation, however, the activity done (or omitted) is viewed
as having a greater degree of strictness. These are the responsibilities that we
shall call duties.

The four theories disagree over the number and types of corporate responsibilities that exist for both senses of the term. They disagree over the nature and
number of corporate duties as well as over those nonduties that still demand a
rendering. In this work we shall be primarily concerned with the concept of
responsibility that is broader and thus employs a less strict view of the degree
of accountability of corporations. This will enable us to keep our discussion
more general and comprehensive at this early stage in the treatment of this subject.
Using the broader concept will also permit us to discuss corporate conduct that
is taken by some theorists as obligatory. If this strategy proves to be too questionable, we can always narrow our examination further at another time if we
have good reason to believe that an institution's legitimacy is based solely upon
the discharging of its social, moral, or institutional duties.

The present definition of the concept is thus meant to be as synthetic or
integrative as possible. That it is not fully so, however, can be seen from
the fact that it does not include a reference to the independent decision-making sense of the term. The present account implies the possibility of an
arena of discretionary action for executives for which they need not give an
accounting, even when they exercise independent decision making. For some
theorists, this arena may be quite wide, while for others it is virtually non-
existent. But admitting the possibility of such an arena demands that we reject the analytic connection that is alleged to exist between being responsible
and exercising independent decision making. This means then that we shall
overlook here (and thus treat as secondary) the sense of the term urged by
certain existential thinkers, such as Sartre, whereby one is said to be responsible or accountable to oneself to be authentic and to avoid being in bad
faith. The reader will see that the interpersonal concept of accountability advanced here admits certain excuses and vindications that are not permitted
within the existentialist account of this notion.

In addition, we have largely ignored the capacity sense of the term. For the
present, such a capacity is assumed in the definition of the concept offered here.
In chapter 15 we shall examine an aspect of this assumption when we consider

works that address the question of whether corporations themselves can be held morally responsible for their actions.

We can see then that in general there are three types of corporate conduct normally thought of as requiring a rendering from executives: (1) actions performed that go beyond the corporation's domain of authority or permissibility, (2) the nonperformance of acts within the corporation's domain of responsibility, and (3) the inferior performance of acts within this latter domain. Conduct, omissions of conduct, or poor performance of conduct that fit the above descriptions respectively as well as the failure to give a rendering of such acts or omissions, are the principal, if not the sole, reasons for considering a corporation or its executives to be irresponsible. Outside of the realm of responsibility, though still within the agent's or corporation's domain of authority, lies the arena of the permitted. This includes actions that are purely discretionary, as well as those that are viewed as heroic or supererogatory. The latter type can occur, for example, when an agent exercises a degree of care that is appropriate for a duty in an action that is otherwise purely discretionary.

REFERENCES

Berle, Adolf A., and Gardiner C. Means. 1968. *The Modern Corporation and Private Property*, rev. ed. New York: Harcourt, Brace and World.

Copp, David. 1979. "Collective Actions and Secondary Actions." *American Philosophical Quarterly*, July, pp. 177–86.

Donaldson, Thomas. 1982. *Corporations and Morality*. Englewood Cliffs, N.J.: Prentice-Hall.

Downie, R. S. 1964. "Social Roles and Moral Responsibility." *Philosophy*, January, pp. 29–36.

Ellin, J. S. 1981–1982. "The Justice of Collective Responsibility." *University of Dayton Review*, Winter, pp. 17–27.

Feinberg, Joel. 1970. *Doing and Deserving*. Princeton, N.J.: Princeton University Press.

Goodpaster, Kenneth. 1984. "The Concept of Corporate Responsibility." In *Just Business: New Introductory Essays in Business Ethics*, edited by Tom Regan, pp. 292–321. New York: Random House.

Hart, H.L.A. 1968. *Punishment and Responsibility*. Oxford: Oxford University Press.

Haydon, Graham. 1978. "On Being Responsible." *Philosophical Quarterly*, January, pp. 46–57.

Serber, Jere. 1983. "Individual and Corporate Responsibility: Two Alternative Approaches." *Business and Professional Ethics Journal*, Summer, pp. 67–88.

Stone, Christopher. 1975. *Where the Law Ends*. New York: Harper and Row.

Werhane, Patricia. 1985. *Persons, Rights and Corporations*. Englewood Cliffs, N.J.: Prentice-Hall.

3

THE TYPES OF CORPORATE RESPONSIBILITY

INTRODUCTION

We have seen in the last chapter that the concept of responsibility is to be explicated in terms of at least four notions—three of which are tied in some way to the idea of accountability. The first involves the initial and general need, expectation, willingness, or demand to give a rendering or accounting of oneself or one's conduct when one is involved in a certain kind of situation. The second focuses upon the conduct or decision making for which one is said to be accountable. The third concerns the individuals or groups to whom an action is directed or an explanation is owed, while the fourth concerns whether or not the responsibility is strict enough to be considered a duty.

In the present chapter we shall consider the second facet of the concept more carefully by reviewing those works whose authors have sought to isolate the principal types of responsibilities that corporate executives are said to have. While we shall mention particular examples of corporate responsibilities in our discussion, our attention will be focused more upon the general types or regions of corporate responsibility than upon the specific activities for which corporate executives are expected to give a rendering.

Theorists have, in general, delimited four broad areas of corporate responsibility: economic, legal, moral, and social. The general ground of these regions is to be found in the basic nature of corporations: they are privately based, economic entities with jural standing whose members are expected and required to make decisions capable of having a relatively significant impact upon other persons and institutions. Not all theorists grant that corporations have responsibilities in each of these areas, however. Some reject the idea that corporations have specifically moral responsibilities at all. Other thinkers grant that firms have such responsibilities but are reluctant to treat them as distinct from their other responsibilities. Still others may view these regions as different in definition but conceive of them as admitting large areas of overlap. In this chapter, we shall not try to arbitrate between these various positions; instead, we shall proceed upon the assumption that relatively clear definitions of these regions can and have been given and shall simply discuss these definitions.

THE ECONOMIC RESPONSIBILITIES OF CORPORATIONS

Whatever else is to be said about it, it can be asserted with confidence that as a business enterprise a corporation is accountable for sustaining and encouraging the production of profit and wealth. This commitment has been viewed traditionally as part of its institutional responsibility—one directed primarily toward the shareholders of the company. In the recent literature, however, it is commonly considered a responsibility that corporate executives may also have toward other select groups of people, perhaps even the public.

The economic responsibilities of corporations have been defined in different ways. A frequent approach is to name an overriding goal or task that is said to be the main economic responsibility of the firm and then cite other tasks directly linked to this main goal. Friedman, for example, says the overriding economic goal of a corporation is to maximize its return to investors (Friedman, 1970, p. 33). To do this, corporate executives must enhance the value of the firm's stock and increase the dividends paid to each stockholder. Manne (and, also at times, Friedman) suggests that the primary economic goal of a corporation is to maximize profit (Manne, 1972, p. 8). Many theorists believe that the goals of maximum profit and maximum investor return will tend to coincide, at least in the long run; they grant, however, that there will often be strains and conflicts between these goals in the short run. While increasing or maximizing its profits, a firm need not immediately increase the value of the dividends given to its shareholders. The revenues received and retained may be reinvested in the firm or used to purchase new companies. This will often directly enhance the financial value of the company's shares in the long run, but this need not happen. It may instead merely make the firm more economically stable and resistant to fluctuations in the marketplace, an outcome that is itself sometimes given as a primary economic goal of a corporation.

With respect to the goal of pursuing profit, theorists like Simon reject the idea that maximizing profit is really a distinct objective of management (Simon, 1957, pp. 204ff.). He contends that because executives must respond to a host of other objectives, factors, and constraints, and must do so in a context he calls one of "bounded rationality," they actually seek to reach merely a *satisfactory* level of profit. Simon calls this the objective of "profit-satisficing."

The definition of economic responsibility in terms of profit maximizing or satisficing requires agreement on the definition of the term *profit*. It is usually defined as the excess of revenues over expenses or costs. But Sawyer, for one, includes social costs in his definition of *costs* (Sawyer, 1979, p. 73). This would make it analytically true that a firm's economic responsibilities coincide with its social ones. Few thinkers grant this point, however. Because of this, in the present work the word *profit* will be defined in terms of the balance of revenues over economic costs directly borne by the corporation. In this way, the coincidence or overlap between economic and social or moral responsibilities will be a matter to be determined by argument and evidence rather than merely by definition.

Shetty and others indicate that goals other than profit maximizing are sometimes seen as primary economic objectives of firms. He mentions as candidates expanding market share, gaining a competitive advantage in one's industry, and inducing growth (Shetty, 1979, p. 74). Business corporations can try to induce growth by some combination of such strategies as expanding sales, increasing the net worth of their assets, moving into new product areas, or purchasing other corporations.

In its first report on social responsibility, the Committee for Economic Development offered another method of defining or determining the economic responsibilities of corporations. It gave an ostensive or extensional definition of the term—one that listed the particular kinds of goals that comprise the economic responsibilities of corporations. The list included such goals as increasing productivity in the private sector, improving the innovativeness of management, enhancing competition, supporting fiscal and monetary policies for steady economic growth, improving the efficiency of the productive process, supplying jobs and career opportunities for individuals, and, providing useful services and safe, reliable products demanded by consumers (Committee for Economic Development, 1971, pp. 13, 37).

THE LEGAL RESPONSIBILITIES OF FIRMS

Because corporations are legal entities established to advance private economic goals, it may be thought that there is ultimately little difference between their economic and legal responsibilities. Since corporate charters typically mention the commitment to economic pursuits, it may be thought that the act of incorporation bonds these responsibilities together so firmly that it is difficult to unravel their separate strands of commitment. Actually, however, these kinds of responsibilities form two relatively distinct classes, though it must be admitted that there is considerable overlap between them. Economic responsibilities uniquely apply in those cases where the pursuit of certain corporate outcomes designed to respond to the stockholders' financial interests need not be specifically required by law. And the class of legal responsibilities, when viewed as distinct from the former class, applies in those cases in which corporations are legally required to take action that compromises their earnings-producing capacity or performance.

Most theorists grant that a firm's economic responsibilities never exceed its legal authority, but some disagree with this. The dissenters maintain that at times a firm is justified in breaking the law to meet certain of its economic responsibilities. For example, Kotchian has argued that executives at Lockheed Aircraft Corporation were justified in disguising payments made to officials of the Japanese government in the 1970s in order to secure a contract for its airplanes in Japan (Kotchian, 1979, p. 74). He reasons that these payments made Lockheed's planes more competitive in international markets and helped the company meet its economic commitments to its workers, stockholders, creditors, and the local communities in which its facilities were located. Whether or not he is correct in his thinking, the very fact that he can meaningfully discuss economic demands that are outside the context of the legal authority of a corporation suggests that we should at a minimum begin with a definition of these two concepts of responsibility that treat them as analytically distinct.

Basic to most of the definitions or descriptions of legal responsibility given thus far in the literature is the view that a corporation's fundamental legal responsibility, broadly conceived, is to obey the statutes, regulations, administrative codes, executive enactments, and court rulings or decrees issued by the various branches of federal, state, and local governments. This area of responsibility covers both civil and criminal law. As we would expect then, there is currently a very broad arena of corporate activity regulated by law: from antitrust activities to product safety issues; from disclosure practices to equal opportunity requirements in hiring, promoting, and firing workers; from pollution abatement policies to antideception practices in advertising. Given the breadth of these concepts and the specific responsibilities they entail, we shall not attempt to specify these responsibilities further here. It can in general be said, however (by way of distinguishing these responsibilities from the moral ones we are about to discuss), that an agent's legal responsibilities, particularly those contained in civil law, do not always involve courses of action that are otherwise avoidable. Nor are they binding upon agents in independence of their actual, and perhaps even their potential, knowledge of the law.

CORPORATE MORAL RESPONSIBILITIES

The next category of responsibilities to consider is the moral. Many theorists have attempted to distinguish moral from nonmoral responsibilities. Some of these definitions of the term are so broad, however, that they do not permit us to isolate the moral from the other types of responsibility. One common definition suggests that the moral realm concerns those factors that prove to have an *overriding authority* on action. But to say this is to say something that does not offer us a very useful way of distinguishing moral from, say, economic responsibilities. For whenever the other types of responsibility are judged as overriding, they automatically become moral responsibilities as well. The approach of this chapter then is to consider accounts of the concept that treat it as a distinct idea. We shall see that there are four features associated with the concept: (1) capacity for sufficient knowledge, (2) relatively significant impact, at least upon others,

(3) power, control, or avoidability, and (4) openness to blame for unacceptable performance.

Held introduces the first feature when she tells us that a moral responsibility is one had or done by an agent who has sufficient knowledge of the nature of an action (Held, 1972, p. 106). By the condition of sufficient knowledge, Held does not mean that an agent must be able to know everything about an action, but he or she must at least have the capacity to know those aspects of it that permit its normative evaluation. If an agent is temporarily or permanently unable to know these things, he or she cannot be said to have a moral responsibility to perform that action. Besides knowing the difference between right and wrong, then, one important class of knowledge about which an agent should be able to be informed to have a moral responsibility includes the typical or likely consequences of a contemplated action.

DeGeorge states the Held condition in another way. He tells us that moral evaluations admit the application of reason and reason giving (DeGeorge, 1981, p. 5). If an issue is not amenable to arbitration by reason (so that the condition of knowledge cannot be met), or if an agent has an insufficient capacity to use reason in deciding how to act, then any responsibilities that apply to such an agent are nonmoral ones. This then indicates a difference between moral and legal responsibilities, for example, for the latter need not always apply to agents who are viewed as having the ability to reason. Even very young children can have legal responsibilities (such as attending school and refraining from shoplifting or drug use), even if these are not conceived of as distinctively moral in nature. It is true that parents are expected to enforce these responsibilities and can be held liable for their infraction, but this is based upon the fact that these things are admitted to be the legal responsibilities of the children in the first place. Truancy, for example, is an activity in which children, not their parents, break the law. This is so even if the children in question are too young to understand the moral nature of what they have done. Besides this case, though, there are numerous examples of individuals being given legal status and responsibility who are not conceived of as moral agents. They or their representatives are legally required to pay their debts or respond to a court order, for example, without the principals' first meeting the conditions of morality considered here. This class includes fetuses and pets, for instance.

DeGeorge also introduces the second feature of the concept when he says that moral issues are those that have an impact on human welfare (DeGeorge, 1981, p. 5). In its present form, however, this condition is stated too broadly; it does not permit us to distinguish clearly moral from legal, economic, or social responsibilities. These others also have some impact upon human well-being. Even minor legal offenses, for example, can affect oneself and others, at least to the extent that such violations contribute to an attitude of disrespect for law. Of greater help would be the concept of having a relatively *significant* or *important* impact upon human welfare. Leaving aside for the moment what constitutes a significant impact, we can see that not all of the legal, economic, or social responsibilities of executives appear to have such an impact. For example, an executive may have responsibilities as a member of a firm to dress in a certain manner while at work or to join certain volunteer groups outside of work, but within limits, he or she would not usually be said to have a moral responsibility to do these things. His or her slight failure in this regard would not typically have a significant impact upon human well-being in general. It would thus not characteristically be held to be the object of moral blame.

Donaldson discusses the third feature when he maintains that for moral matters an agent's decision making must be able to control his or her conduct (Donaldson, 1982, p. 124). Held also reaffirms this condition of control or avoidability when she tells us that activities that admit of moral evaluation are ones in which an agent could have done other than what he or she had done (Held, 1972, p. 106). This condition has been given two interpretations, however—one weaker than the other. The stronger (and more narrow) interpretation defines control as the immediate ability to initiate or prevent an action at the time of the contemplated conduct. The weaker (and broader) interpretation defines control in terms of the general capacity to initiate or prevent actions of that kind in the future but not necessarily at the immediate time of acting. These two ways of conceiving of the condition of control or avoidability are significant for corporations because a corporate official might do something that could not immediately be controlled or avoided by his or her superiors (either because they did not know about the activity or could not coordinate their efforts quickly enough to stop it or its immediate consequences), but they could set up the appropriate monitoring and internal controlling mechanisms to stop actions of this sort in the future. Within the narrower notion of control, the corporation would not be held morally responsible for the initial conduct of its executives; on the broader interpretation, however, it would be held accountable. We shall assume the broader conception of control here, unless otherwise stated.

Finally, Velasquez has advanced a definition of moral responsibility that includes a fourth feature or condition. Using criminal law as a guide, he tells us that moral responsibilities are those for which there is a *mens rea* and an *actus reus*. More specifically, individual moral responsibility involves these conditions: (1) An individual performed or helped to perform an action; (2) he or she did so intentionally; and, (3) finally, the condition with which we are concerned here, if the action is substandard, the agent can be justifiably blamed, censured, or punished in some way (Velasquez, 1983, p. 1). The *mens rea*, or mental component, involves either an explicit intention to bring about a certain outcome and act in a certain way (and thus exert immediate and direct *control* over the action), or it involves at least *sufficient knowledge or foresight* of the risks and dangers involved that one is willing to have others bear these risks as a trade-off for whatever benefits he or she hopes to gain. The *actus reus* involves the physical motions or bodily movements that are necessary to carry out one's control and completion of an action. Because the action in question typically involves the prospect of *significant risk or harm*, a subpar performance is not frequently met with indifference. The action is characteristically disapproved of and the agent is viewed as *blameworthy*. (At a minimum, the failure to render an accounting of oneself in this regard becomes an object of censure.) Thus, we derive the fourth feature of the concept.

In summary, corporate moral responsibilities involve actions that (1) are specifically intended or involve the capacity for sufficient knowledge of the real effects or risks involved, (2) have a relatively significant impact upon human welfare, (3) are brought about by an individual or collective agent who could have chosen to prevent the action or mitigate its negative consequences—at least in the long run, and (4) are done by agents who are open to blame, censure, or perhaps even punishment when the conduct is substandard or otherwise injurious or when no rendering of themselves is forthcoming.

THE SOCIAL RESPONSIBILITIES OF CORPORATIONS

Three broad approaches have dominated the attempt to define the concept of social responsibility: the ostensive or extensional, the metadefinitional, and the intensional. In the first approach, the concept of social responsibility is defined in terms of specific activities or tasks that are said to be socially responsible ones. As it had with the economic and legal responsibilities of firms, the report of the Committee for Economic Development illustrates this approach when it stipulates a set of corporate activities that it views as generally aimed at improving society (Committee for Economic Development, 1971, pp. 37–40).

Against this approach, Strier argues that ostensive definitions are too inflexible and fail to distinguish adequately a corporation's social from its economic or legal responsibilities. Because the concept is a shifting one—changing in nature to meet the newer expectations assigned to corporations by society—no mere list of social responsibilities will provide an adequate definition of the concept (Strier, 1979, pp. 7–8). In recognizing this, Strier is also stressing the point that part of what makes a responsibility social rather than moral in nature is that it is based in large part upon the actual expectations of a group or the public. These expectations may closely coincide with the moral point of view, but they need not do so.

Strier himself bases his intensional definition of the concept upon certain metadefinitional assumptions (Strier, 1979, p. 8). Manne does the same (Manne, 1972, pp. 6ff.). A metadefinitional approach is one that advances conditions that must be met by a first-level definition before it can be considered adequate. Strier contends that and acceptable definition of the notion of corporate social responsibility (CSR) must meet the conditions of (1) flexibility, (2) external determination, and (3) the presence of rational boundaries (Strier, 1979, p. 8). By *flexibility*, Strier means that the definition must be capable of accommodating those changes that periodically occur in society's demands and expectations of corporations. By *external determination*, he means that the definition of this concept must be given to the private sector by individuals outside of the business community, rather than be given to the public by those within business. Strier believes this will add to the impartiality and legitimacy of the concept. Finally, by *the presence of rational boundaries*, he means that the definition must respect other responsibilities of the firm. The concept cannot be so defined that social responsibilities are automatically the overriding ones. We have considered a similar constraint in our discussion of moral responsibilities.

Manne maintains that there are three aspects to any adequate definition of this concept. The definition must emphasize (1) charitable intent (an economic sacrifice done for the public welfare is involved), (2) voluntary effort (the corporate activity cannot be a response to law or to outside economic pressures, especially those brought about by consumers), and (3) the collective nature of the action (the activity must be truly corporate in nature; it cannot involve acts of individual charity or sacrifice done through the corporate conduit) (Manne, 1972, pp. 6ff.).

Theorists like Sethi and Shaffer reject this whole approach, however. Basic to their rejections is the view that some of these stipulations are not really formal, procedural, or metadefinitional in nature. For these authors, the stipulations often involve substantive conceptual matters—matters that address the actual *content* of the definition of corporate social responsibility. As they see it, when Strier says that the concept must be defined within rational economic and legal boundaries, he rejects Shaffer's claim that the concept implies that its responsibilities are overriding ones (Shaffer, 1977, p. 12). Or, when Manne endorses the metadefinitional feature of voluntary effort, he opposes Sethi's view that a corporate social responsibility activity can be done as a response to social expectations and pressures—pressures that may eventually affect the legal and economic conditions in which executives make management decisions (Sethi, 1977, p. 73).

The most common form of definition given in the literature, however, is the intensional form. It has yielded seven dimensions of features claimed to be the necessary or defining characteristics of the concept. For each of these dimensions there is controversy, however. For example, theorists differ over whether the concept must be defined by reference to certain other-directed or public-spirited *motives* of corporate executives. Haas, Loevinger, Manne, and Ackerman and Bauer agree (Haas, 1979, p. 36; Loevinger 1973, p. 389; Manne, 1972, p. 1; Ackerman and Bauer, 1976, p. 6). But thinkers like Davis and Blomstrom, Starling, and Sturdivant disagree. They contend that the concept must be defined with reference to specific *outcomes* or *performances*. For the latter, the emphasis is upon social impact and accomplishment, not upon charitable intent (Davis and Blomstrom, 1980, p. 2; Starling, 1980, p. 232; Sturdivant, 1981, p. 173). This debate mirrors the traditional controversy in moral philosophy between consequentialists and deontologists over the proper place of outcome versus intent in determining one's moral responsibilities.

A second controversy concerns the presence of *voluntariness* in the concept. Manne, Jones, and Wallich maintain that corporate social responsibilities must be entirely voluntary. These tasks cannot be imposed by law or outside economic pressure (Manne, 1972, p. 5; Jones, 1980, p. 59; Wallich, 1972, p. 40). Other theorists disagree. For Strier and Sethi, for example, the essence of the concept is that it is externally imposed upon firms in some way, typically through the power of social expectation. This may manifest itself in terms of market pressures as well (Strier, 1979, p. 8; Sethi, 1977, p. 73).

A third controversy concerns the question of whether the concept involves reference to *economic sacrifice*. Manne and Haas suggest that it does (Manne, 1972, p. 4; Haas, 1979, pp. 34–35). Loevinger contends that such activities need not entail an absolute loss of revenue for the firm, but he does believe their pursuit often closes out more economically attractive options (Loevinger, 1973, p. 389). Bock, and Davis and Blomstrom, on the other hand, contend that there need be no conflict between fulfilling social responsibilities and maximizing profit (Bock, 1979, p. 6; Davis and Blomstrom, 1980, p. 2). For them, the ultimate coincidence of these goals must remain an open question rather than be defined as impossible, as Haas and Manne apparently do.

Another controversy concerns whether the concept of CSR refers to an ongoing *process* or to the *completion* of an activity. This controversy is usually associated with the performance or outcome definition of CSR, but this need not be so. It also applies to motive definitions that make appeal to outcomes in judging or establishing an agent's true intent. Some criticisms of the social tasks of corporations suggest that their lack of warrantedness is based primarily upon management's failure to achieve the stated purposes of these tasks. This seems to imply that successful completion is at least an important, if not a necessary, characteristic of corporate social responsibility. Against this view, however, Starling and Jones contend that the concept refers principally to a process (Starling, 1980, p. 235; Jones, 1980, p. 64). For them the warrantedness of such projects is a matter of degree; it is not determined primarily by appeal to their successful completion.

Fifth, there is the characteristic mentioned earlier that concerns whether these activities are defined so as to override economic tasks or legal duties when there is conflict. Shaffer, for example, maintains that overridingness is a feature of the concept (Shaffer, 1977, p. 12), but most other theorists deny this.

The last two aspects of the concept are advanced by Cooper, who develops them in an effort to distinguish the social from the moral responsibilities of organizations. He believes that actions endorsed as social responsibilities need not always be within the power of the agent to perform; the negative consequences of ignoring or failing to meet one's social responsibilities need not be avoidable. He also contests the idea that there is much point to morally blaming organizations for faulty or injurious decision making in this regard (Cooper, 1968, p. 264). He gives us the example of a failing tennis club as an illustration of a collective enterprise whose members have a social, but not necessarily a moral, responsibility to try to maintain the enterprise. Given the other activities and concerns of the members, their general lack of interest in scheduling matches, and the like, he tells us the club's failure may be unavoidable without its being the moral fault of its members or managers. And given the vicissitudes of the marketplace and the number of business failures per year, particularly for smaller firms, a corporation may also be said to have a social or economic, but not a moral, responsibility to try to stay in business. The top executives of a failed company are not always open to moral blame or censure for their lack of success in this regard.

It should perhaps be mentioned here that this feature is not the opposite of the concept of voluntariness discussed above. It addresses a distinct issue. The latter idea refers to the presence or absence of outside pressures to do a certain type of action. The present concept considers the question of whether an agent can avoid a certain outcome. The concepts can thus be mixed in various ways. For example, corporations may be the targets of social pressure (nonvoluntary) to perform actions whose outcome the executives can otherwise avoid (avoidability), or they may be under no great social or legal pressure (voluntary) to refrain from actions whose outcome the executives cannot avoid (unavoidability) in any case.

A second difference between social and moral responsibilities for Cooper provides us with the final feature of social responsibilities. It is suggested by the discussion of the previous section that moral responsibilities are those that have a relatively significant impact upon human welfare. Social responsibilities, then, need not have such an impact. As we have said, employees may have a social, but not a moral responsibility, to abide by certain constraints of the corporate culture, such as obeying regulations regarding dress or codes of conduct for activities outside the workplace. We would not typically morally blame managers if they sometimes came to work in clothes that clashed somewhat, or if they preferred to play volleyball or softball for one of the local teams than spend more of their free time working for charitable or community organizations. But to the extent that these types of conduct violate the explicit or implicit rules of the firm, the employees in question can then be said to have at least a social responsibility to abide by these rules. They are accountable socially to the organization to give a rendering of themselves and their violations in these areas. But because their actions do not significantly harm third parties (assuming in the second example that the managers in question help charitable or community organizations in some way, at least), Cooper thinks we would not call these infractions violations of moral responsibility. Likewise, corporations may also have activities for which they are socially accountable whose omission need not cause significant harm or be the object of moral blame. Whether or not a particular corporation provides funds for public television may be such an example. Thus, we see that social responsibilities may coincide with moral responsibilities, but they need not do so.

Seven characteristics have thus been closely associated with the concept of corporate social responsibility. Of course, not all theorists have appealed to each of these characteristics or dimensions of the concept in their definitions. Definitions mentioning or addressing only three or four of these dimensions are not uncommon, and theorists may combine these features in various ways. One theorist may advance a definition that mixes the features of voluntariness and charitable intent within a process-oriented approach, while another proposes a definition combining the characteristics of outside imposition and overridingness within a completion-oriented framework.

As defined here for our purposes, social responsibilities are either directly dependent upon the demands or expectations of society as a whole or on one of its organizations, or have (or are intended to have) some impact, even if not a morally significant one, upon the welfare of the group. They can involve conduct that is not otherwise avoidable, and they are not defined as overriding in nature. As for the remaining features, we shall not seek to choose sides in the controversies that concern them. This means that we shall not insist that the concept be defined as voluntary, completion oriented, or involving economic sacrifice; but neither shall we insist on the opposites of these features. Corporate social responsibilities may involve these elements, but they need not always do so. There is usually a voluntary element in the concept, but (positive) social impact can also occur when firms conscientiously carry out their economically or legally imposed rules. As for the feature of completion, a responsibility does not lose its social character merely because it is in the process of being completed. Completions are usually easier to isolate and evaluate than are ongoing processes. But this consideration does not by itself rule out the social character of these processes or activities. Last, some loss or sacrifice of revenue is often involved in carrying out such responsibilities. These projects do not, however, instantly lose their social character if they begin to reap significant financial benefits for a firm and its shareholders.

We can see then that according to the present analysis the same act, or cluster of acts, may involve all or several types of responsibilities—usually with significant overlap but sometimes mixed in various ways. So, for example, the effort involved in seeking to stay in business may be said to be only a social responsibility that the senior managers of a small corporation have toward the public (because the impact of business failure upon each member of the public is negligible). But they may be said to have all four types of responsibility toward their shareholders and workers in this regard (to the extent that meeting the moral dimension of this general responsibility is within their power).

In summary, we see that what distinguishes social from economic responsibilities is that the latter are typically aimed at or respond to the interests or demands of a narrower class of persons, namely those immediately connected to the corporation, especially the shareholders. The former are often aimed at or respond to the interests of the wider public (especially those third parties who are affected by corporate activity). These responsibilities may be at odds with each other, particularly in those cases where minimizing or avoiding corporate harm to these parties would result in lower dividends or fewer jobs. But there is considerable overlap here too. Economic responsibilities coincide with social responsibilities when economic activities have positive social impact (where positive impact also involves lessening harm) or are expected or demanded by the group or the public. Thus, maximizing profit, growth, a return to investors, and the like can be considered as social responsibilities, though they need not be conceived of as the sole or overriding responsibilities of executives. There is also considerable overlap between social and legal responsibilities, though the former need not be imbedded in law. They may, in fact, be in conflict with law. Finally, social and moral responsibilities coincide when socially responsible conduct is otherwise avoidable, has a relatively significant impact upon human welfare, or where substandard performance in this arena would lead to blame or censure. They depart when these conditions are absent.

What we shall see in the coming chapters is that there is a general tendency on the part of the classical theory to emphasize the economic and legal responsibilities of firms. When they do discuss moral or social responsibilities, they tend to interpret them as species of the former types of responsibility. Social activist theorists, on the other hand, tend to emphasize the social and moral responsibilities. They view economic and legal responsibilities as defined in terms of, or at least grounded upon, the social and moral dimensions of corporate decision making. Finally, the remaining two theories take intermediate stands, with stakeholder theorists tending to limit, and social demandingness advocates tending to extend, the importance of the public in determining and discharging the social and moral responsibilities of corporations.

REFERENCES

Ackerman, Robert, and Raymond Bauer. 1976. *Corporate Social Responsiveness: The Modern Dilemma*. Reston, Va.: Reston Publishing.

Bock, R. H. 1979. "Introduction: Modern Values in Business and Management." *AACSB Bulletin, Proceedings*, Annual Meeting, pp. 1–19.

Committee for Economic Development. 1971. *Social Responsibilities for Business Corporations*. New York.

Cooper, D. E. 1968. "Collective Responsibility." *Philosophy*, vol. 43, pp. 258–68.

Davis, Keith, and Robert L. Blomstrom. 1980. *Business and Society: Environment and Responsibility*. New York: McGraw-Hill.

DeGeorge, Richard. 1981. "Can Corporations Have Moral Responsibilities?" *University of Dayton Review*, Winter, pp. 3–15.

Donaldson, Thomas. 1982. *Corporations and Morality*. Englewood Cliffs, N.J.: Prentice-Hall.

Friedman, Milton. 1970. "The Social Responsibility of Business Is To Increase Its Profits." *The New York Times Magazine*, September 13, pp. 32–33, 122–26.

Haas, Paul F. 1979. "The Conflict Between Private and Social Responsibilities." *Akron Business and Economic Review*, Summer, pp. 33–36.

Held, Virginia. 1972. "Moral Responsibility and Collective Action." In *Individual and Collective Responsibility: The Massacre at My Lai*, edited by Peter French, pp. 103–20. Cambridge, Mass.: Schenkman Publishing.

Jones, Thomas M. 1980. "Corporate Social Responsibility: Revisited, Redefined." *California Management Review*, Spring, pp. 59–67.

Kotchian, Carl. 1979. "Case Study—Lockheed Aircraft Corporation." in *Ethical Issues in Business*, edited by Thomas Donaldson and Patricia Werhane, pp. 67–75. Englewood Cliffs, N.J.: Prentice-Hall.

Loevinger, Lee. 1973. "Social Responsibility in a Democratic Society." *Vital Speeches of the Day*, April 15, pp. 388–96.

Manne, Henry (with Henry Wallich). 1972. *The Modern Corporation and Social Responsibility*. Washington, D.C.: American Enterprise Institute.

Sawyer, George C. 1979. *Business and Society: Managing Corporate Social Impact*. Boston: Houghton Mifflin.

Sethi, S. Prakash. 1977. "Dimensions of Corporate Social Performance: An Analytical Framework." In *Managing Corporate Responsibility*, edited by Archie B. Carroll, pp. 69–75. Boston: Little Brown.

Shaffer, Butler D. 1977. "The Social Responsibility of Business: A Dissent." *Business and Society*, Spring, pp. 11–18.

Shetty, Y. K. 1979. "A New Look at Corporate Goals." *California Management Review*, Winter, pp. 71–79.

Simon, H. A. 1957. *Models of Man*. New York: John Wiley and Sons.

Starling, Grover. 1980. *The Changing Environment of Business: A Managerial Approach*. Boston: Dent Publishing.

Strier, Franklin. 1979. "The Business Manager's Dilemma—I. Defining Social Responsibility." *Journal of Enterprise Management*, vol. 2, no. 1, pp. 5–10.

Sturdivant, Frederick. 1981. *Business and Society: A Managerial Approach*. Homewood, Ill.: Richard D. Irwin Press.

Velasquez, Manuel. 1983. "Why Corporations Are Not Morally Responsible for Whatever They Do." *Business and Professional Ethics Journal*, Spring, pp. 1–18.

Wallich, Henry C. (with Henry Manne). 1972. *The Modern Corporation and Social Responsibility*. Washington, D.C.: American Enterprise Institute.

4

THE RELATIONS OF ACCOUNTABILITY

INTRODUCTION

In the last chapter we examined four types of responsibility. They comprise one feature of the general concept of corporate responsibility—that part that addresses the general questions of what corporations are *accountable for*. This involves some concern for another feature—*being accountable to*, but more will be said about this later in the book. In the present chapter, we shall focus our attention upon a third facet of the concept (i.e., the *basis* of an accountability claim) by considering the main types of interpersonal relationship for which there is the expectation or demand for a rendering.

At least eight proposals have been advanced in the literature to suggest the types of interpersonal relationship that lie at the basis of corporate accountability claims. They do not necessarily form an exhaustive list of such relations, as others might perhaps be suggested; but they have played a prominent role in the discussions of corporate responsibility thus far. Because they have emerged from a variety of theoretical and applied disciplines, they have yet to be organized into a systematic pattern or whole. In this work, we shall do little more than describe them and consider their application to the theories of corporate responsibility. We shall treat them as if they are irreducible responsibility—making considerations and shall thus leave them in their present "deontological" state. In some future work, perhaps, their common features or bases might be isolated, and they might then be arranged in some more systematic form—one indicating a lexical ranking, or the like, perhaps. For now they are treated primarily as factual considerations that supply the minor premises from which the specific conclusions of corporate responsibility emerge. It is for this reason that they are expressed in descriptive or factual form. It is, of course, assumed by their advocates that these relationships *deserve* or *demand* respect and that appeal to these relationships should convince an otherwise impartial or reasonable person that an agent is accountable in the case at hand. But the presence or absence of the relationship itself is not a normative or evaluative matter.

The eight types of interpersonal relation are (1) the relation of having promised something to someone or of having given one's consent to something (the promise-keeping model), (2) the relation of overseeing or protecting the interests of others (the stewardship or fiduciary model), (3) the relation of representing someone else, especially when this individual has the power of replacement (the representational model), (4) the relation of affecting another through one's actions (the impact model), (5) the relation of being affected by the actions of another in ways other than replacement (the reverse impact model), (6) the relation of entering into a cooperative effort with others to accomplish a goal (the teamwork or collegial model), (7) the relation of possession or direct control over something (the ownership or dominion model), and (8) the relation of acting in an area of conduct covered by some regulation, code, or law (the regulation model).

As one can see from their initial descriptions, there is considerable overlap between these models. To define one is sometimes to consider one or more of the others. And they all share at least this one feature, of course, that mention of them puts potential agents on notice that they are considering acting in an area that is not a discretionary one for them—one where they can be asked about the way they act or fail to act. The burden of proof would then be upon them to indicate why they have acted in a certain manner. These conceptual and functional ties do not, however, preclude the models from having relatively distinct natures. In this chapter, we shall seek to pinpoint these features.

The Promise-Keeping Model

The first relation to be discussed has had a long history in our legal and moral traditions. It lies at the basis of the law of contracts and has been explained by some philosophers in terms of the activity of an otherwise autonomous, rational will. In summarizing the legal concept of contract or promise, McGuire tells us that four elements are generally present in a legally binding contract: (1) mutuality or reciprocal consent, (2) consideration, (3) legality of object, and (4) capacity of the parties (McGuire, 1986, pp. 202–3). *Mutuality* involves a meeting of the minds. It means that an actual agreement has been reached between the parties, usually through an offer and an acceptance. *Consideration* is the element that distinguishes enforceable from unenforceable contracts. It refers to the activity that the parties agree to do or that element or thing that they promise to forego, even though there is no prior legal duty to do or to forego these things. Thus, for example, in the sale of an automobile, the seller agrees to furnish the car, while the buyer agrees to provide the amount of the purchase price. *Legality of object* means that the object and purpose of the contract must be legally permitted. If its purpose or performance involves the commission of a crime, the perpetration of a tort, or an act that is contrary to public policy, it is not a legally binding contract. Last, *capacity of the parties* means that the parties to the agreement must be legally competent to enter into a contract. Examples of individuals who typically do not meet this criterion are minors, the insane, persons with significantly diminished mental capacity, and those who are under the influence of drugs or alcohol (McGuire, 1986, pp. 203–5).

This way of defining the promise-keeping model shows its affinities to the regulation model. Outside the context of law, however, some moral thinkers have explained the authority of the norm behind promise keeping in terms of the capacity of the will to create responsibilities or obligations for itself. Because such actions or duties are self-imposed, it is thought to be irrational for the will to ignore its own self-appropriated constraints (assuming, of course, there are not prior moral constraints against the purpose or performance of the self-imposition or promise).

Utilitarian thinkers explain the compellingness of the promise-keeping model in terms of the inconvenience, harm, or pain that is caused when parties to an agreement fail to carry out their parts of a bargain. This way of describing it shows its affinities with the impact model. Whatever the ultimate basis of its authority, however, promising places constraints upon a person that require a rendering if he or she fails to perform the promised task properly (Ross, 1939, p. 108).

Some theorists distinguish between promise keeping, which involves mutuality of consent and is usually thought to be more explicit in character, and simple consent for which these features are usually absent. In an otherwise nondiscretionary context where simple consent applies, the consenting individual is, of course, said to be accountable for respecting the arrangement or carrying out the action to which his or her consent is given. This is so whether the consent involved is explicit and informed, or whether it is more tacit in nature and is thus to be inferred from such actions as a party's continued participation in a social institution or relation without protest or rebellion. This means, however, that the party cannot hold others entirely responsible for the action or arrangement in question. Putting this another way, the absence of consent is often thought of as an excusing condition, while the absence of informed consent is often thought of as an appropriate vindication for various accountability claims. We shall include reference to both mutual and nonmutual consensual contexts within the present model.

The Fiduciary Model

The next two models can be found in agency law as well as in other areas of interpersonal decision making. To say that they arise in agency law is not to say that they are mere versions of the regulation model, however. This is because the authority of the norm that stands behind them is not generally seen to be based upon their recognition in or by the law. Agency can be both legal or extralegal in nature. It is a relation in which the actions of one person come to constitute or represent the actions of another. Because of this, the agent is said to be accountable to the principal when he or she acts in this capacity. This concept is illustrated in the relationships of lawyer and client, trustee and estate, worker and employee, and child and parent.

There are two relatively distinct aspects of the agency relationship, however. These, in turn, give rise to the fiduciary (or stewardship) and representational models. In the former accountability claims are grounded upon the interpersonal relationship of overseeing or protecting the interests of others, whether this occurs by choice, appointment, birth, custom, or the like. This model often overlaps with the promise-keeping model because the form of relationship involved here is frequently the product of the explicit consent of the parties. This is the case in standard lawyer-client and doctor-patient relationships, for instance. But the model also applies in certain nonmutually consensual contexts when one is expected to carry out certain actions as a part of one's social roles. This happens when, for instance, grandparents are expected to protect the interests of their orphaned grandchildren or doctors in an emergency room are expected to protect the health of an unconscious accident victim. Certain feminist thinkers such as Gilligan and Blum have emphasized the nonlegal aspects of this type of relationship, where sympathy, empathy, feeling, and nurturance are said to be important facets of the fiduciary's relation to the principal (Gilligan, 1982, pp. 8ff.; Blum, 1982, p. 296). In this work we shall apply the model to those interpersonal contexts in which agents are in some position of authority, superiority, or importance relative to their principals. Their position or status is based upon their superior knowledge, expertise, experience, age, or the like. It is because of these special qualities that they are expected to carefully watch over, guard, and protect the interests of their principals or charges.

Blumberg, and Hay and Gray are theorists who appeal to this relation when discussing the responsibilities of corporate executives. Whatever the precise basis of the role of fiduciary, they tell us that corporate executives do occupy this role and are thus accountable to society and to the shareholders of the corporation to act as effective stewards of the latters' financial interests in the firm (Blumberg, 1983, p. 133; Hay and Gray, 1977, pp. 8ff.).

The Representational Model

The representational model focuses upon another set of interpersonal features from the promise-keeping and fiduciary models. These features are not easy to spell out in a single formula, however. The general idea behind the model is that because the conduct of a certain party represents or reflects in some significant way upon another party or group, the former is said to be accountable to the latter. In addition, the latter is thought to be accountable or liable to third parties for damages the first party might cause while acting in a representational capacity.

This type of relationship applies in at least two distinct kinds of situations. In the first, the former party is said to be a functionary of the latter. A functionary is one who serves at the discretion of another; the latter has power over the functionary, especially the power of removal or replacement. Elected officials and employees are examples of functionaries. While similar in certain respects to the promise-keeping model, the functionary relation need not always be based upon an explicit contract or agreement between the parties. Such was the case in the feudal system of vassalage. And unlike the fiduciary model, a functionary is not always viewed as a steward who watches over the interests of another party in quite the same careful, expert, or professional manner that a doctor or lawyer, for instance, is expected to protect the interests of his or her patients or clients. When functionaries are experts, however, this simply means that they also occupy the role of fiduciaries. Functionaries, as such, typically occupy subordinate positions with limited decision-making power. In organizational life, the activity and success of subordinates is said to reflect upon the status and position of their superiors. They are thus thought to be accountable to their bosses because any error made by subordinates calls into question the supervisory qualities and abilities of their superiors. This is so whether we are discussing government agencies, the church, the military, or the corporation. It seems then that the last two models focus upon somewhat different facets of the account-ability relation, even when they apply to the same social role or function. Thus, for example, members of a school board are functionaries when viewed from the perspective of the parents and citizens of a local community, but they are fiduciaries for the public school children in that district.

Friedman is one theorist who appeals to the functionary concept in defending his view of corporate responsibility. As he sees it, executives must respect the voting power of the shareholders for it is through this that they receive a mandate to carry out their managerial functions without additional or undue interference from the latter (Friedman, 1970, p. 122). Executives are thus typically viewed as being both functionaries and fiduciaries.

In the second kind of situation, which I shall call agency in general, the actions of one individual come to represent or reflect upon the conduct or lives of others. In some sense the actions of the former are taken to be, mirror, signify, or express the actions or choices of the latter. Here the power of removal or replacement is largely absent. Agency in general is illustrated in tribal, clan, or family relationships and is an important facet of many Eastern cultures. In the latter case, the actions of those now living are thought to reflect upon their ancestors. Any disgrace that occurs in the present is said to disgrace all members of the family, both past and present. In the former case, other tribes or clans may hold an entire tribe or clan responsible for the actions of one of the latter's members. In this case the member is thought to be accountable to those who may be penalized for his or her misconduct. And the body or party that may be penalized or punished is held accountable to some other group for the actions of its agents in general. One reason for holding a group or individual accountable for the actions of agents in general is that it is believed that the principal (in general) can exert some influence or control over the latters' actions, but this is not always the case. This can be seen in laws passed in certain states that hold grandparents financially liable for the procreative activity of their unmarried grandsons when both the grandsons and their parents are unable to pay for the support of the child in question. Thus, an agent in general need not be a functionary (a grandparent will not usually disown or remove his or her grandson after the latter has fathered a child he cannot support), nor is an agent in general viewed as an expert or professional who has wide latitude in acting to protect or carefully watch over the interests of the "principal(s)."

The Impact Model

The impact model is supported by theorists such as Fasching and Dahl, as well as most consequentialists in ethics (Fasching, 1981, p. 69; Dahl, 1972, p. 16). It maintains that one is accountable to another to the extent that one's decisions, actions, and even one's chosen omissions of actions influence or affect the interests or well-being of another person—especially when this is likely to be negative in nature. The extent of the accountability relation is usually limited to the area of potential or actual influence.

Some impact theorists restrict these accountability relations so that they include only the direct effects of action (we shall see in a later chapter that this is basic to the stakeholder theory), while others include reference to the indirect effects as well. Some impact theorists consider only the negative effects of conduct, while others include reference to some positive effects as well. Finally, there is the debate between thinkers who reserve accountability relations to only those effects that surpass a certain threshold of impact upon other persons, however this is to be determined. They are challenged by theorists who also include reference to effects that have a much less important or more secondary impact on others. The former theorists believe that one is accountable only for activity that has a relevant and notable impact upon others. Thus, as they see it, we need not explain ourselves if a small bubble of water from a puddle splashes upon others as we walk by them; whereas we are expected to explain ourselves if, in our haste, we cause the entire puddle to splash upon them, thereby completely drenching them and their clothing. If pressed to find a standard of notableness from within this relation itself, it could be suggested that a notable impact is one that is great enough in the single case to counterbalance the burden of having to explain every action done or contemplated that has an impact upon others. Negative impact carries a burden, of course, but so does giving explanations. When the former exceeds the later, an explanation is likely in order.

A facet of the impact model that sometimes has a significant bearing on accountability claims is the precedent one establishes when one repeatedly acts in a certain way. If this kind of regularity contributes to the expectation on the part of others of continued behavior in the future, one is usually viewed as being accountable for having encouraged this expectation in them. Thus, varied behavior in the future may need or demand an explanation. This same point is sometimes also brought out by the teamwork model. When a sudden change in the performance of a certain collective action by a teammate catches the others by surprise and thus lessens the performance level of the team, the individual member will sometimes be called upon to give an explanation of his or her action in this regard.

A relatively distinct facet of the impact theory is endorsed by some deontological thinkers. They tell us that when one's conduct causes considerable harm to another otherwise innocent party, the agent is accountable not only to give a rendering of his or her behavior in this regard but also to make reparation for any damage or suffering that occurred to the other party because of it. The failure to do so also involves a rendering from the agent. Some of the other models also include this demand for reparation.

The Reverse-Impact Model

The reverse-impact model is assumed by theorists like Freeman and Anshen (Freeman, 1984, p. 52; Anshen, 1980, p. 6). The basic idea behind this model is that one is accountable to anyone who has the power to affect an agent in some immediate or important way (other than direct removal). Thus, if a social activist group has the power to embarrass management or otherwise hurt its reputation or economic standing (and is perhaps threatening to do so), the model maintains that management is expected to respond to this group and give a rendering of itself even though the latter may not be one of the traditional constituents of the corporation. The type of responsibility that arises here may often be only a social responsibility, but these theorists argue that some kind of rendering is called for, nevertheless. Thus, the model recognizes the importance of power or influence when one is the recipient of those who have it, just as the impact model recognizes its importance in the opposite situation. As with the impact model, there are versions of this model that are concerned with only a certain type or level of reverse impact.

The reverse-impact model typically focuses upon the expectation of present and future conduct, but some deontologists also urge a version or facet of this model that focuses upon the reverse impact of past behavior as well. People who have affected agents in certain specific ways in the past are said to deserve special consideration from these agents. The latter may even be expected to give a rendering of themselves directly to these people in this regard. Thus, for example, when other people have shown unsolicited kindness or generosity to an agent, we are told that, other things being equal, the recipient of this is accountable to show these people gratitude and its attendant commitments. In this work, the demand for gratitude in these situations will be treated as an aspect of the reverse-impact model.

The Teamwork Model

The teamwork model is discussed by Harrison, Pletta and Gray, Dyer, and others (Harrison, 1952–1953, p. 110; Pletta and Gray, 1983, p. 60; Dyer, 1987, pp. 6ff.). This model focuses upon the relations of loyalty, harmony, and contribution that are needed when people organize themselves in a cooperative effort to achieve a collective goal. It holds that one is accountable to the other members of the working group (the team) to do his or her part to gain the goal. From within the standpoint of this model, failure to do one's part in the project (freeriding or freeloading) or opposition to the group's effort (disloyalty or rebellion) are not, other things being equal, perceived as legitimate activities for group members—nor is conduct that violates the standards or regulations of the group. Members are expected to give an accounting of themselves if they violate or ignore these, even those that are informal or otherwise implicit in nature. This can be said to be part of at least the social responsibility that members have to the group.

Jackall tells us that the teamwork model emphasizes the importance of conformity, continued affability, and social finesse in the life of the modern manager (Jackall, 1988, p. 59). It is an integral part of the fealty relations that develop in bureaucratic organizations. As Jackall sees it, these fealty relations exist in a context of considerable conflict and instability in the corporation. Thus, managers form into "managerial networks"—mini-teams if you will—that are webs of association created to address some of the uncertainty and contingency in their work situations.

Some theorists connect this model to the impact model; they emphasize the considerations of performance or fairness implicit in it. They point out the degree to which overall group performance is hurt when members fail to do their part. This is especially true for teams with interdependent members, like a baseball or basketball team. If a pitcher cannot throw or a guard cannot pass or rebound well, the performance of the other team members will also likely suffer.

Other theorists connect it to the promise-keeping model. They view the authority of the norm behind the teamwork relation as resting upon the promise made by most members in initially joining the group or team, or the one implicitly, but frequently, reaffirmed by them as they stay in the group. Because various accounts of its authority are possible, we shall treat the relation as an irreducible one—at least for the purposes of this work.

As for its connection to the promise-keeping model, however, it is somewhat unclear how far to extend the notions of consent or promise within the teamwork model. In the narrower sense of the term—found in the concept of explicit consent—members of a team do not necessarily agree to abide by the stated rules of the group; nor can it be said that they explicitly agree to all of its unstated rules or norms (often found in the group culture, for example). They may, in fact, be ignorant of many of these rules or norms. In the broader sense of the term, found in the concept of implied promise or tacit consent, it is difficult to determine what members have implicitly promised to do after having joined a group. It seems to make sense to say that they have promised or chosen to obey only some of the group's regulations. They may actually disagree with certain standards or disregard certain regulations without automatically being considered renegades or poor team players. Not all members will be treated this way, of course. Individuals seen as "superstars" or "the franchise," however, can usually get away with bending a few rules. This suggests that the performance element is an important facet of the teamwork model; its authority is not then solely explained by its connection with the promise-keeping or regulation models.

Another dimension of the teamwork model is developed by thinkers like Werhane who prefer to speak of collegiality (Werhane, 1985, p. 99). Collegiality is a relation of mutual effort that involves individuals perceived of as equals, or near equals, in status or function. When applied to professional groups, it involves a relation of close scrutiny over potential members, a fuller measure of autonomy and self-regulation after one has been admitted to the profession, and a dedication to serve the good of the public (as well as that of the profession). The teamwork model in general need not involve these features. Teams may be hierarchically organized, permit little or no autonomous decision making, and have no clear commitment to the public good. They need not even be entirely or explicitly voluntary. One can simply be told to be a member of a team—as are those who are drafted into the military, called for jury duty, or assigned to a team in gym class.

Finally, we should mention that this model is emphasized in the work of certain feminist thinkers who focus upon the relationship of nurturing and helping others who are counting on one for support, direction, or encouragement, whether this be found in a formal organization like a firm or a less formal one like a family or a friendship.

The Ownership or Dominion Model

The possession, ownership, or dominion model typically focuses upon accountability claims that arise over a party's relationship to nonpersonal, nonhuman, or inanimate objects. But it can also refer to one's general control over any thing, characteristic, or object. When it is applied to those areas of personal control involving either individual discretion or interpersonal accountability, it is felt that any (significant) intrusion into the moral or decisional space of another—into his or her volitional territory—requires a rendering. In this sense, the present relation is like the territoriality instinct found in lower animals. Those who wander into the territory of another animal or pack of animals are "accountable" to them for this intrusion. They will be driven off—often times even after they have shown the appropriate degree of submissiveness, deference, or nonhostility. The present model is also thus aligned with the impact model, which also urges the idea that intrusion or impact generally requires a rendering.

Whatever the ultimate basis of the authority of this relation, however, two things follow when one is said to own, possess, or have dominion over something. First, in cases of single possession, the owner is held uniquely accountable for the condition, status, use, and existence of the thing or quality owned or controlled. Others cannot be asked to explain why it remains unused, is left to deteriorate, or leads to harm or abuses, for example. This is so whether we are discussing physical property or personal characteristics like charisma, intelligence, or expertise. Neither is it usually within the latters' domain to be financially rewarded or morally praised if the condition of the object or quality is enriched or otherwise improved upon. Second, it implies that others are accountable to the possessor or owner if they try to interfere with or trespass upon the object or quality owned. They cannot legitimately destroy the nature or value of property, objects, or qualities they do not possess. Finally, like the other relations, if nonowners do interfere with or trespass upon the property or dominion of others, they are at a minimum expected to give a rendering or explanation for such an encroachment to those who have dominion over this property.

Some philosophers have sought to ground this relation upon the idea that the owner has a moral right to his or her property. The latter is said to be the basic concept. We shall not follow this view here. In the first place, not all social theorists accept the idea of a basic moral right to privately held property. Second, the concept of a moral right is a normative one, while the types of relationship that we are discussing in the present context are more descriptive in nature. Last, it is somewhat unclear which of these notions is the more primitive. We shall take as more basic the naturalistic descriptive relations involved in noticing things; using, altering, or improving them; trading them; fighting for and protecting them; or, bequeathing them or giving them away. It can thus perhaps be as cogently said that we hold or possess our rights as that we have a right to hold our possessions. At some point having possession or dominion (over) seems to be an irreducible notion, whether it directly applies to property or to the moral right to hold property. The latter is still urged or claimed to be "one's own."

We see the application of the possession or dominion model in various games or sporting events, where, for example, perhaps only the team holding the ball can score. In football, for instance, there is an important difference between holding the ball and fumbling it. The prerogative goes to the team with the ball; the team cannot lose points if it keeps possession of the ball and stays out of its own end zone.

The possession or ownership model might be thought to be so close to the next model about to be discussed as to be a mere version of it. This is particularly true when the regulation model focuses upon the laws of the land. It might be thought that ownership is a relationship that is respected only when a governing body recognizes and enforces the legal title to property. This interpretation is further reinforced by appealing to the concept of eminent domain, in which a governing body stipulates that all private property is held conditionally, that ownership comes under the general condition that it not interfere with the public welfare. This might suggest then that governments can override possession. But does it show that their laws create or ground the authority of the ownership relation, or the norm behind it, in the first place? In overriding the authority of ownership in these circumstances, the doctrine of eminent domain does not necessarily suggest that ownership involves no authority in its own right. Over-ridingness is not the same as cancellation. Appeal to the doctrine may, in fact, be based upon certain ownership relations that the general public is said to have and that are disregarded if a single party claims a monopoly over certain resources or holdings. Appealing to the doctrine in its normative form may then suggest that private possession or dominion, however it is conceived or applied, has at least prima facie authority. Otherwise, why compensate the previous private owners for their property?

There are, however, added reasons to think that this model is conceptually distinct from the regulation model. State-of-nature examples indicate that pos-session or ownership need not be viewed as a strictly legal concept. Property can be held in such a state or condition without governments' enforcing this holding. In such a state there may still be the need or expectation that a ''tres-passer'' give an accounting to a property holder of his or her conduct, without this being reinforced by a legal sanction from a government. This suggests that typically governments merely *recognize* dominion or possession as an important basis for legal title without at the same time *creating* the relation (or its authority) in the very act of assigning this legal title. (This view accords with at least one interpretation of the legal doctrine of adverse possession, though some theorists hold that ownership on this basis ultimately has a statutory foundation, after all.) According to this interpretation, having legal title to property merely adds to the authority of the relation of possession; it does not create this authority in the first place. The law involves social recognition and the possibility of socially sanctioned punishment for property violators. But it does not create dominion or property; nor does it entirely explain the presence or need for an accounting in this area.

Some states distinguish between ownership and possession. They define own-ership in terms of possessing legal title to an object; possession on the other hand, involves a power or control over an object but not necessarily ownership. For those who accept this distinction, the present model includes both dominion or possession as well as mere ownership in the legal sense.

The Regulation Model

As we have seen, the regulation model is perhaps the broadest of the eight models, having significant overlap with several of the other relations. Basic to the model is the idea that the very presence of a regulation, broadly conceived, puts actual (and potential) violators on notice. The burden is usually upon them to explain why they are (or are thinking of) ignoring or violating a regulation. This burden is present irrespective of the procedural basis or justification for the regulation. It does not matter from the perspective of this model whether the regulation is established within a broadly democratic framework or whether it arises within the hierarchical bureaucracy of a dictatorship. The very presence of the regulation itself is meant to constrain in some way the otherwise discretionary activities of those to whom it applies.

The types of regulation considered within this model include such things as the explicit laws of government, the conventions of language, the customs of social etiquette, and the implicit rules of a voluntary organization. As with the teamwork model, advocates of this model tell us that members of the latter type of organization have at least a social responsibility toward it to abide by its rules and regulations. To disobey or directly challenge the rules is thus often perceived as tantamount to trying to get rid of them. As long as they are in place, however, members are otherwise expected to obey them. We shall see this model in use when examining whistleblowing later in the book for on this question some thinkers appeal to the regulative aspects of an employee's occupational roles to put potential whistleblowers on the defensive. We shall also see it utilized by those classical theorists who support the "game theory" of business decision making for the standard of conformity to law that plays a major role in their theory is a specific application of this model.

There may, however, still be some doubt about whether this really constitutes a distinct model of accountability. It seems so close to some of the other models that it may appear to be simply reducible to these. Of even greater concern, perhaps, is the possibility that the model is nothing more than a restatement of one of the four general types of responsibility itself. Against this latter concern, however, it can be said first that the model is meant to include all forms of regulation, even those that are not connected to governmental or publicly enforced sanctions. Second, with respect to those regulations that are in fact embodied in law, no evaluative judgment is made here about their quality. By taking no normative position in this regard, we preserve the value-neutral character of the present relation of accountability and we leave as an open question whether one may have a responsibility (in one or other of the four senses) to disobey or override a regulation. For those who still cannot accept this broader notion of regulation, I ask that they conceive this model as applying to only those regulations of society or its institutions that have no legal or jural standing in themselves. Whether this narrower concept implies that this model is further reducible to some combination of the other seven models of accountability is, however, a question that need not further detain us at this time.

These then are the eight relations or models of accountability that have played a prominent role in discussions of corporate responsibility. Other relations might also be mentioned, perhaps, but, so far as I can tell, most either reduce to one or other of these eight relations, or there are other problems with appealing to them. Thus, for example, discussions about organizational communication and the quality of corporate disclosure are often guided by the principle of accountability that those who stray from the truth, or the facts as they have occurred, are obligated to give a rendering of themselves. The general duty of truth telling is felt to stem from this root. But this model, as a relation of accountability, is inappropriate in the present context because it makes use of a normative concept (or normative standards of evidence) and thus cannot function as a descriptive premise in arguments concerning specific corporate responsibilities. If, on the other hand, it is looked upon as a descriptive relation, it can be treated as a version of the possession or ownership model insofar as one may be said to be accountable for his or her possession of the facts (or the truth) to avoid ignoring or distorting them. It can also be dealt with by the impact model.

Finally, it should be noted that not all theorists who appeal to these relations believe in the importance of all eight of them. Nor am I aware of any theorist who believes they are all equally important. Part of the difference between one theorist and the next depends upon how they rank these relations. Part also depends on how the relations are blended and interwoven in the substantive arguments that occur in this field.

The relations of accountability constitute an important set of assumptions in the corporate responsibility debate. Equally important, however, are the assumptions that concern the nature of the corporation.

REFERENCES

Anshen, Melvin. 1980. *Corporate Strategies for Social Performance*. New York: Macmillan Publishing Company.

Blum, Lawrence. 1982. "Kant's and Hegel's Moral Rationalism: A Feminist Perspective." *Canadian Journal of Philosophy*, June, pp. 287–302.

Blumberg, Phillip I. 1983. "Corporate Responsibility and the Employee's Duty of Loyalty and Obedience." In *Ethical Theory in Business*, edited by Tom L. Beauchamp and Norman E. Bowie, pp. 132–38. Englewood Cliffs, N.J.: Prentice-Hall.

Dahl, Robert. 1972. "A Prelude to Corporate Reform." *Business and Society Review*, Spring, pp. 17–23.

Dyer, William. 1987. *Team Building: Issues and Alternatives*, 2d ed. Reading, Mass.: Addison-Wesley.

Fasching, Darrel J. 1981. "A Case For Corporate and Management Ethics." *California Management Review*, Summer, pp. 62–76.

Freeman, Edward. 1984. *Strategic Management*. Boston: Pitman Books.

Friedman, Milton. 1970. "The Social Responsibility of Business Is To Increase Its Profits." *The New York Times Magazine*, September 13, pp. 32–33, 122–26.

Gilligan, Carol. 1982. *In a Different Voice: Psychological Theory and Women's Development*. Cambridge, Mass.: Harvard University Press.

Harrison, Jonathan. 1952–53. "Utilitarianism, Universalization, and the Duty To Be Just." *Proceedings of the Aristotelian Society*, pp. 105–34.

Hay, Robert, and Ed Gray. 1977. "Social Responsibilities of Business Managers." In *Managing Corporate Social Responsibility*, edited by Archie B. Carroll, pp. 8–16. Boston: Little, Brown and Company.

Jackall, Robert. 1988. *Moral Mazes: The World of Corporate Managers*. Oxford: Oxford University Press.

McGuire, Charles. 1986. *The Legal Environment of Business: Commerce and Public Policy*. Columbus, Ohio: Charles E. Merrill Publishing Company.

Pletta, Dan, and George Gray. 1983. ''Engineering Accountability—Corporate Responsibility.'' In *Beyond Whistleblowing: Defining Engineers' Responsibilities*, edited by Vivian Weil, pp. 56–70. Chicago: Illinois Institute of Technology.

Ross, W. D. 1939. *Foundations of Ethics*. Oxford: The Clarendon Press.

Werhane, Patricia. 1985. *Persons, Rights and Corporations*. Englewood Cliffs, N.J.: Prentice-Hall.

5

MODELS OF THE CORPORATION—I

INTRODUCTION

At the foundation of the corporate responsibility debate exist certain assumptions that concern the nature of the corporation (beyond the legal features mentioned in chapter 1) and the precise mode of justification that is thought to be needed in defending the legitimacy claims of social institutions. In this and the next chapter we shall examine the first of these sets of assumptions. Since the business corporation is a complex institutional structure with a varied set of functions, it is amenable to different kinds of treatment. Various metaphors or models have emerged. While some of these pictures are overlapping in character, others have led to incompatible views on the nature of corporate responsibility and legitimacy. Frequently, theorists endorse aspects of two or more of these models, sometimes without apparent awareness of this fact or the possible incompatibility that it might cause. In fact, many of the important differences of opinion arising in the corporate responsibility debate are traceable to differences over these models. Unfortunately, there is no clear suggestion in the literature of how to resolve conflicts that occur when the nature of the corporation is itself in question.

There are several bases for these models. Some models are grounded upon certain features of the corporate *structure* that are taken as fundamental, for example, the relation of ownership or the pattern of rights and duties that exists in the corporation. Others rely more upon *functional* properties such as the power or influence of modern corporations. Still others are based upon features that concern the *origin* (real or apparent) or the *initial purpose* of corporations, such as the characteristic of being brought about by individual agreement. These and other bases have inspired specific paradigms or metaphors for the corporation. Thus, the structural basis has given rise primarily to the metaphors of the corporation as a piece of property and an organic body. The functional basis has led in the main to the metaphors of a machine or tool, a nation-state, a mental or moral agent, and an enterprise for the fulfillment of significant or basic needs; the last basis has led primarily to the metaphor of the corporation as an arena of private agreement or of public consent. These metaphors play an important role in the corporate responsibility debate for not only do they emphasize certain corporate features with which the relations of accountability are said to be connected, they also typically stress various internal and external groups of persons toward whom the corporation is alleged to have its most direct, pressing, or dominant set of responsibilities.

THE PRIVATE PROPERTY MODEL

The private property model portrays the ownership relation as the most dominant structural characteristic of the corporation and thus treats the corporation as essentially a piece of property. Friedman, for example, is one theorist who contends that this relation is the primary consideration in determining how revenues should be spent within the firm (Friedman, 1970, pp. 33, 122). This model ultimately applies to the stock of corporations, but it is perhaps best illustrated in the act of one corporation's buying out another. The first completely takes over the second and can dictate such aspects as the resources it has available to it, its personnel matters, strategy, product lines, and the like. The second becomes then a (mere) subsidiary of the first; it becomes an acquired set of assets—assets that can be manipulated. For instance, the management of the parent firm can decide to milk or bleed the resource; it can decide to sell or discard it; or, it can decide to integrate the resource within its enterprise and enrich it.

Downie treats the corporation more as a juridical than a physical asset (Downie, 1980, p. 429). For him, the ownership relation involves a certain legal status—one entailing special legal obligations, rights, and benefits. Owners have a juridical claim to papers or documents (shares) guaranteeing or entitling them to the fruits of their investment. The present financial worth of these documents is based partly upon the current revenue and dividend-producing capacities of the firm in question and partly upon the assessment of other investors or their advisors as to the firm's expected wealth-producing capacity in the future.

Outside of this legal context, business corporations are viewed by their owners as vehicles for investment, vehicles that are capable of producing considerable public and private wealth. The capacity to produce wealth has always been present in some form or another in different economic systems, of course, but it reaches its apex in private form in capitalism. The participation in the production of private wealth has been viewed in two conflicting ways, however. The most common opinion is that it involves a *right* that owners have when, in a legally appropriate way, they exchange money or something of monetary value for shares in a corporation. Friedman and others have advanced this view (Friedman, 1968, pp. 13ff.). Advocates of the social contract model of the corporation, on the other hand, typically view it as a kind of *social permission or privilege* that owners have to gain benefits from these distinctive wealth-producing ve-hicles. This is a permission given to them by the rest of society.

Implicit in these diverse perspectives is a difference of focus in the corporate responsibility debate. The possession of a right typically implies an obligation on the part of the rest of society to respect the claims of the holder contained in the right. Other parties must not legally or morally interfere with these claims or interests. This is especially true of the managers of business corporations whose task it is to augment the wealth-producing capacity of their firms. On this interpretation, their primary responsibilities would usually be economic and legal ones directed to the shareholders. Friedman, for one, concludes from the rights interpretation of the property model that the *sole* social responsibility of corporate managers in their occupational capacities is to maximize the financial return to the shareholders of the enterprise, without of course using fraud or deceit and while acting within the bounds of other laws and certain other generally accepted ethical standards (Friedman, 1970, p. 33). Those who view this participation as largely the product of social permission, however, contend that the chief obli-gation of corporate managers is to be responsive to the needs of those from whom this permission is ultimately received—the general public. Between these two views are works that blend these positions in various ways.

THE PRIVATE CONTRACT MODEL

Closely connected to the property model of the corporation is the private contract model in which the corporation is seen as a form of association involving a complex network of private agreements that exist among and between its internal and external constituents. In this model when shareholders decide to invest their money in a corporation, they agree to abide by the terms of the contract, terms that specify the rights, privileges, and duties of holding stock in the corporation. It is of course the possession of something of wealth that permits one to enter into this type of agreement in the first place. But within this model the ownership relation is seen as being less crucial to the existence of the corporation than are such relations as consent, promise making, voluntary as-sociation, and the like. To oversimplify a bit, ownership originates, but a contract sustains.

Of all the contractual relations involved in the corporation, the most important set is that which contain the network of formal agreements made by corporate members—agreements spelling out the basic institutional rights, privileges, and duties of the shareholders, workers, and managers of the firm. For without the commitment that emerges from these latter agreements, the corporate form of business enterprise could not be sustained. If the consent and commitment of the workers were lost, the firm would have no labor; if the consent and com-mitment of the managers were gone, it would have no center of planning and direction; and if the shareholders were to reject the agreements into which they once entered, the corporation would not only lose its current stock of capital, but in all likelihood it would have little chance in the future of securing further suitable investment as well. Without suitable investment, labor, and managerial direction, the corporation would collapse.

It may still be wondered, however, whether the present model of the corporation may not ultimately be reducible to some form of the property model. Even such advocates of the model as Hessen and Friedman (who are also quite sympathetic to the property model) suggest that the right to hold and control property is a fundamental right assumed in the making of economic agreements (Hessen, 1979, p. xiii; Friedman, 1968, p. 13). No economic transaction could occur unless the parties to the agreement are assumed to have sufficient control over the assets they offer in the transaction. This applies even to the workers for when they agree to give their time and energy to the corporation in exchange for the firm's promise of wages, salaries, fringe benefits, and the like, they are letting their organizational and productive efforts become assets of the firm. Since at least the time of John Locke, it has been urged by some thinkers that our activities, and even our bodies, are our possessions or property. Whether applied universally to all humans or not, it was held that individuals own and uniquely control their bodies. In this view these activities would then be said to be the assets that workers offer in making their economic contracts with others. On this view, then, there seems to be little or no difference between the property and the private agreement models of the corporation. Both metaphors ultimately rely upon ownership relations.

It should be noted, however, that some theorists such as Hosmer and Werhane warn that there are disadvantages to defending the identity of these models in this way. While not Marxists, these thinkers restate an argument advanced by Karl Marx more than a century ago. They tell us that when one conceives of the relation between corporations and their employees as one in which the former are said to "own" the latters' activities, there may be a strong temptation to treat not only their labor but the employees themselves as mere commodities and thus to view them solely as a means to corporate ends (Hosmer, 1984, p. 324; Werhane, 1985, p. 86). Such reduction in human dignity and respect is said to be inconsistent with certain moral beliefs strongly held in our society, however. This suggests that the term *property* should be restricted to one's external possessions and should not apply to one's activities and physical nature. Thus, while a firm can consider the pledged activities of its work force as a valued resource, these activities are not, strictly speaking, its property.

On the other hand, some theorists believe that even though employees or their work effort are not to be viewed as property, they are often treated in this way by managers. Such theorists are most likely then to develop some version of the conflict side of this model to be discussed shortly.

Whatever one's ultimate view of the definition of property, however, the present model differs at least in emphasis from the earlier one. The earlier model focuses upon the basis of an economic transaction—the alleged commodities exchanged—while the present model stresses the nature of the exchange process itself and the moral and legal commitments that make these transactions work.

One of the most sustained recent defenses of the private contract model is that offered by Hessen, who views the corporation as simply an extension of the partnership form of business enterprise (Hessen, 1979, pp. 17ff.). Although, as we have seen, the former is typically distinguished legally from the latter in terms of possessing entity status, virtual infinite duration, and limited liability for its owners, Hessen thinks that these features are not entirely unique to corporations. He tells us that certain forms of partnership can function as single entities when one, or a small number of partners, is given legal title to property or control. This individual, or small group of individuals, can then carry on certain legal functions, such as bringing suit, as a single unit. Hessen rejects the idea proposed by some that the assignment of responsibility differs for these two forms of enterprise. He denies the thesis that corporate responsibility is *collective* in nature, while responsibility in partnerships is *aggregate* in character (Hessen, 1979, p. 41). For Hessen, collective responsibility does not exist. All responsibility in business organizations is divisible; it is an aggregate of the individual responsibilities of their members. The same is true of rights: the rights of the corporation are simply the rights possessed by its individual members (i.e., the right to form voluntary agreements, associate for peaceful purposes, invest one's wealth, or hold property). Hessen contends that no rights are gained or lost when individuals join together in voluntary corporate ventures. And by introducing certain stipulations into the initial business agreement, partnerships can exist virtually as long as corporations. Thus, length of existence is not necessarily a distinguishing mark of the corporate form of business enterprise. Finally, he suggests that while partnerships typically do not involve limited liability, they can be set up in such a way that only the active partners can be held accountable for debt and tort liabilities.

Hessen grants that state agencies demand certain requirements be met before a business venture can be recognized as a legal corporation, but he contends that in this instance the government does not *create* the corporation in question. It merely certifies or legally recognizes its prior existence—an existence it owes to the presence of private agreement (Hessen, 1979, pp. 26ff.). The information that is required in the articles of incorporation is much like that demanded in a birth certificate or a marriage license. He believes that by disclosing the name, purpose, and duration of the business; the number of its shares and the voting rights connected to them; the amount of paid-in capital in the firm; and the names of its registered agents, incorporators, and its first group of directors, the state gives no more notice or legal protection to potential investors and creditors than it gives to potential suitors of those for whom it has given marriage certificates. For Hessen, then, corporations differ from partnerships only in degree, not kind.

Finally, it should be mentioned that the relation that Hessen thinks is basic to the corporation is that of agent and principal. Thus, his account strongly emphasizes the fiduciary status of managers as well as the promise-keeping context of the corporation's origin. The agent-principal relation applies, in fact, even to the nonmanagerial employees of the company. They, too, have an obligation to serve the interests of the principals (the shareholders).

In explaining the fundamental obligations of agents to principals, Blumberg says that the former are expected to be loyal and obedient. They are expected to obey all reasonable demands made by their employers. These are, in general, those demands that do not violate law or the common standards of business or professional ethics (Blumberg, 1983, p. 133). To fail to discharge these obligations puts the burden upon workers to explain themselves. Part of the reason for this, however, is also found in the nature of the agreement between workers, particularly non-union ones, and management that gives management significant power of replacement. Thus, we see the representational (or functionary) model of accountability developed here as well.

On the private agreement model, then, top-level executives are viewed as stewards of the corporation's assets who have promised to protect the investment of the shareholders and who recognize that if they fail in this regard, they can be replaced by the shareholders or their representatives. This general view has come to have an important place in the classical theory of corporate responsibility.

Hay and Gray, among others, maintain, on the other hand, that the private contract model also suggests that executives must protect certain interests of those parties with whom they have entered into direct voluntary agreements. They refer to this as the trustee model of management (Hay and Gray, 1977, p. 9). We have called it the stakeholder theory of responsibility. In any case, as trustees for the corporation, managers are required to consider and protect the interests of shareholders and employees as well as customers, suppliers, creditors, professional groups, government agencies, and perhaps even the broader community (though the responsibility to this last group is explained in this model only to the extent that *actual* agreements have been made between the corporation and the community). As Hay and Gray see it, a private agreement entails reciprocal duties for the contracting parties. The loyalty and obedience that is expected from employees, for example, must be matched by the managers' showing loyalty and consideration for the workers' interests as well.

Mention of the responsibilities of agency law imply what might be called a darker side to the private agreement model. Conflict theorists, for instance, emphasize areas in which there is lack of agreement among or between the various constituents of the corporation. Thus, Marx has emphasized the class conflict present in corporations between workers and owners—one in which the latter are said to treat the former as mere commodities. In this view, just as corporations may be seen as the product of private agreement, so also can their nature be seen as determined by private disagreement and opposition of interest. Morgan reminds us that organizations like the corporation often involve deep-seated conflicts of interest and hidden agendas on the part of their members. As specialization of function has become a dominant feature of organizations, divergence has also tended to predominate. Thus, divergence of opinions, values, backgrounds, and interests has contributed to an internal environment in which dissent, coalition building, the presence of outside interests, and working from expediency play nearly as strong a role in the functioning and motives of organizational life as do agreement and the desire for mutual cooperation. Members of organizations often align themselves into rival groups whose goals or interests may at times be perceived by their members to be as important as the overall goals of the organization itself. They sometimes form temporary coalitions to perform a certain corporate task and then dissolve back into their rival factions after the task has been accomplished (Morgan, 1986, pp. 142ff.). Morgan develops these insights while advancing the metaphor of an organization as a political system, but they remind us that the unique nature of a particular corporation depends upon the distinct blend of member agreement it possesses and conflict it tolerates. Various corporations thus combine these elements in different ways. This same view is advanced by Jackall in his discussion of managerial networks, which are formed to help offset the contingency and instability in the occupational situation of managers (Jackall, 1988, p. 38).

Finally, it should be noted that just as the positive version of the present model has often been used to defend the classical or the stakeholder theories of corporate responsibility, the negative or conflict version is usually associated with some form of the social demandingness or activist theories. Which view is endorsed will depend in great part upon the other assumptions that are held by a particular theorist.

THE ENTERPRISE MODEL

The basic insight behind the enterprise model is that the corporation, like many other social institutions, is an important vehicle for creatively satisfying basic or significant human needs. The model has been endorsed by certain humanistic psychologists or theorists influenced by them. They have typically focused their attention upon the needs of the employees of the corporation. Other versions have also emphasized the point that the structure of the corporation encourages creative and effective responses to the needs of shareholders and those outside the firm as well. The works of Maslow, Argyris, and McGregor fit into the former category, while the work of Hayek fits into the latter. The works of Drucker, and Peters and Waterman fit into both categories.

Morgan has brought out an important aspect of the model in his comparison of organizations to cultures. Such a metaphor also applies to the public power and organic models of the corporation. The culture paradigm emphasizes the shared values, histories, codes of behavior, informal rules, and loyalties that apply to corporations when seen as effective enterprises for advancing individual and collective aspiration (Morgan, 1986, pp. 112ff.).

When developed by humanistic psychologists, the model emphasizes that corporations are more that just sources of income for employees. Maslow, for example, maintains that they are also vehicles to satisfy other needs, such as belongingness, self-respect, and personal growth and fulfillment (Maslow, 1971, pp. 207ff.). In the modern world much of a person's view of self and self-worth stems from the work that he or she performs. In providing jobs to individuals, Maslow maintains that corporations supply their employees with responsibilities and challenges that affect the workers' sense of esteem and personal fulfillment.

Beesley and Evans stress this same point when they suggest that corporations are expressions of human aspiration. Given the fact that employees spend a large share of their lives in their occupations, the tasks and responsibilities they are expected to perform in their careers typically demand a large proportion of their intellectual and emotional commitment (Beesley and Evans, 1978, p. 16). The corporation thus becomes the focus of the accumulation of mastery and power, and the self-esteem and personal gratification that comes from exercising power wisely and effectively. The worker's sense of self-esteem and fulfillment is thus entwined with his or her success in achieving the organization's goals. Maslow calls this relation synergy, by which he means the process whereby a person's actions serve both individual and group needs (Maslow, 1971, p. 202). For corporations to be the foci of synergistic aspiration, reciprocal responsibilities must be respected and carried out: the corporation must respond to the employee's need for self-esteem and actualization, and the worker must respond to the survival and prosperity needs of the organization.

Argyris follows Maslow in believing that corporations are centers of individual and collective aspiration. He believes, however, that there is a strong tendency for the goals of the group to conflict with those of the individual (Argyris, 1957, p. 49). It is important then for the organization to treat its members as adults. He tells us that mature adults differ from young children with respect to their goals and attitudes. While the young child is content to experience passively the outside world, the adult typically seeks an active engagement in the world; while the child remains in a dependent and subordinate position, relying upon the effort and direction of adults for a considerable length of time, the adult typically seeks a great degree of mastery over his or her environment through self-chosen goals; while the child usually behaves in only a few ways, the adult responds to the world more flexibly and creatively; while the child's interests are for the most part casual and erratic—offering a basis for only temporary engagement and short-run perspectives—the adult's interests are deeper and more durable—providing the basis for the development of long-term perspectives. Argyris contends that although most employees in an organization wish to have their adult needs met, the organization often treats them in a more child-like way (Argyris, 1957, p. 53). This tends to reinforce their attitudes of dependence, subservience, passivity, inflexibility, and of short-term thinking. Argyris maintains that such attitudes not only harm the individual employee, they also hurt the performance and effectiveness of the organization. He suggests then the need for "reality leadership," whereby executives seek to minimize the incongruence that exists between the needs of individuals and those of the formal organization (Argyris, 1957, p. 205).

McGregor continues in the tradition of Maslow and Argyris when he distinguishes between theories X and Y. Both make certain assumptions about human nature and work. Theory X assumes that humans have little ambition. They dislike work and will try to avoid it if they can. They must be coerced to work through the use or threat of various penalties in order to achieve organizational goals; without such prodding, they will generally shun effort and responsibility. In terms of Maslow's theory, this view proposes that humans are primarily driven by lower-level physiological and security needs (McGregor, 1960, pp. 33ff.). Theory Y assumes that humans are driven by what Maslow calls higher-level needs for self-esteem, competence, fulfillment, and recognition. It maintains that work and effort is a natural part of living and that humans will exercise considerable self-direction toward the objectives to which they are committed. External prodding and coercion is not usually needed to motivate them; the rewards that come from successful achievement are typically sufficient to enlist their commitment. Humans thus often seek out new challenges and responsibilities that engage their ingenuity and creativity (McGregor, 1960, pp. 45ff.). McGregor concedes that our modern industrial society usually requires from workers only a small fraction of the skills and abilities they could contribute to their organizations. And, like Argyris and Maslow, he believes that corporate organizations are capable of doing much more to advance the self-confidence, competence, growth, status, and public recognition of employees. He calls for integrative management, which is designed to further the needs of both the organization and its individual members (McGregor, 1960, p. 55).

Drucker also supports the enterprise model. He has argued that corporations are essentially the products and vehicles of human effort and achievement that satisfy human needs in uniquely effective and creative ways (Drucker, 1946, pp. 30ff.). This has committed him to the view that managers must consider and encourage the creative abilities of workers (Drucker, 1985, pp. 231ff.). Peters and Waterman suggest that this is an essential ingredient in managers who search for excellence in their business decision making (Peters and Waterman, 1982, pp. 238ff.).

The enterprise model as advanced by these theorists emphasizes the collaborative and reciprocal relations that exist between employer and employee, superiors and subordinates in the corporation. But, like the private agreement model, there is also a more negative side to this paradigm. Just as the corporate flow chart can map out the geography of career ascent, so also can it portend the various occupational termini of the individual employees of the firm. Failed opportunities, missed promotions, frustrated aspiration, and ruthless colleagues or superiors can contribute to negative feelings toward the firm or its members. As Morgan points out in comparing organizations to political systems, employees can become so burned out by their jobs, or harbor such personal resentment toward their firms, that they come to derive satisfaction from doing less rather than more work (Morgan, 1986, p. 156). And they may get the respect of many other employees like themselves for this behavior. Their attitude is captured by an autoworker who said he worked only four days a week because he could not financially afford to work merely three days.

Recognizing that even productive enterprises can have their countercultures, it must still be admitted that the basic thrust of the present model is positive in nature. Clearly, Argyris and McGregor realize the dissatisfying aspects of institutional life, but they choose to focus upon the enabling, fulfilling, and actualizing features of organizations. Because we have already addressed these points of organizational conflict while discussing the negative version of the private agreement model, we shall merely note the possibility of a negative side to the present model and shall focus instead upon the positive features brought out by the authors mentioned above.

In addition to concern for the internal constituents of the firm, the model also addresses the relationship between the corporation and society in general. Hayek, for example, argues that the private sector of the economy offers us something that could not exist in a fully planned society: spontaneity, innovation, and creativity. He tells us an unique kind of order exists in the marketplace—one that is far superior to any that could come about through deliberate organization (Hayek, 1976, p. 110). When humans follow their individual interests, whether egoistic or altruistic in nature, they inevitably further the aims and needs of individuals who were never considered in the initial action. Of course, the initial conduct creates certain benefits for individuals on its own, but it also causes people to respond to it in divergent and sometimes creative ways. These responses in turn encourage further novel and creative patterns of response in others. The innovation fostered in this kind of system permits flexibility and pluralism in the satisfaction of human needs in general. The spontaneous order involved here Hayek calls "catallaxy" (Hayek, 1976, p. 108). For Hayek the corporation, like the other units or members of the private enterprise system, is an institution that permits and encourages its members to contribute to the catallactic order existing in the marketplace. It owes its existence to catallaxy in that the goals of the organization are themselves furthered by the innovative and flexible (though ultimately largely self-interested) actions of its members. It owes its legitimacy in great part to its superior performance in producing a spontaneous and creative pattern of achievements in the social and economic order (Hayek, 1948, pp. 7ff.). This point implies that high-level executives of a corporation should avoid patterns of planning and organization that stifle the creativity of subordinates. They should be willing to delegate authority and decentralize their power in order to permit genuine response and planning at the lower levels of the corporation. This is a point also mentioned by Drucker (Drucker, 1946, pp. 46ff.). It implies that because this kind of order could not be produced by centralized planning and, in fact, would be jeopardized by it, the roles of government regulation found in the public sector and bureaucratic planning found in the private sector should be limited ones. This is, of course, a central tenet of Hayek's work

(Hayek, 1976, pp. 110ff.). Whether the former or latter point is emphasized, however, the assumption of these theorists is that the corporation is a center of largely positive human effort and enterprise that is aimed at the satisfaction of needs in an effective and often creative manner.

THE SOCIAL CONTRACT MODEL

Influenced by the contractarian model of social institutions in political thought and opposed to the private contract model of the corporation is the social contract model. Basic to this model is the view that social institutions in general, and corporations in particular, get their legitimacy or authority from society. This permission may be given explicitly through the activities of federal, state, and local governments when, for example, they grant charters of incorporation, issue licenses, enter into contracts with corporations, and the like, or the permission may be more tacit or implied. The latter is said to occur when both members and nonmembers of a corporation cooperate with some or all of the ends of the firm, or at a minimum when they do not interfere with corporate activities aimed to achieve these ends.

Generally speaking, the advocates of this model focus upon the three legal characteristics of corporations mentioned in the first chapter—entity status, limited liability, and virtual perpetual existence. They argue that these features owe their existence to the consent of the public. Because of this, corporate executives are responsible for considering the interests of those from whom this permission is granted.

Since the model views the corporation as a separate entity under the law, it can also be called the legal entity model; it is a social invention with a distinct legal status grounded upon public consent. In this it is somewhat like the private contract model, which also views the corporation as a legal entity, but the latter's individualistic roots lead its advocates to deny the irreducibly social character of the corporation.

Fasching, like other advocates of the model, tells us that corporations are social inventions; they are organizations established to serve public purposes by pursuing their private interests (Fasching, 1981, p. 64). Especially important in his account are the features of limited and diffuse liability. By pooling individual effort, while permitting both the limitation of financial responsibility and the diffusion of individual moral or social responsibility, corporations put persons in the general society at somewhat greater risk. There are certain important advantages to be gained from this, especially in the area of economic productivity, but Fasching believes that this creates an added responsibility on the part of managers not to abuse the limited liability of their corporations. He maintains that they must limit the negative impact of their transactions (particularly to third parties who are not directly involved or represented in the corporations' explicit contracts) and serve more effectively the public good (Fasching, 1981, p. 69).

Some theorists contend that the consent of the public makes corporations into citizens. They believe that in possessing this status, firms must act like other citizens in obeying the laws and respecting the rights of persons. And because they gain private benefits through the use of various public services, executives are obligated to consider social needs in their corporate decision making. Sohn refers to this view as the citizenship theory of corporations (Sohn, 1982, p. 142).

Anshen argues that since business corporations function within a social system—one that gives them legitimacy, defines their rules of performance, and limits the boundaries of their acceptable activities—corporations must be responsive to the social will (Anshen, 1980, p. 6). By the *social will* he means the consensus of opinion that emerges in a society indicating its needs and values. In the area of corporate responsibility, the social will is determined by such factors as the type of legislation and regulation that exists in a society, by the nature and direction of its judicial decisions, and by such less formal sources as opinion polls, interviews, and the like (Anshen, 1980, p. 7). He tells us that this theoretical construct does not establish a rigid set of rules that corporations must follow. Rather it should be viewed as suggesting a set of understandings or general guidelines within which corporations are expected to function.

Anshen believes that business corporations were once expected to be solely or primarily economic institutions whose basic purpose was to maximize profit or economic growth. Now they are operating within a different set of assumptions. He tells us they are now expected to contribute to the quality of life as well as to its quantity. They are expected to respond to the social needs of the public by minimizing the negative social effects of some of their activities and introducing policies that actually enhance the noneconomic dimension of social life (Anshen, 1980, pp. 8ff.). He tells us further that it does not matter whether an individual manager agrees with these expectations; he or she is required to respond to them simply because they state the conditions under which the members of this society have given their continued permission to the corporate form of business enterprise.

Nader and Green also argue that business corporations are created by government in the act of incorporation. This process gives corporations certain privileges. As they see it, since the agreement involved here is a three-party one between corporate managers, shareholders, and a governmental body, the permission to incorporate entails certain private and public responsibilities for the corporation. The public responsibilities of a business corporation include such activities as providing adequate disclosure, eliminating bribes and fraudulent practices, respecting the rights of employees, and engaging in more competitive practices in the marketplace (Nader and Green, 1976, p. 252). These authors believe that the system of state chartering set up in the United States has proven to be inadequate to guarantee that corporate executives meet these responsibilities. They thus appeal to the social contract model in suggesting a dual system of chartering for many American firms—one that takes place at the federal level as well as the traditional process of incorporation, which occurs at the state level.

Finally, Donaldson believes with other social contract theorists that corporations exist only through the cooperation of the public and that an implied agreement exists between corporations and members of society. Because corporations have special privileges that permit them to act as single agents, hire employees, own scarce minerals, and limit certain of their responsibilities, they have implicitly agreed to perform certain tasks or functions for society (Donaldson, 1982, p. 43). He believes that the minimum demand that society places upon corporations follows from the principle of justice or fairness, namely, that no party to an agreement should be made worse off by it (Donaldson, 1982, p. 44). Thus, at a minimum, the benefits for society of having business corporations should outweigh the detriments.

Donaldson compares the benefits involved in a society like ours in which many of its private productive units are incorporated with one where people produce and work alone. By permitting individuals to work collectively and pool their resources into a single agency that can exist continuously with limited liability in certain areas, other members of society gain the benefits of improved economic efficiency, stable levels of output and distribution, and increased resources to insure the liability requirements of firms. Those working for business corporations are able to increase their income potential, diffuse personal liability, and adjust and stabilize their personal income allocation (Donaldson, 1982, p. 47). Productive units organized in corporate form can also have the disadvantages of depleting resources; polluting the environment; diffusing individual moral responsibility; wielding great, perhaps even excessive, political power; and disposing many workers to lose control over their work lives. But so long as the benefits of incorporation outweigh the detriments to society, corporations meet the minimum condition of fairness and can, to this extent, be justified as legitimate social institutions. For Donaldson, this means that as long as corporations avoid deception and fraud, respect their workers as human beings, and do not systematically worsen the lives of a particular group or segment of society, they meet the necessary conditions justifying their existence as productive organizations (Donaldson, 1982, p. 53). Corporations may have added obligations applying to them, but Donaldson believes the present account provides their moral foundation when viewed as productive institutions.

As Donaldson sees it, the social contract theory has traditionally been used by its advocates as a reform theory. When advanced in political thought as an explanation of the legitimacy of government, contractarians have sought to show some of the duties governments have toward their subjects. This general tendency is also present when social contract theory is applied to corporations. It can be said that in general theorists who appeal to this view advocate a more activist policy of social and moral responsibility for corporations.

REFERENCES

Anshen, Melvin. 1980. *Corporate Strategies for Social Performance*. New York: Macmillan Publishing Company.

Argyris, Chris. 1957. *Personality and Organization*. New York: Harper and Row.

Beesley, M., and Evans, T. 1978. *Corporate Social Responsibility—A Reassessment*. London: Croom Helm.

Blumberg, Phillip I. 1983. "Corporate Responsibility and the Employee's Duty of Loyalty and Obedience" in *Ethical Theory in Business*, edited by Tom L. Beauchamp and Norman E. Bowie, pp. 132–38. Englewood Cliffs, N.J.: Prentice-Hall.

Donaldson, Thomas. 1982. *Corporations and Morality*. Englewood Cliffs, N.J.: Prentice-Hall.

Downie, R. S. 1980. "Moral Problems in a Market Economy: A Reappraisal of Adam Smith." *The Dalhousie Review*, September, pp. 424–36.

Drucker, Peter F. 1946. *The Concept of the Corporation*. New York: The New American Library.

———. 1985. *Management: Tasks, Responsibilities, Practices*. New York: Harper and Row.

Fasching, Darrell, J. 1981. "A Case for Corporate and Management Ethics." *California Review of Management*, Summer, pp. 62–76.

Friedman, Milton. 1968. *Capitalism and Freedom*. Chicago: University of Chicago Press.

———. 1970. "The Social Responsibility of Business Is To Increase Its Profits." *The New York Times Magazine*, September 13, pp. 32–33, 122–26.

Hay, Robert, and Ed Gray. "Social Responsibilities of Business Managers." In *Managing Corporate Social Responsibility*, edited by Archie B. Carroll, pp. 8–16. Boston: Little, Brown and Company.

Hayek, F. A. 1948. *Individualism and Economic Order*. Chicago: University of Chicago Press.

———. 1976. *Law, Legislation and Liberty*, vol. 2. Chicago: University of Chicago Press.

Hessen, Robert. 1979. *In Defense of the Corporation*. Stanford, Calif.: Hoover Institution Press.

Hosmer, Larue Tone. 1984. "Managerial Ethics and Microeconomic Theory." *Journal of Business Ethics*, November, pp. 315–25.

Jackall, Robert. 1988. *Moral Mazes: The World of Corporate Managers*. Oxford: Oxford University Press.

McGregor, Douglas. 1960. *The Human Side of Enterprise*. New York: McGraw-Hill.

Maslow, Abraham. 1971. *The Farther Reaches of Human Nature*. New York: Viking Press.

Morgan, Gareth. 1986. *Images of Organization*. Newbury Park, Calif.: Sage Publications.

Nader, Ralph, and Mark Green, et al. *Taming the Giant Corporation*. New York: W. W. Norton and Company.

Peters, Thomas J., and Robert H. Waterman, Jr. 1982. *In Search of Excellence: Lessons From America's Best Run Companies*. New York: Warner Books.

Sohn, H. F. 1982. "The Corporate Social Responsibility Debate." *Journal of Business Ethics*, May, pp. 139–44.

Werhane, Patricia. 1985. *Persons, Rights and Corporations*. Englewood Cliffs, N.J.: Prentice-Hall.

6

MODELS OF THE CORPORATION—II

THE PUBLIC POWER MODEL

A point raised by many social contract theorists is the power of business corporations. Fasching, Anshen, Donaldson, and Nader and Green, for example, develop this point in advancing their contractarian views on the responsibility of corporations. The public power model differs from the social contract model, however, in that it focuses attention upon the principle of accountability espoused by impact theorists, namely, that the responsibility of an agent is, other things being equal, proportionate to his or her power or control over a situation or action. The validity of this principle is said not to depend upon the existence of an explicitly or implied agreement between corporate executives and other members of society. The emphasis here is not upon consent. It is upon influence. In fact, for most public power theorists, the focus is upon the need to protect individuals from the real or potential abuses resulting from what these theorists take to be excessive corporate power.

The main area of concern expressed by the public power theorists involves the externality effects of corporate decision making. As Nader and Green express it, state and federal governments were not as concerned to limit or regulate corporate power in the nineteenth century because it was widely believed that sufficient countervailing power (to use Galbraith's phrase) was exerted by the parties with whom corporate executives made explicit agreements (i.e., customers, workers, suppliers, shareholders, creditors, and in some cases workers). But in the twentieth century this view is widely disputed (Nader and Green, 1976, p. 63). Nader and Green believe that there are insufficient protections for individuals who do not enter into explicit agreements or transactions with corporations. Whether we are considering the negative effects of monopolistic business activities, inadequate disclosure policies, questionable hiring and firing practices, hazardous working conditions, or insufficient attention to environ-mental concerns, these authors contend that the interests of third parties must be more effectively protected. Their general approach is thus to look to increased federal regulations to protect these parties.

Dahl is also sympathetic to both the social contact and the public power models of the corporation. He argues that since corporations exist because society allows them to, they must be responsive to the needs of the public. But he also maintains that business corporations are formidable political and social enterprises (Dahl, 1972, p. 16). Corporate leaders exercise considerable power over the lives of others. Dahl says that their decisions concerning the quality of the environment and the workplace can cause death, injury, disease, and pain to both members and nonmembers of these organizations. Their decisions on employment criteria and practices and on plant relocation can deprive many persons of their economic well-being and personal freedom. And their use of advertising, promotions, and the like can have a powerful effect upon shaping public opinion and values (Dahl, 1972, p. 18). Dahl thinks that as a public institution, the business cor-poration is justified only by reference to its fulfillment of public purposes, many of which are in the economic arena. But Dahl is concerned that firms are not as responsive and responsible as they should be in the social and political arenas.

Dahl suggests an analogy appropriate to this model is that between corporations and nation-states. This has also been developed by other writers. For example, in writing about ITT's activities in the sixties and seventies, Sampson contends that its leaders conducted themselves as if they were heads of state, appealing to the interests of ITT over those of any other institution. And he alleges that they pursued many goals usually associated with nation-states, even to the extent of jeopardizing the political systems of several countries (Sampson, 1973, pp. 104ff.). He further maintains that there are several business corporations that rival nation-states in their size. ITT, for example, in the early 1970s em-ployed 400,000 people and its gross income was larger than the gross national product of Portugal or Chile (Sampson, 1973, p. 104). Sampson stresses the analogy between corporations and nation-states because he wishes to offset the view that the former are merely private citizens and thus deserve virtually all of the protections afforded legal persons under the law. For Sampson, viewing corporations as virtual or quasi nation-states involves a paradigm shift requiring that we take more seriously the assertions of our rights and prerogatives relative to corporations.

In advancing his version of the public power model, Dahl mentions the ability of the corporation to influence public opinion and values, a theme that is echoed in the work of other writers. Bremer, for example, argues that business values have become a dominant part of our culture. He tells us that business is the most significant force in American life and the strongest influence in determining the everyday values of the average citizen. The values of corporate managers have become the operative values in the nonbusiness aspects of life (Bremer, 1971, p. 121). By *business values* Bremer means such attributes as efficiency, productivity, profitability, and the use of quantitative criteria to judge the acceptability of a program of action. He tells us these values are spilling over into other facets of life when, for example, we speak of an efficient lesson plan or sermon, a productive member of a family, and a profitable friendship, or when we judge our well-being principally in terms of our income. As Bremer sees it, such values have a common root—the basic assumption of economics that a person seeks to maximize his or her own interests (Bremer, 1971, p. 123). His worry is that the egoism involved here conflicts with the values of compassion and fairness traditionally urged in the church and family.

Whitaker agrees with Bremer that the values of the business and corporate world have come to play a dominant part in American life. He believes that this supremacy has coincided with the waning of the traditional sources of value found in the family, community, and the church (Whitaker, 1974, pp. 92ff.). For Wilson, the American business system is more than just an economic system. It is an entire cosmology that entails assumptions concerning the external world, human nature, art, beauty, justice, and a host of other matters. Wilson contends that insofar as the business world is fundamentally a materialistic one, emphasizing such activities as production, capital formation, and the like, the individuals working within business institutions are required to focus upon these values in their institutional decision making (Wilson, 1975, pp. 36ff.). This has had a strong tendency to affect their values, attitudes, and decision making in noninstitutional and noneconomic settings. Thus, the corporate culture has become a dominant force in the shaping of the general culture.

Not all theorists who discuss the power that corporations have to affect the values of individuals focus upon the negative side of this influence, of course. In addition to Wilson, Birdzell discusses the positive aspects of this impact. He maintains that as a business organization, the corporation is organized to pursue cooperative economic effort. Thus, part of its importance in modern society involves the normative or moral system upon which it is grounded. The system emphasizes such positive values as cooperation through commitment, free exchange, frugality, and a meritarian conception of justice, in addition to the traditionally recognized values of productivity, efficiency, and profit maximization (Birdzell, 1975, pp. 75ff.).

Thus, whether the positive or negative aspects of the power of corporations are discussed, the point beyond dispute among these authors is that corporations constitute significant centers of influence and power in American society.

THE CORPORATION AS A MACHINE OR TOOL

The next model of the corporation has arisen in part as a result of addressing the question of whether corporations can be said to be the valid subjects of moral evaluation. Two views have emerged on this question. One accepts the idea that corporations are moral agents, while the other rejects this idea, contending that corporations are not the proper subjects of moral evaluation. They should be looked upon simply as private instruments created to serve economic and social purposes. They should not be treated as distinct agents who can act in behalf of themselves.

The machine or tool model has been developed in several ways. Hayek advances it as an implication of methodological individualism. And although their theories are more often associated with the property or private contract models, even Friedman and Hessen have hints of the machine model in their works for they, too, are methodological individualists. This latter theory contends that only the individual human members of a corporation are the proper subjects of moral assessment. To speak of the corporation itself as good or bad is merely an abbreviated way of passing moral judgment upon its key decision makers. Such theorists view corporations as complex social instruments created primarily to serve economic purposes. The test of their legitimacy is determined by how effectively they fulfill these purposes.

Another way the machine model has been advanced is illustrated in the works of Ladd and Taylor. For Ladd, business corporations constitute formal organizations. Formal organizations are those that have their own unique internal structure, a structure that dictates the logic of the key normative concepts applying to them. By a formal organization, Ladd means one that distinguishes the official and public capacities of its members from their private capacities. The formal organization is concerned only with the former. Its positions are largely impersonal in nature; the individuals filling these positions are able to be substituted or replaced easily by other persons (Ladd, 1970, p. 488). When these individuals act, it is the public role that dictates and dominates their decision making. They are neither expected nor encouraged to make decisions as private persons— persons seeking to maximize their own individual and family interests. They are required to suppress their feelings and personal concerns for the needs and demands of the organization. Ladd tells us that corporate members must accept the values of the firm as data. The public capacity of their roles requires them to abdicate their own private values in order to secure the goals of the organization in a nonpersonal way (Ladd, 1970, p. 494).

Since the goals of the organization provide the value premises upon which corporate decision making takes place, the ideal of rationality applying here is an instrumental one. Concepts such as moral integrity and rightness do not apply to the conduct of the corporation or its members when they are functioning in their official capacities. For Ladd, conduct is right only if it serves the goals and values of the corporation. To refer to a decision of a corporate executive acting in an official capacity as *morally* right or wrong is thus to make a category mistake (Ladd, 1970, p. 500). It is like referring to a corporation as handsome or slender because its members are handsome or slender. Thus, Ladd's form of methodological individualism not only eschews the applicability of moral concepts to corporations, it rejects the idea that the members of a corporation can be morally evaluated when they are acting in an official capacity.

In addition to the primary goals for which the organization is developed (i.e., growth, stability, profit maximization, and the like), Ladd believes that the main internal values of a firm are efficiency and administrative impartiality (Ladd, 1970, pp. 500, 507). It is by these nonmoral values that the conduct of corporate managers is judged. Ladd further contends that business corporations, like other formal organizations, are structures set up to pursue their primary goals. So the comparison to tools or machines is appropriate. There are two facets to the instrumental character of corporations: the corporate structure itself is a social instrument or tool created to pursue economic ends, and the individuals who belong to the corporation are, in their official capacities, mere instruments to fulfill these ends.

Taylor assumes this model in proposing his theory of scientific management (Taylor, 1911, pp. 10ff.). He tells us that the functions of workers should mirror those of a well-run machine. Tasks should become routine and repeatable; they should be broken down into their simplest parts with individuals performing specific functions until they are completely mastered. Supervisors should be available to check, rate, and correct worker performance. This requires that a hierarchy of staff and line positions be implemented, much like that established in the military. The primary purpose of such a mechanistic arrangement is to insure organizational efficiency.

It is in its emphasis upon the instrumental character of the workers' tasks and lives within the corporation that the machine model primarily differs from the enterprise metaphor with which it is sometimes associated. The enterprise model treats workers and their career goals as intrinsically valuable rather than treating them like mere instruments. And since it emphasizes the teleological dimensions of organizational life, the enterprise model does not remove the conduct of managers and workers acting in their official capacities from the arena of moral discourse and evaluation. Even its view of the organization itself differs from the tool model. Since the enterprise model appeals to the team concept, it usually treats the network of interconnected purposes found in the corporation as ends in themselves rather than as mere instruments. Put differently, the enterprise model tells us that members play for the team (or corporation) rather than the team being merely an instrument of the members' play. Both the team and its members are valued in themselves within the enterprise model, which is not usually the case within the tool or machine model.

One of the chief implications upon the corporate responsibility debate that the instrumental theory has had thus far is to discourage the idea that executives should or will voluntarily endorse an activist policy of fulfilling noneconomic responsibilities when this might conflict with the principal economic goals of the corporation. Ladd, for example, tells us that if we were to expect firms to pursue such objectives, this expectation must be translated into the primary goals or values of the corporation. This would need to be done through external pressures, primarily through the force of law or consumer response (Ladd, 1970, p. 508).

THE ORGANIC MODEL

The organic model is one of the oldest theories of social organization. The model was first applied to political and religious bodies and has been especially prominent in the discussions of the nature of the church by Christian theologians. Basic to the model is the view that a social entity should be looked upon as a living organism, with parts arranged for the continued existence, health, and well-being of the whole. Some recent organizational theorists who apply this model to corporations present the theory in terms of the following theses: the teleological, the nonreductivist, the interdependence, and the systems.

Like advocates of the enterprise model, organic theorists stress the idea of purpose in business organizations (Andrews, 1971, p. 162). Purpose can be seen in nearly every phase of the organization—from its corporate charter or mission statement to the preface or introduction to its most recent annual report; from its periodic strategy sessions to its market forecasting; from its rules on bribery to its parking regulations. And, like advocates of the machine model, organic model theorists believe that the purpose of the parts are largely determined by the functions they play in the whole.

The present feature of the organic model implies another: the purposes and good of the whole cannot be reduced to the purposes or good of the parts. This is what Ackoff means, for example, when he says that organicism contends the whole is greater than the sum of the parts (Ackoff, 1981, p. 15). One does not guarantee a whole will function effectively by simply bringing together parts that work well separately. The function of the parts must be tempered or made consonant with the operation of the whole. Too much growth by a part might hinder the effectiveness of the whole and impede the growth of less developed parts; the resulting imbalance might even jeopardize the survival of the whole itself. Like the human body, a social entity has certain objectives that are treated as *sui generis*, such as survival, homeostasis and growth. None of these goals apply to the parts in quite the same way that they apply to the whole.

The organic model also stresses the idea that the parts of a whole are uniquely interdependent. Like the organs of the body, they cannot in normal circumstances function independently. Just as the liver or heart cannot function on its own outside the body, so the finance, research, or public relations departments of a corporation would typically have difficulty operating entirely on their own. This model insists that the functioning of each of the parts affects the functioning of the other parts. In the strict sense, no one part has an entirely independent effect upon the whole. But it also typically emphasizes the need for the parts to specialize themselves in terms of their relatively distinct functions.

Ackoff also tells us that this model demands that we view corporations as components of an ever-widening system of purposes (Ackoff, 1981, pp. 19ff.). The system begins with the web of moral and interpersonal projects and relations that provide a basis for the goal setting of single firms. Beyond this is the wider system of relations and social institutions of which particular corporations form a part. He maintains that without reference to the end states sought by this network of social institutions, no judgment of the effectiveness or legitimacy of specific management decisions can be made (Ackoff, 1981, pp. 19ff.).

Morgan reminds us that, like systems theorists, contingency theorists also stress the need to balance the internal needs of the organization with the environmental circumstances it faces. They believe there is no one best way to organize a company. The appropriate form must consider the fit between the organization itself and its external environment (Morgan, 1986, p. 49). This theory thus emphasizes flexible and creative management to respond to the changing environment of opportunity, risk, and uncertainty that the corporation faces.

Another version of the organic model can be seen in the population ecology of Hannan and Freeman, with its emphasis upon studying those variables that explain the number and stability of various kinds of organizations and the correlations that exist between these types and the various conditions found in their environments (Hannan and Freeman, 1977, pp. 440ff.). It can also be seen in the sociotechnical or organizational ecology model of Trist and Bamforth (Trist and Bamforth, 1951, pp. 20ff.). Trist, for example, focuses upon the role of collaboration between and among the various internal and external constituents of an organization with a view to helping organizations adjust to their turbulent environments while still permitting the management of the social system as a whole (Trist, 1979, pp. 440ff.). These last theories, each in its own way, remind us of a comment made by Friedrich Nietzsche that the health of the organism can often be determined by the diseases it has overcome.

Finally, the model is also endorsed by management theorists, such as Post and Ouchi. The former maintains that the responsibilities of managers cannot be determined without first considering the impact that their fulfillment would likely have upon the other institutions in society (Post, 1986, pp. 51ff.). The latter tells us about the advantages of corporate organizations founded upon a holistic conception of integrated institutional goals, where the health and interdependent effectiveness of the entire organization is the paramount concern of the members. He calls these Z organizations and maintains that they are to be distinguished from traditional corporations on the basis of having more consensual or participative decision-making processes, mutual respect and trust among members, and an integrative and long-run goal-setting structure (Ouchi, 1981, pp. 66ff.)

The present model resembles the enterprise and machine models in important respects, but there are some notable differences as well. Unlike enterprise theorists, for example, organic thinkers often contend that the objectives of the whole supercede the individual goals and projects of the parts. They are thus more likely to believe that just as an individual organ may need to be sacrificed or removed to preserve the health and well-being of the entire body, specific members of a corporation, or their individual work projects, may need to be replaced or withdrawn in order to ensure the attainment of the organization's overall objectives. A second difference concerns the analogies or metaphors that lie at the root of these models. The metaphor of the human body typically grounds the organic model. The enterprise model, on the other hand, is based upon the kind of harmony and integration of parts often found in human creations, like a great painting or symphony, where creative fulfillment is the guiding end rather than the overall stasis of the entity or the health or survivability of the organism.

Like advocates of the machine model, organic theorists typically believe that the purposes of the parts are largely determined by the functions they assume in the whole. Unlike such advocates, however, they are unwilling to grant that these functions exhaust the contributions that members make to the whole. Theorists such as Jennings believe that the personal goals of members contribute to the latters' organizational effectiveness. These goals have value, even if it is only or primarily secondary in nature (Jennings, 1971, p. 29). They further differ from advocates of the machine model in rejecting the idea that the roles that workers play in a corporation are so impersonal that this precludes the assignment of individual responsibility, though they are often inclined to think that collective responsibility is something over and above the responsibilities of individuals within the organization.

THE CORPORATION AS MENTAL OR MORAL AGENT (OR PERSON)

A case can be made for believing that the last model of the corporation is really a combination of at least two distinct metaphors for, to put it simply, a mental agent need not be conceived of as a moral one. It might be contended that since minds cannot act as moral agents because they have no *actus reus* or physical means of bringing about consequences in the world, they should not be treated as full-fledged moral beings. But because mental agents can be said to make decisions, they are in need of some criteria by which to make these. And since some of these may have a significant impact upon at least other minds, some of the criteria to which they appeal will be partly moral in nature. The impact need not be physical to be significant or relevant to moral decision making. So, we shall construe what others take to be the different types of mental or moral agency as simply the various degrees or levels of moral agency.

We begin however with a somewhat unlikely candidate. Morgan tells us that organizations can be conceived of as brains (Morgan, 1986, p. 78). What he means by this is that organizations are centers of (1) information gathering and processing, (2) intelligent decision making, and (3) self-correction. Clearly, organizations are centers of information processing and gathering. They both receive and disseminate information from and to their internal and external constituents and they utilize this information on behalf of their decision-making. They thus consider and weigh alternatives and formulate policies and strategies in terms of which they implement their actions. Morgan reminds us that some theorists, such as Simon, maintain that corporations exhibit only bounded rationality. They do not have perfect knowledge and often excessively fragment their information. And often too they are not in the best situations to achieve their objectives to the fullest extent. He tells us then that they seek profit satisficing rather than profit maximizing (Morgan, 1986, p. 82).

Finally, corporations have the capacity for self-correction. Morgan tells us that they are like holographs in that their parts have both specialized and generalized features—each part is able to do or duplicate the activities of other parts. Each is thus a reflection of the whole. The built-in redundancy permits parts to refer to or consider the contribution of the other parts to the whole (Morgan, 1986, p. 104). The reflective capacity involved here permits self-correction by independently monitoring the functions of the parts with a view to serving the goals of the whole. Corporations that have work teams with members who can perform the tasks of the other members is one salient example of this capacity or mode of organization.

As we have already indicated, Morgan treats these as brain-like functions, but, in fact, they appear to be more appropriate to mind. But, however they are conceived, implicit within the execution of these functions is the model of corporations as agents or decision makers whose decisions are capable of having a moral impact.

This last point is also brought by Goodpaster. He contends that corporations are distinct subjects of moral discourse. They are members of the moral community and are thus amenable to moral evaluation, an evaluation that is independent of the assessment of their members. They are capable of independent moral choice or action and are the subjects of distinct moral obligations and privileges. We have seen that it is a well-accepted principle of law that corporations are at least juristic persons. They are the subjects of rights under the law. But as juristic persons, they are fictitious entities—mere creatures of the state. The logic of this traditional legal view suggests something like the private contract or social contract models of the corporation. Goodpaster, Werhane, and French wish to go beyond these models, however.

Goodpaster believes that the nature of corporate responsibility is a broader matter than that which arises for corporate executives in their private capacities. He contends that corporations are themselves moral agents who have their own discernible responsibilities. His position is based upon an analogy between corporate and individual moral responsibility (Goodpaster, 1984, p. 301). For Goodpaster, two things are necessary for a person to be the subject of moral evaluation: rationality and respect for others. By rationality, he means the capacity to pursue one's projects and purposes with careful attention to the means and ends, the alternatives and consequences, and the risks and opportunities of action. By respect for others, he means the ability to consider the interests of other agents or parties, especially those who are likely to be affected directly by one's actions. We respect others then when we treat them as ends in themselves (Goodpaster, 1984, p. 301). A subject of moral assessment is considered an active agent when he or she has the requisite perceptual, reasoning, coordinating, and implementing abilities to translate conception into decision making and action. Since corporations, through the activities of their members, manifest these abilities in their decision making, Goodpaster concludes that they should be treated as distinct moral agents. He calls the principle that yields this conclusion the principle of moral projection.

Werhane also believes that corporations are distinct subjects of moral evaluation, but she does not think they are metaphysically distinct from the moral agents who compose them. She refers to them as *secondary* or *dependent* moral agents (Werhane, 1985, p. 58). For Werhane, corporate acts are secondary ones; they are attributable to the corporation through the primary actions of persons who work for, or come to represent, the corporation (Werhane, 1985, p. 53). Corporate acts can validly be called "corporate" only if they receive a certain kind of authorization. This authorization comes primarily from the corporate structure with its charter, bylaws, and rules of procedures that spell out its goals, policies, and basic makeup. Such a structure collectivizes and incorporates the separate actions of individual members, thus rendering their activity corporate in form. What emerges is something that, while it depends upon individual conduct and intention, is more than the sum of the parts. Werhane believes that corporations manifest distinct intentional action, even though this collective intent is dependent upon the separate intentions of their members. Ultimately, it is this type of intent that permits the independent moral appraisal of corporate conduct (Werhane, 1985, p. 56).

Like Goodpaster and Werhane, French also believes corporations are not mere creatures of the state; they have a distinct existence beyond the legal sphere. For French, they are full-fledged moral persons; they are both the holders and administrators of moral rights. They can act in behalf of their rights in ways not reducible to the activities of their members (French, 1984, p. 38).

A moral agent for French is anyone who can act intentionally, or at least who has the capacity to responsively adjust his or her conduct in the light of past action. An agent acts with intention or responsive adjustment (self-correction) whenever he or she appeals to certain considerations as reasons for acting. These considerations, in conjunction with certain beliefs about empirical matters, produce or help to bring about an initial or responsive action (French, 1984, p. 40). When a moral agent is capable of doing this in a way that is not reducible to the activities of other agents, we have what French calls a moral person. By a moral person, he means a non-eliminitable subject of moral ascription (French, 1984, p. 38). Corporations are such non-eliminitable subjects.

French offers two primary considerations in behalf of this conclusion. First, corporations have their own internal decision structures, which provide evidence that they can act intentionally or responsively. Second, although human persons are necessary for the working of these decision structures, the actions that result thereby are amenable to distinct moral ascription. They are not mere products of the decisions or actions of the human agents who are members of the corporation.

The internal decision structure includes these elements: (1) the set of offices and positions, spelled out in the corporate flow chart, through which corporate decisions must pass and be ratified; (2) procedural rules that must be followed for an action to be considered a corporate one, rather than a merely random or private action of a corporate member; and, (3) the policies that articulate the general objectives or goals of the firm. These last may be given in the corporate charter, or more usually they can be seen or derived from the past practices of the firm. (They involve such activities as providing maximum investor return, being a leader in technological innovation, pursuing a policy of conservative financial management, providing a safe working environment, and the like.) As French sees it, the corporate internal decision structure organizes the inputs from the various human members of the firm and thereby marks a particular decision or action as a corporate one (French, 1984, pp. 51ff.).

The type of decision or action that emerges is distinct from the individual decisions and actions of corporate members. A corporate action need not depend upon the working of any one individual or group of individuals in the firm, for particular individuals may be replaced without change to the corporate action. In fact, it is possible in certain cases that a particular corporate action does not accurately reflect the intent of any single person in the firm. It is thus the product of incorporated intelligence. It follows that corporations may be the subjects of unique moral ascription; they may be individually blamed, for example, while none of their members are blamed (French, 1984, p. 31). It thus may be appropriate to consider their intentions or dispositions and to apply the language of a virtue ethic to them.

French has suggested that corporations give evidence of moral agency and personhood even in cases where they could not be said to have *intended* a particular outcome to have occurred (French, 1984, pp. 156ff.). The fact that they have *responded* after an untoward event to correct it indicates that they are sufficiently amenable to reason giving to be considered full-fledged moral persons. For French, this implies that corporations have all of the privileges, rights, and duties that are usually accorded to all members of the moral community (French, 1984, p. 32).

The mental or moral agent model suggests that corporations should be held accountable for the same kinds of conduct for which any moral agent is held responsible. One cannot, for example, claim that corporations are subject to economic and legal duties but are immune from strictly moral or social obligations or responsibilities that apply to other moral agents. This conclusion does not by itself entail an activist policy with respect to social or moral responsibility, but it places the burden of proof upon those who would seek to restrict more narrowly the social and moral duties of corporations to show why these arenas should be so restricted. And it seeks to bring into sharper focus the kinds of consideration that are thought to be appropriate in arguing for a narrower range of corporate social or moral responsibilities.

Last, we should not overlook another facet of the mental or moral agent model that is brought out by another metaphor advanced by Morgan. Like some of the other models, this too has its negative side. He tells us that as mental entities, corporations may become psychic prisons for their members, much like Plato's cave did for its inhabitants (Morgan, 1986, pp. 199ff.). Whether corporations imprison their members within patterns of rigid decision making, exhibiting excessively bounded rationality, whether their structure and regimentation commit them to an obsessively restricted pursuit of efficiency, or whether the presence of unconscious forces and defense mechanisms mask the real nature of the interpersonal relations that exist in organizational life, Morgan's metaphor reminds us of a darker side to the mental-like entities telelogically created or constructed within or for social life. The self-correcting functions of these creations must constantly be used to monitor and offset their tendencies to be cages or prisons for their members—whether these be mental, psychic, or moral ones.

A final word of caution about these models is in order. It will be seen in both the general and specific discussions of corporate responsibility presented in the coming chapters that not all of these eight models or their variations are equally represented. In fact, a few theorists whose work will be discussed do not even commit themselves to a distinct model, but where a theorist is so committed, the point will often be noted. The reader will then be able to see how a theorist's view of the nature of the corporation often disposes him or her to advocate a particular kind of theory of corporate responsibility. It should also be noted that some theorists have sought to reduce one or other of these models to another. Thus, for example, they have suggested that a private contract can be viewed as emerging from a higher-level social contract, or a social contract can be viewed as an asset or piece of property, or property can be viewed as a right of a moral agent, or rights can be viewed as very serious or important interests or goals, and so on. These reductivist attempts will be largely ignored in the coming chapters, however.

REFERENCES

Ackoff, Russell L. 1981. *Creating the Corporate Future: Plan or Be Planned For*. New York: John Wiley and Sons.

Andrews, Kenneth R. 1971. *The Concept of Corporate Strategy*. Homewood, Ill.: Dow Jones-Irwin.

Birdzell, L. E. 1975. "The Moral Basis of the Business System." *Journal of Contemporary Business*, Summer, pp. 75–87.

Bremer, Otto. 1971. "Is Business the Source of New Social Values?" *Harvard Business Review*, November-December, pp. 121–26.

Dahl, Robert. 1972. "A Prelude to Corporate Reform." *Business and Society Review*, Spring, pp. 17–23.

French, Peter. 1984. *Collective and Corporate Responsibility*. New York: Columbia University Press.

Goodpaster, Kenneth E. 1984. "The Concept of Corporate Responsibility." In *Just Business: New Introductory Essays in Business Ethics*, edited by Tom Regan, pp. 292–323. New York: Random House.

Hannan, M., and J. H. Freeman. 1977. "The Population Ecology of Organizations." *American Journal of Sociology*, vol. 82, pp. 429–64.

Jennings, E. E. 1971. "The Worlds of the Executive." *TWA Ambassador*, vol. 4, pp. 28–30.

Ladd, John. 1970. "Morality and the Ideal of Rationality in Formal Organizations." *Monist*, vol. 54, pp. 488–516.

Morgan, Gareth. 1986. *Images of Organization*. Newbury Park, Calif.: Sage Publications.

Nader, Ralph, and Mark Green, et al. 1976. *Taming the Giant Corporation*. New York: W. W. Norton and Company.

Ouchi, William. 1981. *Theory Z: How American Business Can Meet the Japanese Challenge*. New York: Avon Books.

Post, James E. 1986. "Perfecting Capitalism: A Systems Perspective on Institutional Responsibility." In *Corporations and the Common Good*, Robert B. Dickie and Leroy S. Rouner, pp. 45–60. South Bend, Ind.: University of Notre Dame Press.

Sampson, Anthony. 1973. *The Sovereign State of ITT*. Greenwich, Conn.: Fawcett Publications.

Taylor, F. W. 1911. *Principles of Scientific Management*. New York: Harper and Row.

Trist, E. L. 1979. "New Directions of Hope: Recent Innovations Interconnecting Organizational, Industrial, Community and Personal Development." *Regional Studies*, vol. 13, 439–51.

Trist, E., and K. W. Bamforth. 1951. "Some Social and Psychological Consequences of the Longwall Method of Coal Getting." *Human Relations*, vol. 4, pp. 1–38.

Werhane, Patricia. 1985. *Persons, Rights and Corporations*. Englewood Cliffs, N.J.: Prentice-Hall.

Whitaker, John H. 1974. "The Supremacy of the Business Ethic." *Business and Society Review*, Summer, pp. 91–96.

Wilson, James A. 1975. "Morality and the Contemporary Business System." *Journal of Contemporary Business*, Summer, pp. 31–58.

7

THEORIES OF INSTITUTIONAL LEGITIMACY

ACCOUNTABILITY AND LEGITIMACY

We have suggested in chapter 1 that as social institutions corporations can be put on the defensive to show the legitimacy of themselves or their actions. Generally speaking, if they are seen as legitimate institutions, they will be the recipients of continued support and encouragement by society. But if their legitimacy is seen to wane, the loyalty of members and nonmembers alike will often lessen as well, and, like many of the previous governments in Eastern Europe, the survival of these institutions will be put in jeopardy or abridged. We also suggested in the preface that there have been times in the recent past when the public has expressed great disappointment with corporate legal, social, or moral performance. Hence the importance of understanding the concept of legitimacy as it has been applied to corporations and their conduct. The purpose of this chapter then is to examine certain discussions of the concept with an eye to advancing a theory of its meaning and to consider the main strategies of justification that have been offered to show or prove the legitimacy of such a social institution as the corporation.

THE NATURE OF LEGITIMACY

Various theorists have sought to define the concept of legitimacy. Weber, for example, defines it as valid domination (Weber, 1968, vol. 1, pp. 212ff.). In this view a legitimate institution is one that has developed a pattern of offices, rules, or procedures that can validly claim the obedience and loyalty of its members. Aligned to this concept is one proposed by Berger, who defines legitimacy as the rightful possession of power (Berger, 1981, pp. 83ff.). For corporations to be viewed in this way, their executives must convince the general public that they exercise their power in a justified manner. They must show that they have developed offices and procedures that justifiably claim the loyalty and the obedience of members, as well as the support and endorsement of nonmembers. Werhane agrees with Berger that legitimate institutions command the loyalty of their members and the support of nonmembers. For her, institutional legitimacy is defined in terms of the network of relations and reciprocal duties that exist among and between these members and nonmembers (Werhane, 1983, pp. 16ff.). To the extent that these are respected within and by the institution, it is viewed as being legitimate in nature.

The accounts of Bock, Hurst, and Farmer and Hogue agree with that offered by Werhane. They too define institutional legitimacy in terms of the existence of a social consensus that supports the institution, gives it legal sanction, and perhaps even offers it special privileges (Bock, 1979, p. 7; Hurst, 1970, p. 60; Farmer and Hogue, 1985, p. 18). This means at a minimum that both members and nonmembers will refrain from condemning, boycotting, or seeking to dismantle the institution or oppose its policies. For the corporation, it means that nonmembers will encourage the growth of corporations, permit individuals to be enlisted as members, and perhaps even directly pay for part of this enlistment and training; they will also permit individuals to be recruited to the ranks of those primarily affected by the corporation's decisions (consumers, shareholders, suppliers, creditors, and the like); and, in general, they will respect the other legal rights and privileges of the corporation.

Finally, Bell contends that the concept of legitimacy concerns the limits of an institution's authority (Bell, 1977, p. 15). Within its domain of authority, the institution has inspired sufficient confidence and trust that members and nonmembers alike will often refrain from even demanding a rendering for the individual actions of the institution. Extensive authority thus implies extensive independence and the relative absence of institutional defensiveness. This degree of authority has some controversial features, though, as Simon indicates. He tells us when members of an organization fully accept the authority of their superiors, they continually permit their behavior to be directed by the latters' decision making, usually without independently examining the merits of this. The superiors' decisions become the subordinates' ones or, as Simon tells us, the latter simply abdicate their choice (Simon, 1965, pp. 11, 126). In this domain of decision making the demand for accountability is only virtually present, since it is typically left unexercised. But beyond this realm of authority, the institution is frequently questioned about its decisions or conduct.

The definitions of Weber, Berger, and Bell remind us of the normative aspects of this concept—that legitimate institutions *deserve* consideration and support. These institutions can justify their place and function in society in general in such a way that they need not continually defend their individual actions.

Whether defined descriptively or normatively, however, legitimacy is not an all-or-nothing concept; it admits of degrees. Minimally, legitimate institutions stay, or deserve to stay, in existence; there is no perceived need to overthrow or eliminate them, though they may need to be altered or reformed. When individuals in society begin to show a lack of confidence in an institution, however, they indicate by their lessened support that the institution's legitimacy is being called into question. When implicit criticism and complaint turns to active protest, the structure or function of the institution may be significantly changed, or it may be more closely watched and regulated by other organizations. Finally, if decentralized protest escalates to socially organized rejection or rebellion, we have a full-scale assault upon the organization, one whose resolution may mean the elimination of the institution in question. For the corporation, theoretically this could involve the public's demand either for the immediate liquidation or confiscation of a company's assets—the collective equivalent of capital punishment—or at least for the exclusion of that group of investors, to the extent to which they can be isolated and regulated, from incorporating or doing business in the country in question in the future—the collective equivalent of exile.

This discussion suggests that we can place institutions into various categories or levels of legitimacy when viewed more descriptively. Outside of these categories are organizations or groups that are viewed as illegitimate. They get some support from their members, of course (otherwise they could not be referred to as a group or social entity, in the first place), but they get virtually none from outsiders. Their existence is, in fact, usually the object of serious and direct challenge within the society as a whole. Illegal organizations, like a drug ring, or socially aberrant groups, like a coven, fit this description.

Category one organizations are seen as having a minimal degree of legitimacy. They are, of course, accepted from within—sometimes with great vigor and sincerity. And they are also usually accepted from without, at least to some extent—sometimes, again, with considerable zeal and earnestness. But they are often rejected by large numbers of individuals outside the group who view them as illegitimate. Examples of category one groups include such organizations as the Students for a Democratic Society and the Palestine Liberation Organization (during much of its history) as well as a newly established dictatorship.

Category two organizations receive internal and external support, in general, but they are closely watched or regulated by other organizations or their members. Unlike category one organizations, their continued existence is not in jeopardy in the general society, but they must frequently justify their nature or conduct to these other organizations—particularly in certain areas or circumstances. Regulated monopolies fit into this category, especially as concerns their pricing powers, as well as dictatorships that are more well entrenched than those in category one.

Category three is where most business corporations currently fit. They have a broad base of constituent and social support. Internally, they are only very infrequently challenged by their members, especially the subordinates. Externally, individual corporations have social sanction and authority in general but are still often asked to explain themselves in specific circumstances both before and after they have acted. Such a request or demand may be made more frequently in some societies or historical periods than in others. Category three organizations are typically watched or regulated by outside groups or agencies, again to varying degrees of scrutiny at different times. But the nature of the regulation is not usually as constraining as that typically given to category two institutions. In addition to private corporations, each of the three branches of the federal government also constitutes an example of a category three institution. Each is watched closely by the other two to guarantee that the power of a single branch does not become excessive or oppressive. Finally, we also see this type of institution illustrated in the main political parties that exist in a democracy.

Category four institutions have a good deal of latitude and autonomy. Members and nonmembers have great trust in these enterprises, in part because they are, or are at least perceived to be, characteristically dedicated to the common good. For some of these organizations, their autonomy is also grounded upon the perception that outsiders lack the specialized knowledge or expertise that it usually takes to regulate them effectively. Their status and autonomy does not, however, prevent them from being questioned at times by outsiders. But more often than not, the questions concern the conduct of individual members or administrations in the organization, rather than the actions of the organization itself. Some professional groups and religious organizations and certain world governments belong to this category.

Finally, category five organizations have the greatest institutional autonomy and internal authority. They are accepted by both members and nonmembers alike, but it is especially with members that their distinctive "authority" can best be seen. Members are not likely to question in any way the rules, procedures, or actions of the institution or its primary representatives. It is here that Simon's phrase about the abdication of choice is most appropriate. In this, they resemble certain types of category one organization, where loyalty to the group's cause or mission is perceived as the highest virtue possessed by the individual members and where disloyalty is viewed as treasonous and perhaps even deserving of death. Category five organizations do not, of course, typically treat disloyalty as a capital offense, and they are more widely accepted as legitimate institutions by those outside the group. But with respect to internal authority, there are some significant parallels between category one and category five organizations. In both cases, there is a certain form of internal smugness or arrogance. The authority of the organization is so fully accepted by members that those who question it are themselves put on the defensive. And the degree of defensiveness can be quite great here, as can be seen by the contempt, and even the loathing, that members of various religions or religious committees have expressed toward individuals whom they have perceived as being heretics, religious persecutors, or even merely doubting Thomases. Thus, certain religious groups or communities, such as the Knights Templar or the Capuchins, have belonged to this category at certain times in their history.

This last example indicates that having institutions with category five legitimacy is not necessarily authoritative or beneficial socially. The complete faith shown in the organization by its members, whereby they forfeit their choice, is now generally seen as a weakness of organizations. It is felt that when members are encouraged to cede their critical faculties for the goals and activities of the group, the organization may have advanced in its level of legitimacy but it has diminished in its overall authority. It is for this reason that the question of subordinate responsibility is so closely connected to the general issue of corporate legitimacy. Those who argue for some degree of check upon the power of superiors by subordinates—even perhaps to the extent of blowing the whistle on them—advance a position that guarantees that corporations cannot have category five legitimacy.

But even if an added degree of legitimacy is not always socially beneficial, it can be seen from the perspective of the organization that having a great degree of legitimacy is *prima facie* beneficial for both society and the organization itself—at least up to the fourth category. One way to look upon the corporate responsibility debate then is to view it as a struggle to determine what category of legitimacy, or sector of a category, corporations do or should belong to when considering the activities of both their superiors and subordinates.

INSTITUTIONAL AND ACTIONAL LEGITIMACY

Thus far we have been discussing the concept of institutional legitimacy. Some thinkers tell us that this is only one aspect of the concept, however; another aspect concerns actions. Rawls, for example, maintains that these aspects involve somewhat distinct modes of justification (Rawls, 1971, p. 54). Thus, an illegitimate or lower-level institution may perform acts that are otherwise unobjectionable. It is possible, for example, for what amounts to an unregulated monopoly in the United States to charge prices comparable to those established by competitive market forces. And clearly it is possible for otherwise legitimate institutions to perform questionable acts. For Rawls, institutional legitimacy concerns the validity or authority of a public system of rules, rules that define various positions and offices and the rights, duties, powers, and immunities that accompany them. This kind of legitimacy relates to the legitimacy of conduct (actional legitimacy) by stipulating those actions that are permitted, those that are in some way constrained or required, and those that are unjustified or forbidden of institutional members (Rawls, 1971, p. 55).

There are then two distinct ways to conceive of institutional legitimacy, when looked upon as a normative concept. Looking at it from the degrees of legitimacy perspective, corporations are more (authoritatively) legitimate as they come closer to being category four institutions. Looking at it from the relations of accountability perspective, corporations are (authoritatively) legitimate to the extent that they effectively satisfy those who demand a rendering from them. This last point suggests that legitimacy claims made for corporations at the institutional level must, at a minimum, show that a world lacking the corporate form of business enterprise (if the legitimacy of the general system of corporate capitalism is in doubt), or one devoid of a particular corporation (if the legitimacy of a single firm is in question), is a world wherein the needs, interests, or claims of those individuals capable of demanding or deserving an accounting from corporate executives would not be respected as fully or satisfied as effectively as they are in the present world. This reminds us again of the important role that the relations of accountability play in addressing the question of institutional legitimacy, for how one conceives of these relations strongly influences how one is inclined to determine such legitimacy.

Actional legitimacy differs from institutional legitimacy in being directed toward specific instances of conduct. Put very generally, a collective action is legitimate when it accords with the policies or regulations of legitimate institutions and either contributes to achieving the institution's goals or inspires the confidence and trust of others in its own right. Other individuals either ask for no rendering of the action at all or at least are satisfied with the rendering that is given, however incomplete it may be. The concept of actional legitimacy can be applied to the conduct of either institutions or individual human agents acting within or for the institution. For a corporation, the justification first proceeds by showing that a particular action is in the corporation's domain of authority. Then it must be shown that the act is, or will be, performed in an appropriate, responsible, or conscientious manner—that is, as we have said, one that contributes to securing the goals of the corporation or inspires the confidence of others in its own right.

By the phrase "domain of authority," I do not mean quite what Bell or Simon mean by this phrase. I do not mean a realm of actions for which virtually no rendering is expected or demanded. Some actions within this domain may need no special justification, but most are, or can be, given a rendering. And this rendering is often sufficient to justify the action. Actually, the importance of the phrase is in terms of what it excludes for beyond this realm or domain are the arenas of the impossible, the unjustified, and the forbidden (*ultra vires*). The last two domains figure prominently in the corporate responsibility debate. Classical theorists, for example, often argue that extensive involvement in social projects is beyond the responsibility of corporations largely because it is beyond their domain of authority. And we shall see that certain social activists contend that firms too often have a difficult time keeping their actions from intruding into the arena of the forbidden.

The test of legitimacy for individual action within an institutional context is like that for collective conduct. The action must be within the institution's domain of authority and be authorized by the institution's policies or regulations, contribute to achieving the collective's goals, or inspire, in and of itself, the confidence of others. Actions done by individuals that are outside of an institutional context are not then considered to be legitimate or illegitimate. They may be good or bad, right or wrong, but according to the present account, the concept of legitimacy (or illegitimacy) does not apply to them.

The justification for any proposed corporate action thus depends upon the domain or arena into which it fits. If a proposed action cannot be done or is forbidden, its nonperformance requires no special explanation. If, however, it is within the domain of the responsible or the required, explanation or justification must be given for its nonperformance or for the manner of its performance, if done. Finally, if it is in the arena of the discretionary or permitted, justification must be given only if its performance interferes with other actions required in some way of the firm. In this case, the quality of the performance may need to be explained or justified. Finally, we can see that legitimate conduct involves either discretionary institutional acts (with interpersonal impact) or institutional acts for which a rendering is to be given but that are done appropriately or conscientiously.

A word about discretionary acts is in order. It should be mentioned that there are at least three kinds of discretionary conduct. The first involves actions whose principal or sole impact is upon the agent; the second involves actions that manifest unsolicited beneficence or kindness, or involve supererogation; and the third occurs when an agent must choose between two conflicting responsibilities, each of which is equally compelling or warranted. As for the first, one rarely needs to justify one's choice of a tie or blouse to wear for the day. As for the second, those who go beyond the call of duty, for example, are not further called upon to explain themselves to others in this regard, unless in their zeal they overlook or disrupt a more pressing obligation. Nor are gift givers generally required to give a rendering of their generosity, unless it is suspected that they have done so largely from an ulterior motive. Generally speaking, it is up to the benefactor to determine when and how a gift will be bestowed. Finally, a company president need not explain himself or herself to others in making a specific choice of how to spend the company's limited charitable funds. If he or she chooses to give the money to only a few institutions that appear on a list of organizations representing equally worthy causes, whatever choice of an institution is made is, within reason, (equally) warranted.

It thus seems that, like legitimacy, the discretionary quality of an action is often a matter of degree as well. Some acts involve a lesser degree of accountability, while others, which may demand a rendering, can possess significant discretionary features. A rendering is to be given then only for conduct that requires it and then only to the degree to which it is appropriate or necessary, given that type of action.

Various proposals have been offered that indicate the nature of the justificational process that is ultimately involved in providing such a rendering. In the next sections of this chapter we shall discuss these proposals as regards their application to institutions. As with some of the other assumptions already considered, most of the strategies to be examined here were first advanced for political or religious institutions, but the literature of corporate responsibility has come to recognize their role in the question of corporate legitimacy as well. The focus of the coming sections will be upon those theories of justification that have been used to defend the legitimacy of the corporate enterprise in general, but it should be noted that these strategies can also be used to defend the legitimacy of particular corporations as well. As with the models of the corporation, theorists sometimes endorse or appeal to several different strategies of justification to show the legitimacy of corporations. And at times they appear not to recognize the possible areas of conflict that might exist between the strategies they assume or advocate. Nine general strategies of justification will be considered in this chapter. Although not necessarily exhaustive, this list does include the more prominent or frequently endorsed strategies.

THE POWER THEORY OF LEGITIMACY

Some theorists reject the idea that the concept of legitimacy is a normative one at all. For them it is primarily or exclusively descriptive. The most common descriptive account of legitimacy is that which associates it with power. One of the most prominent early advocates of this view was Niccolo Machiavelli when he argued that rulers establish the legitimacy of their political dominion or leadership over states only when they solidify their power and control over the members of these states. Such a view still dominates relations between nation-states. The most common practice is for one nation-state to recognize as the legitimate head (or heads) of a foreign government that individual, or body of individuals, who exercises effective control over the making and executing of its laws. One version of the power theory has been used to defend certain religions or religious groups. In this version, the power of a supernatural being (in intelligence, will, imagination, and the like) is said to ground the purposes and functions of the group. Another version focuses upon the abilities, expertise, or charisma of a leader (or leaders) and seeks to ground institutional legitimacy upon these meritocratic qualities or factors.

Chatov, a recent theorist who applies the power strategy specifically to corporations, concedes that in his theory corporations do not have legitimacy in the same way that nation-states do. They do not make and execute the laws of the land; nor do they have the kind of power that governments have to punish those who violate these laws. But Chatov contends that they do have sufficient power to influence the legislative process, and they can have a significant impact upon the type and degree of enforcement that accompanies these laws (Chatov, 1975, p. 87). Internally, of course, they can behave very much like nation-states. Like those who urge the public power model of the corporation, Chatov believes that corporations have immense economic and social power as well. Unlike many of the public power theorists, however, Chatov holds that the legitimacy of corporations is grounded upon this power. For Chatov, the pattern of reasoning used to defend the legitimacy of the corporate form of business enterprise is a descriptive and empirical one. The major premise consists of a statement equating or associating legitimacy with power; the minor premise consists in an empirical statement that is meant to report the power and influence that corporations collectively or specifically have.

Two conclusions can be drawn from this model of justification. Assuming that corporations do in fact have significant power, the first is that they are legitimate institutions, and that is the end of the matter. No persuasive attack upon their legitimacy can be made. They are legitimate institutions (at least in the category one sense of that term) if for no other reason than because they have enough power to determine what responsibilities they must meet and the terms and conditions of their accountability. Such a conclusion can then be used to justify, say, a minimalist theory of social or moral responsibility for corporations.

Chatov looks to another conclusion, however. He is sympathetic to the idea that firms should be more active in the social sphere. But he believes that this will not be accomplished by the general public's merely persuading corporate leaders to pursue moral or social responsibility goals on a voluntary basis. The former should not appeal to the normative notion of legitimacy. They must realize that only outside pressure, only a greater external power, can move corporate leaders to pursue these goals. To some extent, this can be done by public opinion, but it is most effectively accomplished through the force of law. He believes that the idea of corporate responsibility is so important that it cannot be based upon the powers of moral persuasion only; it must be legislated (Chatov, 1975, p. 87).

Chatov's conclusion makes reference to a second view of legitimacy—conformity to law. It suggests that firms must obey the laws of the land if they are to be viewed as legitimate institutions. This second view is quite distinct from the first in those cases where the institution in question is not powerful enough to dominate the making and enforcing of laws. This point implies that legitimacy and power are not equivalent concepts, that other factors must be considered in determining the legitimacy of social institutions.

LEGITIMACY AS CONFORMITY TO LAW

I am aware of no discussion of the responsibilities of corporations that limits these responsibilities to mere conformity to law. Several works appeal to this standard along with other criteria, but none propose the idea that the legitimacy of corporations is grounded simply upon their law-abidingness. Although Friedman endorses the view that the social responsibility of firms is to maximize profit in conformity with law, he also suggests that they must conform their actions to the commonly accepted ethical standards of their society (Friedman, 1970, p. 33). In this view, conformity to law is at least a minimal condition of corporate legitimacy. Shaffer also proposes a view in which law-abidingness is a necessary feature of corporate legitimacy, but, like Friedman, he adds a performance criterion. Corporations must perform their economic functions effectively to be considered legitimate institutions. Shaffer is especially concerned with their efficiency. Any activity not mandated by law that jeopardizes the efficiency of corporations is not within their sphere of authority or responsibility. According to Shaffer, if corporations persisted in performing such actions, their legitimacy would be in question (Shaffer, 1977, p. 15). Carr has also suggested that an important aspect of corporate legitimacy is that corporations abide by the laws of the land. He compares these laws to the rules of a game (Carr, 1968, p. 145). He seems to believe that as long as firms play by the rules of the game and compete successfully against their rivals, they are legitimate institutions.

Not all theorists accept the idea that conformity to law is even a minimum or necessary condition of corporate legitimacy, however. While they agree that an entrenched or widespread violation of the law usually disconfirms a corporation's claims to be a legitimate social institution, conformity to law by itself does little to bestow institutional legitimacy. For them, legitimacy is grounded more upon the types and bases of the laws themselves rather than upon the mere following of law. Gillespie, for example, argues that certain actions allowable under law may yet be morally objectionable (Gillespie, 1975, p. 1). And DesJardin and McCall contend that the present theory of legitimacy is indifferent to the procedural justice involved in the legislative process itself (DesJardin and McCall, 1985, p. 12). Respect for law is presumably as compelling a principle of legitimacy in a dictatorship as it is in a democracy. These objections have led some theorists to look further for the standard of legitimacy.

CONFORMITY TO CURRENT STANDARDS

Closely associated with the last position is the conformity to current standards strategy. This position states that the legitimacy of institutions is ultimately based upon whether the actions of an organization or its members accord with the current standards of acceptable behavior. These standards may be found in the law, encountered in actual executive practice, based upon the expressed standards of a profession, or determined by the current mores and customs of society. Whatever their basis and however they are ascertained, they involve matters that can usually be discerned by observation. We can tell, at least theoretically, whether the actions of accountants or lawyers accord with current professional practice in their respective fields or the present mores of society without having to make independent assessments of the conduct itself. Thus, like the two views already discussed, this theory is naturalistic. And since the accepted standards of conduct for one group or society may differ from those of another, the theory is relativistic as well.

Consistent with the distinction between actional and institutional legitimacy, the advocates of this theory usually question the legitimacy of specific institutions only when a pattern of questionable actions has become so imbedded in an organization that it appears to be beyond reform. When this point has been reached is often a controversial issue among these theorists, however. We shall see that this strategy of defense is often used by social demandingness theorists to justify their theory of corporate responsibility.

The conformity to current standards theory has recently been endorsed by Richman, Bradshaw, and Lodge, and it is implicit in certain aspects of the discussions of collective responsibility found in the works of Cooper and French. The former theorists correlate legitimacy with responsibility and go on to base their views about the responsibilities of executives upon the current expectations of society, though they differ somewhat on the precise nature of these expectations (Richman, 1977, pp. 52ff.; Bradshaw, 1974, p. 24; Lodge, 1970, p. 46). The latter argue that one cannot typically fault members of a group or collective for following its generally acceptable practices or customs, even when the actions that emerge from this tradition have otherwise unfortunate consequences (Cooper, 1972, p. 88; French, 1984, p. 15). Because this theory admits the presence of varied, if not conflicting, standards of conduct in different groups and societies, it can give rise to ambiguous positions on the question of institutional legitimacy. This has led other theorists to look for a more universal standard to arbitrate these disputes. One such approach is the procedural strategy.

PROCEDURAL THEORIES OF LEGITIMACY

Procedural theories are similar to the two conformity theories in contending that legitimacy is not a function of the specific content of an action or policy of an institution. They hold rather that it is a function of the processes or procedures whereby institutions (or their actions or policies) come into being in the first place. Since the most frequently advanced procedural theory is the contractarian or consent theory, we shall restrict our discussion to it in the present section. This theory can take several forms.

One form has been advanced by Ross when he speaks of the obligatory nature of keeping our promises (Ross, 1939, pp. 108ff.). As we have seen, in the act of promising we commit ourselves to abide by the constraints of the promise or contract; we give our consent to these terms as free agents. The other party to whom we give our promise has a legitimate claim upon our conduct relative to the terms of the agreement. Ross contends that the fact that we promise to do something does not, however, always mean that the demands of this promise are overriding. The demands are, as he says, *prima facie* in nature. They are compelling unless overridden by more authoritative demands. And Sidgwick tells us that the simple act of promise making does not always impose a moral demand upon the promiser. We have seen that promises are not even *prima facie* binding if they directly conflict with previously made agreements or if the conduct required by them interferes with actions demanded by other moral (or legal) principles (Sidgwick, 1966, pp. 305ff.).

Classical economic theorists argue that what motivates individuals to keep their promises and abide by their agreements is the fact that, as free and informed agents, they have chosen to bind themselves and another party to a relationship that is perceived to be mutually advantageous. Rational self-interest is thus the compelling factor that bestows legitimacy upon the relationship. It is this economic model of contract, rather than the moral theory advanced by Ross and Sidgwick, that has usually been applied to corporations. It is largely because of this model that classical theorists often believe that parties to a contract can buy or compensate their way out of a previously binding agreement without thereby causing significant adverse effects to the agents or individuals involved. All they need do is to find a way to encourage the other party to also wish to break the agreement. The equilibrium point that is thus arrived at after the appropriate compensation is given is then seen as an illustration of the principle of mutual consent, in a somewhat enlarged form, of course, endorsed in the present strategy. As we have seen in an earlier chapter, Hessen argues that contractual commitment grounded upon perceived mutual advantage is the very basis of the corporation itself. Shareholders, executives, and workers are bound by a web of agent-principal agreements having just this basis (Hessen, 1979, pp. 26ff.). And Friedman and Buchanan have maintained that this is also the basis of the agreements made between the corporation (or its members) and those outside the corporation (Friedman, 1970, p. 122; Buchanan, 1975, p. 43). For these theorists, corporations are legitimate institutions and can make legal claims upon other people because their activities are largely founded upon this type of conditional, revisable, or revocable contract.

Opponents have pointed out various failings in this largely egoistic account of legitimacy. Ross, for example, contends that these agreements should and often do take a back seat to other considerations (Ross, 1939, p. 111). Their *prima facie* character thus prompts us to look for the other factors that ground the claims corporations make upon other people. In addition, a commonly raised objection to this version of the consent theory maintains that it is insufficient to explain the commitment that outsiders have to respect the conditions of corporate agreements or transactions to which they are not parties. This is especially true of those transactions that have a negative impact upon these outsiders.

To respond to these points, contractarian or consent theorists have appealed to the notion of tacit consent. Two-party agreements involve explicit consent, while many-party agreements usually involve hidden or implied consent. Locke, for example, argued this point when discussing the legitimacy of government. The fact that citizens enjoy any part of the dominion of a government and do not emigrate from it or openly oppose its policies by rebellion or revolution indicates that they implicitly accept its authority over them (Locke, 1952, pp. 68ff.). The same can be said of other institutions, such as corporations. The fact that individuals do not openly oppose corporations or their actions, the fact that they buy the corporations' products or are employed by them, indicates that they at least implicitly accept them as legitimate institutions.

But as Pritkin has suggested, the notion of tacit consent is a vague one. If purchasing a firm's product suggests consent, what does nonpurchase indicate? Pritkin contends that until we are clear about the meaning and evidence for tacit nonconsent (or tacit rebellion), we must be cautious in inferring too much from the mere fact that individuals do not frequently or openly challenge corporations or their policies (Pritkin, 1972, pp. 58ff.).

Recent versions of the consent theory, such as those of Buchanan and Rawls, stress hypothetical consent. While we shall discuss Buchanan's theory in the next chapter, we will treat Rawls's view here. Rawls's position is developed in an attempt to determine the nature of just institutions. For him, only just institutions can claim to be legitimate. To be just, they must conform to principles accepted by individuals who pursue their rational self-interest while being unaware of the particulars of their lives (Rawls, 1971, p. 136). In this "veil of ignorance" atmosphere of what Rawls calls the original position, individuals are unaware of such things as their economic, political, or social position in life; the era in which they live; their gender; the nature and extent of their natural assets and abilities; their conception of the good; and the level that civilization or culture has achieved during their lives. Rawls believes that the character of the veil of ignorance in this hypothetical situation ensures the impartiality of the contractors' decisions. And the risk-averse and rational facets of their nature or character lead them to choose two principles of justice that must be met by all institutions. These principles are stated in the order of their importance. First, each person is to have an equal right to the most extensive liberty compatible with a like liberty for others. Second, social and economic inequalities are to be arranged so that they are both reasonably expected to be to everyone's advantage and attached to positions open to all (Rawls, 1971, p. 60). Thus, Rawls makes use of hypothetical consent to defend an egalitarian conception of the social contract. We shall see in the next chapter that Buchanan uses it to advance a non-egalitarian view.

There are, of course, some important similarities between this and the previous theory. If there is consensus on the current standards to be used in determining appropriate corporate behavior, consent is then brought into the earlier theory in an important way. It must be admitted that agreeing to abide by the current practices and standards of society, or a profession, or the like, even though one does not agree with every rule found in these standards, is itself a kind of metaconsent—a consent to the second best position, perhaps. We see then that building or relying upon a consensus is an important feature in both of these strategies of legitimation. But then, as we have noted, the previous theory often yields inconsistent consensuses; and its empirical or descriptive nature is incompatible with the normative versions of the procedural theory. Similar objections also apply to the present interpretation of the procedural theory.

FORMAL THEORIES OF LEGITIMACY

Formal theories of legitimacy are like consent or conformity theories in that they seek to explain the concept of legitimacy without regard to the specific content of the principles or practices followed by social institutions. What counts most is the form of the principle to be followed. They differ from consent theories in that they are not necessarily concerned with whether the individuals affected by the principles have given their actual or hypothetical consent to them. The rational character of the structure of the principles is itself sufficient to explain their normative compellingness.

A formal theory of legitimacy was explicitly developed by Kant when he advanced the first formulation of the categorical imperative. In suggesting that individuals are to act so that the maxim of their action can be willed as a universal law, he was specifically focusing upon the consistency and internal coherence of the rules that guide our actions. Rules of conduct that have incoherent or chaotic consequences if universally willed or carried out are structurally flawed and cannot be compelling to a rational mind (Kant, 1964, pp. 88ff.).

Recent theorists, such as Singer, have followed Kant in endorsing a formalist principle called the generalization test. According to this test, actions are to be avoided if the consequences of everyone, or nearly everyone, doing that action in similar circumstances would be disastrous or undesirable (Singer, 1971, p. 4). Singer maintains that he advances this principle in an attempt to unearth important features of the logic of moral discourse.

Another theorist who has advanced a formalist criterion is Hare, who believes that this criterion is the sole principle of justification in ethics. He suggests that there are only two features that mark the logic of moral reasoning—prescriptivity and universality (Hare, 1963, p. 89). The first feature consists in the fact that moral discourse attempts to guide conduct. It seeks to indicate to people what should be done. The second consists in the fact that, like descriptive discourse, it is meant to apply to all persons and situations of a similar nature. Thus, if it is morally wrong for one person to do a certain kind of action, it is wrong for all persons to do that action in relevantly similar situations. From these two logical properties, Hare advances a formalistic criterion of conduct that he calls the "golden rule test" (Hare, 1963, p. 138). If a person has certain desires and interests that lead him or her to judge that some action is good or should be done, the logic of moral discourse requires one to recognize that this action is to be preferred in all relevantly similar situations. Thus, for example, if one person does not wish to be lied to and discourages this activity when he or she is the recipient, that person is logically compelled to admit that lying is wrong, even in cases in which he or she is the agent. The thrust of this test is to demand impartiality in one's moral judgments and conduct.

Donaldson and Waller specifically appeal to the golden rule test in their discussion of the legitimacy of administrative acts and organizational codes of conduct (Donaldson and Waller, 1980, p. 49). As they see it, administrative actions are legitimate to the extent that they have passed this role-reversal test. Such a test requires that the agent put himself or herself in the place of the recipient (with the recipient's values and interests). If the agent can approve of the action after applying the role-reversal test, the action is a legitimate one

(Donaldson and Waller, 1980, p. 50). Legitimate corporations are those who perform legitimate actions.

Against the golden rule test, Lundberg has argued that it has no clear application to business (Lundberg, 1968, p. 40). He believes that its intelligent application requires managers to know more about the recipients of their actions than they can justifiably come to know (given their other responsibilities). Beyond this, it has been argued that appeal to formal criteria cannot be the sufficient test for corporate legitimacy, in any case, for the test authorizes actions that may be harmful to others (if they have interests that condone such actions). One way to avoid this criticism is to appeal not the *actual* interests of recipients but to their *ideal*, *rational*, or *best* interests. The problem with this response, however, is that in appealing to the ideal or best interest of individuals, one is actually bringing in an added criterion of legitimacy that is itself in need of explication. This same point can be seen with reference to the concept of a relevantly similar situation (or person or action) that forms part of the generalization and golden rule tests. Additional criteria are needed to delineate relevantly similar from relevantly different situations (or persons, etc.).

PERFORMANCE THEORIES

Performance theories judge the legitimacy of social institutions by reference to the outcomes of their actions or policies. In moral theory this position has traditionally been referred to as consequentialism. Consequentialism in ethics is the theory that argues that the rightness or obligatoriness of a course or policy of action is determined solely by reference to the (nonmoral) consequences that it produces or is likely to produce. That action or policy of action that has, or is likely to have, the greatest balance of good over bad consequences is regarded as right and is usually considered to be the agent's duty.

As a theory of legitimacy, consequentialism has two versions—one stricter than the other. In the stricter version, legitimacy requires that the *best* balance of good over bad consequences be achieved. On this version, there is usually only one legitimate action to be performed, or policy of action to be followed, by the members of a social system in any particular situation. And ultimately there can be only one legitimate system of social institutions. On the weaker version, legitimacy requires that only a *balance* of good over bad consequences be achieved. This is sufficient to show accountability and to gain the confidence and support of the members of a social system. In the weaker view, several social systems may be seen as legitimate. Performance standards can also be used to specify the kind or level of performance needed to determine the degree of legitimacy of a social institution. We shall follow the second version in this work.

Consequentialists have argued for different kinds of experiences, actions, or values as constituting the nature or criterion of (nonmoral) good, but the most common criterion proposed is either pleasure or actualization (the development of human potentials and capacities). There are two principal forms of consequentialist theory. Egoistic consequentialists contend that the good that is to be promoted is solely that of the agent, while universal consequentialists (also known as utilitarians) maintain that the (nonmoral) good in question is that of all of those individuals affected by an action or policy of action.

Carr mentions a theory that is egoistic in its performance aspect. According to this theory, actions or policies are legitimate to the extent that they best promote the interests or development of the agents within the corporation (Carr, 1968, p. 153). He also seems at times to suggest that they are legitimate when they best promote the interests of the corporation itself (Carr, 1968, p. 144). That these views are not equivalent can be seen from the fact that the interests of corporate members (for higher pay, greater job security, a better chance for promotion, etc.) may at times be in conflict with the interests of the corporation (for greater efficiency and control through lower wages, more flexible patterns of hiring and firing, fewer promotions, etc.). If corporate self-interest is alleged to take precedence over member self-interest, the theory in question is moving toward utilitarianism for it is holding the good of the corporation to be more important than the good of one or more of its individual members. Utilitarianism takes this point one step further when it advocates that the good of society, all humankind, or all living beings overrides the good of any segment or individual member of these groups.

Some performance theorists have argued that this standard, when viewed only in economic terms, is what ultimately gives legitimacy to corporations. They argue that these institutions are specifically developed for economic performance and the good produced from this performance far outweighs any of its negative consequences. Friedman endorses this economic performance view and uses it to argue that a firm's sole social responsibility is to pursue the goal of maximum financial return for the shareholders (Friedman, 1970, p. 33). And, as we have seen, Hayek emphasizes the benefits of the creative order of relations that arises spontaneously and unpredictably in a society that encourages its various business enterprises to pursue their economic advantage freely and without undue outside interference (Hayek, 1976, p. 110). Other theorists, like Shaffer and the writers of the Committee for Economic Development's report on social responsibility, mention such advantages as efficiency, productivity, fuller employment, greater job security, and more advanced technology as being key facets of economic performance (Shaffer, 1977, p. 15; CED, 1971, pp. 37ff.).

Critics of corporate performance, on the other hand, emphasize some of the negative effects of management's actions or policies. Velasquez, for example, mentions such factors as imperfectly competitive markets, inequities that prevent certain members of society from fully participating in the marketplace, and such negative externalities as pollution, deceptive advertising, concealed product hazards, fraud, bribery, and the like (Velasquez, 1982, pp. 17–18). To the extent that these effects are not minimized or eliminated, either the legitimacy of corporations is jeopardized or at least their degree of legitimacy is lessened.

Other theorists question the idea that the effects of corporate actions are the sole or most important determinant of their legitimacy. They contend that corporations are responsible to respect the rights of those affected by their conduct.

LEGITIMACY AND RIGHTS

Thinkers identified as rights theorists generally challenge the assumptions of consequentialism, though some consequentialists have advanced their own interpretation of the rights theory. When the latter occurs, consequentialists usually define rights in terms of the interests of those affected by an action. Brandt, for example, identifies them as those interests to do, have, or enjoy that are strongly justified to be maintained and encouraged by society (Brandt, 1983, p. 40). Traditionally, consequentialists have viewed rights as those interests that are most highly valued in a specific situation. Thus, for example, the interests that are protected in having free speech or a fair trial are thought to be important enough by most of these theorists to deserve special consideration. Consequentialists will call these interests rights because they believe that their satisfaction generally produces much better consequences than does their violation. But rights like these need not take precedence in every situation. It is a common feature of the consequentialist analysis of rights that if they are defined as those interests that are preemptory over other considerations, it is only because these interests are expected to produce the best balance of good over bad consequences in the specific situation, or type of situation, under consideration. Consequentialists are thus usually reluctant to point to any one interest as always being an overriding one. Only a utilitarian calculation can determine what takes precedence in particular circumstances. When rights are not defined as preemptory, they are viewed as instruments. The assignment of rights is merely a means to remind agents of the importance of certain considerations in the calculation to determine the greatest balance of satisfaction (or excellence) over dissatisfaction (or lack of excellence).

A recent version of the consequentialist analysis of rights has been put forth by Demsetz and Posner (Demsetz, 1967, pp. 351ff.; Posner, 1981, pp. 48ff.). It has come to be called the economic theory or analysis of rights. On this view, rights are based upon considerations of efficiency or wealth maximization. These theorists reject the idea that a pattern of rights can be assigned independently of these considerations. Thus, the right (or alleged right) of a person to be free from attack is not initially any more compelling than the alleged right of an attacker to terrorize a victim (Demsetz, 1967, p. 351). We assign a right to the victim rather than the attacker because protection of the former's interests will likely bring about a more efficient distribution of resources than will protection of the latter's interests. Since violence and unexpected attack usually undermine productivity and planning and entail high protection costs, it is generally more efficient, and thus more agreeable to those in society, to assign a noninterference right to would-be victims. Applying this theory to corporations, these theorists ground the legitimacy of corporations upon their willingness and ability to protect those interests that encourage efficiency and productivity in the distribution of society's resources.

Nonconsequentialists offer a different definition and theory of rights. They usually identify rights with certain kinds of claims. Feinberg, for example, defines them in the basic sense as valid claims or entitlements (Feinberg, 1973, p. 66). Werhane suggests that these entitlements are universal and based upon the belief that human beings have inherent value (Werhane, 1985, p. 5). She tells us that their validity is grounded neither upon their being protected by law, nor upon their being recognized by members of society. Rights in the basic sense are valid then in independence of these considerations. Fried views rights as categorical moral entities whose violation is always wrong (Fried, 1978, p. 108).

For these theorists then rights are preemptory moral entities that override consequentialist considerations. Even if a greater balance of nonmoral advantage over disadvantage could be attained by violating a basic right, the wrongness of this violation "trumps" these consequentialistic advantages. Nozick refers to rights as side constraints upon action (Nozick, 1974, p. 29). Or, as Fried puts it, consideration of rights screens out certain factors from ever being admitted into our moral calculations in the first place. Rights act as a kind of calculative or reflective censor, offering us exclusionary rules. Whatever is inconsistent with the demands of basic rights is excluded from our moral assessments (Fried, 1978, p. 136).

When a right is identified with a claim or an entitlement, it is usually viewed as a three-term relationship consisting of an action or response between an agent or person and a right holder or claimant. The kind of response demanded by the right depends upon its nature (whether negative or positive) and the nature of the situation and the agent (or respecter of the right).

Werhane tells us that negative rights are rights to be left alone (Werhane, 1985, p. 10). They typically do not demand any specific action from an agent or respecter of the right. They may be very general (like the rights to freedom or privacy) or they may be more specific (like the rights to vote or participate in government). Positive rights require some definite action on the part of agents. These rights demand more than mere respect for the freedom or decisional space of right holders. They call for conduct that is instrumental in having claimants seek to achieve the objects of these rights. Thus, Fried suggests that a right to a fair share in the distribution of scarce resources is the only positive human right (Fried, 1978, p. 110). The framers of the United Nations manifesto on rights, on the other hand, claim that such rights as that to work, to have protection against unemployment, to receive fair remuneration for work, and to have equal access to food, clothing, and medical care are added moral rights that all persons have (UNESCO, 1949, p. 61). Some rights theorists believe that only negative rights are truly rights. Even those theorists who accept the existence of positive rights, however, realize that their demands may not always be satisfied in a world of scarce resources.

Rights are often thought to entail obligations on the part of the respecter of rights. These duties are taken as the correlative of rights. Thus, it is said that if X has a right to Y, then Z is obligated to *respect* this claim and to *act* in the appropriate manner toward X (if positive action is required). But since some positive rights demand responses that may be impossible to fulfill (scarce resources may make it virtually impossible to satisfy everyone's claim to a job or medical care), certain theorists suggest that not all rights entail duties. Other theorists, like Feinberg, prefer to call these more demanding positive rights "manifesto rights." He excludes them from the correlative hypothesis (Feinberg, 1973, p. 95). Such "rights" are then ideal rights; they constitute valid claims only in a world where the basic needs of people can be met.

Some rights theorists distinguish absolute from nonabsolute (or *prima facie*) rights. Feinberg tells us that absolute rights are those that are exceptionless and nonconflictable. A nonconflictable right is one that does not conflict with other rights of its own kind, and if it does conflict with rights of a different kind, it will always take precedence over these other rights (Feinberg, 1973, p. 95). *Prima facie* rights are those that may be overruled in specific situations. There is much discussion about which rights, if any, are absolute rights. Feinberg believes that perhaps the right not to be treated inhumanely or not to be the subject of exploitation and degradation are examples of absolute rights (Feinberg, 1973, p. 96).

Rights theorists do not apply their theory to the corporate responsibility debate in a uniform way. The application depends upon the types of rights they accept and the level of stringency that they assign to these rights. Those thinkers who treat rights as conventions created by law (legal rights), convert the rights aspect of their position into a conformity to law theory of legitimacy. Those who distinguish legal from moral or human rights, but who deny that there are positive rights, emphasize the demands of noninterference and freedom. Hessen and Friedman, for example, stress the rights of freedom of choice, of association, and of property or ownership in their discussions of corporate responsibility (Hessen, 1979, p. xiii; Friedman, 1970, p. 33). Their focus is thus upon the responsibilities that corporate executives have toward shareholders, which leads them to advocate the classical theory of corporate responsibility. Theorists like Werhane, on the other hand, who focus upon the rights of stakeholder groups (like workers or consumers) advance a more demanding position on social and moral responsibility for corporations (Werhane, 1985, pp. 144ff.). Last, theorists like the framers of the United Nations manifesto on rights, who advocate both positive and negative rights, tend to advance the most demanding theory of social or moral responsibility. The egalitarian aspects of the latter theory would entail profound changes in the structure and practice of modern corporations if they were fulfilled or discharged.

The presence of such diversity in the analysis and application of rights has given rise to doubts about the workability of this theory when applied to the question of corporate responsibility. Determining which groups have what rights, and the stringency of these rights, has led some theorists to look more deeply for the basis of rights themselves.

LEGITIMACY AND RESPECT FOR PERSONS

The respect for persons theory is not always easily distinguishable from some of the theories of legitimacy already discussed. It has strong affinities to the consent, formalistic, and rights theories, and it sometimes makes use of the concept of intrinsic good that is central to most consequentialist theories. But the way its fundamental moral concepts are typically organized is not precisely like that of the other positions.

There is much discussion among these theorists about the type of conduct demanded by the respect for persons principle. The principle states that one should never treat any person, including oneself, as a mere object or instrument for the satisfaction of another person's needs or interests. Thus, organizations are legitimate to the extent that they obey this principle. There is general agreement among these theorists that the reason for this is the unique value or dignity that persons are said to have. Both Fried and Werhane, whose positions were discussed under the rights theory, suggest that the basic rights of persons are grounded upon this unique worth (Fried, 1978, pp. 20, 118; Werhane, 1985, p. 5). There is some disagreement, however, over the precise feature of people that makes the response of respect appropriate. Pollock emphasizes the rationality and autonomy of people (Pollock, 1974, p. 261). Because people can choose ends according to a rational plan and because they can impose upon themselves rational ends of conduct, they are self-regulating members of the moral community. The respect that we have for the laws of morality requires us to respect the self-regulating activities of rational beings. Since other animals and plants do not have this capacity, they are not full-fledged members of the moral community. We are then at times justified in using them solely as a means to human ends. To use other people as mere means, however, is to seek to impose one's will upon them. It is to seek to destroy the very feature of people that makes morality and the moral law possible. A will that seeks to impose itself upon another mature, rational will is an inconsistent or incoherent one (Pollock, 1974, p. 261).

Gewirth and Harris ground the appropriateness of respect for people upon the capacity of people to develop themselves. In addition to freedom and rationality, there are other capacities that comprise a person's well-being (Gewirth, 1979, p. 141; Harris, 1966, p. 119). Such attributes as artistic, physical, and social capacities are included here. For Gewirth, to intrude upon a person's freedom or well-being is to do something that cannot be coherently willed for such an intrusion, if practiced generally, would threaten the development, and perhaps the very existence, of the will that sought to so impose itself upon another

(Gewirth, 1979, p. 145). We can see then that this theory has strong affinities to formalism.

For Harris, respect for people not only demands that we avoid treating people as mere obstacles or expendables; it requires sympathetic consideration of their interests and projects. Since the choices and projects of people are unique sources of value, people are in essence creators of intrinsic worth. Thus, to show sympathetic consideration for people is to show sympathetic consideration for intrinsic value itself (Harris, 1966, p. 116). This point is also urged by certain feminist thinkers such as Gilligan. She tells us that a relation of respect involves the sympathetic consideration of the feelings, attitudes, beliefs, and projects of other people and maintains that this type of response to others is an important aspect of the moral development of many women (Gilligan, 1982, pp. 8ff.). This suggests that the principle of respect for persons demands more than just noninterference with others. It demands at times that positive steps be taken to encourage the development of the value-producing aspects of human nature. MacLagan endorses the same conclusion. He maintains that the demand to respect persons is more than a demand for mere impartiality or friendship. It requires definite regard for the welfare of others because they are the possessors of intrinsic worth (MacLagan, 1960, p. 289).

We are led then to two interpretations of the respect for persons principle—one entailing only negative duties and the other entailing positive obligations as well. The first interpretation is consistent with the consent and the (negative) rights theories of legitimacy. As Pollock puts it, to respect another's freedom is to avoid using that person in a manner to which he or she would not consent (Pollock, 1981, p. 10). It is to respect his or her negative right not to be interfered with. The second interpretation is consistent with the (positive) rights theory and certain forms of consequentialism for it demands positive concern for the welfare of others. Because they have often been advanced with reference to the generalization test, both interpretations have formalistic aspects. But Pollock and others have argued that since the principle of respect demands respect for the *objective* ends of people (rather than merely their subjective choices), it has a content that is not generally included in the formalistic theory.

As with the rights theory, the two interpretations of the respect for persons theory give rise to different views on the nature of corporate responsibility. The first interpretation is often associated with the classical or stakeholder theories of corporate responsibility for it simply demands that corporate executives not interfere with the freedom of other people. Thus, if corporations respect the interests of shareholders, obey the laws of the land, and avoid fraud and deceit, or if they refrain from conduct that involves negative externalities on certain other individuals, they will in general meet the legal, moral, and social demands placed upon them, and they will be viewed as legitimate. The second interpretation, however, is usually associated with at least three of the four positions on corporate responsibility to be discussed in coming chapters. The determining feature here is the group of people whose welfare is primary. The classical theory focuses upon the shareholders, while the stakeholder theory focuses upon those added individuals who have a special interest in or connection to the corporation. Social activist theories focus upon the welfare of all individuals who are affected in some way by the acts or omissions of corporate executives.

Before moving on to treat briefly the connection between these views and the relations of accountability discussed earlier, we should stop momentarily to consider these strategies. It seems that they can in general be correlated with the categories or levels of legitimacy that we discussed previously. We cannot always say precisely into what category a certain group or organization will fit, given a certain strategy of defense used to show its legitimacy, but we can usually determine the highest category it is likely to reach, given that type of defense. Thus, the power strategy is not likely to get an organization much beyond category one legitimacy; the conformity to law defense could establish an organization as belonging marginally to category three, but it typically is a defense used for category two institutions. The performance, rights, and respect for persons strategies, however, admit of wide variation in application, depending upon how they are developed. There are versions that can be used to show that certain institutions belong to category four and in rare instances, they have even been used to seek to establish category five legitimacy for some institutions. Naturally, since the quality of an institution's defense is usually enhanced by a mixture of these strategies, the type of legitimacy established depends as much upon the particular blending of strategies employed as it does upon the compellingness of any specific strategy of argument itself.

THE STRATEGIES OF LEGITIMACY AND THE RELATIONS OF ACCOUNTABILITY

One way to look at the connection between the eight strategies discussed thus far and the relations of accountability is to view the former as ways of telling us why the latter are authoritative at all. They also tell us about the latters' degree of authority. They are said to offer us the normative grounds for these accountability relations. Thus, those who advance only a single strategy of legitimation try to reduce these relations to a single compelling feature or ground upon which they are said to rest (whether this ground is said to be the likely impact of an action, or the rights or consent behind it, for example). Relations that lack this feature are thus to be rejected. Theorists who appeal to several strategies reduce the normative bases of these relations to the features mentioned in the strategies advocated. There is, of course, some circularity or duplication in this way of looking at the present connection (i.e., consent authorizing the promise-keeping model—promises are otherwise authoritative because they involve consent or promise; the performance model authorizing the impact model— impact involves accountability because of its likely overall effects or impact). But this seems not to be a significant enough problem to jeopardize altogether the usefulness of this view of the connection.

There is, however, another way to look at the connection between these factors. One can treat the relations of accountability (whatever their final makeup and number) as *sui generis* in authority, view them as both partially descriptive and partially normative in nature and define institutional legitimacy in terms of an organization's meeting its responsibilities—in terms of its meeting the demands of the relations of accountability that apply to it. The eight strategies of legitimacy would then be seen as factors that direct our attention to the types of relationship that deserve an institutional accounting. And we have then a ninth model of institutional legitimacy. In the chapters ahead we should keep all nine of these strategies in mind.

Actually, this ninth strategy is itself amenable to two interpretations. On the first, an institution is legitimate when it meets those responsibilities that are deemed its duties. This restriction emphasizes responsibilities that, if unmet, result in blame or punishment for the institution in question. This often means in general that the focus of the strategy is upon legal and moral responsibilities. This view is typically used to defend organizations with category two or three legitimacy. In the second interpretation, institutions are legitimate if they meet all the responsibilities assigned or applicable to them. This includes responsibilities that are duties as well as those that are nonduties. For corporations this involves the full range of economic, legal, moral, and social responsibilities. This restriction, or strategy of legitimation, is capable of showing that the corporations to which it accurately applies are strong category three institutions; they may, in fact, be institutions that possess some category four credentials. Such organizations would thus deserve greater respect and autonomy and would seem to need less outside supervision or regulation. This second interpretation is assumed in the present work when considering this ninth strategy.

It should be pointed out that this way of looking at this issue implies, however, that the first eight strategies of legitimation discussed here are not meant to apply to every institutional action or decision. The relations of accountability provide us with a restricting consideration: outside of the area of choice directly linked to these relations is an arena of institutional choice and authority that is discretionary in nature.

One final point should also be mentioned. As previously said, not all theorists accept each of the relations of accountability or strategies of legitimation. Some rely upon a few and blend these relations and strategies in various ways. Friedman, for example, combines the first three models of accountability within a generally performance-oriented strategy of legitimation (Friedman, 1970, pp. 33ff.). Gulick, on the other hand, appeals to the regulation model of accountability but only when the laws considered arise within a consent or democratically oriented strategy of legitimation (Gulick, 1982, p. 38). And Donaldson relies upon the promise-keeping model of accountability but develops this within the framework of a fairness or consent theory of legitimacy (Donaldson, 1982, p. 44). We shall need to be cognizant of these various combinations and positions when discussing the theories of corporate responsibility in coming chapters.

REFERENCES

Bell, Daniel. 1977. "Dilemmas of Managerial Legitimacy." In *Proceedings of the First National Conference on Business Ethics*, edited by W. Michael Hoffman, pp. 13–24. Waltham, Mass.: Bentley College Press.

Berger, Peter. 1981. "New Attack on the Legitimacy of Business." *Harvard Business Review*, September-October, pp. 82–89.

Bock, R. H. 1979. "Introduction: Modern Values in Business and Management." *AACSB Bulletin, Proceedings*, Annual Meeting, pp. 1–19.

Bradshaw, Thorton F. 1974. "Corporate Social Reform: An Executive's Viewpoint." In *The Unstable Ground: Corporate Social Policy in a Dynamic Society*, edited by S. Prakash Sethi, pp. 19–29. Los Angeles: Melville Publishing Company.

Brandt, Richard. 1983. "The Concept of a Moral Right and Its Function." *Journal of Philosophy*, vol. 80, pp. 29–45.

Buchanan, James. 1975. *The Limits of Liberty: Between Anarchy and Leviathan*. Chicago: University of Chicago Press.

Carr, Albert. 1968. "Is Business Bluffing Ethical?" *Harvard Business Review*, January-February, pp. 143–53.

Chatov, Robert. 1975. "Corporations, Economics, Legitimacy and Fear." *Business and Society Review*, Fall, p. 87.

Committee for Economic Development [CED]. 1971. *Social Responsibilities of Business Corporations*. New York.

Cooper, David E. 1972. "Responsibility and the System." In *Individual and Collective Responsibility: The Massacre at My Lai*, edited by Peter A. French, pp. 83–91. Cambridge, Mass.: Schenkman Publishing Company.

Demsetz, Harold. 1967. "Toward a Theory of Property Rights." *American Economic Review: Papers and Proceedings*, October, pp. 347–359.

DesJardins, Joseph R., and John J. McCall. 1985. *Contemporary Issues in Business Ethics*. Belmont, Calif.: Wadsworth Publishing Company.

Donaldson, John, and Mike Waller. 1980. "Ethics and Organization." *The Journal of Management Studies*, February, pp. 34–55.

Donaldson, Thomas. 1982. *Morality and Corporations*. Engelwood Cliffs, N.J.: Prentice-Hall.

Farmer, Richard N., and W. Dickerson Hogue. 1985. *Corporate Social Responsibility*, 2d ed. Lexington, Mass.: Lexington Books.

Feinberg, Joel. 1973. *Social Philosophy*. Englewood Cliffs, N.J.: Prentice-Hall.

French, Peter. 1984. *Collective and Corporate Responsibility*. New York: Columbia University Press.

Fried, Charles. 1978. *Right and Wrong*. Cambridge, Mass.: Harvard University Press.

Friedman, Milton. 1970. "The Social Responsibility of Business Is To Increase Its Profits." *The New York Times Magazine*, September 13, pp. 32–33, 122–26.

Gewirth, Alan. 1979. "Starvation and Human Rights." In *Ethics and the Problems of the 21st Century*, edited by K. E. Goodpaster and K. M. Sayre, pp. 139–59. South Bend, Ind.: University of Notre Dame Press.

Gillespie, Norman. 1975. "The Business of Business Ethics." *University of Michigan Review*, November, pp. 1–4.

Gilligan, Carol. 1982. *In a Different Voice: Psychological Theory and Women's Development*. Cambridge, Mass.: Harvard University Press.

Gulick, Walter B. 1982. "Is It Ever Morally Justified for Corporate Officials to Break the Law?" *Business and Professional Ethics Journal*, Spring, pp. 25–47.

Hare, R. M. 1962. *Freedom and Reason*. Oxford: Oxford University Press.

Harris, Errol. 1966. "Respect for Persons." In *Ethics and Society*, edited by Richard DeGeorge, pp. 107–22. New York: Doubleday.

Hayek, F. A. 1976. *Law, Legislation and Liberty*, vol. 2. Chicago: University of Chicago Press.

Hessen, Robert. 1979. *In Defense of the Corporation*. Stanford, Calif.: Hoover Institution Press.

Hurst, James W. 1970. *The Legitimacy of the Business Corporation in the Law of the United States: 1780–1970*. Charlottesville: University Press of Virginia.

Kant, Immanuel. 1964. *Groundwork of the Metaphysics of Morals*, translated by H. J. Paton. New York: Harper and Row.

Locke, John. 1952. *Second Treatise on Government*. Indianapolis: Bobbs-Merrill.

Lodge, George Cabot. 1970. "Top Priority: Renovating Our Ideology." *Harvard Business Review*, September-October, pp. 43–55.

Lundberg, Craig C. 1968. "The Golden Rule and Business Management: Quo Vadis?" *Economic and Business Bulletin*, January, pp. 36–40.

MacLagan, W. G. 1960. "Respect For Persons As a Moral Principle—II" *Philosophy*, October, pp. 289–305.

Nozick, Robert. 1974. *Anarchy, State and Utopia*. New York: Basic Books.

Pollock, Lansing. 1981. *The Freedom Principle*. Buffalo, N.Y.: Prometheus Books.

Posner, Richard A. 1981. *The Economics of Justice*. Cambridge, Mass.: Harvard University Press.

Pritkin, Hanna. 1972. "Obligation and Consent." In *Philosophy, Politics and Society*, vol. 4, edited by Peter Laslett, W. G. Runciman, and Quentin Skinner, pp. 45–85. New York: New York University Press.

Rawls, John. 1971. *A Theory of Justice*. Cambridge, Mass.: Harvard University Press.

Richman, Barry. 1977. "New Paths to Corporate Social Responsibility." In *Managing Corporate Social Responsibility*, edited by Archie B. Carroll, pp. 52–68. Boston: Little, Brown and Company.

Ross, W. D. 1939. *Foundations of Ethics*. Oxford: The Clarendon Press.

Shaffer, Butler D. 1977. "The Social Responsibility of Business: A Dissent." *Business and Society Review*, vol. 17, pp. 11–18.

Sidgwick, Henry. 1966. *The Methods of Ethics*. New York: Dover Publications.

Simon. Herbert A. 1965. *Administrative Behavior*, 2d ed. New York: Free Press.

Singer, Marcus George. 1971. *Generalization in Ethics*. New York: Atheneum.

United Nations Educational Scientific and Cultural Organization [UNESCO]. 1949. *Human Rights, A Symposium*. New York: Alan Wingate.

Velasquez, Michael. 1982. *Business Ethics: Concepts and Cases*. Englewood Cliffs, N.J.: Prentice-Hall.

Weber, Max. 1968. "The Types of Legitimate Domination." In *Economy and Society*, 3 vols., edited by G. Roth and C. Wittich. New York: Bedminster Press.

Werhane, Patricia. 1983. "Accountability and Employee Rights." *International Journal of Applied Philosophy*, Spring, pp. 15–26.

———. 1985. *Persons, Rights and Corporations*. Englewood Cliffs, N.J.: Prentice-Hall.

PART II

THE FOUR THEORIES OF CORPORATE RESPONSIBILITY

8

THE CLASSICAL THEORY OF CORPORATE RESPONSIBILITY

INTRODUCTION

In this and the next four chapters we shall examine the four theories of corporate responsibility and shall consider how they answer the question of the proper balance between the economic and noneconomic responsibilities of corporations. As we have said, the focus of these discussions will be upon the conduct or decisions of executives for which they must give a general rendering. They will only at certain times be concerned with those responsibilities also considered to be legal or moral duties.

Six criteria have been suggested in the literature as essential to the discussion of the differences among these four positions. They include these considerations, which I have posed in the form of questions. (1) *Motive*: For corporate executives to carry out their responsibilities, especially their social and moral responsibilities, must they act from a certain motive or set of motives? Must they act with the intent of helping some individuals other than themselves or some group of persons other than the corporation's stockholders? Do some of their responsibilities involve performing actions that are entirely voluntary, that is, not required by law or strong social pressure? (2) *Relation to profit*: Are there corporate responsibilities that sacrifice the revenue-producing capacity of firms or is a corporation's overriding responsibility an economic one? (3) *Group affected by decisions*: Are corporate managers required to directly help individuals other than the stockholders of the company? If so, what individuals or groups are to be benefitted? (4) *Type of act*: What is expected or required of corporate managers—just general noninterference with the goals and decisions of others or is positive assistance in attaining these goals also expected? (5) *Type of effect*: Must managers consider only the direct effects of their actions or must they consider the indirect effects of these as well? (6) *Expressed or ideal interests of the group affected*: Whatever one's answer to question three, are corporate executives accountable to respond to the expressed interests of the group or groups affected by or involved in their decisions or are they responsible to respond to their justified or best interests?

As previously said, the four approaches that have thus far emerged on the general questions of corporate responsibility are the classical, stakeholder, social demandingness, and social activist theories. In this and following chapters we shall examine these theories in more detail and focus upon the arguments advanced in their behalf. At the end of our discussion of each of these theories, we shall consider the assumptions they typically make regarding the models of interpersonal relationship that ground accountability claims. We shall also consider those models of the corporation and strategies of justification for the legitimacy of social institutions that are most often associated with each of these positions. The emphasis of these discussions will be upon the interplay of the four types of corporate responsibility mentioned in chapter 3. With the exception of chapter 12, I shall say little about the particular responsibilities corporations encounter in specific situations. However, from these discussions and analyses one could derive a picture of how the four models would characteristically be used to decide virtually any issue in the corporate responsibility arena.

THE CLASSICAL THEORY

Various theorists have offered definitions and analyses of the classical theory of corporate responsibility. Jones, for example, describes the theory as one in which economic performance can best be achieved when corporate executives respond only to the economic interests of the company's stockholders. This is what will secure greater efficiency and productivity in the marketplace. Since society is better served by the specialization of function of its various institutions, corporations can best serve society by focusing exclusively upon their institutional economic functions. Because managers are not specifically trained to pursue social goals, they should confine their institutionalized power to limits set by their management expertise. This means that executives should protect and promote the economic interests of the stockholders who directly or indirectly elected them and who, in effect, are their bosses (Jones, 1980, p. 61).

Sethi tells us that the classical theory (which he calls the social obligation model) confines the question of legitimacy to legal and economic criteria only. It maintains that legitimate corporations are those that perform their economic functions well and do not violate the laws of society. It contends that corporate executives are ultimately accountable only to the stockholders whose interests they have promised to protect. Legitimate firms, in this view, will normally seek to maintain the legal status quo, at least as far as shareholders expect or demand this of them. They will likely oppose government attempts to internalize certain costs presently assigned to outside parties. Since social programs not mandated by law are for the most part costly to initiate and manage, such firms will not usually pursue them. In fact, they will rarely go beyond the letter of the law for those social programs that are legally mandated (Sethi, 1977, p. 74).

From the perspective of the classical theory, if the members of society strongly desire some good or service not provided by the market, they should either seek to build a market for it (Shaffer, 1977, p. 13), or they should urge government either to provide the good directly or at least to supply firms with the necessary motivation to provide the good. They should not expect firms to provide it voluntarily at the risk of failing to meet their economic objectives.

These definitions and descriptions apply to one version of the theory. In a second version, executives are responsible to respond to the *wishes* of the shareholders relative to the firm. It is generally assumed that these two versions coincide, but as mentioned in chapter 1, this need not be so.

In the classical model a manager's first obligation is to the shareholders. This relationship defines the principal sphere of the manager's legitimate activity. All other corporate responsibilities, even the legal ones, are at best secondary or derivative in nature. For example, the obligation to pay back a creditor is based ultimately upon the need to continue the firm's economic functions effectively. Or, to take a different example, duties toward workers are viewed as compelling only or primarily insofar as their discharge brings an economic return to the shareholders. As classical theorists see it, the stakeholder interests described by stakeholder theorists are compelling largely to the extent that their satisfaction is demanded by law, especially contract law; ultimately, however, their compellingness is grounded upon their helping to meet the financial demands of the company's shareholders.

In summary, according to this theory corporate executives have a primary and positive economic responsibility toward the shareholders to secure the latter's financial goals or to respond to their wishes relative to the corporation. They also have negative responsibilities toward the shareholders to avoid undue interference with their wishes relative to the firm or to otherwise harm them through violating the law or committing fraud or deceit. In addition, they have a set of negative responsibilities toward stakeholders and the general public that are similar to these latter responsibilities and that are grounded upon their economic responsibilities. Any positive social or moral responsibilities they may have toward these latter groups are at best secondary or derivative; they owe their justification to their ability to help fulfill the positive economic responsibilities owed to the shareholders. In the end, most classical theorists endorse some form of laissez-faire capitalism as the most legitimate type of economic system for, as they see it, it best respects the freedom of market participants while encouraging the virtues of efficiency and productivity.

ARGUMENTS FOR THE CLASSICAL THEORY: PERFORMANCE

Among the many arguments advanced for the classical theory, perhaps the most prevalent is that from economic performance. It is argued that when firms respond to shareholders by focusing upon improving their economic condition—when executives concentrate upon lowering costs and increasing revenues, sales, or profits—the company and society both benefit (Davis, 1977, p. 40).

Various accounts of the performance argument have been advanced. In the recent literature, we find that the position of methodological individualism is basic to both an important version of the performance argument and to the classical theory of responsibility it is used to support. The specific reasons for this are too numerous and complex to state in the present context, but in general it can be said that methodological individualism is believed to permit theorists to show the legitimacy of an economic system built upon private property and wealth maximization without apparently jeopardizing the scientific status of the discipline of economics. Theories, such as utilitarianism, that judge performance in terms of the promotion of certain values purported to be universally or intrinsically valid are seen as too ideological to preserve the value-neutral status of economics. They also do not allow interpersonal comparisons of satisfaction or preference. Theories that are more subjective in nature may not be powerful or convincing enough to justify a particular economic system. Methodological individualism is believed to thread between these difficulties.

The concept of methodological individualism has two meanings, however. As a position about the nature of responsibility, it is defined by Hessen as the theory that holds that only the individual is the proper subject of moral obligation. Duties or responsibilities allegedly assigned to collections of individuals, even when these collections are highly organized and institutionalized, are ultimately reducible to responsibilities that apply solely to the group's members (Hessen, 1979, p. 41). This is not the sense of the term that we shall treat in this chapter; rather, it is its definition as a normative ethical theory that concerns us here.

As a normative theory, Buchanan defines it as the position that holds that the individual is the center of a value system. All value judgments spring ultimately from the interests of the individual; only the individual can reliably judge his or her own satisfaction and value (Buchanan, 1975, p. 1). The optimal state that an individual strives for is the satisfaction of all of his or her interests. When an economic system helps individuals to aspire to or attain this condition, it is said to be moving toward a Pareto optimal or efficient state. The most efficient economic system is one in which an alteration of any kind would not bring about an increase in the personal satisfaction of the participants of the system and would, in fact, decrease it for at least one individual.

Because most methodological individualists assume that no reliable quantitative measure of pleasure exists that permits accurate interpersonal comparisons of satisfaction, they have sought to rely solely upon a grading mechanism that permits ordinal or rank comparisons of different satisfactions for a single individual. If we assume with them that a person's willingness to relinquish a certain resource (like money, effort, or possessions) to gain the pleasure of having a good can itself be used as a basis for ranking pleasures for that individual, we can under certain circumstances make comparative judgments about the person's satisfactions, without needing to have direct access to or an exact quantitative measure of his or her pleasure in itself. Thus, for example, if we know that an individual is willing to exchange two dollars to obtain one type of good but is at the same time willing to trade only one dollar to obtain another, we have a basis for expressing the relative priority of these goods for this individual. We do not need to determine the precise level of intensity of pleasure that these goods bring, or are expected to bring, to their owner. We need not even determine the precise degree of difference in ranking of these goods. Their relative position or ranking for an individual can be determined with considerable accuracy by simply observing his or her trading or exchanging behavior over a broad range of choices and times. The profile of choice thus derived directs us to an area of relative stability for the person—an equilibrium point (or points) in his or her market life. From this point of stability, we can theoretically plot the points where this individual cannot be induced by any exchangeable commodities, services, or experiences to change his or her current position or status in the market.

The account thus far views efficiency in terms of the actual or potential choices of market participants. But it has left out an important psychological truth accepted by most classical economic theorists since the end of the nineteenth century, namely, that the more we have of an item or an experience, the less we tend to value additions to it. This truth has given rise to the relational concepts of marginal cost and marginal benefit. Thus, it is said that a producer will not produce an item beyond the point where its marginal revenues for him or her are equal to or less than its marginal costs; a consumer will not purchase goods beyond the point where their marginal costs are equal to or greater than their marginal benefits; this concept holds for shareholders, workers, and so forth. A system that encourages all market participants to function at an equilibrium point established by the assessment of the marginal costs and benefits for various goods for them is one that fosters efficiency. Thus, if all market participants are brought to a point where they have no incentive to engage in transactions that take away something that they already have in exchange for something they do not have, it can be inferred that their staying at the equilibrium point—standing pat, if you will—indicates they are satisfied with where they are relative to these choices. The equilibrium point that is established by imagining them to "stand pat" on all future market choices is the point of optimality or efficiency for them. Any change they make from this point is perceived by them to make them worse off. A Pareto-efficient system is one in which all members of the system function at this point.

This is, of course, a static portrayal of efficiency that is problematic when we consider a dynamic market economy. But even here, methodological individualists argue that the classical theory promotes the greatest value. Because it permits more latitude for all market participants, it facilitates the transition to new optimum points for them. This is especially true of corporate managers who are freed from certain noneconomic constraints in their decision making by the classical theory. The point of "standing pat"—particularly for shareholders—takes on greater significance in a system with this kind of latitude.

Various theorists have endorsed the classical theory because they believe it leads to the most efficient economic system, as thus conceived. Friedman, for example, endorses such an "invisible hand" argument. He maintains that an economic system with limited corporate social activities best satisfies the interests of all market participants. Shareholders are better off because they come to realize a greater or more secure return on their investment—a return that is available for immediate spending or for further investment. They are thus not inclined to sell the shares they own in a particular firm and are, in fact, constrained in their choices to buy more shares in this firm primarily by the attractiveness of the shares of other firms—firms whose managers also follow the guidelines of the classical theory. Consumers are more satisfied because firms have an incentive to respond to their demands for various goods or services with products that are priced more attractively because the firms are not reducing net earnings or their assets by spending on social causes. A more demanding theory of social or moral responsibility would leave consumers at a point from which they would willingly move to one where prices could be lowered. Considerable corporate social expenditure thus leaves shareholders and consumers at a temporary "equilibrium" point from which they would like to move. The new point is also along the equilibrium line of managers, if they merely reduce the level of their social spending. The new point, if reached, thus represents a more optimal point of equilibrium for society because it improves the condition of shareholders and consumers without worsening the condition of managers.

In addition, workers would be more satisfied because financially successful firms have the incentive and wherewithal to hire more of them and to provide them with better wages, salaries, working conditions, and other benefits. Workers employed in such firms are more likely to stay at a fairly fixed equilibrium point relative to these considerations. Finally, society benefits when all firms seek to be economically competitive and constrain their social spending because prices and profit will allocate the resources of society in the most nonwasteful manner (Friedman, 1968, pp. 133ff.). Efficiency, as thus understood, is one universal value of the methodological individualist.

Shaffer develops the invisible hand argument in a somewhat different direction. He tells us that the pricing system forces producers to respond to high-demand areas of the market. To produce goods for which there is insufficient demand is thus to waste resources. Social goods are goods for which a private market has not been presently or sufficiently developed. To use resources to satisfy the small demand for these goods is to squander them. It is to devote them to areas of decision making where the incentive to reduce costs is less clear and compelling (Shaffer, 1977, p 15).

Davis reminds us of another (more nationalistic) facet of this argument. He tells us that when the firms of a certain country focus their attention upon the goal of profit maximization, such a policy helps to improve that country's balance of payments. Since social projects add costs to products or services, such added costs may serve as disincentives to foreign buyers. Economically sound and efficient firms that focus upon cost reduction will tend to stimulate foreign trade. The *prima facie* compelling benefit of a favorable balance of trade with other countries will usually result from this (Davis, 1977, p. 42).

Carr advances his own version of the "invisible hand" argument. For Carr, business life is like diplomacy or judicial advocacy. It involves public activities not regulated by the usual principles of private or religious life. While bluffing and exaggerating, for example, are usually viewed as somewhat deceitful by those championing the claims of these latter principles, Carr tells us that they are perfectly legitimate strategies demanded by the business game. In comparing the activity of business to a game, Carr maintains that corporations and their members must play to win. They will do better if they identify success in business life with the goal of maximizing profit. Certain departures from the usual standards of morality or social norms are thus permitted in order to pursue the goal of winning. In poker, for example, a kind of deception is allowed—this makes the game a more competitive and interesting one. And Carr tells us that as long as one plays by the rules of poker, strict adherence to the principles of honesty, compassion, impartiality, and mutual aid are not expected aspects of one's game strategy. The same is true in business. As long as one obeys the laws of the land, the only demand is full commitment to achieving the ends of business life—success or profit (Carr, 1968, p. 148).

Classical theorists believe that when managers commit corporate funds to social causes not directly linked to their primary economic mission, they impose an undue cost upon their shareholders, workers, customers, and fellow citizens. They raise the level of their marginal costs without generating a corresponding increase in their marginal revenues or benefits. They produce a system that individuals would be reluctant either to choose or remained fixed at, a non-Pareto efficient system in which they would judge themselves to be worse off.

A second universal value assumed by methodological individualists is, as we have seen, freedom or noninterference. The laissez-faire economic system envisioned by classical theorists is said to best promote the freedom of individuals. First, it assumes the need for freedom in the formation and actualization of values. Freedom is needed to ensure that the actual interests of the individual are determined and advanced. And it is also required for the satisfaction of many of these interests as well. Without economic freedom, the choices of market participants would be too coerced or otherwise biased to be used to judge accurately the efficiency of an economic system as a whole. The fact that participants stray very little from a certain (equilibrium) point in those choices that involve the gaining and distribution of their income, revenue, assets, or the like could not then be used to justify the optimality of this point for those individuals. It might merely reflect the dominance of an outside agency or power to force these individuals to choose in certain specified, habitual, or ritualized ways.

In addition, Hayek contends that a system that demands that managers respond primarily to the financial interests of shareholders gives executives the greatest degree of freedom and latitude (Hayek, 1976, pp. 107ff.). It permits various types of business units to contribute to the development of a new social and economic order, one that is only possible when the decisions of managers are left relatively unconstrained. This catallactic order can best occur when the primary purpose of these business units is not diluted. Thus, the two universal values endorsed by methodological individualists—efficiency and freedom—are said to be effectively promoted and protected by the classical theory.

Not all classical theorists are methodological individualists, of course. Some, like Birdzell and Novak, contend that the classical theory best preserves certain values that have an independent social or moral foundation. Birdzell, for example, believes that the theory best promotes the values of commitment, free exchange, distributive justice, frugality, and profit (Birdzell, 1975, pp. 79ff.). And Novak argues that it most effectively supports a situation in which the economic, cultural, and political systems of a society exist in harmonious balance (Novak, 1982, pp. 50ff.).

LOYALTY TO SHAREHOLDERS

A second line of argument for the classical position turns its attention away from the alleged ineffectiveness of pursuing noneconomic or social ends. It focuses instead upon certain nonconsequentialist features of the relationship that exists between the shareholders and the managers of a business corporation. This nonconsequentialist line of argument has several dimensions.

One dimension focuses upon the ownership status of the shareholders and the rights that are said to attach to this. Pilon, for example, tells us that because shareholders have an equity, and typically a voting, interest in a corporation that is based upon their positive right of ownership, they have a special claim to the loyalty of the managers (Pilon, 1982, pp. 31ff.). In the early period of capitalism, it was not hard to see the primacy of the property rights of owners. Since the owners were in general also the managers of business enterprises, the connection between profit and property rights or ownership was a relatively clear one. Owners invested their resources in these enterprises to enhance their wealth. Few questioned the legitimacy of the economic decisions of owners because these decisions concerned matters that affected the wealth-producing capacity of their own property. As long as their initial assets were assumed to be legitimately earned, the fruits of their investment were viewed as rightfully earned as well. Decisions concerning the development and profitability of these enterprises were seen as wholly within the domain of the owners. In this view, those outside the enterprise were the ones to be held accountable for respecting the property rights of the owners.

In the modern era, however, ownership and management have come to be viewed as distinct aspects of corporate life. Still, most classical theorists remind us that an important basis of the accountability relation between managers and shareholders is founded upon the ownership status and rights of the latter. The market authority of managers is thus in large part grounded upon the legitimate claim that shareholders have to the assets used in market transactions.

The second dimension of the loyalty argument focuses upon the fiduciary role of managers. Friedman and others tell us that as fiduciaries, managers are expected to be good stewards of the shareholders' assets or interests. They have a definite and overriding obligation to protect and augment the property interests or wishes of stockholders (Friedman, 1970, p. 122).

The stewardship role of managers is itself sometimes viewed as the outgrowth of two additional facets of the relationship between managers and shareholders. Friedman considers the first of these when he stresses the voting power of shareholders whereby they elect representatives who, in turn, select the top executives of the corporation (Friedman, 1970, p. 122). Because the latter are thus indirectly chosen by the shareholders to protect their interests, executives are viewed as the representatives, surrogates, or functionaries of the owners in their dealings with various market or nonmarket individuals or groups. The second facet of the stewardship role is seen by some classical theorists as resulting from the managers' consent. By giving their consent to the fiduciary role when hired, the managers have in effect promised to abide by the constraints of their contracts. Sawyer tells us that continued respect for their fiduciary role is also based in part upon the past obedience of managers. By responding to the financial needs, wishes, and interests of shareholders in the past, managers contribute to the expectation of respect for this role in the future as well (Sawyer, 1979, p. 32).

Pastin and Hooker tell us that the responsibility or duty that applies here can be ignored or overridden only in the most compelling of circumstances (Pastin and Hooker, 1984, p. 467). For corporate executives to decide unilaterally to use the shareholder's resources for social or moral projects that may offer little or no financial return to the company is for them to renege on their promise to the owners, undermine their professional role as the latters' fiduciaries, and endanger their position as functionaries of the shareholders. Finally, it shows a measure of disrespect for the property rights of the stockholders that is otherwise incompatible with their stewardship responsibilities. Most classical theorists believe that the pursuit of such social or moral goals is not justified, or, as Friedman puts it, it constitutes an unfair tax upon the shareholders (Friedman, 1970, p. 122).

THE CONSTRAINT ARGUMENT

A third argument emphasizes the economic constraints on managers. Manne, for example, tells us that corporate executives have little discretionary funding available to them with which to carry out noneconomic programs (Manne, 1972, pp 13ff.). He contends that if corporate social or moral spending can be assumed to follow the pattern of private giving for charitable causes, only about 3 percent of a corporation's taxable income would be available for spending in social areas. He also indicates that the actual amount is much less than this. (More recently, Useem has stated that corporations typically give between 1 to 2 percent of their pre-tax net income in donations to nonprofit organizations (Useem, 1988, p. 77). For Manne, the economic realities of the marketplace dictate that the actual level of corporate charitable or social spending is less than either of two considerations. Assuming that the marketplace is made up of otherwise rational participants, the amount for social or moral spending will be less than the increase in capital accumulation costs that would occur if large numbers of shareholders sell off their shares of the corporation. And it will be less than the expense involved in some individual or group's seeking to take control of the firm by takeover, merger, proxy fight, or the like (Manne, 1972, p. 14).

As Manne sees it, since shareholders, especially institutional investors, view with disfavor any corporate expenditure that reduces their wealth position, they will sell their shares of stock if they believe that a policy of corporate spending for noneconomic programs has appreciably reduced, or will likely reduce, the value of their equity interest. As they sell off the company's shares, the value of its stock drops and the expense of its capital accumulation rises. Thus, the economic limit of social or moral spending is the point at which its level matches that of the relative increase in the expense of accumulating capital in the future.

In another scenario, the level of spending will not likely exceed the transaction costs of someone's displacing management or its policies by a proxy fight, takeover bid, or the like. Manne believes that as actual or potential investors realize the corporate earnings to be gained by a policy of lowering or eliminating the current social or moral spending of a particular corporation, they will have an incentive to institute such a corporate policy. This will occur when the gain involved in the change in policy exceeds these transaction costs (Manne, 1972, p. 19).

Finally, Manne suggests that even very large companies rarely have more than $100,000 to $150,000 of discretionary revenue available to spend on an annual basis for noneconomic programs. He believes that this figure is far less than what corporate activists often ask of, or demand from, firms (Manne, 1972, p. 23).

LACK OF EXPERTISE

In addition to having qualms about the abilities of corporations to pay for social projects, classical theorists also express concern over whether corporate executives have sufficient expertise to perform such projects. Davis mentions that classical theorists believe that managers are trained more fully in the economic than in the social sciences. Such theorists are thus reluctant to encourage activity that is outside the executive's area of expertise (Davis, 1977, p. 41). Shaffer contends that executives can use the test of efficiency to judge the success of economic projects, but social or moral projects are not amenable to such a test. Shaffer thinks that because executives have no special expertise in judging the merit and success of these latter projects, they should restrict themselves to areas of decision making for which they do have training and expertise (Shaffer, 1977, p. 15).

Lundberg adds that the test often used to defend moral or social spending—the golden rule test—is not clear on what it demands of corporate executives (Lundberg, 1972, p. 240). This suggests that the kind of expertise needed to understand and apply various standards of decision making to specific cases is not one that can be easily claimed by people. Such expertise, if it exists at all, is not apt to apply to business leaders any more than it does to educators or government regulators.

This realization has divided classical theorists into two camps. The first urges little or no government involvement in social or moral projects that have a strong economic impact upon market participants, while the second accepts a somewhat more active role for government in the social arena. The first group, represented by Friedman and Shaffer, doubts that expertise in social decision making even exists. They are thus suspicious of government intrusion into various areas of private decision making. They recommend that government have a limited role in these areas (Friedman, 1968, pp. 22ff.; Shaffer, 1977, p. 17). But other classical theorists seem to accept the idea that expertise in social, political, and moral areas of decision making might exist. They thus appear to grant that training or education in these areas is possible and that expertise is more likely to apply to political and social leaders who have this training than to business leaders who typically do not. This leads Levitt and others, for example, to permit a somewhat more extensive role for government decision making in the social areas of life (Levitt, 1958, p. 46).

Finally, Manne provides us with an example of what can happen when programs of social or moral spending are initiated by individuals who lack the relevant expertise. He tells us of a case where the introduction of certain corporate social measures actually hurt a share of the group these measures were meant to assist. Examples of this sort are not infrequently found in the literature of the classical theory. He tells us that Coca-Cola, in an effort to respond to criticism concerning the living conditions of migrant workers working in the company's orange groves in Florida, sought to improve these conditions by increasing the migrants' wages and medical benefits. The program was costly, though, and in an effort to keep prices in line with their competitors, executives at Coke introduced automated methods of orange picking that eventually put one third of these migrant workers out of work (Manne, 1972, p. 28).

CONCERN FOR CORPORATE POWER

The last argument for the classical position that we shall review in this chapter moves in the opposite direction from the managerial constraint argument. The earlier argument stressed the idea that corporate executives have limited funds available for social or other purposes. The present argument is concerned with the power firms would have if they were to become major providers of social services. Levitt, for example, argues that in such a situation our society would become a monolithic one. He believes that if people became more dependent upon corporations for their social as well as their economic well-being, corporate values would become the primary values in society. And as corporations took on these greater social roles, they would become dominant centers of economic, political, and social power, much like the feudal estates or fiefs of medieval times, or like certain modern nation-states (Levitt, 1958, p. 44). Levitt believes that this form of corporate statism would be unhealthy and unwise. It would have an unhealthy effect upon the pluralistic aspects of our democratic society because it would tend to homogenize values. And it would be unwise because it would dilute the advantages that come from having specific political, social, and economic institutions carry out specialized responsibilities and functions (Levitt, 1958, p. 47). Like some of the other classical theorists, Levitt believes that important social goods or services should be primarily provided by government.

A variation of this argument is mentioned by Davis. He tells us that since corporate executives are not directly accountable to the general public, they should not be given more power by being assigned social tasks (Davis, 1977, p. 43). Social power without social accountability is an imprudent political policy. Until the lines of their social accountability can be clearly established, executives must refrain from an aggressive pursuit of social goals.

THE ASSUMPTIONS OF THE CLASSICAL THEORY: ACCOUNTABILITY RELATIONS AND MODELS OF THE CORPORATION

Having reviewed the main arguments for the classical position, we are now ready to examine some of its main assumptions. These assumptions are schematically provided in Figure 8.1.

The classical theory makes appeal in some way to all eight types of interpersonal relationship, but the manner of this appeal is what primarily distinguishes this theory from the other positions on corporate responsibility. Clearly, they typically appeal to the promise-keeping, fiduciary, and representative (functionary) relationships. They view corporate managers as agents of the shareholders who have implicitly or explicitly agreed to protect the latters' financial interests or wishes. And since the shareholders have the power of replacement, corporate executives must give priority to these interests and wishes. Classical theorists generally reject the application of these relations to the other market participants served or affected by the corporation.

Theorists like Friedman and Hayek appeal to the impact model in their argument that corporations can best promote both the good of shareholders and the common good when corporations focus their attention upon discharging their

Figure 8.1
The Classical Theory (Principle Assumptions)

Relations of Accountability	Models of the Corporation	Strategies of Legitimization
1. Promise-Keeping or Consent**	1. Private Property**	1. Power*
2. Fiduciary**	2. Private Contract**	2. Conformity to Law**
3. Representational**	3. Enterprise**	3. Conformity to Current Standards*
4. Impact**	4. Social Contract*	4. Procedural*
5. Reverse-Impact*	5. Public Power*	5. Formal*
6. Teamwork or Collegial*	6. Machine or Tool**	6. Performance**
7. Ownership or Possession**	7. Organic*	7. Rights**
8. Regulation**	8. Mental or Moral Agent*	8. Respect for Persons*
		[9. Relations of Accountability]

 * can or does play some direct role in defining or defending the theory

** plays a significant role in defining or defending the theory

immediate and specific institutional responsibilities. Shaffer, Lundberg, Manne, and Levitt, each in his own way, bring out the negative impact that would occur if corporations were to become more socially or politically active. They also point out that the demands of meeting economic and legal responsibilities coupled with a lack of the relevant expertise excuses corporate executives from being held accountable for not initiating social or moral projects. And Sawyer mentions the impact that the past activities of managers have had upon the shareholders. Since they have acted as loyal agents of the shareholders in the past, they have established the precedent of acting in this way—one that implies their continued loyalty in the future. But with the exception of strict consequentialists, the general tendency of the classical theory is to avoid directly grounding corporate responsibility claims upon the impact or reverse-impact models of accountability. It is true that they contend that their theory has a greater positive impact upon society as a whole than any other theory of corporate responsibility. But they deny that it is, or should be, the immediate or overriding intention or purpose of managers to bring about this impact. If this were the managers' primary purpose, it would also require executives to consider the interests of all of the other parties affected by their decisions to be initially on a par with those of the shareholders. This would imply that those injured by corporate decisions have a claim to compensation (beyond that required by law) that is equal in normative standing to the financial claims of the shareholders. This point is typically denied by classical theorists, however. The point of the invisible hand argument is that the connection between positive social impact and the fiduciary motives of managers is a natural or automatic one. It occurs without executives' trying to bring it about. Strict consequentialists, on the other hand, appeal to the impact model by ignoring the purposes or intent of managers. For them it does not matter what executives plan or try to achieve. What is important is what executives actually accomplish. In their view, if the classical theory has the best balance of social benefits over detriments, it is justified from the standpoint of the impact model.

The same point holds for the reverse-impact model. Those classical theorists who are not strict consequentialists typically deny that it is the primary purpose of managers to consider the countervailing power that groups other than the shareholders exert over them. They believe that responding to the shareholders' financial interests will, in fact, on balance satisfy the interests of the public and will thus lessen the latter's incentive to pressure, regulate, or control corporate executives. But they hold it is not the basic motive of managers to blunt the potential of others to exert this countervailing pressure or influence upon corporations, except to the extent that such pressure is directed toward expanding the regulation of the firm by government. The latter form of pressure is inconsistent with the laissez-faire aspects of the classical theory. Once again, strict consequentialists believe that the classical theory appeals to the reverse-impact model because they believe that following it would lead to a satisfied (and thus less intruding and regulatory-minded) general public. Manne, of course, appeals to the reverse-impact model when he suggests that shareholders will not look kindly upon an active program of corporate social or moral spending. They will use their discretionary financial power (rather than their voting power) to sell their shares if such a program is perceived as being too costly to the company.

Such theorists as Hayek and Friedman appeal to the teamwork model of accountability, but they seem to apply it in only one direction. They do not use it to defend the idea that upper-level management has a distinct and compelling set of duties toward lower management or workers that rivals their duty to the shareholders. Instead they use it to defend the obligation that all employees are said to have toward the company and its shareholders. This is an important element in their defense of the loyalty of subordinates to be discussed later in the book. In addition, they apply the teamwork concept macroeconomically when they argue that an institutionalized specialization of function brings about the most productive and balanced economic and social system.

Classical theorists, like Friedman and Pilon, assume the ownership model when they insist upon protecting the ownership status and rights of shareholders. This permits them to single out shareholders for special management consideration. And Friedman and Carr assume the regulation model when they maintain that executives must play by the rules of the game, avoid fraud and deceit, and in general obey the other laws of the land. But as we have seen, they generally reject the idea that regulation, especially government regulation, is, as such, beneficial and thus more of it is needed. In this respect, the model receives only a grudging endorsement.

As regards the models of the corporation, it is clear from the first two arguments that classical theorists assume some combination of the private contract (primarily in its positive form), private property, enterprise, or machine models of the corporation. These theorists typically believe that corporations are largely the result of private agreements that are built upon the ownership and control of private wealth. Upon establishing these private agreements, an economic institution is created that is designed to be a wealth-producing instrument or machine—one owned by the shareholders and controlled through the web of these agreements. Last, these private economic creations have proven to be effective tools for the advancement of freedom, creativity, efficiency, productivity, and wealth. Classical theorists usually maintain that no political institution could be as successful in promoting these values.

While it is possible for classical theorists to assume the public power, organic, mental or moral agent, or social contract models of the corporation, they are less likely to do so. The public power model usually carries with it the implication that power should be correlated with responsibility. This could suggest added social or moral responsibilities for corporations. It would also be difficult to advance the managerial constraint argument while assuming this model, though it should be added that some classical theorists endorse the positive version of this model. And, as we have seen, Levitt advances an argument that stresses the dangers involved in corporations' becoming too socially or politically powerful.

The assumptions of methodological individualism that involve mechanism and associationism usually preclude the endorsement of the organic model of the corporation. Some classical theorists do, however, accept the macroeconomic implications of the model, whereby corporations are to be assessed from the standpoint of their role in the wider society. They do this because they believe in the positive catallactic effects of socially decentralized economic or corporate decision making. But they usually abjure the attempt either to portray these effects teleologically or to picture the wider society as some kind of superorganism. Furthermore, they characteristically reject certain microeconomic features sometimes thought to go along with the organic model that entail that members of the corporation be viewed and treated as ends, and not merely as means, by the other members of the firm.

Nor is the mental or moral agent model likely to be assumed by classical theorists. To accept this model is to view the corporation as an agent or person who is distinct from its members. This implies that the interests and good of the corporation may at times be distinct from the interests and good of the shareholders. But this implication is in conflict with a basic principle of the classical theory, namely, that the interests or wishes of the shareholders should dominate the decision making of corporate managers. In addition, this theory is at odds with methodological individualism (when viewed as a theory of the nature of responsibility) for the mental or moral agent theory tells us that an ascription of responsibility to a collection of individuals is not always reducible to an ascription of responsibility to their members. Methodological individualists typically view corporations as fictional legal agents rather than real moral agents.

Two aspects of the mental agent model that classical theorists are not reluctant to accept are the brain and psychic prisons metaphors suggested by Morgan. They can thus view corporations as centers of information processing that may at times be guided by the bounded rationality of its members. But they are not as likely to endorse the idea that corporations have self-correcting processes that function independently of the thought processes of their members. And while they may agree that certain corporations can or have become psychic prisons for their members, especially the inefficient or poorly run ones, they do not believe that it is in the nature of corporations to be or become such prisons.

Few classical theorists accept the social contract model of the corporation because, as it is usually presented, it implies that society expects that corporations will be more active in the noneconomic arena. One notable exception to this is Buchanan. In his defense of the classical theory, he accepts the social contract model and combines this with the consent theory of legitimation. He denies, however, that the terms of the social contract demand greater levels of corporate social activism (Buchanan, 1975, p. 37). As he sees it, the contractors expect corporations to pursue something like the "game ethic" of Carr.

THE ASSUMPTIONS OF THE CLASSICAL THEORY: STRATEGIES OF LEGITIMATION

The two principal theories of legitimacy assumed by classical theorists are the performance (or consequentialist) and rights theories. As we have seen, these theorists stress the overall positive consequences that are alleged to result from a policy of limited corporate social activity. And they argue that their theory best respects the property and fiduciary rights of stockholders and the right of freedom of choice for all market participants.

Classical theorists are, however, sympathetic to the conformity to law and current standards theories, though they are unlikely to endorse these as the sole or primary norms for the legitimacy of social or economic institutions. They do believe that the fact that a corporation has not violated the law and has otherwise conformed to the current moral or social standards of society are strong indications of its legitimacy—as long as this latter conformity does not significantly interfere with the revenue-producing capacity of the firm. Their enthusiasm for these models is dampened, however, when others seek to use them to expand the grip that law and morality have over corporate decision making.

Classical theorists could assume the power theory of legitimation and argue that the extent of corporate power in society permits corporate leaders to determine what constitutes the noneconomic arena of activity. This would justify executives in defining a limited social role for corporations. But it could also be used to permit them to define a more extensive moral or social role for the corporation, should they so choose. And this point is generally inconsistent with the classical theory. This suggests that the power theory cannot by itself provide the basic framework for the defense of the classical position. It is also inconsistent with those aspects of the argument for the classical theory that are based upon concern for excessive corporate power. Finally, its descriptive nature opposes the normative assumptions of the classical theory of corporate legitimacy. And, even if successful, the power strategy would place corporations at a level of descriptive legitimacy that is well below that envisioned by most classical theorists.

Formalistic theories of legitimation cannot be applied to the classical theory in an unambiguous manner. Classical theorists accept at least one tenet of formalism. They believe that the values of freedom and efficiency are universalizable values, and they have no difficulty in universalizing the maxim that a social or economic institution should focus upon its own unique abilities and functions. But there is one version of formalism that they are likely to reject. In general, they urge that the golden rule test not be applied to business decision making. As Lundberg indicates, some believe that the test is too vague to be useful in business life (Lundberg, 1972, p. 240). Some also take exception to the version of the test that requires executives to refrain from any business transaction that they believe would leave other parties in a relatively worse position. This role-reversal test would presumably disqualify such transactions because executives could not accept the agreement if they were the parties who were negatively affected to a significant degree. Some classical theorists believe, however, that such a test would nullify many business agreements. Part of the incentive for making an economic agreement is the belief, whether justified or not, that it will give one a relative advantage over some other party, including at times the one with whom one is making the agreement. By seeking to eliminate such agreements, theorists who advocate this version of formalism might unwittingly undermine important aspects of the business community by cancelling many of the agreements of its members.

Some classical theorists appeal to the respect for persons theory of legitimacy, but only when respect is equated with the negative duties of noninterference and nonharm. They maintain that a restricted system of corporate social activity best respects the freedom and dignity of all market participants. The so-called positive duties of mutual aid and benevolence are not required of corporate executives by these theorists. When the argument for the common good is used to defend the classical theory, however, we have seen that it is frequently framed in consequentialist rather than deontological terms as constituting a significantly advantageous feature of the classical theory. In this view, the emphasis is placed upon this relative advantage rather than respect for persons as such. This is so even when executives are not held to be obligated to promote directly the common good.

This brings us to the procedural or consent theory. Most classical theorists agree with the two-party version of the consent theory. All market transactions demand this kind of consent and promise keeping, and if this type of consent could by itself confer legitimacy, corporations and their private agreements would clearly meet the requirements. In the previous chapter, though, we considered reasons to doubt the validity of this version of the theory. Some consent theorists have of course advanced other versions of the theory, including one for multi-party agreements. In general, however, classical theorists have avoided appealing to this version because to them it implies that corporate executives should actively promote the interests of parties with whom no explicit agreements have been made (otherwise corporate activities and structures would not receive support from these groups of people).

One theorist who seeks to defend the classical theory within the framework of the multi-party version of the consent theory is Buchanan, who believes that our social institutions should be viewed as emerging from a two-step process of social decision making. In this process a set of agreements arises to which every participant gives his or her rational consent. The first step involves an agreement that is consistently applied to all members to lay down arms and accept certain restrictions on their behavior. It involves the delineation of property rights for the possession and use of resource endowments and stocks of goods, and it determines the rules under which the collectivity will operate in providing and financing public goods (Buchanan, 1975, p. 72). Only unanimous agreement at this level can permit a rational transition to the next step in negotiations (Buchanan, 1975, p. 48).

The second step involves agreements that establish the specific constitution of property relationships. It is at this level, if at all, that participants agree to create and support business corporations. Buchanan believes, though, that a strong commitment to social or moral activism by corporations is not one of the conditions of their social existence. Nor would it be rational for members of society to expect corporations to allow social or moral goals to supplant their traditional economic functions.

Buchanan believes that the fairness and rationality of these agreements is based upon the fact that individuals can withhold their consent if they are unhappy with them. What helps to gain their support is not just the advantages of collective organization in general; nor is it the specific advantages of these business units. It is also the ability of participants to make specific trade-offs, side payments, and other forms of compensatory stipulations to the agreements (Buchanan, 1975, p. 65). Thus, as long as individuals agree to the assignment and execution of corporate property rights, either directly or through the inducement of these side payments and transfers, the corporate structure has a legitimate claim upon the allegiance of the participants. And as long as the policies and actions of corporations are within the bounds of the negotiated agreements, both members and nonmembers alike must respect the firm's claims to legitimacy.

The outcome of these hypothetical negotiations can then be said to be rational, in the Pareto-efficient sense of this term. As a methodological individualist, Buchanan cannot ground their rationality upon the specific goods or material values they are alleged to promote. He grounds it instead upon the presumed fact that they will satisfy the interests of all the participants (whatever these interests turn out to be). The satisfaction of the participants is assured because they give their unanimous consent to the agreements, indicating thereby that they believe they are better off in the post-agreement context than they were in the pre-agreement stage (Buchanan, 1975, p. 29). A Pareto-efficient bargain is not necessarily the best one that can be reached for each participant, but it is rationally justified nevertheless because a change from the agreement (without compensation) will make some individuals worse off (Buchanan, 1975, p. 47).

We see then that it is also possible to ground the classical theory of corporate responsibility upon the assumptions of the social or public contract model of the corporation and the multi-party version of the consent theory of the legitimation of social institutions. To do so, however, one must also believe that individuals in society have not given their actual or rational consent to the idea that corporations should be significant centers of social or moral change.

REFERENCES

Birdzell, L. E. 1975. "The Moral Basis of the Business System." *Journal of Contemporary Business*, Summer, pp. 75–87.

Buchanan, James M. 1975. *The Limits of Liberty*. Chicago: University of Chicago Press.

Carr, Albert Z. 1968. "Is Business Bluffing Ethical?" *Harvard Business Review*, vol. 46, no. 1. January–February, pp. 145–53.

Davis, Keith. 1977. "The Case For and Against Business Assumption of Social Responsibilities." In *Managing Corporate Social Responsibility*, edited by Archie B. Carroll, pp. 35–45. Boston: Little, Brown, and Company.

Friedman, Milton. 1968. *Capitalism and Freedom*. Chicago: University of Chicago Press.

———. 1970. "The Social Responsibility of Business Is To Increase Its Profits." *The New York Times Magazine*, September 13, pp. 32, 33, 122–26.

Hayek, F. A. 1976. *Law, Legislation and Liberty: The Mirage of Social Justice*. Chicago: University of Chicago Press.

Hessen, Robert. 1979. *In Defense of the Corporation*. Stanford, Calif.: Hoover Institution Press.

Jones, Thomas M. 1980. "Corporate Social Responsibility Revisited, Redefined." *California Management Review*, Spring, pp. 59–67.

Levitt, Theodore. 1958. "The Dangers of Social Responsibility." *Harvard Business Review*, September–October, pp. 41–50.

Lundberg, Craig C. 1972. "Is the Golden Rule a Useful Guide to Business Decision-Making?" In *Issues in Business and Society*, edited by George A. Steiner, pp. 237–42. New York: Random House.

Manne, Henry (with Henry Wallich). 1972. *The Modern Corporation and Social Responsibility*. Washington, D.C.: American Enterprise Institute.

Novak, Michael. 1982. *The Spirit of Democratic Capitalism*. New York: Simon and Schuster.

Pastin, Mark, and Michael Hooker. 1984. "Ethics and the Foreign Corrupt Practices Act." In *Business Ethics: Readings and Cases in Corporate Morality*, edited by W. Michael Hoffman and Jennifer Mills Moore, pp. 463–67. New York: McGraw-Hill.

Pilon, Roger. 1982. "Capitalism and Rights: An Essay Toward Fine Tuning the Moral

Foundations of the Free Society.'' *Journal of Business Ethics*, February, pp. 29–42.

Sawyer, George C. 1979. *Business and Society: Managing Corporate Social Impact.* Boston: Houghton Mifflin Company.

Sethi, S. Prakash. 1977. ''Dimensions of Corporate Social Performance: An Analytical Framework.'' In *Managing Corporate Social Responsibility*, edited by Archie Carroll, pp. 69–75. Boston: Little, Brown and Company.

Shaffer, Butler D. 1977. ''The Social Responsibility of Business: A Dissent.'' *Business and Society*, Spring, pp. 11–18.

Useem, Michael. 1988. ''Market and Institutional Factors in Corporate Contributions.'' *California Management Review*, Winter, pp. 77–88.

9

THE RESPONSE TO THE CLASSICAL THEORY

THE PERFORMANCE ARGUMENT: FREEDOM AND THE GAME ANALOGY

Various theorists have responded to the classical theory of corporate responsibility. In this chapter we shall examine the argument of several of these opponents. Our treatment of this issue will be quite extensive, both because the literature on this question is considerably large in size and because such a treatment will help to introduce the diverse perspectives of the other theories. We shall not then seek to examine the criticisms of the other theories in quite this focused or careful a manner.

We have seen that classical theorists argue that the specialization of function that occurs when managers focus upon their economic responsibilities toward the shareholders provides the overall social system with a synergistic, creative, and productive order. But opponents to the theory reject or question various aspects of this performance claim. Some, such as Goldman and Velasquez, simply reject the idea that the classical theory leads to the most fair and effective social system (Goldman, 1980, p. 268; Velasquez, 1982, p. 149). As they see it, it has resulted in a host of negative consequences. Velasquez, for example, tells us that it has often led to unchecked negative externalities or social costs and harms to otherwise innocent third parties, poor product quality, excessively high prices, and inferior working conditions (Velasquez, 1982, pp. 149ff.).

Nearly all of the opponents argue that their model of corporate responsibility best serves the overall social system. Some, in fact, contend that their model best promotes two of the very values that classical theorists claim for their own position—productivity and efficiency. But we shall postpone our discussion of the positive arguments for each of these claims until the appropriate place in the coming chapters. For the present, however, we shall discuss four added points that opponents reject in the performance argument.

First, against Friedman and Hayek, they argue that the classical theory does not best preserve the freedom or liberty of all parties in the social system. Pichler, for example, contends that the liberty principle demands greater respect for the decisions of other constituents than is typically given in the classical theory (Pichler, 1983, p. 22). He maintains that concern for the freedom of workers, consumers, and others requires, at a minimum, a more demanding policy of accuracy and completeness in corporate disclosure than is often thought justified by classical theorists. He tells us that many corporations need to restructure themselves to encourage greater participation in decision making and to reduce restrictions on the flow of certain information. Many need to establish audit and review committees at the board level to facilitate the executive power of board members, especially the independent ones. And they need to provide more relevant information to workers, consumers, and shareholders to help them exercise their freedom by making more informed decisions. Pichler tells us that parties to contracts with management should be provided with complete information about transaction terms. Thus, consumers should be given full information by management on the hazards of a particular product. Workers should be given full freedom to organize. Employers should not limit the ability of employees to utilize personal time for discussion of wages, hours, or working conditions. Nor should they hinder the workers' attempts to solicit the cooperation of other workers for the purpose of collective representation. Pichler further believes that management should eliminate or minimize the negative effects of its actions upon third parties—especially in such areas as the environment and plant closings (Pichler, 1983, p. 23), though he grants that the primary obligation of managers is to the owners of the company. In this sense, his theory is somewhat analogous to the classical theory. But he insists that management cannot overlook the rights and freedoms of other stakeholders, even if this should prove to be somewhat costly to the shareholders (Pichler, 1983, p. 25). Management should consider the choices and preferences of certain other groups to be roughly on a par with the interests and needs of the shareholders.

Second, opponents of the classical theory reject the game analogy of business that is advanced by Carr. The point of this analogy is to suggest that management is justified in engaging in certain otherwise morally questionable practices, so long as these practices conform to the law and contribute to the economic success of the business. It is to be inferred from this that economic performance or success is an ultimate corporate value. It is to be further inferred that both individual firms and society are better off when managers view business decision making as a game.

Opponents criticize the game theory in various ways. Some question the belief that Carr's account accurately portrays how executives actually make management decisions. It is maintained against Carr that most business transactions are grounded upon the expectation of nonlegally imposed trust and honesty (Blodgett, 1968, p. 163; Purchell, 1975, p. 45; Wokutch and Carson, 1984, p. 457). According to this view, these values rival economic success in the role they play in management decision making. Firms that repeatedly violate these values by lack of disclosure, exaggeration, or the like, face the threat of retaliation by customers, creditors, suppliers, and others. In effect, such firms often put themselves at a competitive disadvantage. It is further contended that most firms realize that the small temporary gain received from an occasional violation of this expectation is rarely worth the loss in trust that might ensue for future transactions.

Others argue that even if exaggeration, lack of disclosure, and other questionable game strategies were commonly or universally practiced by business executives, this would not in itself justify these practices. Thus, James and Gillespie contend that a practice does not acquire such justification by the simple expedient of being made more widespread (James, 1982, p. 287; Gillespie, 1975, p. 1).

Some theorists indicate that Carr's theory fails to do justice to the distinction between constitutive and regulative rules of conduct. As Carr sees it, most of the important rules of corporate conduct are constitutive in nature; they merely define the practice in question. But this simply leads us to ask the question of whether the business "game" should be played at all.

DesJardin and McCall raise this objection in another way. They reject the analogy advanced by Carr and the pattern of argument in which it functions. They contend that this type of argument could be used to support the alleged authority of several otherwise questionable rules or principles of decision making. As they see it, since many areas of decision making have their own institutional rules of winning, each may then be said to constitute its own "ethic" (DesJardin and McCall, 1985, p. 12). This could yield such "systems" of ethics as the dictator or the playboy ethic, for example.

They also contend that Carr's position that executives are expected to abide by the laws of the land indicates an inconsistency in his theory (DesJardin and McCall, 1985, p. 12). They suggest that the formation, execution, and adjudication of law in society rests upon values other than success and freedom. A basic component of the idea of law is the value of procedural justice or fairness. Thus, for example, to take the case of the judicial system, those corporate executives who may be supposed to follow "the game ethic" in business expect nevertheless to be treated impartially in civil or criminal litigation. They expect decisions to be made on the basis of the evidence rather than upon the personal whims or mere self-interest of the judge or jury. This demand for impartiality implies that persons can transcend their private roles, and the alleged game facets of their institutional public roles, to render fair and informed verdicts. It implies as well that when they show respect for law, executives are at the same time demonstrating respect for certain values that call into question the soundness of the game theory itself.

Other opponents to this theory also question the analogy between business and a game like poker. Thus, Solomon and Hanson contend that although business is a competitive practice, it is not a game (Solomon and Hanson, 1983, p. 109). Some of the business executives responding to Carr's article felt that the game analogy trivialized business life. The stakes involved in business activities for executives, shareholders, workers, and consumers are considerably greater than those won or lost in a game of cards, for example (Blodgett, 1968, p. 165). Gillespie, and Solomon and Hanson argue that business life has no clear point of beginning or end, like the game of poker does. Business decisions made many years ago may still have an impact on people's lives (Gillespie, 1975, p. 1; Solomon and Hanson, 1983, p. 109). Workers not informed of hazardous materials in the workplace, consumers not told of safety-related defects in products, the public not apprised of toxins in their air or water are not like the gambler who raises a bid while not knowing the cards in his opponent's hand. They are not voluntary participants willing to risk their health or safety. James thinks that because business has such an extensive second and third-party impact, it bears little resemblance to a game like poker (James, 1982, p. 287).

Finally, there is an objection to the present analogy from a different point of view. It can be argued that business is unlike poker in that economic success often breeds political success. Winning in business sometimes permits executives to influence the making and administering of the laws and codes regulating their economic conduct. For example, by working to secure import quotas to diminish the availability of foreign goods, by gaining stricter licensing requirements to screen out potential competitors, or by seeking to lower environmental standards to postpone installing expensive pollution-control equipment, certain firms show their ability to change the "rules of the game" in their own favor. The analogy to poker would be somewhat closer, contend opponents, if the players were allowed to use their winnings to "buy" new rules for the game. By altering the rules in their favor, initial victors could thereby make continued success more likely. But of course in this situation few early losers would wish to continue playing. What this shows, critics contend, is that there is an important difference between a game like poker, which has a degree of fairness built into by a set of stable and impersonal rules, and the arena of business decision making, which requires that a certain number of nonlegal restrictions be placed upon management's ability to change the laws of the land to its own liking.

PERFORMANCE AND EFFICIENCY

A third major objection raised to the performance argument concerns the willingness of most classical theorists to equate the concept of performance with that of efficiency. Opponents of the classical theory question the concept of Pareto efficiency. They also question some of the assumptions of methodological individualism upon which the concept is framed. Cirillo, for example, tells us that the Pareto concept is meant to apply to a static market situation (Cirillo, 1979, p. 51). It is useless in cases where a managerial action or policy of action has both winners and losers. The Pareto criterion cannot be used to arbitrate the dispute between the various positions on corporate responsibility discussed in these chapters. Some people will be made worse off whether managers tighten their loyalty to the shareholders of the company or whether they respond more directly to the interests and needs of other groups of people. In a situation like this, where some individuals are made worse off while others are made better off, we would like to know *how* much better or worse off, so that we might judge the overall welfare, performance, or fairness of the alternative proposals. But it is just such interpersonal comparisons of utility or value that are ruled out by the Pareto principle. It permits the ordinal ranking of satisfaction for single individuals, but it excludes any form of interpersonal comparison of utility or value. This suggests to opponents of the classical theory the need for, if not the presence of, other performance criteria that are not based solely or primarily upon individual preference.

Brandt criticizes the subjectivism that is implicit in both the Pareto concept and the position of methodological individualism in general (Brandt, 1967, pp. 23ff.). In the latter theory, an individual's values are based upon his or her own preferences in situations where an exchange of items or goods is possible. For the methodological individualist, a goal is not chosen or preferred by an individual because it is authoritative; it is authoritative for that person because it is preferred by him or her. But classical theorists admit two exceptions to this general view—the values of freedom and efficiency are not themselves said to be grounded upon their being preferred by individuals. They are authoritative whether or not individuals choose to pursue or respect them. Critics of the classical theory question the coherence of a position that permits these exceptions, but they will admit no others. If certain values can, in principle, be admitted to be valid in independence of human preference, opponents wonder why methodological individualists limit such values to only these two.

Hodgson criticizes the theory of choice of methodological individualists. He rejects their attempts to offer mechanistic and value-neutral explanations for economic phenomena (Hodgson, 1983, p. 237). As he sees it, methodological individualists shun the language of reasons, purposes, motives, and values in favor of the language of preference, satisfaction, efficiency, marginal utility and equilibrium. For Hodgson, methodological individualists view persons as centers of equilibrium who are driven by antecedent causes to balance their competing interests and preferences with resource availability. In such a view, the marginal utility of choice is that point of homeostasis at which the satisfaction of gaining a good or service is equal to the pain or dissatisfaction of having to pay for it (Hodgson, 1983, p. 242). Two goods have equal utility for a person, then, when that person is indifferent in preference toward them.

In response to this theory, Hodgson proposes a return to a teleological and normative-based view of choice. Choice, in the strict sense, implies for him the belief that the object of choice is desirable and thus should be preferred (Hodgson, 1983, p. 246). Unlike the methodological individualist, who sees choice as the mere product of prior causes, Hodgson contends that choice is based upon a concept of worth—where the worth or value of an object is only in part determined by the current long-run plans and purposes of the individual agent. Such a theory challenges the notion that economics can be a science like physics or chemistry, but Hodgson believes that it conforms more closely to human nature and to the phenomenology of choice and conduct.

An added criticism concerns the nature and authority of the method of proof that is used to show that one policy of action is, in fact, more efficient than another. It is contended that problems arise when the response to personal preference is defined as the standard for judging efficiency. It is asserted that as the forces of technology and specialization advance, consumers, workers, and the general public cannot be presumed to have sufficient or adequate knowledge to discern and protect their interests. Thus, the assumption of the sufficiently informed consumer, worker, or manager becomes practically, if not theoretically, impossible to defend. This entails that an individual's assessment of personal satisfaction is too tainted or otherwise problematic to be straightforwardly used as proof either of Pareto optimality or of the effectiveness or justice of the overall system.

This objection calls into question the authority or justified character of the preferences or choices of people as seen within the context of methodological individualism. To help defend or guarantee this authority, methodological individualists have traditionally assumed that market participants are *rational* (at least to the extent of being able to protect their own interests) and are sufficiently *knowledgeable* on the relevant issues to make informed choices. Some opponents, influenced by the work of Freud, Marx, or other theorists, question the alleged rational character of the preferences or choices of market participants. They believe that many market preferences are the product of nonrational or irrational factors. Unlike classical theorists, they do not believe that a recurrent or stable pattern of market preference should automatically be used as an indication of the Pareto efficiency of a system satisfying these preferences. Such a pattern may simply indicate a compulsive or otherwise unhealthy psychological condition in market agents themselves.

The point of this objection is to suggest that the preferences of market participants may be in error. Another way for critics to advance this thesis is to question the other aspect of the classical assumption about market participants— the alleged informed character of their market preferences. Opponents suggest that because knowledge and information are themselves scarce commodities, they have become basic items for sale in the marketplace. This means that some market participants have an incentive to exploit this scarcity for their own benefit. They will provide or sell information only to those who are willing to pay for it. In deciding whether or not to obtain such information, other market participants cannot automatically be assumed to be sufficiently informed to make a wise or prudent purchasing decision. This is particularly true of decisions about acquiring information that has an immediate bearing upon an agent's present desires or preferences. Information that suggests that his or her preferences are mistaken or should be changed in some way is unique information. The very fact that an agent contemplates purchasing such a relatively scarce commodity indicates that the agent believes that he or she is not yet a sufficiently informed market participant. Hence the need for the purchase. It also indicates that the agent's present decision and the preferences upon which it is based can be in error. It will almost certainly be in error if he or she has made incorrect purchasing decisions about such information in the past. Opponents believe that to maintain otherwise is to fail to explain the justified character of present market preferences, or it is to become involved in regress. They suggest that if the proof of the wisdom or prudence of a present market decision of an agent in obtaining information of this kind is propagated upon the assumption of the wisdom or prudence of like decisions having been made in the past, how then can the wisdom or prudence of these past decisions be independently established? Their enlightened character must be based upon the assumed wisdom or prudence of informational purchasing decisions made in the agent's still further past. Because this regress extends indefinitely, or at least to the point where the wisdom or prudence of the agent can no longer be assumed, opponents believe there can be no independent or nonproblematic defense of the assumption of the informed choice of market participants. Informed choice is not a given in the marketplace; it too must be proven. This entails that the present or stable preferences and satisfactions of agents cannot be the *sine qua non* of market theory. Since these preferences may themselves be in error, their ordinal ranking is of little use to one who is seeking to establish the optimal character of certain micro and macro aspects of the economy.

Along these same lines, theorists like Knight and Galbraith contend that the "dependence effect" of advertising biases the assessment of personal satisfaction in the direction of the wants or values of the advertisers (Knight, 1923, p. 585; Galbraith, 1976, p. 136). They maintain that the satisfaction of consumer demand is not sufficiently indicative of optimal results occurring at the microeconomic level. Since the preferences upon which the test of optimality is based are largely products of the system, the appeal to the satisfaction of these preferences proves to be somewhat circular. A more independent test of effectiveness and fairness is needed. Presumably, it would be one grounded less exclusively upon the direct reports of material satisfaction of market participants. It would perhaps be directed more toward interpersonal comparisons of well-being generally.

Finally, when efficiency is defined in straightforward quantitative terms, critics of the classical theory reject the argument of Shaffer that when management responds to groups other than the shareholders of the company, the form of decision making they are involved in rarely results in cost-effective practices or programs. Brummer, for example, has argued that considerations of cost and waste can be one facet of the socially responsible character of socially or morally motivated projects (Brummer, 1983, p. 119).

PERFORMANCE AND SOCIAL RESPONSIBILITY: SOME EMPIRICAL STUDIES

The last criticism of the performance argument to be discussed here concerns a basic belief of classical theorists that the financial interests of the stockholders are best served when management focuses primarily or exclusively upon economic matters. Opponents argue instead that a more extensive involvement in corporate social responsibility projects may make good business sense. Thus, for example, Bock suggests that social responsibility goals need not interfere with corporate economic performance (Bock, 1979, p. 13). And theorists like Freeman and Starling, who endorse the strategic planning approach to corporate responsibility, argue that a firm's overall performance suffers when managers implement only the classical theory (Freeman, 1984, p. 65; Starling, 1980, pp. 224ff.).

As Arlow and Gannon have indicated, the empirical studies that have examined the bearing of corporate social responsibility upon economic performance have yielded mixed results. They tell us that some studies show a positive relation, others a negative one, while still others suggest little or no correlation at all (Arlow and Gannon, 1982, p. 238). On the positive side is the work of Sturdivant and Ginter, Bragdon and Marlin, Eilbert and Parket, and Bowman and Haire.

Sturdivant and Ginter found that in the years between 1964 and 1974 growth in earnings per share of some twenty-eight firms studied was positively correlated with firms that were identified as socially responsible companies by Moskowitz, the editor of *Business and Society Review*. Conversely, they found that of the firms studied those that were rated the lowest in social responsibility by Moskowitz in 1974 had lower levels of growth in earnings per share (Sturdivant and Ginter, 1977, p. 38). Bragdon and Marlin found that paper companies judged by them as having a favorable pollution-control performance record were in general found to be the more profitable firms in the industry as well (Bragdon and Marlin, 1972, p. 17). Eilbert and Parket compared the economic performance of eighty firms judged to be more socially responsible (because they voluntarily responded to the survey of the authors (with certain other firms listed in the *Fortune* 500. These authors used four measures of economic performance: (1) net income, (2) net income as a percentage of sales, (3) net income as a percentage of stockholders' equity, and (4) earnings per share. They found that the median values on all four dimensions were higher for the firms judged to be more socially responsible (Eilbert and Parket, 1975, pp. 9ff.). Finally, Bowman and Haire examined the annual reports of eighty-two firms in the food processing industry to determine which firms had the greatest amount of space devoted to the topic of social responsibility. They found that those firms that had some discussion of the topic performed better economically than those that had no such discussion. This was determined by appealing to the mean and median return on equity for these firms five years before the study began. They found further, however, that when these firms were subdivided into high-, medium, and low-mention categories for reporting their social responsibility, the firms in the high- and low-mention categories performed more poorly economically than did the medium-mention firms. The authors conclude that too strong a commitment to social responsibility goals may inhibit the economic stability and growth of corporations (Bowman and Haire, 1975, p. 53).

On the negative side, there are two studies conducted by Vance. In one he compared fourteen firms identified as socially responsible by Moskowitz in 1972 with certain firms listed in the *New York Stock Exchange Composite Index*, the *Dow Jones Industrials*, and the *Standard and Poor's Industrials*. He judged them in terms of the percentage difference in their stock values recorded on the dates January 1, 1972 and January 1, 1975. He found that thirteen of the fourteen firms studied had poorer records of stock performance than did the other firms studied (Vance, 1975, p. 20). Again, consulting information from two 1972 issues of *Business and Society Review*, he compiled a list of forty-five companies ranked by business leaders as firms most fully committed to social responsibility goals and fifty firms ranked for their commitment to social responsibility projects by graduate business students surveyed by the journal. He compared the percentage change in stock value of these firms on the dates January 1, 1974 and January 1, 1975. He found a negative correlation between their stock value performance and their ranking with respect to social responsibility (Vance, 1975, p. 22).

Last, there are studies that show no significant correlation between the commitment to social responsibility and economic performance. Folger and Nutt, for example, examined the stock performance of nine paper companies between March, 1971 and March, 1972 that reported their record of pollution control efforts. They found that a company's rating on pollution control bore little relation to the value of its common stock or to the purchase of its stock by mutual funds (Folger and Nutt, 1975, p. 157). Alexander and Bucholz used the same social responsibility rankings as Vance, but they adjusted the rates of return for risk. After reducing Vance's original sample to forty-one companies that sold common stock, they too found no significant relationship between social responsibility ranking and stock market performance (Alexander and Bucholz, 1978, p. 483). Abbott and Monsen, who studied 450 companies in the *Fortune* 500, compared the investor returns during the years 1964 and 1974 with the companies' commitment to social responsibility goals as measured by their reported social activities. They concluded that social involvement seems neither to strengthen nor weaken a company's return to the investor (Abbott and Monsen, 1979, p. 514). Finally, in their study of thirty commercial banks in Texas, Kedia and Kuntz concluded that there is virtually no evidence of a strong correlation between social behaviors, good or bad, and the usual indicators of economic performance (Kedia and Kuntz, 1981, pp. 8ff.).

Studies conducted or reported in the 1980s have reaffirmed the results of those conducted in the 1970s. Several researchers have pointed out the weaknesses of the earlier studies and have sought to develop more inclusive or sophisticated methods of determining corporate social or moral responsiveness and of measuring corporate financial performance, but this has not altered the overall results to any appreciable degree. Some studies show a negative, some a positive, and others a weak or neutral correlation between these variables (however they may be measured or determined in a specific study).

For example, the work of Becker and Olson and Kleiner and Bouillon show a negative correlation. Becker and Olson studied the financial performance of 1,200 companies. They divided these firms into unionized and non-unionized categories, where unionization, however it came about, could be used as one indication of the social responsiveness of firms. They discovered that on average the unionized firms gave a lower return to the investors than did the non-unionized companies. The former gained in some way because shareholders of these companies bore less risk, according to the authors. The risk was shared with the unionized workers. But they concluded that the benefits of risk sharing do not seem great enough to compensate for the lowered return to the shareholders (Becker and Olson, 1989, p. 256).

Kleiner and Bouillon sent surveys to 106 firms in 1984 and correlated the returns on these with independent financial data concerning the firms studied. The surveys asked whether or not the firms in question provided information to their production workers on such factors as the financial condition of the company and the workers' productivity and relative standing in the labor market. Since many unions get this material on their own, non-unionized firms that voluntarily provided this information to their workers could be viewed as being more morally or socially responsible than firms that did not share this information with their workers. These authors found that such information sharing was positively related to the level of wages and benefits for the workers in both unionized and non-unionized companies but was unrelated to their productivity. More important for our purposes, it was to a statistically significant degree negatively related to profits and cash flow in the non-unionized firms (Kleiner and Bouillon, 1988, p. 616).

Jones's work indicates that a slightly positive relation exists between social responsiveness and productivity. The type of company he studied was the business cooperative. He sent surveys to fifty British firms in the retail industry in which executives were to indicate whether workers financially participated in the company (with profit-sharing programs and the like) or whether workers sat on the company's board of directors. As with the other two studies, it is assumed that such employee programs or corporate structuring policies indicate that a firm is more socially responsive, at least to this particular stakeholder group. Jones then correlated these results with measures of worker productivity in the firms. If this latter variable increases, it is inferred that the firms' financial performance will be otherwise improved. He found that those firms that had workers on their boards had moderately increased levels of productivity over those cooperatives that did not. But he also found that firms whose workers participated financially in the cooperative had reduced levels of productivity.

The net impact of all of this was small but involved a slightly positive correlation overall (Jones, 1987, p. 79).

Finally, the work of Wokutch and Spencer and Cochran and Wood indicates that the relationship between these variables is very complex—perhaps too complex to say at this time whether their correlation is positive or negative in nature. Wokutch and Spencer studied the financial and social performance of 130 large manufacturing firms. They determined the social responsiveness of these firms in part by sending 6,000 questionnaires to executives in which the latter were asked to rank only those firms in their own industry for social performance. This was checked against *Fortune* magazine's ratings of firms in 1983, especially in the area of responsibility to the community and the environment. They further examined these firms for their criminal records (1980–1983) and their record of corporate philanthropy relative to the other firms in their industry. This gave these authors a fourfold matrix of corporate behavior for these firms: *saints* were corporations that had no record of criminal behavior in the period considered and gave relatively high contributions to charity; *pharisees* were firms with no crimes but that had lower levels of corporate giving; *cynics/repenters* were companies with criminal records that gave relatively high contributions to philanthropy; and, finally, *sinners* were firms that had both a record of crime and were rated as low in corporate charity. The financial performance of these firms was determined by using the measures of return on total assets and return on sales compiled from *Fortune*'s annual listing of the 500 largest firms (1978–1982).

These authors found that of the seventy-four firms included in the final determination, those deemed saints and those considered cynics/repenters were rated the highest in social responsiveness by their peers in the questionnaires. But the saints had significantly lower returns on assets and returns on sales, which suggests a negative correlation between social and financial performance. But since the other three groups performed about the same financially, it shows that some firms that were rated highly in the area of social responsiveness performed about as well as those ranked low in this regard (Wokutch and Spencer, 1987, p. 72).

The work of Cochran and Wood also indicates that a complex set of relationships exists between the variables of social responsiveness and financial performance. These authors studied the performance of thirty-nine firms during the 1970–1974 period, and thirty-six firms during the 1975–1979 period. They used a combined Moskowitz list as a reputational index for determining the social responsiveness of these firms in the periods studied. Finally, they used three types of accounting returns as their measures of financial performance: (1) the ratio of operating earnings to assets, (2) the ratio of operating earnings to sales, and (3) the excess market valuation. The performance of the firms studied in these areas was checked against the performance of other firms in the same industry.

What Cochran and Wood found was that firms ranked highly in the area of social responsibility financially outperformed those rated as poor in this regard, when the second and third measures mentioned above were used as the basis for comparison. When the ratio of operating earnings to assets was used, however, a nonstatistically significant correlation emerged (Cochran and Wood, 1984, p. 51). These authors did find that within industry groups the financial variable that correlated most strongly with corporate social responsiveness was asset age. Generally speaking, the older a company's assets, the less socially responsible it was perceived to be. Cochran and Wood believe that this relationship must be considered in future studies in this area. They conclude that after appropriate controls are in place, there is at best a weak correlation between corporate social and financial performance.

Questions have been raised about the divergent nature of these empirical results and about the methods used in these studies to determine both the economic and social performance of the corporations examined. Questions have also been raised concerning whether the researchers have properly isolated social performance as a causative factor in their studies and have investigated the relation of social to economic performance over a long enough period of time to draw relatively conclusive inferences about the true nature of the relationship existing between these variables. Even the more recent studies can or have been questioned in these regards. What these studies do suggest to opponents of the classical theory, though, is that when managers respond directly to the needs and interests of individuals other than the shareholders, they do not necessarily injure the financial interests of the corporation. Thus, these thinkers view the performance argument for the classical theory as an unsuitable base from which to criticize the other theories of corporate responsibility.

In addition to the performance argument, there is a deontological side to the defense of the classical theory. One such argument emphasizes the loyalty relation existing between managers and shareholders.

THE LOYALTY TO SHAREHOLDERS ARGUMENT

Classical theorists argue that a special relation exists between management and shareholders that requires that the former always give precedence to the interests of the latter in their business decision making. The ground of this special responsibility is said to be found in some unique feature of the management-shareholder relationship—whether this be the presence of ownership rights or voting power by the shareholders, or whether it be the consent of management or the representative and fiduciary nature of the latter's agency role.

As regards property rights, critics of the classical theory raise several arguments against the idea that ownership is the basis of an overriding relation between stockholders and corporate managers. Goldman, for example, questions the idea that stockholders are owners in the true sense of the term, with full-fledged property rights. He likens their status to that of gamblers (Goldman, 1980, p. 284). He tells us that they do not have a special relation to managers that overrides the relation the latter have to bondholders or to other creditors. Corporate managers are legally obligated to reimburse the creditors of the corporation within a certain period of time agreed upon in the contract. No such legal requirement exists with respect to dividends paid to the stockholders. It is a management strategy of some corporations that earnings available for dividends are retained and reinvested in the firm. And even for those corporations that normally distribute quarterly dividends, their management can decide to skip the dividend in any given quarter if it believes this will best contribute to the corporation's well-being.

Bowie reminds us that the courts have ruled in *Dodge v. Ford Motor Company* (1919) that management is under a general obligation to pay dividends to shareholders (Bowie, 1982, p. 19). But the very fact that there may be exceptions to this general rule, indicates that there are certain relationships to individuals other than the shareholders of the company which sometimes take precedence in the decision making of management.

Classical theorists do not deny that payments to workers, suppliers, bondholders, and other creditors normally take precedence over the dividends paid to shareholders. Their contention, however, is that this is done largely as a means of gaining long-run prosperity for the firm and its stockholders. These theorists believe that the ultimate economic relation is still that which exists between the shareholders and the managers of the company.

It is open to critics of this theory, however, to question the type of proof that can support this view. If payments to certain individuals with whom the corporation is bound by contract almost always override the payment of dividends to shareholders, how can it be said that the former are done merely to serve the interests of the shareholders? How can the ultimate motive of managers be determined in these cases? Classical theorists might respond by suggesting that if the discharging of a contract payment were an end in itself, more firms would seek to prepay the debt involved in these contractual relations. The fact that they typically do not emphasizes the importance of the shareholder relation. But opponents may point out, finally, that the most this shows is that various groups of constituents have an equal claim upon the decision making of corporate management.

Critics of the classical theory raise other objections to the ownership defense of the primacy of shareholders. They maintain that there are types of interpersonal relationships that have a bearing upon the nature of the responsibilities of managers other than those suggested by the ownership and fiduciary models. Managers are not simply fiduciaries or respecters of the ownership rights of shareholders; they are also policy makers whose decisions can have a direct and significant impact upon thousands, if not hundreds of thousands, of persons. In addition, they believe that shareholders are not like property holders in the traditional sense of the term. They grant that the traditional notion of property holder implies that accountability claims generally attach to nonproperty holders to be responsible to avoid actions that would otherwise reduce the quality or value of property they do not own. They do not typically attach to the owners themselves. But these thinkers deny that the owners of corporations (or their surrogates) are justified in ignoring the quite extensive impact that many of their business decisions have upon other people. For example, Bowie and Werhane maintain that in their zeal to satisfy the shareholders' financial interests managers should not overlook the other groups to whom they are accountable (Bowie, 1982, pp. 24ff.; Werhane, 1985, pp. 27ff.). And Sturdivant suggests that the role of the fiduciary vis-à-vis the owners does does not automatically supplant the role of promise keeper to workers or consumers or the role of rights respecter of the other stakeholders of the company (Sturdivant, 1981, pp. 181ff.).

Even if the controlling or managing party of modern corporations were the owners themselves, this would not eliminate or place in a secondary role the responsibilities that they have to creditors, workers, consumers, and the like. Owner-managers still have accountability relations with these other groups of people. Thus managers have responsibilities to individuals other than the shareholders because shareholders have these responsibilities in the first place. When they purchase stock in a corporation, they "buy into" these responsibilities, and as their fiduciaries, managers are expected to respect and discharge these added responsibilities as well.

SHAREHOLDERS AND THE AGENCY ARGUMENT

Classical theorists question the view of Goldman that shareholders are really akin to gamblers. We saw that Friedman, for example, points out that most stockholders have corporate voting rights (Friedman, 1970, p. 122). They have, among other rights, the power to remove current management and replace it with a new management team. This suggests a different basis for the special relation alleged to exist between managers and shareholders, a basis we earlier referred to as the representational or functionary model.

Opponents of the classical theory, such as Freeman, question the idea that the power of replacement is an overriding consideration in determining the responsibilities of managers. He tells us that many groups of constituents have the power to affect the security, reputation, and well-being of a company and its managers (the reverse-impact model). It is true that these groups cannot directly replace managers by utilizing the kind of voting power typically possessed by the stockholders, but they can still initiate action that might lead to the replacement of management (Freeman, 1984, p. vi). As opponents see it, if classical theorists ground their position upon the functionary model of accountability relationships by stressing the stockholders' power of replacement, they are bound to admit that any group of individuals that has the power to affect a company in a major way merits the serious consideration of management. In Freeman's view, such a group deserves the same initial consideration as the shareholders.

Beyond this, opponents contend that the representational model suggested by certain classical theorists is greatly oversimplified, if not definitely misleading.

Stone and Bock, for example, tell us that in many corporations, especially the larger ones, managers function in relative independence of the shareholders' voting power (Stone, 1975, p. 126; Bock, 1979, p. 10). This is so for several reasons. First, given the total number of outstanding shares of voting stock in large corporations, it generally requires a large block of shares to effectuate a change in corporate policy or in senior personnel. Second, with few exceptions, members of the board of directors, who directly represent the shareholders, do not have the staff and resources necessary to sufficiently research management proposals to determine if they square with the shareholders' wishes (assuming that these can be determined without great difficulty). Third, members of the board of directors are for the most part nominated by management. This has given rise to the charge that the upper-level management of most modern corporations typically constitute a self-perpetuating oligarchy. Finally, it is argued that since a good deal of stock is now owned by institutional investors who are oftentimes more concerned with short-run stock performance than with exercising their voting power in a drawn-out battle to replace current management, the latter typically need not fear replacement. They do, nevertheless, need to consider the implications of having these investors find more suitable companies in which to invest.

In their appeal to the voting rights of shareholders, classical theorists do not of course merely mean to stress the shareholders' power of replacement. There is an added consideration that introduces a new dimension to their argument. They believe that when top-level managers are noted into power by the shareholders—however indirectly or imperfectly this process may take place—these executives' promise or consent to represent the latters' interests in a special way. It is the unique character of this promise that supplies an additional basis for their function as agents or stewards of the shareholders' assets.

Opponents to the classical theory raise various caveats and objections to the agency argument and to the promise-keeping model of accountability upon which it is based. In the first place, they point out that this promise, whether real or alleged, need not override the other commitments and agreements made by management. Bowie and Alpern, for example, contend that these other agreements can override the fiduciary promise made by management to the shareholders (Bowie, 1982, p. 27; Alpern, 1984, p. 470). Second, Michalos and Alpern tell us that not all promises carry (equal) moral weight. Not all are to be discharged. Thus, a promise to do wrong carries no moral weight whatsoever (Michalos, 1979, p. 345; Alpern, 1984, p. 470). The classical theorist's appeal to the promise-keeping model can at best explain why certain actions that are initially of a discretionary nature become mandatory. But opponents of this theory maintain that it cannot explain the circumstances in which managers should make promises in the first place; nor can it account for the alleged supervenience of the specific promises managers have actually made to the shareholders.

Third, there is the argument from agency law. Theorists of agency law, such as Michalos, Jacobs, and Blumberg, remind us that although executives do have many legal duties toward the corporation and its shareholders, there are times when other considerations override these agency duties. In specifying some of the principal agency duties of executives, Michalos tells us that agency law requires that in business matters agents act in good faith toward their principals. They are expected to exercise due care and skill in protecting the principals' interests, especially their financial interests. They are to keep proper accounts of the principals' assets and restrict, or at least clearly detail, the conditions of delegating authority to others. Finally, they are to avoid situations in which a conflict of interest between agent and principal might arise (Michalos, 1979, p. 344). In this last area, agents must avoid even the appearance of impropriety in the handling of trade secrets and other privileged or confidential information.

Jacobs indicates that corporate law demands from the fiduciary constant and largely unqualified fidelity (Jacobs, 1973, p. 1070). The corporation is also entitled to the agent's undivided loyalty in the seizure of corporate opportunities. There should be no interference with business relations resulting from an agent's pursuit of his or her own self-interest. The agent must avoid conduct that deprives the principal of profit or harms the principal in some other way due to this apparent conflict. In fact, no harm need actually occur to the principal. It is sufficient that the pursuit of self-interest appears to impair the agent's judgment in protecting the principals' interests (Jacobs, 1973, p. 1080). And Blumberg adds that the legal duties of loyalty and obedience cover all employees of the corporation (Blumberg, 1983, p 133). They are not permitted to speak disloyally of their employer or reveal confidential information gained through their employment, except in certain circumstances.

It is in the recognition of these exceptional circumstances, however, that statutory and case law rejects the idea that the highest legal duty of an agent is uninterrupted loyalty to the principal's interests. Thus, Blumberg tells us that agency law permits certain acts that may be perceived as disloyal—particularly in the area of disclosure of confidential information. This occurs when the secrecy of the information covers up a crime committed by the employer, when it interferes with the otherwise natural demands of the employee's self-interest (the secrecy brings an employee into the web of crime, for example, making him or her liable for prosecution), or when it protects some other act or practice conflicting with the public interest (Blumberg, 1983, p. 134). It is this last consideration in particular that suggests a broader responsibility (if only a legal one) for corporate managers than that of acting as the loyal or obedient agents of the company's shareholders.

THE CONSTRAINT ARGUMENT

The constraint argument suggests that management has little discretionary power to pursue goals that may conflict with its fiduciary obligations to the shareholders. There are two aspects or theses to this argument, one of which is more general than the other. The first involves the broad assertion that management decision making is under financial constraints. This thesis, or part of the argument, is in general accepted by critics of the classical theory. Where they disagree with certain classical theorists, however, is in that aspect of the argument that advances a specific calculation of these constraints. Critics contend that classical theorists like Manne have exaggerated the limits of such constraints. In addition, they reject an important assumption about the motivation of investors that classical theorists characteristically endorse.

In the first place, theorists such as Bock, and Hay and Gray maintain that the degree of separation of ownership and control that has occurred in modern business corporations has given management considerable discretionary power to pursue social goals (Bock, 1979, p. 10; Hay and Gray, 1977, p. 9).

Other critics maintain that an appeal to statutory and case law shows that the discretionary power of management is a well-entrenched facet of modern business life. Thus, Stone, Jones, and others point out that the language of corporate charters is typically quite open ended and gives power to management to carry out any legitimate business or economic function (Stone, 1975, p. 79; Jones, 1980, p. 61). And Bowie and others cite the case of *A. P. Smith v. Barlow* (1953), where the court ruled that the giving of charitable contributions is a legitimate economic activity of management (Bowie, 1982, p. 19).

Hay and Gray contend that this separation has given rise to an entirely different theory of corporate decision making. In the newer view, managers are concerned with responding to a broad range of interests of different constituents and are not simply concerned with responding to the financial wishes or interests of the shareholders (Hay and Gray, 1977, p. 9).

Second, opponents like Sethi maintain that many investors favor social or moral responsibility practices for firms, even if these should reduce somewhat the economic return on their investments (Sethi, 1977, p. 72). Thus, he denies an important assumption of the constraint argument as it is advanced by Manne. He rejects the idea that shareholders always view with disfavor any corporate expenditure that reduces their financial position.

Another theorist who rejects Manne's argument is Wallich, who suggests that because a large number of investors have an equity stake in many corporations either because they have directly purchased stock in these corporations or because they participate in institutions, such as pension or mutual funds, that invest in diverse corporations—they have nearly as strong an interest in promoting the well-being of the economic system as a whole as they do in promoting the well-being of single firms (Wallich, 1972, pp. 52ff.). Since Wallich believes that many social projects contribute to the well-being of the overall economic system, he maintains that rational investors will favor these projects, even if they reduce the corporate earnings of a particular firm in the short run (Wallich, 1972, p. 55). Wallich does not base this kind of support upon the presumed existence of altruistic sentiments of the part of shareholders. He grounds it instead upon what he takes to be the enlarged self-interest of these diversified investors.

Rudd agrees that investors take on some added costs and risks when they use noneconomic criteria to influence their portfolio decisions, but he maintains that the risks and costs involved here need not act as strong disincentives for such decision making (Rudd, 1981, p. 60). Rudd tells us that two recent studies indicate that the added risks involved when certain investors sold their stock of companies doing business in South Africa and replaced them with the stock of other companies were not significant. These investors had to bear the expense of the transaction costs for the replacement, of course, and they bore a slightly greater risk that the long-term economic performance of the firms whose stock they purchased would be poorer than the performance of the companies whose stock they sold, but the costs and risks involved in this case did not seem to exceed the expected overall gain in social performance that the investment decision did or could produce. Rudd tells us that certain factors can decrease the risk of social or moral responsibility investment. Risk is lessened if there is a diversity of social responsibility firms in the market in which to invest, if these firms pursue both social and economic goals in their corporate decision making, and if the number of investors using this criterion does not change appreciably (Rudd, 1981, pp. 57ff.). Like Sethi, Rudd thus questions the assumption that investors are motivated only by a narrow concern for the economic performance of a company.

Finally, opponents to the constraint argument contend that many social projects requested of corporations are not expensive to perform. Some projects involve voluntary activities sponsored by the corporation but performed by workers and managers during their lunch hours or free time. Other proposals, such as restructuring the board of directors or increasing the level and quality of the firms' social reporting, do not necessarily require a substantial monetary investment. Some of these projects may not be considered moral or social responsibility projects by Manne and others, but few opponents of the classical theory accept the particular definition of social responsibility (discussed in chapter 3) proposed by Manne.

THE EXPERTISE ARGUMENT

Many critics of the classical theory reject the idea that the planning and execution of social projects requires a distinct type of expertise that corporate managers lack. In summarizing arguments in behalf of corporate social responsibility, Davis indicates that one prevalent view is that corporations have valuable resources that can be applied to social problems (Davis, 1973, p. 316), which include capital resources, management talent, and functional expertise. Since business is often praised for its innovative ability, business leaders may be able to provide the necessary spark for solving some otherwise intransigent social problems.

A somewhat different response to the expertise argument is given by other critics, who contend that even if it were true that corporations currently lack the requisite expertise to solve certain social or moral problems, this does not excuse them from carrying out social or moral tasks. Assuming that the other arguments for corporate social involvement are compelling, then the present argument would exempt business leaders from engaging in social or moral projects only if it was theoretically or practically impossible for them to gain the necessary expertise. Solomon and Hanson, for example, tell us that if management is under a general obligation to initiate certain social projects, it has a more specific duty to orchestrate its resources to accomplish these social tasks effectively (Solomon and Hanson, 1983, p. 247). This is one aspect of the concept of responsibility itself. Beyond this, Preston and Post, and Purchell imply or contend that if a corporation does not have the necessary experts in social or ethical planning, it should hire them (Preston and Post, 1975, pp. 106ff.; Purchell, 1978, pp. 42ff.). Thus, it should hire individuals with such skills as interpreting social indicators, reporting and assessing social or ethical performance, and evaluating strategies of future social involvement.

Against the argument of Lundberg that questions the existence of expertise for ethical or social planning, Purchell contends that there are individuals who, by education and training, are more sensitive to the ethical implications and complexities of various management decisions. He recommends that these people, whom he calls "angel advocates," be hired as consultants to management and perhaps advise members of the board of directors on controversial issues (Purchell, 1978, p. 43). Beyond this, Donaldson and Waller contend that the golden rule or role-reversal test criticized by Lundberg does not involve the level of controversy and ambiguity that Lundberg alleges (Donaldson and Waller, 1980, p. 52).

For the most part, opponents to the classical theory concede that corporations cannot be expected to provide leadership in every area of social or moral involvement. They do contend, however, that management should focus upon those areas in which they can be most effective. Sturdivant and Davis, among others, argue that this is the best method of utilizing the relevant expertise within a context of relatively scarce resources (Sturdivant, 1981, p. 163; Davis, 1975, p. 23). In this way, one firm can set an example for others. It can show others how to distinguish effective from ineffective social or moral projects without the level of resource overextension that would otherwise occur—a level of extension or depletion whose cumulative effect upon society's resources might prove to be a major disincentive for further corporate involvement in these areas in the future.

An added argument for developing the relevant corporate expertise in social or moral decision making is advanced by Jones, who contends that nearly every corporate decision that managers make has a moral or social impact of some kind (Jones, 1980, p. 61). Since managers can rarely avoid the noneconomic aspects of their decision making, they are responsible or obligated to assess the overall impact of their policies, at least with an eye to lessening or minimizing the adverse social or moral consequences of these activities. Whether executives decide to introduce a new method of advertising or marketing, open or close a plant, divest the firm of one of its subsidiaries, lobby for or against a bill setting stricter requirements for the disposal of toxic wastes, or initiate a tender offer for the acquisition of another company, it is nearly impossible to separate the purely economic from the largely social or noneconomic implications of these alternatives. The impact model of accountability implicit in this objection suggests that managers are responsible for both the economic and the noneconomic consequences of their corporate activities. Ignorance of the relevant social or moral impact is thus no excuse, nor is it a good reason for giving the noneconomic responsibilities a secondary status.

Last, opponents of the classical theory argue that if corporate executives ignore the social or moral impact of their corporate decisions, or if they refuse to initiate social or moral programs (for whatever reason), greater levels of government regulation can be expected in these areas. They maintain that the growth in government regulation that has occurred over this century is in large part due to the perception that businesses are unwilling or unable to regulate themselves, especially in those areas of greatest social impact. If executives wish at least to preserve their remaining discretionary power (and the current status of their corporation's legitimacy), they must consider both the economic and noneconomic impact of their activities (Davis, 1973, p. 314).

THE CONCERN FOR CORPORATE POWER ARGUMENT

Classical theorists, such as Levitt, argue that if corporations perform both economic and noneconomic functions, they would become too powerful—both in the making of law and the shaping of personal opinions and values.

Opponents give various responses to this argument. First, they repeat the objection made above that the economic side of management decision making cannot be readily distinguished from its social or moral side. They contend that since even areas of decision making that appear to be purely financial or economic in nature have noneconomic aspects to them, management must also decide how to function in a responsible manner in these latter areas as well. The issue is thus not *whether* to take on greater social or moral responsibility, it is *how* to direct the course of such responsibility (since it is already present in management decision making anyway).

Second, Jones contends that utilizing one's power for the sake of promoting freedom and pluralism in society is itself a basic feature of the social or moral responsibility of corporations (Jones, 1980, p. 61). If corporate executives have the power to lessen or undermine the influence of other groups in society, the demands of responsibility may require that they refrain from doing so, or, at a minimum, it requires that they exert their power in a manner that is consistent with the demands of economic and political freedom and pluralism.

Third, from a somewhat different perspective, opponents such as Nader and Green, and Dahl argue that corporations are already great centers of power (Nader and Green, 1973, p. vii; Dahl, 1973, p. 11). As they see it, we need not worry that only if corporations take on social or moral tasks will their power become excessive. They maintain that all members of society should consider what economic and noneconomic responsibilities are expected from corporate executives. And they should actively advocate and share their views with legislators, regulators, other citizens, and managers themselves.

Last, Galbraith raises an objection to the power argument that differs in certain respects from that raised by Nader and Green. He believes with them that, if unchecked, corporate power would become excessive. But he maintains that there are other decision-making groups and institutions in society, such as government agencies, that can exert countervailing power over firms to help avoid this outcome (Galbraith, 1952, pp. 108ff.).

REFERENCES

Abbott, W. F., and R. J. Monsen. 1979. "On the Measurement of Corporate Social Responsibility: Self-reported Disclosures As a Method of Measuring Corporate Social Involvement." *Academy of Management Journal*, vol. 22. pp. 501–15.

Alexander, J. J., and R. A. Bucholz. 1978. "Corporate Social Responsibility and Stock Market Performance." *Academy of Management Journal*, vol. 21, pp. 479–86.

Alpern, Kenneth D. 1984. "Moral Dimensions of the Foreign Corrupt Practices Act." In *Business Ethics: Readings and Cases in Corporate Morality*, edited by W. Michael Hoffman and Jennifer Moore, pp. 468–75. New York: McGraw-Hill.

Arlow, Peter, and Martin J. Gannon. 1982. "Social Responsiveness, Corporate Structure, and Economic Performance." *Academy of Management Review*, vol. 7, no. 2, pp. 235–41.

Becker, Brian E., and Craig Olson. 1989. "Unionization and Stockholder Interest." *Industrial and Labor Relations Review*, January, pp 246–61.

Blodgett, Timothy. 1968. "Showdown on Business Bluffing." *Harvard Business Review*, May–June, pp. 162–70.

Blumberg, Phillip. 1983. "Corporate Responsibility and the Employee's Duty of Loyalty and Obedience: A Preliminary Inquiry." In *Ethical Theory and Business*, 2d ed., edited by Tom Beauchamp and Norman Bowie, pp. 132–38. Englewood Cliffs, N.J.: Prentice-Hall. (First published in *Oklahoma Law Review*, vol. 24, no. 3, August 1971.)

Bock, R. H. 1979. "Introduction: Modern Values in Business and Management." *AACSB Bulletin Proceedings*, Annual Meeting, pp. 1–19.

Bowie, Norman. 1982. *Business Ethics*. Englewood Cliffs, N.J.: Prentice-Hall.

Bowman, Edward H., and Mason Haire. 1975. "A Strategic Posture Toward Corporate Social Responsibility." *California Management Review*, vol. 18, no. 2, pp. 49–58.

Bragdon, Joseph H., and John A. T. Marlin. 1972. "Is Pollution Profitable?" *Risk Management*, April, pp. 11–19.

Brandt, Richard. 1967. "Personal Values and the Justification of Institutions." In *Human Values and Economic Policy*, edited by Sidney Hook, pp. 22–40. New York: New York University Press.

Brummer, James. 1983. "In Defense of Social Responsibility." *Journal of Business Ethics*, May, pp. 111–23.

Cirillo, R. 1979. *The Economics of Vilfredo Pareto*. London: Frank Cass and Company.

Cochran, Philip L., and Robert A. Wood. 1984. "Corporate Social Responsibility and Financial Performance." *Academy of Management Journal*, March, pp. 42–56.

Dahl, Robert. 1973. "Governing the Giant Corporation." In *Corporate Power in America*, edited by Ralph Nader and Mark Green, pp. 10–24. New York: Grossman Publishers.

Davis, Keith. 1973. "The Case For and Against Business Assumption of Social Responsibilities." *Academy of Management Journal*, vol. 16, no. 2, pp. 312–22.

———. 1975. "Five Propositions for Social Responsibility." *Business Horizons*, June, pp. 19–24.

DesJardin, Joseph R., and John J. McCall. 1985. *Contemporary Issues in Business Ethics*. Belmont, Calif.: Wadsworth Publishing Company.

Donaldson, John, and Mike Waller. 1980. "Ethics and Organization." *The Journal of Management Studies*, February, pp. 33–55.

Eilbert, H., and I. Parket. 1975. "Social Responsibility: The Underlying Factors." *Business Horizons*, vol. 18, no. 4, pp. 5–10.

Folger, H. R., and F. Nutt. 1975. "A Note on Social Responsibility and Stock Valuation." *Academy of Management Journal*, vol. 18, pp. 155–60.

Freeman, Edward. 1984. *Strategic Management*. Boston: Pitman Books.

Friedman, Milton. 1970. "The Social Responsibility of Business Is To Increase Its Profits." *The New York Times Magazine*, September 13, pp. 32, 33, 122–26.

Galbraith, John Kenneth. 1952. *American Capitalism: The Concept of Countervailing Power*. Boston: Houston Mifflin Company.

———. 1976. *The Affluent Society*. New York, Houghton Mifflin Company.

Gillespie, Norman C. 1975. "The Business of Ethics." *University of Michigan Business Review*, November, pp. 1–4.

Goldman, Alan H. 1980. "Business Ethics: Profits, Utilities and Moral Rights." *Philosophy and Public Affairs*, vol. 9, no. 3, Spring, pp. 260–86.

Hay, Robert, and Ed Gray. 1977. "Social Responsibilities of Business Managers." In *Managing Corporate Social Responsibility*, edited by Archie B. Carroll, pp. 8–16. Boston: Little, Brown and Company.

Hodgson, Bernard. 1983. "Economic Science and Ethical Neutrality." *Journal of Business Ethics*. November, pp 237–53.

Jacobs, Leslie W. 1973. "Business Ethics and the Law: Obligations of a Corporate Executive." *The Business Lawyer*, vol. 28, no. 4, July, pp. 1063–88.

James, Gene G. 1982. "Crisis of American Ethics." *Journal of Business Ethics*, vol. 1, no. 4, November, pp. 285–91.

Jones, Derek. 1987. "The Productivity Effects of Worker Directors and Financial Participation by Employees in the Firm: The Case of British Retail Cooperatives." *Industrial and Labor Relations Review*, October, pp. 79–92.

Jones, Thomas M. 1980. "Corporate Social Responsibility Revisited, Redefined." *California Management Review*, Spring, pp. 59–67.

Kedia, Banwari, and Edwin C. Kuntz. 1981. "The Context of Social Performance: An Empirical Study of Texas Banks." In *Research in Corporate Social Performance and Policy*, vol. 3, edited by Lee E. Preston, pp. 3–12. Greenwich, Conn.: JAI Press.

Kleiner, Morris, and Marvin Bouillon. 1988. "Providing Business Information to Production Workers: Correlates of Compensation and Profitability." *Industrial and Labor Relations Review*, July, pp. 605–17.

Knight, Frank. 1923. "The Ethics of Competition." *Quarterly Journal of Economics*, vol. 37, pp. 579–624.

Michalos, Alex. 1979. "The Loyal Agent's Argument." In *Ethical Theory and Business*, edited by Norman Bowie and Tom Beauchamp, pp. 338–48. Englewood Cliffs, N.J.: Prentice-Hall.

Nader, Ralph, and Mark Green, ed. 1973. *Corporate Power in America*. New York: Grossman Publishers.

Pichler, Joseph A. 1983. "The Liberty Principle: A Basis for Management Ethics." *Business and Professional Ethics Journal*, Winter, pp. 19–29.

Preston, Lee E., and James E. Post. 1975. *Private Management and Public Policy: The Principle of Public Responsibility*. Englewood Cliffs, N.J.: Prentice-Hall.

Purchell, Theodore, 1975. "A Practical Guide to Ethics in Business. *Business and Society Review*, Spring, pp. 43–50.

———. 1978. The Need for Corporate Ethical Specialists." *Review of Social Economy*, April, pp. 41–53.

Rudd, Andrew. 1981. "Social Responsibility and Portfolio Performance." *California Management Review*, vol. 23, no. 4, pp. 55–61.

Sethi, S. Prakash. 1977. "Dimensions of Corporate Social Performance: An Analytical Framework." In *Managing Corporate Social Responsibility*, edited by Archie B. Carroll, pp. 69–75. Boston: Little Brown.

Solomon, Robert C., and Kristine R. Hanson. 1983. *Above the Bottom Line: An Introduction to Business Ethics*. New York: Harcourt, Brace, Jovanovich.

Starling, Grover. 1980. *The Changing Environment of Business: A Managerial Approach*. Boston: Kent Publishing Company.

Stone, Christopher. 1975. *Where the Law Ends*. New York: Harper and Row.

Sturdivant, Frederick. 1981. *Business and Society: A Managerial Approach*. Homewood, Ill.: Richard D. Irwin.

Sturdivant, F. D., and J. L. Ginter. 1977. "Corporate Social Responsiveness: Management Attitudes and Economic Performance." *California Management Review*, vol. 19, no. 3, pp. 30–39.

Vance, S. C. 1975. "Are Socially Responsible Corporations Good Investment Risks?" *Management Review*, vol. 64, no. 8, pp. 18–24.

Velasquez, Manuel. 1982. *Business Ethics: Concepts and Cases*. Englewood Cliffs, N.J.: Prentice-Hall.

Wallich, Henry C. (with Henry Manne). 1972. *The Modern Corporation and Social Responsibility*, edited by Robert Goraski. Washington, D.C.: American Enterprise Institute.

Werhane, Patricia. 1985. *Persons, Rights and Corporations*. Englewood Cliffs, N.J.: Prentice-Hall.

Wokutch, Richard E., and Thomas L. Carson. 1984. "The Ethics and Profitability of Bluffing in Business." In *Business Ethics: Readings and Cases in Corporate Morality*, edited by W. Michael Hoffman and Jennifer Mills Moore, pp. 457–62. New York: McGraw-Hill.

Wokutch, Richard E., and Barbara Spencer. 1987. "Corporate Saints and Sinners: The Effects of Philanthropic and Illegal Activity on Organizational Performance." *California Management Review*, Winter, pp. 62–77.

10

THE STAKEHOLDER THEORY

DEFINITION OF THE THEORY

The stakeholder theory differs from the classical theory in several important respects. As Sethi and Bock tell us, it holds that there are groups of individuals other than the shareholders of a corporation to whom corporate managers are directly responsible (Sethi, 1977, p. 74; Bock, 1979, p. 12). The individuals in question are those who are, or who are likely to be, directly affected by the decisions of a corporation or have an explicit contractual relationship with it. They are thus said to have a stake in the corporation. These theorists typically contend that corporate executives are responsible to consider the interests of stakeholders to be on a par with those of the shareholders. Executives are said to owe them more than just noninterference or general good will, however; they are also responsible for providing them with certain benefits. Stakeholder theorists differ somewhat on the precise nature of these benefits, just as they disagree over whether these benefits should reflect the expressed or ideal interests of stakeholders, but in general they believe that the benefits in question should be at least sufficient to permit these individuals to carry out effectively their distinct stakeholder roles or functions.

Stakeholder theorists recognize that managers may act from various motives. It is not then a usual or necessary feature of their position to demand that only certain motives count. As they see it, corporate executives may respond to the interests of stakeholders principally from the motive of corporate or individual self-interest, or because such a response is demanded by law or by public pressure. Managers might also respond voluntarily from a genuine desire to benefit the lives of stakeholders. These theorists recognize, however, that when managers are urged to act primarily from the motive of corporate or shareholder interest, the stakeholder theory moves far closer to the classical theory in its emphasis. And when managers are urged to respond to the claims of stakeholders because of a widespread or concerted social pressure to do so, the position moves closer to the social demandingness theory. Recognizing the presence of mixed management motives in these cases thus implies that stakeholder theorists can define their position without having it collapse into one of the other theories of corporate responsibility. But it also implies that the presence of a specific motive is not the distinguishing feature upon which the stakeholder theory depends.

Many stakeholder theorists recognize that the interests of noninvesting stakeholders do not always override the financial interests of shareholders. They believe such a view could seriously compromise or jeopardize the economic function of the firm. Bock and Starling, for example, define the theory in such a way that striving for a certain minimum level of profit performance is a prerequisite to corporate decision making (Bock, 1979, p. 12; Starling, 1980, p. 234). Having achieved this level, executives are freer to respond to the interests of the other constituents of the firm. In fact, theorists like Jones and Sherwin, define the concept of stakeholder in such a way that beyond this level the claims and interests of all stakeholders, including shareholders, are equally legitimate (Jones, 1980, p. 61; Sherwin, 1983, p. 184).

There is, however, a difference of opinion among theorists on the question of who are the actual or legitimate constituents or stakeholders of a corporation. All agree that individuals who make explicit contracts with a corporation are among its stakeholders. The disagreement concerns the other consideration used to define a stakeholder—the consequentialist consideration. Theorists such as Anshoff, Ackoff, and Starling contend that only those who are directly or primarily affected by the acts of a corporation are its stakeholders (Anshoff, 1965, p. 33; Ackoff, 1981, p. 30; Starling, 1980, p. 244). But Freeman, on the other hand, tells us that a stakeholder is also anyone who can directly affect the corporation (Freeman, 1984, p. vi.). In this latter definition, however, virtually everyone is a stakeholder of a firm, even those who are usually excluded from such membership, because nearly everyone can affect corporations in some direct way by refusing to buy its products, lobbying against it, and the like. In his further discussion of the concept, however, Freeman narrows the notion to include only those groups that can presently damage a firm or its reputation in some important respect. The initial legitimacy of the group's claims is not a consideration. What makes the group a stakeholder of a firm is its power to affect the corporation in some significant way. Thus, Freeman considers environmentalists, consumer advocates, and even terrorists as stakeholders (Freeman, 1984, p. 55).

While it is to be admitted that Freeman's view is a possible version of the stakeholder theory, it must also be conceded that the inclusion of groups who often see themselves as representatives of the public pushes this theory very far in the direction of the social demandingness position, as it is currently advocated. And if we are to include environmentalists and consumer advocates, it is difficult to see how we could exclude church groups, peace groups, ethnic groups, pro-choice and anti-abortion groups, gays, and a whole host of special interest groups as stakeholders. The combined effects of meeting the demands of these groups is virtually the same as meeting the demands of the social demandingness theory. Finally, it must be admitted that by including terrorists in the category of stakeholder, Freeman's theory may even be construed as moving toward social activism (depending on the demands of the terrorists). Since many of the arguments for this broader version of the stakeholder position are considered in the next chapter, we shall postpone its discussion here and shall focus instead upon the narrower definition of the stakeholder concept in which those who are only indirectly affected by corporate decision making are considered to have no unique or legitimate claim upon the business decisions of a particular corporation—even if they have the power to directly and negatively affect the corporation in some way.

Stakeholder theorists include the following groups of individuals in the category of stakeholder, as thus defined: stockholders, workers, consumers, suppliers, creditors, and competitors of the corporation; members of government agencies overseeing the firm; professional groups representing individuals within the company; and the residents of local communities in which a corporation's facilities or plants are located. Stockholders are considered stakeholders because of many of the factors discussed in chapter 8. Two reasons are typically given for considering members of the remaining six groups as stakeholders: they have usually entered into contractual or contract-like agreements with the firm or its members, or they are directly affected by the decisions of the corporation. This last factor is usually the sole reason given for including the final group of individuals in the stakeholder category.

These two considerations not only specify the kinds of individuals to whom corporate executives are directly responsible, they also set limits for the extent of this responsibility. Thus, corporate managers are said to be responsible to respect only or primarily those interests of the parties with which they have made contractual agreements that are directly connected to these contractual relationships. And they are accountable to respect the interests of those individuals who are otherwise directly affected by their decisions only or primarily in the areas of these effects. This last point suggests that government officials, to take an example of a stakeholder group that has no immediate financial interest in a corporation, are stakeholders solely in the areas where they have legal jurisdiction over the corporation and where corporate decision making (especially when it concerns the firm's obedience to law) has a direct bearing upon the security and effectiveness of these government agents when functioning in their official capacities. Much the same can be said of professional groups with respect to their claimed professional responsibility over various members of the firm.

These two considerations also entail that corporate executives are not directly responsible to provide certain benefits to those who are only indirectly affected, if at all, by corporate decision making. Beyond stakeholder responsibilities is an arena of choice that is guided principally by the personal discretion of management. If executives choose not to implement a corporate policy that would otherwise benefit members of the general public as such, stakeholder theorists believe that they are not expected to give a rendering of themselves relative to this decision.

Some theorists believe a major reason why members of the general public are not considered as stakeholders is that they are not directly affected by the decisions of corporate executives. But the relation between these concepts may perhaps be even stronger than this; perhaps the one defines the other. We should then view the concept of the general public as itself defined in terms of the notion of a direct effect of choice or action. Thus, whoever is not directly affected by the conduct of corporate executives (and, of course, is not involved in explicit agreements with these executives) is, for that action, a member of the general public. Everyone else is a stakeholder. Therefore, the class of individuals designated as members of the general public is a shifting one. A person may be a member of the general public for one corporate action, while being a stakeholder for another. So although these terms have a relatively stable conceptual or intentional component, when viewed in this way, they do permit a considerable degree of variance in their extensional application.

While most stakeholder theorists are clear that one factor used in designating someone as a stakeholder is that he or she is directly affected by corporate conduct, they are less clear on what constitutes a direct effect of such conduct. One suggestion advanced by Ackerman and Bauer, and Post is that direct effects are those that result from the firm's primary areas of economic involvement (Ackerman and Bauer, 1976, p. 10; Post, 1986, p. 58). Primary areas of economic involvement are those that are either based upon the initial charter of the corporation or have developed from the past and present strategic planning, policy making, and conduct of the firm. They are, in short, the principal areas in which the firm receives its revenues.

An important weakness with this way of defining the concept of a direct effect, however, is that it precludes appealing to the stakeholder theory in the determination of what areas of corporate activity should be (or become) the primary ones. In the present view, the stakeholder theory would become a useful guide to making other business decisions only after this initial decision has already been made.

A weakness is still present even if the term *primary* is meant to refer only to economic effects. Even if the only effects with which executives must be concerned are economic ones, this does not tell us how to reconcile disputes between stakeholder groups with different economic relations to or claims upon the corporation. We could, of course, appeal to the other principle in the theory—the contractarian principle—but it is a strange implication of this interpretation of the phrase *direct effect* that consequentialistic considerations play no role whatsoever in reconciling disputes between the various economic claimants of the firm.

A second and more promising way to define the concept stipulates that direct effects are those that occur to individuals without the intervention of the choices or actions of third parties. Thus, for example, when the management of a corporation decides to lay off a number of its workers, the unemployed workers are directly affected by this decision. They are stakeholders in this matter. But friends of the workers who may be affected when the latter choose to change their social or recreational habits are not stakeholders in this instance. This is so because they are affected by the corporate decision, if at all, only through the mediation of the choices of the laid-off workers. Or, again, if corporate executives fail to repay their corporate loans in a timely manner, this delinquency directly effects the creditors of the company. They are stakeholders in this matter. It has, however, only an indirect effect upon potential clients of these creditors who may be affected by the latters' choice to institute a more demanding policy of furnishing collateral or of guaranteeing repayment for all future loans.

Therefore, it can be suggested that the direct effects of action are those that occur to a person independently of the choices of third parties. It does not matter how these third parties have come to be independent of these effects—whether by their explicit choice or by unintentional noninvolvement. The effects are no less direct even if third parties intentionally choose to become uninvolved with the actual impact these effects have upon a particular person. For example, residents of a local community found to be living near an abandoned chemical dump site are directly affected by the chemical firm's policy of environmental decision making. This is so even if the policy was implemented many years earlier and in the interim many people, including officials, have chosen to ignore the health problems the dump site could cause for present or future residents.

The consequentialist or noncontractual side of the stakeholder theory can be stated in terms of either the actual or the likely direct effects of corporate action. Typically these theorists define the position in terms of the likely direct effects, since, among other things, this permits an evaluation of a corporate decision at the time of action. But the position may also be defined so that only the actual direct effects of corporate decision making count. When the likely direct effects are used for determining or evaluating corporate action, executives may be judged as acting irresponsibly even in cases where stakeholders eventually benefit from a corporate action. This would occur, for example, in cases where unexpected or fortuitous conditions blocked or lessened the direct negative effects usually associated with an action of a certain type. In cases like these, it is generally believed that luck or good fortune should not be able to salvage an otherwise poor decision.

Before moving on to consider the arguments raised in defense of this theory, it should be pointed out that not all stakeholder theorists stress the distinction made here between the direct and indirect effects of corporate action. Without this distinction, however, it would seem that such theorists would be unable to distinguish stakeholders from nonstakeholders. The reason for this is offered by both turbulent-wave organization theorists, like Trist, and autopoiesis (or self-referential systems) theorists, like Maturana and Varela. Given that the waves of effects occurring after an action is performed reverberate well beyond the locus of the action's initial effects and often come back to affect the action's author, and given that these effects characteristically become mingled with the choices and interventions of other persons, who may also experience self-referential effects, to produce still further consequences, the stakeholder theorist who does not initially screen out those individuals who are only indirectly affected by a corporate action would be unable, even in theory, to show that a management action leaves these individuals ultimately unaffected. They would thus be required to admit that individuals usually considered to be members of the general public are actual or virtual stakeholders, and they would be unable to distinguish the stakeholder theory from the social demandingness position.

Various compromise positions can be advanced, of course. For instance, one might admit the relevance of the indirect effects of corporate conduct but assign a secondary status to them. Such a position would, among other things, shrink the area of management discretion mentioned earlier, or one could maintain that executives have duties to stakeholders but only general responsibilities to the public. These alternative views show that various hybrid positions can be grafted from combinations of the initial four theories discussed in this book. But it should be pointed out that this recognition does not significantly alter the nature of the arguments for these initial theories. Nor does it significantly change the basic assumptions of the four theories themselves, though it does emphasize the point that they can be combined in ways not specifically discussed here.

In sum, an important part of the stakeholder theory as defined here demands that corporate executives consider the likely direct effects of their decisions on other people—effects that are neither in whole nor in part the product of the choices of other people—whether or not the absence of this third-party influence is itself the product of explicit third-party choice.

ARGUMENTS FOR THE THEORY: POWER AND PERFORMANCE

In this and the next sections of the chapter we shall consider various arguments raised in behalf of the stakeholder theory, using the strategies of legitimization discussed in chapter 7 as the basis of our discussion. Of the strategies discussed there, most directly apply to the present issue in some way. The conformity to law model is not used here, however, for several reasons. In the first place, there are a number of corporate responsibilities urged by stakeholder theorists that are not demanded by law, including such things as offering employee assistance programs for workers and providing broader disclosure of a product's ingredients to consumers. Second, if this were a main argument for the stakeholder theory, it would merely convert this theory into a version of the classical position. To respond to stakeholder interests solely or primarily because it is demanded by law is to do nothing different from what classical theorists endorse.

If stakeholder interests are *uniquely* compelling, it must be for some reason distinct from that urged by classical theorists.

This latter point can also be said about the conformity to current standards theory, though this time the concern is that this defense would convert the stakeholder theory into a species of the social demandingness position. It is true that there is a certain theoretical instability in the stakeholder view; it is a little like a complex element isolated in the laboratory that is unable to retain its unique character in the outside world. The theory has a tendency to be absorbed into the classical theory, especially when good stakeholder relations are seen to promote sound economic health for the corporation. But, as we have just pointed out, its more pronounced tendency is to be assimilated into the social demandingness position. One way for this to happen is to base the need for good stakeholder relations ultimately upon their being endorsed by the current standards of society. It becomes a mere version (or metaversion) of the latter theory. Thus, this strategy of defense is not really appropriate for the stakeholder theory as defined here.

We have seen that the remaining strategies of legitimacy can in general be divided into consequentialist and nonconsequentialist types. In the present section we shall consider two consequentialist strategies of argument—those that emerge from the power model and those that stem from the performance strategies.

The power model of legitimation is rarely endorsed by stakeholder theorists in a self-conscious manner. In fact, theorists who do endorse this model usually combine it with other strategies of argument. Freeman, for one, does however advance a species of the power argument when discussing the stakeholder responsibilities of managers. Although this argument seems to push his overall theory toward the social demandingness position, it is nevertheless relevant to the present context. He contends that when managers respond to stakeholder concerns, they make their firms more resilient to attack from such external groups as consumers, the media, or government officials (Freeman, 1984, pp. 52ff.). This resilience is a sign of the effectiveness of management as well as being a mark of the increased power of the firm. When this power is ultimately used to satisfy the interests of the shareholders, we have ironically a position that is not essentially different from the classical view. Freeman avoids this consequence by advancing other arguments for his theory.

The most commonly endorsed consequentialist argument for the stakeholder theory is the performance argument, which in general, takes two forms. One version is put forth by some strategic management theorists, such as Starling, Sturdivant, and Ackoff, who emphasize the advantages that accrue to firms that follow the stakeholder approach. They believe that the long-term survival and profitability of a firm is enhanced when it responds to stakeholder interests as a major part of its corporate strategy (Starling, 1980, p. 231; Sturdivant, 1981, pp. 16ff.; Ackoff, 1981, pp 29ff.).

Manning and Maslow concur with this view. They advance the performance argument with respect to employees as the main stakeholder group. They tell us that firms that treat their employees with respect and seek to encourage the latters' unique abilities function more dynamically and productively in the marketplace (Manning, 1981, pp. 15ff.; Maslow, 1971, pp. 237ff.).

Various theorists have developed this argument with respect to other stakeholder groups. For example, Peters and Waterman stress, among other issues, the importance of respecting consumer interests. They tell us that consumer-oriented companies are generally the more successful ones in their industries (Peters and Waterman, 1982, p. 14).

In addition to arguing that the stakeholder position leads to better performance for single firms, several stakeholder theorists contend that it also leads to better performance for society as a whole. For example, Ackoff and Starling argue that the various elements of the overall social system function more efficiently and coherently when managers respect the interests of stakeholders (Ackoff, 1981, p. 33; Starling, 1980, pp. 234ff.). They believe that since everyone is a stakeholder of some particular corporation, everyone benefits in certain ways by this theory, without at the same time demanding that corporations meet the typically more exacting social or moral requirements of the last two theories of corporate responsibility. Firms are thus encouraged to be socially more morally active to a certain degree, but they are also urged to perform many of their traditional economic functions as well.

A principal assumption of those stakeholder theorists who endorse the performance argument is that executives are accountable for at least the direct effects of their business decisions. Although few stakeholder theorists give an explicit defense of this assumption, there appears to be two reasons why they believe it is nevertheless warranted: one concerns limitations in the knowledge of managers and the other concerns limitations in their power.

Starling, and Jackson and Aldag (among others) suggest that managers are not sufficiently informed about the indirect effects of their corporate actions to be held immediately accountable for them (Starling, 1980, p. 243; Jackson and Aldag, 1980, p. 30). Cameron tells us that it is extremely difficult, if not impossible, to attribute or trace through the lines of causality that exist when a myriad of interacting elements apply simultaneously to a situation (Cameron, 1986, p. 544). These authors further imply that managers cannot be expected to develop the necessary expertise to gain this knowledge. For them, it is an exacting enough task for managers to determine the direct effects of their actions or the effects of their actions in the chief or primary areas of their business involvement. Coming to know the indirect effects would require that managers know how others will respond to their corporate decisions and how these people will in turn affect the choices and lives of still other individuals. These authors suggest that this demands of managers a knowledge of human nature and psychology that is considerably beyond their expected or usual expertise. In maintaining this, however, they come quite close to aspects of the conformity to current standards theory of legitimacy.

A second reason for restricting the principle of accountability just mentioned to the direct effects of action is that these are more within an agent's power or control. Since persons are accountable only or primarily for those actions that are within their power to perform, it is said that they cannot be held completely or primarily responsible for the effects of actions that occur fully or largely through the influence and choices of other agents. These latter effects must be viewed as being largely within the sphere of responsibility of these other parties. Thus, executives need not give a rendering of them or, at most, they need give them only cursory or secondary attention. This does not mean of course that an agent cannot be held accountable for the effects of actions performed by others with whom he or she is acting collaboratively. In the case of collaborative action or conspiracy, it can be argued, however, that the decisions of an agent's collaborators to do certain actions are important to getting the agent to do his or her part in the collaborative project in the first place. Thus, collaborative action involves shared responsibility. But in cases where no initial collaboration exists, this view holds that it is open to stakeholder theorists to insist that the type of shared responsibility just mentioned does not apply. An agent whose actions influence others to choose and act on their own in certain ways is not required to give a rendering for these secondary or derivative effects. The primary sphere of one's responsibility is thus limited to the sphere of the direct effects on one's actions.

DEONTOLOGICAL ARGUMENTS: PROCEDURAL AND FORMAL CONSIDERATIONS

In chapter 7 we also discussed certain deontological strategies of justification for legitimacy claims. In this section we shall consider two of these: the procedural and formalist lines of argument for the stakeholder theory.

The procedural defense centers upon the act of consent or agreement that is involved in many management decisions. Since a common or frequent relation that exists between managers and stakeholders is a contractual one, it is argued that the mere presence of a contract obligates each party in certain ways—each is thus accountable to the other to fulfill his or her side of the agreement or promise.

There are also theorists who argue that even to the unexpressed facets of an agreement accountability relations may apply. For example, Werhane argues that some of the responsibilities that managers have toward workers are more in the nature of an understanding. They are grounded upon the factor of reciprocity or mutuality found in the employer-employee relation. This is in part why managers are responsible to treat workers fairly and with general respect and consideration (Werhane, 1985, p. 102).

If the procedural defense largely focuses upon the consent or promise making of managers, the formalist defense focuses primarily upon the consent and promise-making capacities of stakeholders. Formalists emphasize the inconsistency or incoherence of treating stakeholders in certain ways. They believe that in order for stakeholders to make agreements with executives at all, it is imperative that they use certain human faculties and abilities. But if managers take action that injures or otherwise jeopardizes these abilities, they not only typically violate the terms of the contract, they also undermine the presence of the institution of contract or promise making itself. Such formalists believe that if one chooses to undermine the very conditions of this choice, one seeks to do something that is inherently incoherent. The principle behind this choice is structurally flawed and has no normative or moral authority whatsoever.

Bowie provides us with a recent example of this mode of reasoning. He tells us that those people who enter into valid contractual relations in business must be assumed to be responsible, autonomous adults. This implies that these people view themselves and are viewed by others as moral agents, that is, they are individuals who have rights that they can claim against others. To enter into valid contracts with other people is to recognize that these individuals have rights that they can assert against an agent (Bowie, 1982, pp. 46–47). Although Bowie emphasizes the rights of contract makers, his argument is nevertheless formalistic because it does not specify what rights must be granted here. To admit any rights at all entails that contract makers or, in this case, managers are accountable directly to those with whom they have made agreements.

The same can be said for a version of the formalist argument developed by Donaldson and Waller. They advance their argument with the employer-employee relation in mind but, like several of the arguments already considered, it can be applied to other stakeholder groups as well. They tell us that an important aspect in the justification of any action is the role-reversal test (Donaldson and Waller, 1980, p. 50). This means that before acting an agent must consider whether he or she would be the willing recipient of a contemplated action—assuming that the agent has basically the same abilities, desires, and interests as the prospective recipient(s). If the agent cannot give his or her rational consent to being such a recipient, the directive behind the act is also structurally flawed and has no authority.

Unlike Bowie's argument, the present line of reasoning does not focus attention uniquely upon the contractual relations in business. Rather, its focus is upon the other feature of business decisions that is relevant to the stakeholder theory, namely, their tendency to have a direct impact upon other people. The argument is formalistic, of course, because these authors give no concrete reason why an action would fail the role-reversal test. The reason emerges in the specific context of the test's application.

Finally, it should also be mentioned that, like Bowie's argument, there are versions of the Donaldson-Waller position that can be used to defend both the social demandingness and the social activist theories. These versions arise in a context in which an agent is expected to apply the role-reversal test even to those who are noncontractually or only indirectly affected by their actions. We shall consider these versions in a later chapter.

DEONTOLOGICAL ARGUMENTS: RIGHTS AND RESPECT FOR PERSONS

The argument advanced by Bowie seeks to defend the idea that certain stake-holders have rights. Other theorists also advocate the rights position. According to most rights theorists, the logic of rights is such that if X has a valid rights claim against Y, then Y is accountable to X in the areas of conduct that affect or are affected by the rights claim. As they see it, if I have a valid rights claim to freedom of movement in certain areas, one who would seek to block or restrict this freedom is accountable to me and others at least to give a rendering of his or her conduct in this regard.

The rights argument has been advanced with various stakeholder groups in mind. We shall illustrate this argument by considering three writers who advance it with respect to workers' rights. Werhane, for example, argues that employees have general rights to fair treatment and respect. This involves providing fair pay for the employee's work, of course, but it also involves such actions as respecting the employees' privacy and safety in the workplace, providing sufficient information to them so that they can perform their work effectively and with their rational consent, and providing a system of due process for workers (Werhane, 1985, p. 102–3). Gibson also contends that workers have rights to health and safety, freedom of speech, and due process, among others (Gibson, 1983, p. 12). Finally, Ewing agrees that workers have rights to freedom, privacy, and due process and proposes a nine-point bill of rights for employees (Ewing, 1977, pp. 146ff.).

Not all theorists who defend stakeholder rights do so entirely or exclusively within the context of the stakeholder theory. Those who argue that these rights are merely legal in nature espouse a position that is closer in important respects to either the classical or the social demandingness theories. On the other hand, those who argue that these rights are moral rights based upon certain features inherent in human nature advance a position that is closer in relevant respects to the social activist model. Gibson's view is closer to the social demandingness model for she contends that the rights of stakeholders are ultimately institutional ones. This means that they are grounded in our social institutions as they have currently evolved. Different institutions would give rise to the development of a different set or pattern of rights. Thus, there is nothing sacrosanct about the present pattern of stakeholder rights. They may change as the social institutions themselves change (Gibson, 1983, p. 124).

Werhane advances two considerations in behalf of worker rights. First, she argues that reciprocal accountability is an important feature of the unique relation that exists between employers and employees (Werhane, 1985, p. 102). This reciprocal accountability may be based upon such factors as the contractual nature of the relationship or it may be because employers and employees are joined together in a common effort to achieve an institutional purpose. Whatever the exact reason, her argument differs from some of the other stakeholder arguments we have thus far examined in that a version of it can be advanced that defends only this theory of corporate responsibility. The unique reciprocal relations of which Werhane speaks are not present among the members of the public or between the public and corporations; they are unique in that they apply solely to those specific types of interpersonal relationship that are either dominated by contract or illustrative of the type of teamwork she mentions. Nor is their authoritative character always recognized in the rules, norms, or codes of our current social institutions. The reciprocal character of the accountability relation is thus seen to follow from the pattern of human relationship itself; it is not viewed as stemming from society's opinions or views about this relationship or about the explicit demands placed upon this relationship by society. It seems then that her position is uniquely stakeholder in nature.

Actually, however, the second argument that she advances for the stakeholder status of workers does, in fact, push her theory toward another position on corporate responsibility, namely, the social activist theory. She believes that employee rights are based, in part, upon certain general features of human nature that are thought to deserve respect and consideration (Werhane, 1985, p 27). Whether these features are said to be autonomy, rationality, self-conscious sentience, or the like, employees are said to deserve respect or to be entitled to initial equal consideration with stockholders, for example, because they possess these characteristics. This argument moves in the direction of social activism because it must be admitted that every individual who possesses these characteristics is entitled to such consideration. It does not matter whether they have contractual relationships with the firm or even if they have direct contact with it; the corporation should treat them with respect just because of their peculiarly human characteristics. So, while employee relations may be more extensively involved in corporate decision making, they are no more authoritative on this account.

Finally, consider again Bowie's argument for this theory of corporate responsibility, now seen as another illustration of the respect for persons defense of the position. We have seen that the formalist side of his argument proposes that the making of a genuine agreement or contract with another person implies that each party relies upon and respect certain characteristics in the other contractor. In Bowie's case, two of the relevant characteristics are autonomy and rationality (Bowie, 1982, p. 47). For Bowie, it is incoherent and self-defeating for an agent to do something to someone with whom he or she has made an agreement that would otherwise jeopardize or harm the very characteristics of human beings that make agreements of this sort possible in the first place. But Bowie also believes that these features are deserving of respect in their own right. Hence, his argument also has elements of the respect for persons defense.

There are two possible interpretations of Bowie's position here. It could be restricted only to those who make *actual* agreements with corporate executives, or it could be applied more broadly to anyone who *is capable of* making such agreements. In the narrower version, it is an argument that defends only the

Figure 10.1
Stakeholder Theory (Principle Assumptions)

Relations of Accountability	Models of the Corporation	Strategies of Legitimization
1. Promise-Keeping or Consent**	1. Private Property*	1. Power*
2. Fiduciary**	2. Private Contract**	2. Conformity to Law
3. Representational*	3. Enterprise**	3. Conformity to Current Standards
4. Impact**	4. Social Contract	4. Procedural**
5. Reverse-Impact*	5. Public Power**	5. Formal**
6. Teamwork or Collegial*	6. Machine or Tool	6. Performance**
7. Ownership or Possession*	7. Organic**	7. Rights**
8. Regulation*	8. Mental or Moral Agent*	8. Respect for Persons*
		[9. Relations of Accountability]

 * can or does play some direct role in defining or defending the theory

** plays a significant role in defining or defending the theory

stakeholder theory. However, in the broader version (the one I think Bowie favors) it can be used to justify the social activist theory. It should be mentioned here that the general impetus of the respect for persons argument is directed more toward the social activist theory and less toward the stakeholder position. Only by admitting an additional premise that limits respect merely to actual contract makers or to those directly affected by corporate decisions can one use the argument solely to defend the latter theory.

THE ASSUMPTIONS OF THE STAKEHOLDER THEORY

We have thus far considered the strategies of legitimation that are most relevant to the stakeholder theory. We shall now examine those assumptions which concern the relations of accountability and the models of the corporation which are also most often associated with the position. The three sets of assumptions are schematically provided in Figure 10.1.

Like the classical theory, the stakeholder view appeals to all eight relations of accountability, but the manner of this appeal is somewhat unique. The various strategies are often used piecemeal to establish the various stakeholder groups. Thus, the fiduciary and ownership models, if used exclusively, are assumptions more appropriate for the classical theory. But when used with some of the other models—models that are used to ground the stakeholder status of other groups— they become the means whereby stockholders are also admitted to have stakeholder status. The fiduciary model is also used to defend the idea that those members of the corporation who have the status of professionals have a special responsibility to protect the interests of certain individuals or groups with whom the corporation deals. Thus, auditors or accountants may be said to stand in a fiduciary relation to creditors, governmental officials, and perhaps fellow workers (as well as the shareholders); and, engineers have a special responsibility to customers or clients to promote the safety of the firm's products. Some top executives may also be lawyers or physicians and may thus have a fiduciary relation to individuals other than the shareholders. Finally, managerial professionals in general are now often viewed as having such relations to certain constituents other than the stockholders. Thus, personnel managers are viewed by some as having a stewardship relation to workers, and public relations personnel are seen as having a fiduciary or quasi-fiduciary relation to those who receive information from the company.

Not only does the ownership relation ground the stakeholder status of shareholders, it is also at least part of the reason why managers are held to be accountable to certain other stakeholder groups. It is believed that the latter have some kind of direct property relationship to the firm (other than being the owner of its assets) that managers are required to respect. For instance, creditors have the funds they have loaned to the firm; consumers have the money they have spent for the firm's products or services; workers have their mental and physical abilities, as well as the investment in the firm of their time, energy, and loyalty; and so on for several of the other types of stakeholders.

But the ownership model is not appropriate when considering members of government agencies or professional groups as stakeholders. Nor is it the primary factor behind the stakeholder status of members of local communities. The stakeholder theory typically requires managers to respect more than just the property of members of local communities. They are also expected to consider their safety, health, and future well-being. It is doubtful whether these expectations can be explained simply or primarily upon the basis of the need for managers to respect the property holdings or rights of the residents of local communities.

While thus a relevant model of accountability for the stakeholder theory, the ownership model cannot be said to play a dominant role here. If it were to be viewed in this way, one would expect to see stakeholder theorists endorsing the idea that the interests of stockholders always supercede the interests of the other stakeholder groups for only they are direct property holders of the firm's assets. As we have seen, however, this belief is not characteristically included in this theory (at least not after a certain level of profit performance has been reached by a firm).

As for the representational model, it is used to defend the stakeholder status of shareholders, but it can also be used to establish such a status for certain professional groups whose members may be affected by the conduct of their colleagues or peers working for a corporation. Since the latter's actions reflect upon such groups, these groups are said to have a stake in these actions. In addition, however, the model can be used to reaffirm the functionary status of corporate professionals—especially those whose professional groups have the power to negate, retract, or otherwise markedly affect their occupational status or professional credentials or standing.

The representative model is also applicable in another way. Some theorists believe that certain activities of stakeholders can be viewed as a kind of ratification process. For instance, when lenders choose to loan money to a corporation, when consumers buy a company's products, or when employees choose to continue working for a firm, each group can be viewed as giving at least a partial vote of confidence in management. But the problem with this way of looking at it is that the ratification procedure considered here is more akin to that found in contract making (the promise-keeping model) than that found in an election or voting process *per se*. In addition, it is difficult to determine what precisely stakeholders are ratifying when they make such choices. Does a customer really reaffirm the social or environmental policies of a firm by simply buying one of its products? His or her decision may actually have little to do with such matters. It is true, of course, that if a sufficiently large enough number of potential consumers refuse to buy the products or services of a company, this action sends a strong message to its management. But it is a message that is more likely to be urged or emphasized by social demandingness than by stakeholder theorists. Finally, the model is inapplicable to the noncontractual stakeholders of a firm, even when it is viewed within the scope of this broader interpretation of the voting process.

The regulation model also applies to this theory. It pertains to the formal rules of a company that are meant to direct the conduct of its internal constituents, and it is pertinent to the informal rules and values that are part of the culture of the corporation. To follow these rules or values is said to be an aspect of the reciprocal obligations that are shared by the managers and workers alike. This implies that managers are responsible to carry out their side of these duties too. The model also applies to the professionals within the corporation who are responsible to respect the relevant and appropriate principles of their profession, and it applies to the obligation of managers to abide by the special regulations that are administered by various agencies of government and are targeted specifically at particular corporations. It does not, however, apply to a situation that would occur were the laws of society in general to come to demand respect for the interests of all of the stakeholders of a company. As we have seen, this is a consideration, were it to arise, that is more appropriate to the classical or social demandingness theories.

The reverse-impact model is assumed by Freeman in defense of his position, but, as previously mentioned, his view is closer to another theory of corporate responsibility. It is clear that managers should be concerned with the response that stakeholders are capable of making to their decisions for otherwise stakeholders might come to demand greater levels of government regulation for corporations. Such a demand is typically a good indication that the legitimacy status of a firm or industry is in the process of being changed to a lower level. And if stakeholders become sufficiently annoyed with corporate decision making or performance, they may refuse to discharge or renew the agreements they have made with management. But it should be pointed out that this latter concern is already covered by the promise-keeping model, and the former concern can equally apply to nonstakeholders as well. Since they too can demand greater levels of government regulation, a firm that responded to this group primarily for this reason would be more attuned to the social demandingness theory. Finally, since the reverse-impact model maintains that managers must respond to the interests of all those whose actions may directly affect the firm, it implies that managers must also be responsible to protect the interests of even those who are only indirectly affected by corporate actions. This idea also belongs more appropriately to the social demandingness position.

This leaves us with the promise-keeping, impact, and teamwork models. The promise-keeping model clearly applies to those who are considered stakeholders of a corporation because they have entered into contractual relations with it. This seems to leave out members of local communities and perhaps representatives of professional groups or government agencies, but the former group can be considered full-fledged stakeholders on the basis of the impact model, and the latter two are involved in at least quasi-contractual relations with members of corporations. This can be seen in the oaths, pledges, signed documents, and the like in which the latter are involved.

As for the impact model, it plays an important role in determining who is and who is not a stakeholder, but is used by Ackoff and Starling to show the overall positive social impact of the theory, it is more appropriate to the social demandingness or activist positions.

Finally, the teamwork model is relevant to those stakeholder theorists who discuss the internal constituents of a firm: such people as stockholders, members of the board of directors, other executives of the firm, and the other employees. Maslow, for example, specifically appeals to the special bond that exists among individuals who pursue a common career or occupational purpose. This also seems to be an important aspect of the reciprocal obligations that Werhane says exist between management and workers.

With the exception of professional groups, the teamwork or collegial model seems less appropriate when considering the external constituents of a firm. It is true that some systems theorists and strategic management advocates who accept the stakeholder theory appeal to the general harmony or public welfare said to occur in society when firms respect the interests of their stakeholders. In this latter use of the teamwork model the stakeholder theory is not alone, however. Each theory of corporate responsibility typically argues that it offers members of society a better chance of achieving their common economic and social goals.

A challenge to this last application of the teamwork model is the difficulty of considering the pluralistic elements of the social and economic systems urged by the stakeholder theory as constituting a team with a common set of overriding purposes. Can the type of society envisioned by these theorists actually function as a team? Can it even be envisioned along collegial lines?

The teamwork model may also be meant to apply to the separate external constituents of a firm themselves. Thus, consumers, creditors, professional groups, government officials, and the like may be viewed as distinct teams with their own specific goals—goals that are blocked or enhanced by the decisions of managers. But, again, given the potential for conflict among these various stakeholder groups, it is difficult to see how this application of the teamwork model squares with the public welfare argument or interpretation we are presently discussing. It seems an open question whether helping one stakeholder group at the expense of another will actually improve the overall welfare of society. At the very least, another model of interpersonal relationship is needed to show which stakeholder "teams" deserve the greatest attention and response from managers.

MODELS OF THE CORPORATION

Of the eight models of the corporation discussed earlier, only five seem to play an important role in the stakeholder theory: the private contract, enterprise, public power, organic, and mental agent models. Stakeholder theories do not assume the primacy of the private property model of the corporation, but, as we have seen, they are not entirely averse to it either. They agree that many stakeholder groups have a property relation to the firm and thus have prerogatives over the holdings that brings them into this relationship. But these theorists do not typically emphasize the property aspects of the stakeholder position. This model is usually associated with the classical rather than with the present theory for, as we have said, the stockholders of a corporation are thought to have the most direct and significant property relation to the firm insofar as they are its owners.

Despite the contractarian elements of the Werhane and Bowie defense of the stakeholder status of certain groups, the social contract model does not ultimately seem to be appropriate as an assumption here, either. This model tells us that the source of management authority is an implicit agreement made between executives and members of society to protect the interests of the latter. But were such an agreement to be made or recognized, it would ultimately require managers to treat all members of society on a par with those with whom management has made its explicit contracts. Such a position grounds the social demandingness theory perhaps, but it is less appropriate for the stakeholder theory. In fact, even a version of the present model that held that the nature of the contract stipulated that only stakeholder claims and interests be respected by management, that it fulfill only its stakeholder responsibilities, would bring us back ultimately to a variant of the social demandingness theory. It would perhaps constitute a distinctive, and even ingenious, version of this theory, of course, but it would be a version of the social demandingness theory nevertheless.

Finally, the machine model has not been explicitly endorsed by stakeholder theories. I believe it is theoretically possible for stakeholder theorists to appeal to the model, but no one to my knowledge has thus far done so. Perhaps one reason for this is that it appears to be more applicable to some of the other theories of corporate responsibility, such as the classical or the social demandingless theories. If the corporation is viewed as a tool used to achieve some overall purpose, the purpose pursued is usually thought to be either wealth maximization or social utility. It is hard to find someone who argues that the corporation is a tool designed specifically or even primarily to respond to stakeholder interests. In addition, the stakeholder theory seems to be so wrapped up with purpose—especially the purposes of the individual internal constituents of the firm—that it is hard to see how the mechanistic elements of the machine or tool model can straightforwardly apply to these teleological components. It is, of course, possible for advocates to assume that many corporations function primarily in routine or standardized ways within structures that have relatively clear lines of authority and a significant degree of specialization, but stakeholder theorists are generally anxious to offset these facets of corporate life. In this case, however, the model is assumed more as a foil than as a metaphor that is willingly embraced by these theorists.

We come now to the models that play a more significant role in the development and defense of this theory. Many stakeholder theorists make explicit appeal to the private contract model. Advocates of this model see the corporation as a web of private agreements existing among its internal constituents and between management and certain outside parties. And since stakeholder theories hold that the presence of explicit contractual obligation is an important feature in defining a stakeholder, they accept the idea that a key aspect of a corporation consists in this network of private agreements. Stakeholder theorists may also appeal to the negative side of this metaphor, but once again it is used more as a foil for them. They realize that the corporation is a source of private disagreement and conflict, but they wish to minimize or overcome this facet of organizational life and believe that their theory can effectively do this.

Much the same can be said for the enterprise model. The negative side of this metaphor, which emphasizes the actual or potential conflict that comes from the pursuit of private career goals, is something that they grant may apply to certain corporations now, but eventually it can or will be overcome by the positive elements brought out by the enterprise metaphor. These play a more dominant role in the stakeholder theory—especially as they concern relations among the firm's internal constituents. Whether because of the presence of contract or the pursuit of a common set of occupational purposes, stakeholder theorists believe that workers and corporate colleagues should be treated with respect. This means in part that upper-level management should, to the extent possible, assist lower-level management and other employees in fulfilling at least their career goals.

And they should encourage the latter's pursuit of self-respect, autonomy, and actualization. This is what is alleged to bring about syncretism within the corporation. And by respecting the claims and interests of the firm's external constituents, social syncretism is also often alleged to result as well.

Stakeholder theorists also assume important elements of the public power model. Advocates of this model are concerned with the impact corporations have upon the laws and values of society. Most stakeholder theorists agree that corporations have significant power over their members and nonmembers alike. They are dominant institutions that have a great impact upon society, and they are to be held responsible for this impact. They differ from other public power theorists, however, in restricting corporate accountability to only the direct aspects or effects of this impact because, as some see it at least, this is the extent of the effective power or influence of management.

Some stakeholder theorists appeal to the organic model of the firm and of society. This is especially true of systems theorists and some advocates of strategic management. First, they view the firm as an entity that is more than the mere sum of its parts, an entity whose existence depends in great part upon the presence of each of its primary stakeholder groups. If stakeholders are not treated as ends in themselves, if management discriminates against them and uses them merely as a means, the corporation itself would be in jeopardy. Beyond this, though, some stakeholder theorists stress the idea that firms are organs of the wider society. They appeal to the ideal of unity or coherence of social purpose in defending the stakeholder theory, even though this line of reasoning might be thought more appropriate to the social demandingness or activist positions. And because they advocate a degree of flexibility in determining specific corporate responsibilities—the list of such responsibilities alters as the interests and demands of various stakeholder groups change—their theory is often endorsed by contingency theorists and advocates of organizational ecology.

Finally we come to the mental and moral agent model. Stakeholder theorists have not specifically mentioned the moral agent model in the defense of their position. This is perhaps because if one were to consider corporations themselves to be distinct moral agents on a par with stakeholders and other moral beings, they would then be seen as deserving of a like respect. This would imply that any corporation that makes agreements with a firm or is directly affected by its actions is a stakeholder. While many stakeholder theorists contend that other firms are stakeholders, they usually believe that competitors are stakeholders for only certain kinds of business decisions, such as those that reflect upon the industry as a whole. For the other decisions, they are not viewed as being entitled to the same consideration or respect that is given or owed to the other stakeholder groups.

Stakeholder theorists do grant or assume certain features of the mental agent metaphor. They grant that corporations are complex centers of information gathering and dissemination that exercise self-correcting functions. Advocates of the argument from limited knowledge of indirect effects may also appeal to the concept of "bounded rationality," which is endorsed by certain thinkers who are sympathetic to the brain or mental agent metaphor. And the conflict that is frequently present in corporations may be perceived to make firms into "psychic prisons" for their members. But, by and large, recent stakeholder theorists have not explored or exploited this metaphor to any significant degree.

REFERENCES

Ackerman, Robert, and Raymond Bauer. 1976. *Corporate Social Responsiveness: The Modern Dilemma*. Reston, Va.: Reston Publishing Company.

Ackoff, Russell L. 1981. *Creating the Corporate Future*. New York: John Wiley and Sons.

Anshoff, H. Igor. 1965. *Corporate Strategy: An Analytic Approach to Business Policy for Growth and Expansion*. New York: McGraw-Hill.

Bock, R. H. 1979. "Introduction: Modern Values in Business and Management." *AACSB Bulletin, Proceedings*, Annual Meeting, pp. 1–19.

Bowie, Norman. 1982. *Business Ethics*. Englewood Cliffs, N.J.: Prentice-Hall.

Cameron, Kim S. 1986. "Effectiveness As Paradox: Consensus and Conflict in Conceptions of Organizational Effectiveness." *Management Science*, May, pp. 539–53.

Donaldson, John, and Mike Waller. 1980. "Ethics and Organization." *The Journal of Management Studies*. February, pp. 34–55.

Ewing, David. 1977. *Freedom Inside the Organization*. New York: E. P. Dutton.

Freeman, Edward. 1984. *Strategic Management: A Stakeholder Approach*. Marshfield, Mass.: Pitman Books.

Gibson, Mary. 1983. *Worker's Rights*. Totowa, N.J.: Rowman and Allanhead.

Jackson, Donald W., Jr., and Ramon J. Aldag. 1980. "Planning for Corporate Social Actions." *Managerial Planning*, September–October, pp. 28–33.

Jones, Thomas M. 1980. "Corporate Social Responsibility Revisited, Redefined." *California Management Review*, Spring, pp. 59–67.

Manning, Frank V. 1981. *Managerial Dilemmas and Executive Growth*. Reston, Va.: Reston Publishing Company.

Maslow, Abraham. 1971. *The Farther Reaches of Human Nature*. New York: Viking Press.

Peters, Thomas J., and Robert H. Waterman, Jr. 1982. *In Search of Excellence*. New York: Warner Books.

Post, James E. 1986. "Perfecting Capitalism" In *Corporations and the Common Good*, edited by Robert B. Dickie and Leroy S. Rounder, pp. 45–60. Notre Dame, Ind.: University of Notre Dame Press.

Sethi, S. Prakash. 1977. "Dimensions of Corporate Social Performance: An Analytical Framework." In *Managing Corporate Social Responsibility*, edited by Archie B. Carroll, pp. 69–75. Boston: Little Brown.

Sherwin, Douglas S. 1983. "The Ethical Roots of the Business System." *Harvard Business Review*, vol. 61, November–December, pp. 183–92.

Starling, Grover. 1980. *The Changing Environment of Business: A Managerial Approach*. Boston: Kent Publishing Company.

Sturdivant, Frederick. 1981. *Business and Society: A Managerial Approach*. Homewood, Ill.: Richard D. Irwin Press.

Werhane, Patricia. 1985. *Persons, Rights and Corporations*. Englewood Cliffs, N.J.: Prentice-Hall.

11

THE SOCIAL DEMANDINGNESS THEORY

DEFINITION

The third theory of corporate responsibility to be discussed here is referred to by different names. Hay and Gray call it the quality of life management theory (Hay and Gray, 1974, p. 138), and Sethi refers to it as the social responsibility model (Sethi, 1977, p. 74). We shall call it the social demandingness theory. I call it the social demandingness theory realizing that there are those who feel that some reference to moral demands should also be included in the title of the theory, but the ensuing discussion will mention the social more often than the moral responsibilities of firms. The chief reason for this is that most of the literature on this theory addresses the issue of the social responsibilities of corporations. Nevertheless, the reader should remember that moral responsibilities are also considered by the theory.

The basic idea behind the theory is that corporations are responsible to carry out those activities that are expected or demanded of them by society. In defining and defending this approach to corporate social responsibility, Finlay, for example, tells us that responsible business decision making is the management process embodying those factors that arbitrate the interplay between corporate resources and *social demands* (Finlay, 1977, p. 59). Boarman says that the normative or ethical side of corporate decision making is supplied by both the market and the moral and social forces in society (Boarman, 1982, p. 534). Thus, this theory differs from the stakeholder position in maintaining that management is in some way directly responsible to society or the general public, that is, even to those who are only indirectly affected by its decisions.

The central theses of the theory can be put forth in either of two ways. First, the position requires that managers solicit and consider the opinions, demands, or expectations of members of the public regarding corporate activity, especially corporate social or moral activity. In doing this, management is expected to consider the opinions of both those who are, and those who are not, stakeholders of the corporation. Second, the theory stipulates that managers are required to respond to the interests and needs of society so expressed. They should seek to promote its general welfare in the areas covered by these social expectations.

There is some disagreement among these theorists about how socially demanding this latter requirement really is, however. Buchanan offers a more minimalist interpretation of the demands of the public. He believes that the social demands placed upon corporations by society are relatively few in number and are primarily restricted in scope to the economic and legal arenas. As he sees it, they are consistent with the demands urged upon corporations by classical theorists (Buchanan, 1975, pp. 72ff.).

Most social demandingness theorists disagree with this, though. Like Anshen and Donaldson, they contend that the public's social or moral demands on corporations have been increasing in the last few decades (Anshen, 1980, pp. 10ff.; Donaldson, 1982, pp. 41ff.). Bradshaw, for example, contends that the public expects firms to provide for cleaner air and water and to protect the health of workers, consumers, and people living near plants, factories, and waste disposal sites. It also expects firms to promote worker self-respect and fulfillment and make it possible for employees and the public to have meaningful leisure and a dignified old age (Bradshaw, 1974, pp. 24–25).

Richman tells us that society expects firms to improve their methods of social and financial accounting and disclosure, to measure and identify social values, and to make appropriate organizational changes for social responsibility. It expects firms to reward socially responsible performance, respect the rights of workers, provide leadership in the area of ethical investing, and lobby government for effective legislation in the social responsibility area (Richman, 1977, pp. 52ff.). Votaw and Sethi agree with this last point and add that society also expects corporations to be more consistently candid and thorough in releasing information pertinent to the public's welfare (Votaw and Sethi, 1973, pp. 183ff.).

Another social demandingness theorist tells us that our business ideology has changed over the course of the twentieth century. Lodge tells us that the traditional ideology in the United States once stressed the values of individualism, property rights, competition, scientific specialization, and a limited role for the state. But this individualistic, laissez-faire ideology has been largely superceded by a more communitarian one, one that emphasizes the importance of the collective, the rights (particularly the nonproperty rights) and duties attached to membership in the group, and the need to respond to the community's welfare in a holistic manner. This communitarian ideology will typically involve an active, planning state and a more socially or morally active private sector (Lodge, 1970, pp. 46ff.). He contends that management must take into account this newer business ideology for it is no longer enough for firms to provide goods and services to the public for profit in the marketplace; they are now viewed as social institutions that have social and moral responsibilities to fulfill.

Finally, Hay and Gray contend that society demands at a minimum that corporations limit or eliminate the negative social impact of management decision making (Hay and Gray, 1974, p. 137). Agreeing with this view, Davis tells us that corporations are expected to restrict the negative social effects that directly or indirectly result from their actions, such as poverty, deteriorating cities, defacement of the landscape, environmental pollution, and disregard for consumers (Davis, 1975, p. 23).

CLARIFICATIONS OF THE THEORY

Before examining the main arguments raised in behalf of the theory, we should first consider three points in its definition. First, the theory is inherently relativistic; it is relative both to time and place. It does not state any specific action that management is always responsible to perform. It does, of course, place management under the general duty to consider the expectations or demands of the public, but the specific social or moral activities expected of corporations can clearly change as society itself changes. In fact, if Zenisek is correct, this flexibility may have an important bearing on the clarity of the theory itself. He tells us that the way firms respond to these demands affects the future expectations of society in such a way that these two dimensions form, as Emory and Trist would say, a turbulent field (Zenisek, 1979, p. 363). This is one where slight changes in the one dimension of social expectation bring about changes in the other dimension of corporate response, which reverberate back to the first again in a continuous process of fluctuation between the poles of expectation and response, and between the poles of high and low social expectation—even, in fact, between the poles of stability and turbulence themselves.

This changeable nature suggests an element of instability, if not unclarity, in the theory itself—an instability that could also have an important bearing upon the overall debate by affecting the cogency, and even the nature of some of the theories of corporate responsibility themselves. It also suggests, however, that the present arrangement of these theories is not meant to be lexical in nature, at least, if by lexical, one means that it is arranged in order from the least to the most socially or morally demanding position. It should also be noted, however, that given the apparent expectations or demands of the public in the last several decades, the present classification does in the main seem to follow this pattern. But, as previously said, society's demands and expectations can change. Members of society may come to wish that firms would merely focus upon their economic functions, which would make the position no more socially or morally demanding than the classical theory, or they might come to place even greater social or moral demands on management than those usually advocated by activist theorists. It all depends on the actual demands or expectations of society.

The next clarification concerns the question of the precise nature of the data or phenomena upon which the theory is based. Are these to be defined in terms of the expectations, the interests, or needs of society; in terms of its norms; or in terms of the welfare of society in general? Social demandingness theorists are in disagreement on this issue. For example, Ackerman and Bauer, Shocker and Sethi, and Zenisek tell us that executives are accountable to respond to the expectations of society in the areas of social or moral responsibility (Ackerman and Bauer, 1976, p. 6; Shocker and Sethi, 1973, p. 98; Zenisek, 1979, p. 362). But Hay and Gray, Jacobs, Finlay, and Davis contend that managers must respond to the demands of society (Hay and Gray, 1974, p. 139; Jacobs, 1973, p. 1076; Finlay, 1977, p. 59, Davis, 1975, p. 19). Along this same line, Drucker, and Atkinson and Atkinson say this theory stipulates that corporate conduct be judged in terms of the prevailing moral standards or norms of society (Drucker, 1981, p. 31; Atkinson and Atkinson, 1980, p. 132). Because some believe that these standards enunciate or represent the primary moral demands that society places upon firms, they would regard this definition as a species of the previous one. Other theorists would treat it as a distinct position, though. Finally, some thinkers, such as Sawyer, and Votow and Sethi, define the theory in terms of the needs, interests, or welfare of society (Sawyer, 1979, pp. 390ff.; Votow and Sethi, 1973, p. 183).

These versions of the theory have somewhat different implications for the corporate responsibility debate. If, for example, executive responsibility is based only upon the demands (including the moral demands) of society, this would likely require them to do solely those actions whose nonperformance would be viewed in very serious terms, perhaps even as being wrong or evil. It would require them to fulfill those responsibilities that are viewed as moral or social duties (nonduties would then be matters of management discretion). It would likely demand, for example, that executives provide truthful information to stakeholders and the public, provide safe working conditions for their employees, and avoid contaminating the water used by surrounding residents or dismissing an employee solely to avoid paying for his or her retirement. Given the current demands of society, this presently seems to be the least socially or morally demanding version of the theory for it permits managers to rely upon their own discretion in deciding all of those corporate matters about which society makes no explicit demands.

A somewhat more exacting version is that which bases social demandingness upon the social and moral expectations of the public. Clearly, a demand is some form of expectation, so there is overlap between these two versions of the theory, but the term *expectation* has a considerably broader meaning than does the term *demand*. Beyond what is demanded, an expectation involves reference to what is good or beneficial to perform but whose nonperformance does not necessarily constitute a serious harm, wrongdoing, or evil. Thus, society might expect firms to donate to educational institutions or to fund the rebuilding of cities, but it may not require or demand these actions of corporations. They would not then be social or moral duties. In the previous version of the theory, corporate executives may not then be currently responsible for such charitable contributions; in the present version, however, they might well be.

Given recent accounts of the actual demands and expectations of society, the version of the theory that places the greatest moral or social constraints upon management, however, is that which equates social demandingness with the promotion of social welfare. This version of the theory comes very close to the social activist position to be discussed shortly in that its moral or social demands are not based upon what the public directly, explicitly, or presently says it generally wants or requires of corporations. They are based instead upon what actually contributes to the expressed interests and needs of society when these are studied or surveyed distinctively or separately. It is typically more demanding than the other two versions of the theory because it makes executives responsible for responding to those interests of the public that the public has not yet even formulated into distinct demands or expectations for corporations. This latter set of responses usually broadens the class of conduct for which corporate executives are already held accountable by the theory. That this is so can be seen in a variety of ways, one of which will be mentioned here. It is quite clear that the expressed demands or expectations of society are affected by a number of variables, such as the public's perception of the ability of corporations to solve social or moral problems in the first place. One reason the public may not specifically or expressly expect or demand a certain activity from management is its belief that management does not at that time have the proper social, moral, or technical expertise or tools to perform the action effectively. And if a corporation develops this expertise, there is usually a time lag before the public knows about this development. The earlier versions of the theory would not require that managers perform the action in question until the public expressly asks for it. The present version would. And it would make executives responsible for shortening the time lag that often exists between such corporate innovation in these areas and society's awareness of this innovation (and the revised expectations or demands of society that depend upon this). And this is so even if the shortening of the time lag would prove to be otherwise costly to the firm, at least in the short run.

There are thus three viable candidates for the definition of the basic data or factors included in the standard behind this theory. In fact, in addition to these versions, there is still another that is also sometimes suggested to be a fourth version of the theory. It is that formulation that equates the public's needs or interests with their ideal, rather than their expressed, needs or interests. But, unlike the last version, because this view appeals to a standard of corporate responsibility that is entirely independent of what people actually say they want or need from firms, we shall consider this to be ultimately a species of the social activist theory and shall postpone its discussion until the next chapter.

The third point of clarification concerns another facet of the problem of determining the precise nature of the data or norms upon which the theory is grounded. There is disagreement about what constitutes a moral or social demand in the first place, and there is a conflict of opinion on the question of what actually constitutes an expectation or interest. Looking at social demands, for example, some theorists equate these with explicit legal demands; others equate them with the expressed demands of the majority of the people in a society. Still others equate them with the expressed demands of a certain segment of the population—a segment whose experiences, educational background, expertise, character, or the like are thought to provide a more impartial expression of society's views. Some theorists take this segment to be the clergy, some to be the media; others take it to be educators or professional groups, still others to be anyone with a college education, and so on. Similar problems also arise in determining the nature of moral demands and of social expectations or interests.

A final controversy concerns the proper method of isolating and measuring the strength of such demands, expectations, or interests—assuming that these can initially be accurately defined. The whole literature of social indicator research, for example, has grown considerably in the last decade and a half in order to address precisely this question.

In mentioning these disputes, it is not my purpose to seek to arbitrate between them. It is sufficient for our present purposes to simply point them out so that the reader will better understand the range of views that fits under the present position.

Finally, then, using the six criteria for defining the positions on corporate responsibility that were given in chapter 3, it can be seen that the social demandingness theory is to be distinguished from the other positions on corporate responsibility principally on the basis of the group toward whom executives are held responsible (in this case, stockholders, stakeholders, and the general public); the type of effect that results from corporate conduct (in this case, corporate executives are responsible for both the direct and indirect effects of their actions); and the type of interest had by the individuals affected by corporate action (in this case, only the expressed interests or expectations of these people are relevant). Since these theorists differ considerably among themselves on the types of action required of executives, their relation to profit, and the motive behind corporate social or moral involvement, these last criteria are not as helpful in distinguishing the position from the other views.

THE ARGUMENTS FROM POWER AND CONFORMITY TO LAW

The social demandingness theory is, of course, closely connected to the conformity to current standards strategy of legitimation. In some of its versions, in fact, it is a mere species of this latter position. But how does its defense relate to the other strategies?

As with the stakeholder theory, the present view assumes the conformity to law model but does not primarily rely upon it in its own defense. Social demandingness theorists believe, of course, that the law provides firms with a idea of the current standards of society, and that firms should obey the law because such obedience is an important element of an institution's legitimacy. The problem is that it could at best perhaps give them only category two legitimacy; so meeting such a requirement would involve fulfilling merely a minimal standard. These theorists believe that firms are expected to do more in the social or moral areas than just what is explicitly demanded by law. A distinct justification is thus needed for these added responsibilities. As was said with respect to the stakeholder theory, this strategy of argument is more appropriate for the classical theory in any case, though there is extensive common ground between the social demandingness theory and the present strategy of legitimation, since both involve a consensus of some sort. On the other hand, when it is believed that the sole or principal reason for responding to the expectations, demands, or interests of the public is that this would best serve the legal requirements of society, then the social demandingness theory has merely become a (complicated) version of the classical theory.

As for the power model, there is a version of the argument from power used to defend the social demandingness position, but there are few such theorists who believe that it is the primary defense for their view. The basic idea behind the power model is that firms should be socially or morally active because (and to the extent that) such conduct contributes to their power and autonomy. The version of the power argument most relevant to the present theory is that which contends that successful corporate response to social or moral demands or expectations will ward off more expanded intrusions of government oversight into the private sector in the future. And this, in turn, will preserve and promote corporate autonomy. We see this argument raised or mentioned in the work of Davis, Wallich, and Loevinger, among others (Davis, 1973, p. 314; Wallich, 1972, pp. 46ff.; Loevinger, 1973, p. 388). Although some social demandingness theorists appeal to this argument, it does not typically play an important role in the theory's defense because the focus of the defense is upon corporate self-interest, while the focus of the theory is usually upon consideration of public opinion or welfare in itself. In those cases where corporate self-interest conflicts with these public considerations, appeal to this defense would drive the theory toward the classical position, making it more difficult to distinguish it from the latter.

THE PERFORMANCE ARGUMENT

As with the classical and stakeholder theories, two versions of the performance argument have been used to defend the social demandingness position. The first equates performance with the benefits that accrue to single business units; the second equates it with whatever contributes to the overall social welfare.

The first version of the argument is advanced by Sawyer, among others (Sawyer, 1979, p. 391). It contends that firms responding to social demands or expectations are better off in the long run than those firms that do not. Being "better off" economically is usually defined either in terms of investor returns (such as higher dividends, greater stock value, or larger capital gains) or in terms of accounting returns (such as greater market share, increased revenues or profits, or a lower debt to equity ratio). But it may also be defined noneconomically in terms of increased levels of autonomy, consumer or employee satisfaction, power, respectability, and so on. When defined in this latter way, the power defense mentioned above can become a species of the performance argument.

Generally speaking, however, this first version of the performance argument plays an ancillary role in the defense of the social demandingness theory. The reason for this is much the same as that which applied to the power strategy—the present strategy relies upon a level of corporate self-interest that is incompatible with the other-oriented nature of the position. In addition, however, the inconclusiveness of the empirical studies in this area makes this strategy more the basis of a continued research project than an important ground of the social demandingness theory. What one typically finds is that it is offered as only one among several considerations raised in behalf of the theory.

Far more important in the recent literature is the argument from systemwide performance. This is a commonly raised argument by systems theorists, such as Post, as well as certain strategic management theorists, like Hay and Gray, and Freeman (Post, 1986, pp. 46ff.; Hay and Gray, 1974, p. 140; Freeman, 1984, pp. 43ff.). This version of the model views performance as improved social or public welfare and argues that this is what determines the level of a corporation's legitimacy. These theorists contend that responding to the interests, demands, or expectations of the public is the most effective way to improve the public welfare. This is so because, unlike the classical and stakeholder theorists who largely condone ignoring the social or moral interests or views of the public, the present theory proposes that executives specifically consider these factors in their corporate decision making.

Parenthetically, it should be noted that the version of this theory that directly endorses promoting the public welfare does not principally rely upon this version of the performance argument. Such an appeal would be either circular or redundant. At best, it would convert a discussion of justification into one of motivation (i.e., the best way to secure the general welfare is to specifically strive to attain it in one's corporate decision making).

One author who also seems to advance a species of the performance argument is Wallich. As we saw in chapter 9, a basic aim of his position is to suggest shareholders have good reason to pressure executives to be more active morally and socially, even when this activity is otherwise economically costly to the firm, at least in the short run. Opposing Manne and other classical theorists who argue that shareholders look with disfavor upon any social policy that will prove to be financially costly to the corporation—particularly in the long run—Wallich contends that many shareholders in recent decades have more than just a financial interest in single firms; they have diversified social and economic interests to match their diversified investments (Wallich, 1972, pp. 52ff.). This means that they will view with disfavor the activities of firms that jeopardize the moral, social, or economic performance of the other firms whose stock they own. As

Wallich sees it, corporate executives are expected by these investors to respond to these wider interests in their corporate decision making and thus to do nothing that would harm the needs or interests of virtually the entire free enterprise system. To the extent that diversified investors are the key public group used to determine social demand or expectation, or to the extent that their interests coincide with those of the public, his view can then be seen as a variant of either the stakeholder or the social demandingness theory. Because he believes that managers are expected to respond in a manner that often ultimately coincides with the expressed and diversified interests of the public, his argument can be viewed as urging the social demandingness position—especially when we note that those diversified interests of which he speaks concern the common good. But it can also be seen as an argument for the stakeholder theory when it is realized that it involves explicit reference to only a particular type of stakeholder group.

An important aspect of the consequentialist side of the social demandingness theory is the belief that managers must consider both the direct and indirect effects likely to result from their corporate conduct. They reject the thesis of stakeholder theorists that because managers cannot be expected to know the likely indirect effects of their actions, they should not be held accountable for them. Social demandingness theorists appeal to the traditional notion of causality under law, which holds that agents are accountable for the results of their actions, even if the conduct of other agents contributes in some way to the occurrence of these results. Thus, contributory causation is a ground of responsibility. Many also further agree with more activist theorists such as Solomon and Hanson that lack of the relevant expertise in predicting indirect effects is not, by itself, a sufficiently compelling excusing condition. They argue that acquiring such expertise may itself be one of the social or moral responsibilities of corporate executives (Solomon and Hanson, 1983, p 247).

Further, it is contended that predicting the likely indirect effects of certain corporate actions is not always a difficult task. Thus, for example, various studies and reports have shown that higher levels of divorce, family tension, alcoholism, and suicide can be expected to occur in economically depressed communities where large numbers of workers lose their jobs through plant closings. Social demandingness theorists hold corporate executives partly responsible for these negative effects, even though they would not have occurred were it not for the actions and choices of the former workers of these plants.

PROCEDURAL ARGUMENTS

The most distinctive argument for the social demandingness theory is the argument from consent—the social contract argument. Unlike consequentialist thinkers, who base the legitimacy of the corporation directly upon its performance, social contract theorists ground corporate legitimacy upon the permission of the public. Performance plays a role in this theory, of course, for the conduct of firms must be within the guidelines set by the public's consent. But, as Fasching and other social contract theorists point out, it is ultimately this consent that gives the corporation permission to operate and to continue functioning (Fasching, 1981, p. 64).

Thus, social contract theorists often focus upon the three characteristics of a corporation that were discussed in chapter 1—entity status, limited liability, and perpetual duration or continuous self-renewal—and seek to show the role that social permission plays in each of these features.

Anshen, for example, tells us that legitimacy is a social concept; it is conferred upon institutions through the consent of individuals in society (Anshen, 1980, p. 6). He identifies this consent with the social will, which he says is determined by such factors as the presence of laws and regulations, the nature and direction of judicial decisions, and other less formal means of expression, such as opinion polls and purchasing trends (Anshen, 1980, pp. 7ff.). As he sees it, the social will is no longer satisfied with evaluating firms solely from the perspective of economic performance. It demands from corporations the provision of social benefits, the carrying of social or moral burdens, and the internalizing of social costs. He maintains that if firms ignore the social demands placed upon them by the public, the public may relinquish their consent and look to other institutions to satisfy their needs.

Nader and Green tell us that in the very act of incorporation, corporations solicit the permission of the public (through their representatives in government) to exist and function as distinct legal entities (Nader and Green, 1976, pp. 63ff.). As a consequence, these authors believe that firms are responsible to protect the interests of those whose permission they have sought.

Chaudhuri agrees with Nader and Green. He bases his view upon an analysis of the notion of property. This analysis reveals that ownership is a three-term relation between a right holder, an obligation holder, and an act of consent between them that spells out the terms of the ownership (Chaudhuri, 1971, p. 274). For Chaudhuri, since corporate property is a governmentally created rational construct existing between shareholders and corporate managers on the one hand, and the general public on the other, corporations must get the permission of the governed in order to exist as distinct entities in a democratic society. They thus function as public or quasi-public agencies that have instrumental (not intrinsic) rights to operate within the jural relations given through this general social permission (Chaudhuri, 1971, p. 280). Like Nader and Green, and Anshen, then, Chaudhuri contends that his theory of corporate property implies that corporate executives are ultimately responsible to the public to meet its general demands and respond to its overall interests.

Although he is cognizant of the role that the social contract plays in legitimizing the other two features of the corporation, Fasching provides an account that focuses upon the second characteristic of a corporation—its limited liability. Corporations for him are social inventions created to serve the public through the pursuit of private gain (Fasching, 1981, p. 64). To encourage the pursuit of wealth, society confers upon corporations certain special features, like that of limited liability for corporate debts and torts. The corporate characteristic that disperses financial liability is thus a social and legal privilege; it is not an inherent right that accompanies ownership. Fasching further contends that this feature is leading some managers to seek to lessen or disperse some of their social or moral liability as well. This he thinks is an unjustified extension of the privilege. The attempt to shirk off these liabilities directly conflicts with the interests of those who permit corporate owners and executives to restrict some of the firm's other liabilities in the first place (Fasching, 1981, p. 67).

Hoffman and Fisher accept Fasching's position on the origin of this special privilege. They develop an argument that is somewhat different from Fasching's position, even though it is still based upon the feature of restricted corporate liability. They tell us that corporations are common, not private, property (Hoffman and Fisher, 1984, p. 144). Private property is something about or over which an individual or group of individuals has a right to exclude others from in its use or benefit and other individuals are also excluded from being assessed liability, should the property become the object of legal suit or challenge (Hoffman and Fisher, 1984, p. 146). Common property, on the other hand, is property for which the second feature is absent. The public may at times be expected to compensate or rescue holders of common property from their debts (as in the case of the Lockheed and Chrysler corporations and more recently many savings and loan institutions) or their torts or potential torts (as in the cases of the Environmental Protection Agency Superfund and the catastrophic insurance offered by the United States government to firms in the nuclear industry). Hoffman and Fisher's argument not only implies that corporations are responsible to the public (because the public is sometimes called upon to satisfy debts and other legal obligations); it implies as well that because members of society have a generalized ownership relation to corporate assets, they also have a responsibility to monitor the conduct of the stewards of these assets for they may be held liable for the latters' poor decisions. There are thus reciprocal, if somewhat distinct, duties here.

Finally, we come to the feature of self-renewal or virtual perpetual existence. Fasching, for one, points out that this characteristic is dependent upon the activity of some governmental body; if the governmental body disappears or withdraws its support, a corporation registered through this body disappears as well (Fasching, 1981, pp. 64ff.). It would reappear only by being accepted by and registered within some other governmental body, one that would then permit it to be incorporated. In this view, corporations are dependent institutions; they cease to exist whenever their authorizing bodies cease to exist. This is not to say that they go in and out of existence with every shift in government, or that they will likely not outlast the lives of their current stockholders or workers. Such continuous self-renewal is not, however, an indication of institutional independence. It is rather an indication that a particular society or country believes that its interests are best served by permitting firms to become so organized. But what society has bequeathed to corporations, it can also take away. This is especially so if the welfare of society is ignored by executives in their corporate decision making.

These three features of the corporation could thus not exist without the consent of the public. For executives to ignore the public's wishes and interests in their corporate decision making is for them to undermine this permission and jeopardize the existence of the very institutions for whom they are acting.

There is another version of the social contract argument that stipulates that corporate executives should respond to the ideal interests of members of society rather than to their expressed interests. It requires consideration of these interests, even if society does not distinctly expect or demand this from corporations. Certain comments made by Anshen suggests that he may accept this view of the social contract (Anshen, 1980, pp. 45ff.), though we can see that it is more appropriate to classify this view as an argument for the social activist position rather than for the present theory.

OTHER ARGUMENTS

Three other arguments for the social demandingness theory should be mentioned here. The first is the argument from fairness, which has two versions. The first emphasizes the fairness of expecting firms to respond to the demands of the public because they have so much power in society. Davis, for example, tells us that corporate responsibility arises from this power (Davis, 1975, p. 20). Davis and Blomstrom formulate this idea into a principle they call the iron law of responsibility. Power and responsibility go hand in hand. Because business decisions have widespread social consequences, corporate executives must then consider the interests of those affected by their decisions (Davis and Blomstrom, 1975, p. 50). These authors also note an egoistic or reverse-impact side to this principle. It tells executives that those who do not use their power in a manner considered responsible by society will tend to lose it.

This first version of the argument can also be used to defend the position of social activism, but the second is usually restricted to the social demandingness theory alone. In advancing the latter version, Donaldson maintains that corporations should seek to solve social problems because they have often played a significant role in causing them in the first place (Donaldson, 1982, pp. 47ff.). To ignore the negative social impact of their actions is for corporations to become free riders. It is for them to seek to gain advantages for themselves at the expense of other members or institutions in society, advantages they would not will or wish all to get.

Another argument that is sometimes advanced for the social demandingness theory is the rights argument. It is contended that since members of the public have certain rights that must be respected, executives are required to consider these rights in their corporate decision making. Usually this argument is raised by social activist theorists, but there is a species of it that can be advanced here.

We find it put forth by thinkers who have some sympathy for libertarianism. They argue that freedom of choice and action is a basic right of persons in this society. To exercise this right people must otherwise be free to think and act as they choose. To respect this right means that individuals will in general avoid interfering with others, even when this interference is thought to be for the others' good. Social institutions, like corporations, are thus generally expected to avoid unduly interfering with the rights, lives, and opinions of other people— especially third parties. They are required to avoid imposing their views upon other people for they thereby seek to interfere with the latters' freedom of thought. They are encouraged to monitor the freely developed views and interests of the public and, other things being equal, respect the actual choices and conduct that emerge from this freedom. Beyond this, however, they are not required to provide assistance to the public in an effort to aid the public in achieving its positive goals.

Finally, there is an argument akin to the respect for persons defense of legitimation. Some theorists believe that the principle of respect for persons simply demands that one respect the independence of others; it does not require that one seek to promote their general welfare. Pollock, for example, maintains that the principle requires that we not use people, or have them act, in ways in which they would not choose for themselves (Pollock, 1981, pp. 13ff.). If the respect for persons model is interpreted in this more minimalist way, it can be seen to demand that one should avoid being paternalistic with others and it requires that one give serious consideration to their interest or need to be left alone. Finally, it demands that corporations not interfere with, or otherwise bias, the process of forming social or moral expectations. Because they show their respect for people by obeying this principle, the principle commits them to following the general guidelines of one version of the social demandingness theory, even though its basis is unlike that typically associated with the position as it is usually advocated.

It should be noted, however, that there are forms of the last two arguments that have also been raised in behalf of the classical theory. This is particularly so either when the basic rights of people are viewed as wholly negative in nature, or when both respect for persons is equated with not interfering with their choices and when property rights are viewed as overriding. There are also versions of these arguments raised in behalf of the social activist position. This is especially true when rights are viewed as being both positive and negative in nature or when respect for persons is equated with respecting their capacity for rational or ideal self-determination. Once again, the lines of demarcation between these theories are not perfectly distinct or evident.

THE ASSUMPTIONS OF THE THEORY

So what are some of the principal assumptions of this theory? We can see from the previous arguments and the table schematically provided in Figure 11.1

Figure 11.1
Social Demandingness Theory (Principle Assumptions)

Relations of Accountability	Models of the Corporation	Strategies of Legitimization
1. Promise-Keeping or Consent**	1. Private Property	1. Power*
2. Fiduciary*	2. Private Contract	2. Conformity to Law*
3. Representational*	3. Enterprise*	3. Conformity to Current Standards**
4. Impact**	4. Social Contract**	4. Procedural**
5. Reverse-Impact*	5. Public Power**	5. Formal**
6. Teamwork or Collegial*	6. Machine or Tool*	6. Performance**
7. Ownership or Possession*	7. Organic**	7. Rights*
8. Regulation*	8. Mental or Moral Agent*	8. Respect for Persons*
		[9. Relations of Accountability]

 * can or does play some direct role in defining or defending the theory

** plays a significant role in defining or defending the theory

that three strategies of legitimation play a primary role in the defense of the position; they are conformity to current standards and the appeal to procedural (consent) and performance criteria. Other strategies apply, of course, but these are the ones most commonly or forcefully associated with the position. The position appears to be a straightforward illustration of the conformity to current standards strategy, but one cannot underestimate the importance of contractarian and consequentialist elements here. As for the other strategies, however, the rights and respect for persons strategies are typically more appropriate for the other theories, although somewhat unorthodox versions of the theory have rested upon versions of these strategies. So the other strategies have some application to it, at least when combined with certain other assumptions.

As with the classical and stakeholder positions, all eight models of accountability apply in some way, though not all play an equally important role in the theory. The theory makes obvious appeal to the promise-keeping model in its assertion of the social contract. And when the demand to abide by the constraints of specific, explicit agreements is seen as grounded partly upon society's insistence that promises be kept, we have such a close connection between the demands of the theory and the present accountability relation that the connection borders on being question begging.

The impact model plays a vital role in the theory. We see this in the "iron law of responsibility" and the concern that corporations are responsible to minimize or eliminate the negative effects of their conduct. And the insistence that both the likely direct and indirect effects of corporate action be considered by management clearly expands the domain of the impact model in determining corporate responsibilities and duties. Finally, the reparation facet of relieving the distress caused by previous corporate decisions makes explicit appeal to the impact model.

The fiduciary model is assumed to the extent that society expects executives to act as effective stewards of the company's assets. But it is not assumed that executives or corporations are agents or fiduciaries of the public in some direct or special way; and it is not assumed that they thus have unique responsibilities toward the public because of this. They are at best only quasi agents because they are the recipients of the social promise. Some social demandingness theorists believe, however, that there is one area of corporate activity in which executives are stewards. They are stewards of the information discovered in and by the corporation because how they convey this information to the public can directly affect the fundamental standard of decision making advocated by the theory, namely, public opinion and expectation. The integrity of this standard is too important and basic for the theory for it to rest simply upon the current demands (or metademands) or expectations of society.

The representational model is much like the fiduciary one. Because in part managers can theoretically be replaced by the shareholders, society demands that executives respect the latters' interests or wishes. In this case, though, it is not the representative relation that is the dominant feature; it is social demand. Beyond this, the model applies by extension only. These theorists do not usually contend that members of society have directly or specifically selected the managers of firms to protect their interests. Some seem to believe, however, that when a governmental body gives a corporation permission to incorporate, this can be likened to a voting process of sorts. But this metaphor does not imply that members of the public meet routinely to ratify or remove the vote of confidence they have given to the managers of a corporation. The decisions of management come under the direct scrutiny of certain groups of people who make up the public, of course. Thus, for example, consumers, lenders, and many workers directly review and confirm or disconfirm (vote for or against) particular decisions made by management. But this way of looking at legitimation leads us back to the promise-keeping model, and it is typically associated with the stakeholder theory. Members of the public functioning in nonstakeholder capacities typically do not get a chance to vote directly for or against a certain corporation or its social policies, except perhaps for those times when they explicitly choose to avoid being one of the corporation's consumers or when they occasionally vote for a bill that directly affects a corporation or industry. The vote that the public exercises in selecting its government leaders could perhaps be viewed as a kind of indirect ratification procedure for the corporations for the latter are monitored and regulated by these leaders, but this indirect procedure is not the kind of direct selecting process characteristically urged within the representative or functionary model. Finally, it should be pointed out that if this model were a dominant assumption of the theory, members of society might even come to believe that it would be justified in having nearly every facet of corporate decision making come under this indirect form of public review. As it now stands, however, such regulation is characteristically restricted to those areas of corporate decision making that either have the potential for a significant impact upon society or relate to its making of legally binding contracts. And social demandingness theorists typically do not urge that this should change.

The teamwork model applies to those social demandingness theorists who defend their view on the basis of the impact that corporate social or moral activity has upon the performance of the overall social system. But again, the model of interpersonal relationship primarily assumed here is the impact model. This is in large part because of the difficulty mentioned earlier of conceiving of society in general as a team (or even a clan) pursuing a clearly delineated set of common goals. Like the representative or functionary model, its application to the theory is primarily indirect (or merely metaphorical) in nature.

Appeal to the possession or ownership model requires one to assume that members of society have first claim to the ownership of a country's natural resources, or at least to the disposition to permit corporations to exist and function under a condition of limited liability. Those social demandingness theorists who appeal to the social contract argument clearly believe that the permission that society gives to a business to function as a corporation is one that is within its jurisdiction to give. Members of society can then be said to initially possess the prerogatives behind this disposition. And, in the case of limiting the financial liability of corporations, members of society or their representatives are viewed as possessing the resources that would be used to insure this limitation, should a corporation be unable to compensate those who bring a debt or tort action against it. Even for those theorists who advance the performance argument and are concerned with the impact corporate decisions have upon society, there is the belief that members of society possess, or otherwise have jurisdiction over, the resources jeopardized by a poor corporate decision. And it is clearly endorsed in the common property argument of Hoffman and Fisher. Thus, when they tell us that corporations are semipublic entities functioning in the social domain, we can see that the ownership model plays some role in the defense of the theory, whether this defense is formulated in consequentialist or deontological terms.

The reverse-impact model is also given some place in the present theory. It plays an anthropomorphic role in the contractarian suggestion that corporate gratitude should be shown to the general public for its permission to incorporate. And it plays a significant role in the speculation of what could happen if society would withhold its consent from corporations or otherwise block the pursuit of some of their goals. We see it also expressed in the "iron law of responsibility" and in the argument from concern for increased government regulation and lessened corporate autonomy. But while it does play a role in these arguments, with the possible exception of concern for gratitude, the reverse-impact model does not typically function as a primary consideration in the theory. To be concerned with what others can do to the corporation at a particular moment is to be largely concerned with protecting corporate self-interest. But, as we have said, the focus of the theory is upon overall social or moral concern or well-being—particularly when this conflicts with corporate self-interest. Thus, the reverse-impact model has only a limited application to the theory.

Finally, the regulation model has a small part to play in the theory unless one views society's demands as formalized in a more or less explicit social or moral code for executives. Otherwise their following the laws of the land or certain professional codes are seen as duties stemming from both the unique origin and legal status of the corporation as well as from the demands of society.

MODELS OF THE CORPORATION

We come now to the assumptions involved in the eight models of the corporation. We can see from what has been said thus far that social demandingness theorists do not in general view the corporation solely or primarily as a piece of private property. Most of these theorists are anxious to point out the common or public aspects of corporate existence rather than its private character. Nor do they view it principally as a consequence of private agreement for it would be difficult to defend the social consent argument on this basis (though they do realize that private disagreement or conflict often plays a role in corporate life).

In addition to the social contract model, these theorists characteristically assume the public power, organic, and tool models of the corporation. The public power model is assumed primarily by those social demandingness thinkers who believe that corporations are powerful centers of choice and action that possess their own cultures. They are thus required to use the considerable power that they have to rectify or alleviate the negative effects of their past actions and to promote social welfare. This view is typically found in the work of those thinkers who endorse the impact model of accountability relations while advancing the performance argument for the social demandingness theory. We see it also endorsed in the "iron law of responsibility."

The organic model is assumed by those who take a systems view of society and see it also as an organism. They believe that corporate conduct must be judged in part by its contribution to the goals of this broader organism. This model holds that since the part depends upon the whole for its survival, health, and prosperity, it must respond to the latter's goals. It leads us to the social demandingness theory when, in addition, it is held both that the prosperity of the group (i.e., society) is typically determined by the explicit demands or expectations of its members and that society does in fact make unique social or moral demands upon firms or have distinct expectations for them beyond their responding to their stakeholders. In this network of concepts, the organic model of the corporation can play an important role in the theory.

The tool model also plays some role in the work of social contract theorists. Like Fasching, many assume that the corporation is largely a socially created instrument or tool to serve the purposes of the public. But social demandingness theorists characteristically avoid the issue most often associated with the tool metaphor, namely, whether or not corporations are to be treated as distinct moral agents that directly bear certain unique responsibilities not reducible to the responsibilities of their members (see chapter 15), and they typically reject the mechanistic features of the tool model wherein efficiency and administrative impartiality are considered the primary or sole values of the corporation.

The enterprise model is not entirely inapplicable to the social demandingness theory. It suggests that the corporation is a complex unity of the purposes of its members. This model frequently emphasizes the private or personal career goals of corporate members, however, such as gaining financial security or advancement, peer or superior respect, social status, occupational satisfaction and fulfillment, and the like. But if the model is extended to view society itself as an enterprise whose members have their own personal and career goals that deserve consideration and respect by corporate managers, we have a unique application of the enterprise model to the theory. A more straightforward application occurs when the moral goals of the members of the corporation are viewed as their dominant personal goals and when it is assumed that benevolence, pursuit of social welfare, and respect for the opinions of the public are taken to be cardinal virtues by the members. This generates a somewhat different version of the theory—one where the enterprise metaphor plays a key, if somewhat unorthodox, role.

The mental agent side of the moral agent model does play a role in the theory. Social demandingness theorists do at times view corporations as psychic prisons—at least to the extent that such organizations are often seen as directed by "bounded rationality" and inflexible or outdated patterns or strategies of decision making. The theory itself is meant to be quite flexible in structure and current in its design—the present (and continually changing) demands or expectations of society make up its dominant standard. Thus, these theorists are more anxious to overcome or minimize these inflexible features than they are to dwell upon them as important and persistent characteristics of corporate life.

The mental agent model applies in another way. Since corporations are viewed as centers of information, they have a special and distinctive obligation to follow in the gaining and disseminating of information—one that is not itself based upon social expectation. They must not unduly interfere with the formation of public opinion and attitudes about corporations for such interference would impair or jeopardize the basic criterion upon which the theory rests.

Finally, the moral person side of the moral agent model could at best apply to this theory only by extension. When the model is interpreted as asserting that corporations are literally full-fledged moral persons, it is not usually associated with the presentation or defense of this position. The theory does not typically treat the corporation as a self-sustaining and intrinsically valuable component of our moral universe. As we have seen, it holds instead that corporations are social creations; they are manufactured entities that have merely instrumental value.

One version of the moral agent model does not treat corporations as moral persons, however. Like the position of Goodpaster, it urges that responsibility claims apply to corporations as if they were moral persons. Since this version makes no specific claim about the intrinsic value of the corporation, it is possible for an advocate of this version to endorse the social demandingness theory. I am familiar with no social demandingness theorist who presently holds this view, however.

REFERENCES

Ackerman, Robert, and Raymond Bauer. 1975. *Corporate Social Responsiveness: The Modern Dilemma*. Reston, Va.: Reston Publishing Company.

Anshen, Melvin. 1980. *Corporate Strategies for Social Performance*. New York: Macmillan Publishing Company.

Atkinson, Christine, and Adrian Atkinson. 1980. "Corporate Social Responsibility: A Philosophical Appraisal." *Journal of Enterprise Management*, vol. 2, pp. 131–35.

Boarman, Patrick M. 1982. "Business Ethics." *Vital Speeches*, June 15, pp. 532–35.

Bradshaw, Thorton F. 1974. "Corporate Social Reform: An Executive's Viewpoint." In *The Unstable Ground: Corporate Social Policy in a Dynamic Society*, edited by S. Prakash Sethi, pp. 24–31. Los Angeles: Melville Publishing Company.

Buchanan, James M. 1975. *The Limits of Liberty*. Chicago: University of Chicago Press.

Chaudhuri, Joyotpaul. 1971. "Toward a Democratic Theory of Property and the Modern Corporation." *Ethics*, vol. 81, July, pp. 271–86.

Davis, Keith. 1973. "The Case For and Against Business Assumption of Social Responsibilities." *Academy of Management Journal*, vol. 16, no. 2, pp. 312–22.

———. 1975. "Five Propositions for Social Responsibility." *Business Horizons*, June, pp. 19–24.

Davis, Keith, and Robert L. Blomstrom. 1975. *Business and Society: Environment and Responsibility*. New York: McGraw-Hill.

Donaldson, Thomas. 1982. *Corporations and Morality*. Englewood Cliffs, N.J.: Prentice-Hall.

Drucker, Peter. 1981. "What Is Business Ethics?" *Across the Board*, October, pp. 22–32.

Fasching, Darrel J. 1981. "A Case for Corporate and Management Ethics." *California Management Review*, Summer, pp. 62–76.

Finlay, J. R. 1977. "Rethinking the Corporate Social Predicament." *Business Quarterly*, Summer, pp 59–69.

Freeman, Edward. 1984. *Strategic Management: A Stakeholder Approach*. Marshfield, Mass.: Pitman Publishing.

Hay, Robert, and Ed Gray. 1974. "Social Responsibilities of Business Managers." *Academy of Management Journal*, March, pp. 135–45.

Hoffman, W. Michael, and James V. Fisher. 1984. "Corporate Responsibility: Property and Liability." In *Business Ethics: Readings and Cases in Corporate Morality*, edited by W. Michael Hoffman and Jennifer Mills Moore, pp. 142–49. New York: McGraw-Hill.

Jacobs, Leslie, W. 1973. "Business Ethics and Law: Obligations of a Corporate Executive." *The Business Lawyer*, July, pp. 1063–88.

Lodge, George Cabot. 1970. "Top Priority: Renovating Our Ideology." *Harvard Business Review*, September–October, pp. 43–55.

Loevinger, Lee. 1973. "Social Responsibility in a Democratic Society." *Vital Speeches of the Day*, April 15, pp. 388–96.

Nader, Ralph, and Mark Green. 1976. *Taming the Giant Corporation*. New York: W. W. Norton Company.

Pollock, Lansing. 1981. *The Freedom Principle*. Buffalo, N.Y.: Prometheus Books.

Post, James E. 1986. "Perfecting Capitalism" In *Corporations and the Common Good*, edited by Robert B. Dickie and Leroy S. Rounder, pp. 46–55. South Bend, Ind.: Notre Dame University Press.

Richman, Barry. 1977. "New Paths to Corporate Social Responsibility." *Managing Corporate Social Responsibility*, edited by Archie B. Carroll, pp. 52–68. Boston: Little, Brown and Company.

Sawyer, George C. 1979. *Business and Society: Managing Corporate Social Impact*. Boston: Houghton Mifflin Company.

Sethi, S. Prakash. 1977. "Dimensions of Corporate Social Performance: An Analytical Framework." In *Managing Corporate Social Responsibility*, edited by Archie B. Carroll, pp. 69–75. Boston: Little, Brown and Company.

Shocker, Allan D., and S. Prakash Sethi. 1973. "An Approach to Incorporating Societal Preference in Developing Corporate Action Strategies." *California Management Review*, Summer, pp. 97–105.

Solomon, Robert C., and Kristine R. Hanson. 1983. *Above the Bottom Line: An Introduction to Business Ethics*. New York: Harcourt, Brace, Jovanovich.

Votaw, Dow, and S. Prakash Sethi. 1973. *The Corporate Dilemma*. Englewood Cliffs, N.J.: Prentice-Hall.

Wallich, Henry C. (with Henry Manne). 1972. *The Modern Corporation and Social Responsibility*. Washington, D.C.: The American Enterprise Institute.

Zenisek, Thomas. 1979. "Corporate Social Responsibility: A Conceptualization Based on Organizational Literature." *Academy of Management Review*, vol. 4., pp. 359–68.

12

THE SOCIAL ACTIVIST THEORY

THE DEFINITION OF SOCIAL ACTIVISM: THE FIRST THESIS

In this chapter we shall complete our discussion of the four theories of corporate responsibility by considering the social activist theory. There are two important points to this position. The first is that there exists a universal standard for determining responsible corporate conduct that is independent of the interests of stockholders and the claims of stakeholders. Although the standard demands concern for the welfare of the public, it is concern for their welfare as an expression of their ideal or rational interests rather than merely their present or expressed interests that is of importance. The second thesis is that this standard often demands greater social or moral activism from corporate leaders than has been provided by many of them in the past or is currently demanded of them by the other theories of corporate responsibility. Thus the theory can also be referred to as moral activism, but we shall continue to refer to it here as the social activist position.

Returning to the first thesis, social activist theorists believe that the standard of responsible corporate conduct is independent of the current expectations, demands and, often even the current interests of the various groups of individuals served or affected by management decision making. They refer to this standard then as universal or independent in nature. As Wilkins puts it, it is an absolute standard (Wilkins, 1975, p. 62) for it is not relative to the actual demands or expectations of society at any one time. Purchell tells us that the standard is not a personal or private one; it is not subjective or context bound (Purchell, 1975, p. 43). Most social activist theorists also believe it is comprehensive and all encompassing; it applies to all decisions and actions. Hence, Purchell contends that it deals with both economic and noneconomic matters (Purchell, 1975, p. 44).

The standard that typically requires greater levels of corporate activism may be said to have an ethical, religious, or metaphysical basis. Goldman and Rawls, for example, view the basis as primarily ethical in nature (Goldman, 1980, pp. 261ff.; Rawls, 1971, pp. 7ff.). Purchell views it in religious or supernatural terms since for him it is ultimately connected with or grounded upon God's will and reason. Finally, Gewirth treats it as ultimately resting upon certain metaphysical features of human nature (Gewirth, 1979, pp. 142ff.). Some social activists treat these accounts as overlapping, while others view them as more distinct or exclusive in nature. In this chapter we shall rely principally upon the version of the theory that grounds the standard upon an ethical foundation. It is to be understood, however, that this account can also apply to the other versions. In any case, the important point for social activist theorists is that the standard be independent of what people presently think about it. And, although it is usually thought to capture what is the public's real welfare, it is also independent of what members of the public actually think is, or is in, their welfare.

Of the two theses that make up this theory, the first claim just considered is not particularly helpful in distinguishing this position from the other theories of corporate responsibility, however. This is so because it is also possible to combine this thesis with the classical or stakeholder accounts. This happens whenever these latter theories are said to be defended by appeal to an independent normative or ethical standard. Thus, as we have seen, a classical theorist such as Birdzell contends that corporate decision making is responsible and justified when (and to the extent that) it promotes certain values. Birdzell himself mentions the values of commitment, free exchange, distributive (meritocratic) justice, frugality, and profit (Birdzell, 1975, pp. 79ff.). In addition, recent libertarian thinkers, such as Novak and Hayek, argue that the corporate form of business enterprise, structured as it is to pursue profit or enhance shareholder wealth, is an ethically justified aspect of our overall social system. And even certain stakeholder theorists have maintained that their theory has an independent moral or ethical warrant.

This first thesis is, however, generally helpful in distinguishing this theory from the social demandingness position. This is so, even though it must be admitted that there is at least one way to combine this thesis with the latter view. This can be done only by arguing for a metaprinciple that suggests that it is always ethically justified for corporate executives to respond to the expressed desires or interests of members of the public. Theorists who oppose paternalism and who stress the importance of having individual autonomy to form and act upon personal opinions and values are generally sympathetic to this view. But few social activist theorists actually contend this. They do not accept this metaprinciple as supervenient; they typically believe that even the expressed opinions or interests of the public may be in error. As they see it, society can be too lenient toward firms at one time and possibly even too demanding of them at another. In either case, the standard proposed by activist theorists is seen by them as helping to correct the public's attitudes or views because it expresses criteria that are said to have an independent normative foundation. It can thus be said to provide a stable set of values from which to judge current social demands and opinions.

THE SECOND THESIS

Of more help in distinguishing this theory from the other views of corporate responsibility is the second thesis. It consists of the assertion that the standard we have just been discussing often requires a greater commitment to social or moral activism on the part of corporations than has been provided in the past or is currently demanded of them by the other theories. This greater commitment to social or moral activism may be a matter of kind (when, for example, it is advocated by some activist theorists that major changes are required in the slaughtering and meatpacking industries), or it may be a matter of degree (when it is urged by these theorists that executives should notably increase their corporate charitable donations). In any case, the activist standard requires that executives be social and moral leaders in the corporate community rather than the moral followers they would be if they followed the lead of the other theories.

Because it demands an anticipated response to potential social problems, Sethi, and Ackerman and Bauer refer to this theory as the social responsiveness model (Sethi, 1977, p. 73; Ackerman and Bauer, 1976, p. 6). Because it focuses more upon the actual conduct of executives in the social arena than it does upon merely what they plan to do, Carroll calls it the social performance model (Carroll, 1981, pp. 3ff.).

Whatever it is called, it must be admitted that activist theorists are not entirely in agreement on the precise nature of the independent standard used to judge corporate conduct. There are various ways in which they express it. Some cast it more in consequentialist terms; others view it more deontologically; still others view it dispositionally in terms of corporate virtues. Thus, for example, traditional utilitarians tell us that executives are required to promote the common good. Singer formulates the standard in terms of relieving avoidable pain or suffering (Singer, 1982, p. 360). Camenish tells us that corporate executives are responsible to contribute to human flourishing generally (Camenish, 1981, p. 64). And Williams contends that the present standard of corporate responsibility requires executives to optimize the welfare of everyone, while they also promote harmonious relationships in society (Williams, 1982, pp. 15ff.).

Theorists who view the standard in more deontological terms include Purchell, who tells us that responsible management conduct preserves and advances human dignity and freedom generally (Purchell, 1978, p. 41). Goldman contends that corporate decision making is irresponsible when it involves a severe infringement on the rights of individuals (Goldman, 1980, p. 286). Rawls formulates an egalitarian standard. He tells us that just institutions are those that have offices and positions open to all. They are justified in considering or treating people differently only when this contributes to the welfare of the least advantaged members of society (Rawls, 1971, pp. 60ff.). Trowbridge formulates the standard of responsible corporate conduct in terms of the concept of impartial review. He says that executives are responsible to perform actions that can be justified before an impartial board of inquiry whose members are technically competent in the field in question (Trowbridge, 1975, p. 18).

And as we would expect, there are theorists who seek to combine the consequentialist and nonconsequentialist approaches in various ways. Thus, for example, the activist aspect of Fasching's theory makes appeal to a standard formulated in terms of consent and abiding by one's promises as well as the standard of alleviating distress (Fasching, 1981, p. 62). In addition, he also makes appeal to the principle that corporate executives should seek justice in their cost-benefit allocations (Fasching, 1981, p. 69).

More recently, some theorists have followed the lead of MacIntyre, Wallace, and Peters and Waterman. They have spoken of the virtues involved in personal and organizational life, such as excellence, conscientiousness, and integrity (MacIntyre, 1984, pp. 181ff.; Wallace, 1978, pp. 39ff.; Peters and Waterman, 1982, pp. 8ff.). In fact, the approach of the present work may be seen as an attempt to unpack the concept of corporate conscientiousness, but because I believe that this approach ultimately must make appeal to one or other of the two earlier positions, I shall focus my attention upon these theories in the rest of the chapter.

ACTIVIST PROPOSALS

This brings us to the question of what specific suggestions on corporate conduct have emerged from within the social activist theory. What types of decision making are demanded by the activist standard, however it is finally conceived?

Activist theorists have offered various proposals, many of which are similar to those made by the other theorists of corporate responsibility. But when this is true, the proposals are usually viewed as resting upon the normative foundation that is somewhat different from that assumed by the other theories. And they are typically urged as a particular facet of a broad array of activist proposals rather than being meant to stand alone or to be part of a small group of suggestions aimed at benefiting principally one group or constituency served or influenced by the corporation.

We begin with the suggestions of Murphy. He tells us that firms are responsible to do these things: to disclose voluntarily the contents of their products, so that consumers may know those ingredients or components that can adversely affect their health or contaminate the environment; to establish a department of consumer affairs in their organizations; and, to examine actively the ethical impact of their actions. They are to disclose the results of their social activism in social performance reports available to shareholders and the general public. Finally, they are to restructure the corporate board so that independent members sit on its key committees (such as, the Nominating, Compensation, and Audit and Review Committees) and give adequate staff and funding to these committees, so that they can carry out their trustee and watchdogging functions effectively and fairly (Murphy, 1978, pp. 19ff.).

Carroll and Blumenthal contend that corporations are responsible for developing and implementing a code of conduct in their organizations. They should be willing to use ethical considerations in their criteria for performance and promotion (Carroll, 1978, p. 9; Blumenthal, 1976b, pp. 14ff.). Carroll tells us that superiors should set realistic economic performance goals for their subordinates. This might reduce the pressure and temptation for subordinates to reach their goals by using illegal or otherwise questionable means (Carroll, 1981, p. 8). Blumenthal suggests that corporate executives should be willing to discuss openly and frankly social issues with their critics, rather than avoid them or respond defensively to their suggestions or complaints (Blumenthal, 1976a, p. 33).

Purchell, Raelin, and Steiner believe that corporations should hire specialists or professionals in social or ethical decision making to occupy various positions in their organizations. They should also nominate to the board of directors individuals who, by special training or otherwise, show that they are particularly sensitive to, or knowledgeable of, moral matters (Purchell, 1978, p. 43; Raelin, 1987, p. 173; Steiner, 1976, pp. 5ff.).

Jones and Sawyer contend that corporations should conduct social impact studies before important business decisions are made (Jones, 1980, p. 65; Sawyer, 1979, p. 389). Other theorists, like Bauer and Finn, and Abt, agree with another point mentioned by Murphy that executives should report their corporation's social performance (Bauer and Finn, 1972, pp. 2ff.; Abt, 1972, pp. 138ff.). They further imply that executives are responsible for studying and improving the various methods of social performance reporting and planning that have already been developed, so that more reliable instruments of corporate reporting and planning may be forthcoming.

Jones contends that corporations should be more active in lobbying government agencies to frame and execute laws with positive social impact and be more generous in their corporate donations (Jones, 1980, p. 64). Solomon and Hanson agree with this. They believe that giving corporate donations in support of the arts is an especially important area of corporate social activity (Solomon and Hanson, 1983, pp. 232ff.).

Many theorists have offered or reviewed suggestions for the structural or organizational changes that are thought to be needed if firms are to be more sensitive and responsive to social and moral concerns. In addition to suggestions about restructuring the board of directors, theorists have proposed that corporations should develop the proper offices to implement social responsibility planning. McAdam, for example, considers the advantages and disadvantages of three approaches to this question—the task force, the social responsibility officer, and the social responsibility committee (McAdam, 1973, pp. 14ff.). Ackerman tells us that social activist firms are those that have sought to bring concern for social responsibility down to the ranks of middle and lower-level managers (Ackerman, 1973, p. 95). Fasching and Purchell add that one way this can be done is to implement an ongoing program of management seminars on social and ethical issues (Fasching, 1981, pp. 71ff.; Purchell, 1980, p. 262).

Finally, Sturdivant and others suggest that this theory may require even more radical changes in the structure of corporations—some of which have been tried in other countries. He suggests that firms should move more vigorously in the direction of organizational democracy where nonmanagement workers have the opportunity to participate directly in management decision making (Sturdivant, 1981, p. 192).

Of course, these suggestions do not exhaust the list of proposals made by social activist theorists, but they do provide us with an idea of the kinds of programs or activities for which these thinkers believe executives are responsible. That some of these ideas may also be proposed by non-activist theorists does not necessarily jeopardize their activist character; as we have seen, this is established by the nature of their normative foundation and the holistic and comprehensive character of the entire body of proposals of which they typically form a part.

In conclusion, we see then that there are several factors that distinguish social activism from the other theories of corporate responsibility. It holds that executives are responsible for pursuing social or moral goals from voluntary motives, even when doing so compromises the firm's profit performance (at least in the short term). Corporations or their members are required to perform acts that benefit shareholders, stakeholders, and the general public, both in the primary areas of their business decision making (where the direct effects of their actions are more likely to be noticed) and in secondary and tertiary areas as well (where the indirect effects become more prominent). Last, in considering the interests and welfare of others, corporate executives are to respond to the formers' ideal or rational interests rather than merely their expressed or current interests.

ARGUMENTS FOR SOCIAL ACTIVISM: THE FIRST THESIS

In this section we shall consider some of the activist arguments raised principally against the social demandingness position. We shall be particularly concerned with those used to defend the first thesis of social activism. In the next three sections we shall examine the arguments that social activists advance in opposition to the other two theories of corporate responsibility. This will take us to a defense of the second thesis of the theory.

As we have seen, activists agree with social demandingness theorists that corporate executives must at least consider the interests of the general public in their business decision making and are to be held accountable for both the likely direct and indirect effects of their actions. Many of these theorists disagree with advocates of social demandingness, however, on the question of whether corporate executives are responsible for relieving distress or suffering that they did not cause. They also disagree on the nature of the standard that guides corporate conduct and the type of public interests to which they should respond. Why do activists typically believe that this standard is independent of the actual social demands or expectations that members of society have expressed toward corporations?

The answer to this question can be found in the work of many theorists who oppose relativism in ethics—especially that form that used to be referred to as cultural relativism and now is sometimes called conventional ethical relativism. The names of various moral philosophers come to mind here, including those of Kant, Mill, Moore, Ewing, Ross, and Rawls. Rather than review the particular arguments of each theorist, I prefer to present here a summary of the main strands of the argument, parts of which can also be found in the recent work of Wilkins, Williams, Purchell, and Almeder, among others (Wilkins, 1975, p. 62; Williams, 1982, pp 15ff.; Purchell, 1975, pp. 43ff.; Almeder, 1980, pp. 10ff.). The main contention of the argument is that the relativist standard proposed by social demandingness theorists is too unclear, vacillating, and biased (or circular) to be a reliable guide for determining the true responsibilities of corporate executives.

The standard is unclear whenever members of society fail to express an explicit or universal opinion, demand, or expectation about corporate responsibilities on a particular social or business issue. Activist theorists contend that this is precisely what happens with the controversial moral and social questions facing business today. Controversial issues are controversial in large part because no one view on how to solve them has clearly won out in society. For example, what are the demands or expectations expressed by society toward corporations in these areas: ending apartheid in South Africa, rebuilding our cities, hiring the chronically unemployed, or thoroughly restructuring the upper echelons of their organizations? Activist theorists tell us that no clear social consensus has thus far been reached on these issues. Thus, on the very social or moral questions for which executives most need direction in their decision making, the theory implies that none is forthcoming.

Activist theorists also remind us that the standard of the social demandingness theory is unclear in another respect; no consensus has been reached by these theorists on the nature of social consensus itself. That is, as we have seen in the last chapter, social demandingness theorists have come to no agreement on the question of how their normative standard is itself to be empirically determined. Is this by present law, majority opinion, media response, random sampling and opinion polls, the current mood of legislators or judges, or the views of some other select group in society? Activists believe then that the social demandingness theory is unable even to propose a sufficiently clear principle to enable us to distinguish the relevant social or moral demands from those that are irrelevant to business decision making.

Second, activist theorists argue that even if the standard of corporate conduct proposed by these theorists on particular issues were sufficiently clear and univocal in a single society, this standard may at times conflict with the demands expressed in other societies. But to try to rely on both standards for direction in corporate decision making would be to vacillate on a particular social or moral issue. Nor is it always possible to avoid this problem by acting one way in one society and another in a different society. For example, if executives of an American-based firm were to consider giving payments to foreign government officials to facilitate its business in another country—one that did not openly oppose the giving of such payments—they would still risk violating the demands of this country (as expressed now in law in the passage of the Foreign Corrupt Practices Act of 1977). And they may thereby risk other values endorsed cross-culturally, such as honesty, fair play, law abidance, and the like.

Third, some activists also argue that the standard of corporate conduct proposed by social demandingness theorists is otherwise circular or biased. To advance this view, these theorists rely on an argument raised by Knight and Galbraith, mentioned earlier in this book, which concerns the "dependence effect" of public opinion and expectation (Knight, 1923, pp. 603ff.; Galbraith, 1976, p. 136). The argument suggests that since the formation of public opinion about corporations and their social responsibilities has already in large part been influenced by the corporations themselves (in the form of advertising, press releases, annual reports, and other publications), the appeal to the standard of public demand or expectation cannot be viewed as an entirely disinterested one.

Another way to express this concern was also brought out in the discussion of the last chapter. We saw there that social demandingness theorists are committed to respecting and protecting the independence and initial impartiality of public opinion. If these attitudes and expectations are tampered with, the authority of the theory would be jeopardized. But this implies that the validity of at least one standard of corporate choice is not itself based upon whether members of the public currently expect or demand that corporate executives abide by it. Its independent authority suggests an inconsistency in the social demandingness theory itself.

Thus, activist theorists, such as Solomon and Hanson, believe that something other than appeal to the present or expressed demands of the public is needed here. They maintain that the standard for which corporate executives are responsible is the same standard that applies to other agents in decision-making situations (Solomon and Hanson, 1983, p. 232). Whether this standard is formulated in terms of respecting rights, acting compassionately, virtuously, or justly, promoting the greatest good, or whatever, these theorists believe that the choices of executives are not to be given special treatment. They are not considered exempt from the principles and rules of common morality applicable to all humans in decision-making situations. As Hoffman and Moore indicate, executives are otherwise ordinary people with the usual responsibilities of common morality to fulfill (Hoffman and Moore, 1982, p. 293).

Goldman expresses this point by contending that the functions of corporate executives are not strongly role-differentiated ones (Goldman, 1980, p. 260). A strongly role-differentiated function is one that can at times supercede the considerations of common morality. For Goldman, this means in particular that it can override concern for the rights of others. He believes, however, that an executive's duty to the shareholders is not supervenient over his or her obligation to respect the rights of workers, consumers, and members of the general public. In part, he maintains this because he believes that executives do not owe shareholders a return on their investment. The latter do not have a right to receive dividends from the company. When they invest in a firm, their position in the corporation is more like gamblers than like bondholders or creditors (Goldman, 1980, p. 284). In part, too, he maintains this because of his view on rights. As he defines them, rights are moral claims that cannot be overridden by simple concern for utility or welfare. He believes that while it may be beneficial that executives enhance shareholder wealth in their business activities, this utilitarian concern does not itself supercede the rights of others. Executives are not then justified in maximizing profit if this involves seriously infringing the rights of other people (Goldman, 1980, p. 282).

ARGUMENTS FOR THE SECOND THESIS: THE EXACTING STANDARD

The rights argument of Goldman takes us to the defense of the second thesis of social activism. Why do social activists believe that the universal standard mentioned in the first thesis is socially or morally activist in nature?

The answer they give to this question is a simple one—the standard is activist because it is founded upon the principles of common morality, which can themselves be very normatively demanding and exacting of persons.

But what then are the principles of common morality? For activists, they are directives of conduct meant to apply to all agents as such. Five of these directives are of particular interest to us because they reflect or represent five of the strategies of institutional legitimation discussed in an earlier chapter. These are the consent, respect for persons, formalist, rights, and performance models. We shall briefly consider the application of each of these models to the activist position.

The consent model grounds an argument found in the activist aspects of the works of Nader and Green. They contend that when members of society, through their representatives in government, give their permission to corporations to function as single entities under the law with limited liability for debts and torts, they expect corporations to assist them in reaching their own social goals to the extent possible (Nader and Green, 1976, pp. 63ff.). Executives are thus not only expected to avoid harming society in their decisions, they are also required to go beyond reparation to relieve distress they themselves may not have brought about. And they may be required to perform various acts that otherwise benefit society, even though there may be no present market for them. As Nader and

Green see it, this is the real nature of the understanding spoken of by social demandingness theory that is said to exist between representatives of corporations and members of the public. So, if executives are to remain true to their side of the agreement, they are responsible to take certain actions not currently demanded by society.

Bowie develops an argument grounded upon the consent, formalist, and respect for persons models. We have already discussed part of this argument in chapter 10. Bowie maintains that one reason corporate executives are obligated to abide by their contracts and be responsible to the interests of certain stakeholder groups is that they must respect those characteristics of human agents that permit them to enter into contracts in the first place. Of particular importance in this case are the characteristics of self-determination and rational thought (Bowie, 1982, pp. 46ff.). The argument implies that more than just avoiding harm is expected here. It also suggests that corporate executives should give positive assistance to those with whom they have made agreements, especially when this bears on the conative or rational capacities of these agents.

Taken this far, the present argument defends part of the stakeholder theory. But it is extended by Bowie and others, like Goodpaster, to include all agents who might be affected by corporate decisions (Bowie, 1982, pp. 46ff.; Goodpaster, 1984, pp. 301ff.). This is done by urging that all human beings have these capacities and thus deserve such consideration and treatment. It does not matter whether they are actual contract bearers or stakeholders of the corporation. It is at this point that the consent model blends with the respect for persons model (though the argument can, of course, be advanced solely from within the assumptions of the latter framework).

There is also a formalist side to this argument, which can be seen when it is urged that it is inconsistent, or otherwise incoherent, to permit an agent to rely upon or advance a capacity in himself or herself that is meant to directly or systematically eliminate or jeopardize that same capacity in others. It is believed that the maxim behind such a decision cannot be willed universally.

Just as there is a formalist side to Bowie's argument, there is a formalist side to Gewirth's argument. This is so even though he refers to his position as the ''generic rights'' approach. His theory also fits into the respect for persons framework. For Gewirth, moral rights are grounded upon the necessary conditions of purposive agency, namely, freedom (or noninterference) and well-being. He believes that without choice and the conditions of general well-being (i.e., life, physical integrity, mental equilibrium, and certain maintenance and additive goods), action is impossible (Gewirth, 1979, p. 141). Gewirth does not claim that people have rights to a broad range of goods that could add to their well-being (such as a high salary or a free advanced education), but he does contend they have a right to have their well-being respected and not harmed. The generic rights he discusses are primarily negative ones; they demand general noninterference and avoidance rather than affirmative action. There are times when they do require positive action, however. These are cases where a definite and significant harm occurs to others and an agent knows about this and has the power to minimize or help to eliminate it (Gewirth, 1979, p. 145). Gewirth uses the example of alleviating world starvation as an illustration of an activity for which everyone (including corporate executives) is responsible. He believes that the latter are responsible to increase their charitable contributions to the starving and malnourished, and seek to open job markets for these individuals even if their past actions did not originally cause this social or economic problem.

The formalist side of Gewirth's position is brought out by the fact that he believes that the generic rights of which he speaks are equal rights. He claims that contradiction or incoherence results from admitting the need for freedom and well-being for oneself but denying this for others. To claim that freedom and well-being are necessary conditions of choice or action is to admit that they cannot be suppressed. The abrogation or hindrance of choice may of course come from many sources—from physical obstacles, mental problems, environmental restrictions, and social interferences. Gewirth is concerned, however, with those restrictions over which humans have some control, restrictions that are brought about or can be eliminated by choice. He believes that to claim the need for noninterference and nonharm for oneself is to claim that one is entitled to these things insofar as one is an agent. But to deny this entitlement to others is to claim that these conditions are not necessary after all. They are then expendable. The contradiction arises when one seeks to claim these conditions are necessary (for self) and yet expendable (for others), when one implies that some agents, like oneself, are entitled to have these conditions respected, while others are not (Gewirth, 1979, p. 147). It occurs as well in the agent's choice to view and treat as expendable those conditions that make choice itself possible.

Gewirth's argument has activist implications even though he accepts the idea that rights are primarily negative in nature. But theorists who believe in positive rights, such as the framers of the United Nations document on social and economic rights, urge an even more active social and moral role for corporations. They believe that concern for the rights of other people requires executives to actively assist these people in meeting their otherwise valid and rational goals, even if this involves some considerable sacrifice to the economic performance of the firm.

Another theorist who believes that corporate executives are responsible to alleviate the distress of world hunger is Singer. The principle he formulates is consequentialistic or performance-oriented in nature. He tells us that all individuals are responsible for alleviating the suffering of others, when this involves no sacrifice of something of comparable moral value for themselves or others (Singer, 1982, p. 360). Since the lessening or loss of a dividend check is not of comparable moral worth with the suffering and loss of life involved in starvation, he believes that executives cannot appeal to the fiduciary duties to stockholders to excuse their failure to give aid to the hungry or malnourished in the world. They thus have this responsibility even though their decisions may not have caused the problem of hunger in the first place.

In another context, Singer has argued that firms that harm animals in certain ways as a usual or normal part of their business activity are sacrificing something of greater value for something of lesser worth. They are not alleviating suffering but are instead causing it. He believes that the principle formulated above requires that firms make major changes in their policies of experimenting with animals, for example. It also implies that the current practices of cattle and poultry farms and the slaughtering and meatpacking industries are in need of radical transformation (Singer, 1986, pp. 24ff.).

We see then that activist thinkers reject the argument of the other theorists of corporate responsibility that the latters' positions best promote the social welfare. Against the "invisible hand" argument of the classical theory, Almeder maintains that it is hard to believe that society as a whole is made better off when firms seek to gain only their own private economic advantage (Almeder, 1980, p. 14). A similar concern attaches to the stakeholder and social demandingness positions since they advocate seeking to benefit only a certain segment of society, or all of society but only in certain restricted respects.

THE APPLICATION OF THESE PRINCIPLES TO ACTIVIST PROPOSALS

Opponents of activism often feel that a difficulty with the theory is the tendency for some of its principal arguments to be formulated in overly abstract terms. For some, it is difficult to believe that such abstract arguments can be ultimately convincing. I do not propose to resolve the issue or problem here, but I do wish to guide the reader through a somewhat more careful consideration of the defense of two activists proposals to illustrate two other features of these arguments— their complexity and interconnectedness. It will be noticed that the presentation of these arguments is still somewhat abstract, and the discussion is incomplete. It is abstract because activists typically organize their views around the assertion and defense of general principles of choice rather than upon the detailed consideration of specific cases. It is incomplete because the present account deals primarily with the first line of defense for these proposals. Space does not permit the development of response and counterresponse for each of these arguments, which would be necessary to make them more concrete, encompassing, or convincing. Still, the presentation accurately reflects the usual manner of argument of these theorists. The proposals to be examined are (a) corporate executives should upgrade their commitment to the disclosure of corporate social and moral performance, and (b) corporations should increase their charitable contributions to help locate and sustain the hungry of the world. The argument strategies to be examined are taken from the principles of common morality just discussed. They include the strategies of appeal to: (1) basic rights, (2) freedom, (3) promoting the greatest good, and (4) lessening avoidable harm. It should be noticed that both consequentialist and deontological considerations are equally represented here. As we pursue these argument strategies further, both the strengths and some of the weaknesses of the theory should thus become somewhat clearer to the reader.

Before we begin, however, it should be noted that the activist defense as discussed here, particularly on its deontological side, does not necessarily offer a final warrant for a particular proposal. It may merely shift the burden of proof back to thinkers who endorse one of the other theories of corporate responsibility and who thus either reject the proposal in question or at least urge it with some modification.

Basic rights defense. The rights defense of these proposals maintains that they protect certain basic rights of people while not infringing upon the rights of others, or if infringement does take place, it is upon rights that are secondary to those in question. One theorist who advances a rights argument here is Goldman. His argument is designed with the classical theory in mind, but it can be expanded to apply to the other positions. Basic to his argument is the thesis that a greater investment in corporate social or moral performance reporting protects the right of persons (both shareholders and potential shareholders alike) to make informed investment choices while it conflicts with none of the other rights of these individuals. Since, as we have seen, he believes both that shareholders do not have a right to dividends and that rights take precedence over nonrights or matters of mere utility, his argument leads to the conclusion that the right to be informed on certain matters supercedes the benefit of a larger dividend check for the shareholders. We have noted that certain classical theorists take exception to Goldman's thesis about the rights of shareholders, however. They believe that since shareholders have property and voting rights in a corporation, they do have a right to influence or help determine in some way the disposition of corporate revenues, assets, and expenses (including the dispersal of its earnings in the form of dividends). They thus may deserve to receive dividends. But it is nevertheless still open for Goldman to argue that the right to be informed about all the relevant aspects of corporate decision making is more basic than the real or alleged right to determine the level of dispersal of dividends for without the former right being protected, the exercise of the latter is either empty or blind. So even if shareholders have ownership rights in the corporation, these investors' rights are at best secondary in nature to the right to relevant information.

The stakeholder and social demandingness positions also require that various external groups have broad access to corporate information, especially in the social and moral arenas, but the basis of their positions is generally too narrow or suspicious for the rights theorist. Basic rights are compelling and authoritative for these latter thinkers not because of social demand or expectation; these rights even apply in situations where their authority is not specifically recognized. And since their authority is universal, they can be said to apply to all humans, not just to a company's stakeholders.

The proposal to increase corporate support for alleviating world hunger is defended by Gewirth on the ground that a person's generic right to meet the minimum conditions of well-being takes precedence over the more specific property or voting rights of shareholders (which might be used to lessen such corporate donations in favor of more hardy dividends or reinvestment in the firm). For Gewirth, generic rights typically supercede specific rights both because they are more fundamental to human nature and because their denial or abrogation leads to a more extensive or magnified form of suffering, conflict, or incoherence than that usually associated with the denial of a more specific right. We see then both consequentialist and formalist elements to his argument. This also means, however, that although the rights of stakeholders or members of the public for certain nonbasic things are also authoritative, they do not override a third party's right to the minimum conditions of survival. Beyond this, the discussion between Gewirth and his opponents concerns the proper means to respect and fulfill this right.

Freedom defense. Activist theorists who advocate the argument from concern for freedom, such as Purchell and Bowie, argue that a lessened corporate commitment to social or moral performance reporting restricts the freedom of actual or prospective shareholders and stakeholders without encouraging a like degree of freedom for these people in other areas of decision making. These theorists believe that since the absence of such information typically affects the range and quality of a person's investment or business decisions, corporate executives are justified in restricting their social performance reporting only if it will likely promote a greater degree of freedom for all individuals involved. These theorists believe, however, that such a restriction rarely has this effect. Moreover, such a policy is objectionable from another point of view: it jeopardizes the self-correcting function usually involved in the arena of public discussion of social and moral matters. Since unreported information rarely becomes part of this domain, it becomes difficult, if not impossible, to have outside confirmation of a corporation's performance in these areas. This means then that, other things being equal, justification cannot be given to a practice that impedes both the activity of reasoning in a specific case and the process of offering justification or disconfirmation in general. These points indicate to activist thinkers that the burden of proof rests on those theorists who believe that such a restricted policy is warranted. They must show how it responds more effectively to individual rights and produces a greater level of freedom in society as a whole.

Activist thinkers who appeal to the freedom principle argue that it also justifies greater corporate involvement in feeding the hungry. They believe that the kind and degree of freedom that the malnourished and hungry lose in or by their condition is much greater than that lost by the shareholders or stakeholders of activist firms whose net revenues, dividends, or capital gains are made smaller by the practice of corporate giving. Thus non-activist corporations should give more to help these unfortunate people than the 1 to 2 percent of net revenue they typically give to charity.

Promoting the greatest good defense. Some activist theorists who are utilitarian in the traditional sense argue for the practices of expanded corporate social reporting and donations for the starving on the grounds that they produce more good in society than do their opposite or contrary practices. As we have seen, versions of this argument have been advanced within the other theories of corporate responsibility as well. These thinkers believe that by making knowledge of corporate social performance available to shareholders and the public alike, corporations can do more, on balance, to promote good than if they restricted such information as a means of lessening their expenses. While activist theorists believe that it is possible to provide too much information to stockholders and the public, they think that this point is usually reached when the sheer weight of the information disclosed produces the effect of an "information overload" upon the audience (and thus becomes counterproductive) rather than when it merely becomes more expensive for the company to gather and disseminate. Many activist thinkers who argue for the practice of more thorough corporate social or moral reporting contend that few firms are in danger of doing more harm than good by expanding such reporting. Few have reached the point where they either are producing an information overload in their audience or are discouraging prospective shareholders or stakeholders from having confidence in the company because of the expenses involved in this reporting.

Activist thinkers typically recognize some warranted limitations to corporate disclosure, of course. They believe that otherwise confidential or privileged information, such as trade secrets and the like, are usually better left undisclosed, but they also think that the type of information involved in corporate social or moral reporting is rarely of this nature. In opposition to those theorists who suggest that a greater commitment to corporate social or moral reporting is not necessarily correlated with better economic performance by a firm, they can reply that this is but one measure of the overall value or worth of a corporate practice. Even if the charge were true, activist thinkers believe that opponents cannot overlook the other considerations that are relevant to the issue—considerations such as expanded freedom and a more effective arena of public debate—considerations whose value is not easily measured but whose impact they believe to be both real and significant, nevertheless.

Activist theorists who give a utilitarian defense for an expanded program of corporate aid to the starving and malnourished characteristically argue that it produces more good for the unfortunate than it causes pain or suffering for the company, its shareholders, or stakeholders. They grant that while corporate resources are limited, they believe that if executives set spending priorities for those corporate revenues not bound by contract or law that reflect the true economic, moral, and social value promoted by each dollar spent, they would be committed to far greater levels of spending to aid the unfortunate than what they presently give. They do not believe that all of this aid need go directly for food, of course. Some would go for medicines, others for capital expenditures to secure the self-sufficiency of those now starving. But however this money is spent, activists typically think these donations are a better "value expense" than the money given to the more traditional economic or social projects of a firm.

Lessening avoidable harm defense. Much the same argument is advanced by activist thinkers who appeal to the harm principle. Like Singer, they believe that a greater extent and degree of avoidable harm is prevented when corporations aid individuals in meeting their basic needs at this time than when they work to enhance the lives of those whose basic needs have already been met. Along the same line, most theorists relying upon the harm principle believe that withholding information about a corporation's social performance does less in general to avoid harm than does bearing the expense of providing such information. They also believe that few firms have reached the point at which their commitment to social or moral reporting is doing more harm than good.

OTHER ARGUMENTS FOR THE SECOND THESIS

There are added considerations that activists urge in behalf of their position. In the first place, it is logically possible to accept the principle of alleviating suffering in general as urged by Gewirth and Singer, for example, and yet believe that executives who conform to a non-activist theory of corporate responsibility are doing all that can be expected of them in the social or moral arenas. Activist theorists typically respond to this challenge by contending that the current power of corporations implies that executives should be doing more than they are presently doing in these areas. Thus, Davis, James, and Fasching maintain that the enormous power of modern corporations entails that executives have an enormous responsibility to use this power wisely and compassionately (Davis, 1975, p. 20; James, 1982, p. 288; Fasching, 1981, p. 63). We can see then the principle of the ''iron law of responsibility'' is no stranger to social activists.

Starling and Carroll argue that most corporations have the financial and human resources, the know-how in organizational planning and implementation, and the motivational spirit to help alleviate some of the world's most pressing and intractable economic and social problems (Starling, 1980, p. 240; Carroll, 1981, p. 41). They believe that corporate executives are uniquely qualified to be more morally or socially active in their corporate decision making. Some social activists also contend that since no other social institutions or agencies seem able to solve such problems as world starvation and poverty, in the absence of corporate involvement, these problems and their related suffering will likely continue unabated.

In addition, some activists maintain that it is better to act to ward off a social problem before it becomes serious than it is to react to it after it has gotten out of hand. If executives would adhere more closely to the social activist theory, they could carry out planning and response functions that could become models of social anticipation and organizational efficiency in the future.

Last, it should be mentioned that activist theorists recognize that certain firms may be unable to carry out some of the activist proposals considered in this chapter. This is especially true if these firms are not doing well in the marketplace. Similarly, they realize that there are times when the economy itself discourages corporate social activism. In periods of recession or depression not as much can

Figure 12.1
Social Activism (Principle Assumptions)

Relations of Accountability	Models of the Corporation	Strategies of Legitimization
1. Promise-Keeping or Consent*	1. Private Property	1. Power
2. Fiduciary*	2. Private Contract	2. Conformity to Law
3. Representational	3. Enterprise**	3. Conformity to Current Standards
4. Impact**	4. Social Contract*	4. Procedural*
5. Reverse-Impact	5. Public Power**	5. Formal**
6. Teamwork or Collegial**	6. Machine or Tool	6. Performance**
7. Ownership or Possession	7. Organic**	7. Rights**
8. Regulation*	8. Mental or Moral Agent**	8. Respect for Persons**
		[9. Relations of Accountability]

* can or does play some direct role in defining or defending the theory

** plays a significant role in defining or defending the theory

be expected from firms. But even allowing for these periodic cycles in the economy, activists believe that corporations are in general potent sources for positive social change.

THE ASSUMPTIONS OF SOCIAL ACTIVISM

The 3 sets of assumptions applicable to social activism are provided schematically in Figure 12.1. We have seen that activist theorists make direct appeal to five of the eight strategies of legitimation discussed earlier. Their theory can thus be formulated within the context of any of these strategies. They do not appeal to the power, conformity to law, or conformity to current standards strategies. And they reject the formulation of the consent model that demands that executives respond only to those goals or expectations of society for which there exists a social consensus.

They reject the power model because, as we have seen, they believe in the authority of an independent moral or normative standard to guide business decision making. The power model denies the existence or importance of such a standard. Activist theorists are not entirely in disagreement with this latter model, however. They do believe that abiding by the appropriate standard can enhance one's power. But the type of power had in mind here is a kind of psychological power or strength of character to control one's moral development in the future. It is not the kind of external or worldly influence that the power model characteristically emphasizes. And with a few notable exceptions they often believe that the possession of such power is usually an unintended result of responsible decision making rather than being one of its explicit goals or purposes.

They reject the conformity to law model because they believe that law is for the most part only partially indicative of the true standard of corporate responsibility. Whenever conflict arises, current laws must give way to this independent standard. And as with the other theories, they believe moreover that if this model were the sole or dominant framework within which to justify social institutions, there would be no significant difference between it and the classical theory of corporate responsibility.

Last, they reject the social consensus and conformity to current standards strategies for the reasons discussed earlier. Such positions are thought to offer standards that are too unclear, vacillating, circular, or inconsistent to be reliable normative guides to business decision making.

Of the frameworks of interpersonal relationships that bear on accountability claims, activists largely appeal to the promise-keeping, fiduciary, impact, teamwork, and regulation models. The promise-keeping model plays a role in the work of those activist theorists who are contractarians. Within this model, executives are expected to abide by the terms of the implicit agreement they have made with members of society. This implies that they are also viewed, at least to some extent, as being the fiduciaries of those with whom they have made these agreements. Some activist theorists also assume the fiduciary model in another way. They believe that executives, like all moral agents, are trustees or fiduciaries of the moral and social order. They are thus expected to represent and protect this order in all of their corporate conduct.

Activist theorists also assume the impact model in their thinking. They believe that executives are responsible not only to avoid harming others in their decisions; they are also expected to relieve the suffering of others, even if this suffering is not the product of past corporate action. Some activists go farther and contend that executives are responsible to bring about the greatest good within their power. In appealing to each of these versions of the performance model, activist theorists assume that executives are accountable for the impact of their actions.

Activist theorists also assume the teamwork model, both as this concerns the functioning of corporate units together and the behavior of institutional units in the social system as a whole. Their belief is that in general an activist program of respecting rights, alleviating distress, or bringing about good is more effective in producing a harmonious corporate and social order than are those programs sponsored by the other theories of corporate responsibility.

Finally, activist theorists accept the regulation model—at last to the extent that the elements of the moral code assumed by them are seen as constituting a set of authoritative regulations by which to guide corporate decision making. They do not, of course, accept regulations just because they are regulations, but because they grant the authority of certain regulations, they accept this model in some way. They also accept the model to the extent that they believe that conforming to various laws and professional codes will in general lead to alleviating social or moral distress. In this case, they advocate the model not as an end in itself but for its role in helping to secure the social and moral benefits urged by the theory.

Activist theorists typically do not appeal to the representative, reverse-impact, or ownership models. For them, appeal to these models may help explain why certain groups or individuals have some kind of claim upon corporate decision making, but they usually do little to explain for them the unique appeal of the activist proposals. Some would like to see corporate executives be representatives to society of a higher moral order—to be models and exemplars to or for society. But this is not the type of descriptive relation usually envisioned within the representative model. As for its functionary side, activists do not usually contend that executives have been specially selected by members of society to represent the latters' interests. Activist thinkers who accept the consent theory believe, of course, that members of the public have given executives general permission to function within the corporate form of business enterprise. But this type of permission giving is not the same as specifically choosing or voting for an individual to represent one's interests. And it is the latter process that is emphasized in the functionary model.

Activist theorists do not appeal to the reverse-impact model of accountability relations, except that some recognize that corporate activism may stem from a kind of corporate gratitude. Most grant that in general an activist policy will reflect well upon the corporation and that in the long run activist firms will enjoy better public relations than will non-activist ones. But they typically reject the idea that this form of corporate self-interest is the basic goal or rationale for social or moral activism. It is for them at best only a by-product. To push the egoistic side of this model too vigorously is to begin to challenge the basic other-oriented direction of the activist theory.

Finally, activists have not primarily appealed to the ownership model. They have not argued that the property rights of those in distress grounds the executive's responsibility to alleviate their suffering. For them, the latter responsibility stands on its own merits. And unlike the ownership model that implies that the burden of proof rests upon those who seek to interfere with, or otherwise compromise, the property holdings of individuals, the present theory places this burden upon those who think that alleviating avoidable suffering is not the overriding principle of choice. Because activists believe that an executive's primary responsibility is to conform to the latter principle, they give far less weight to the ownership model in this matter.

THE ACTIVIST ASSUMPTIONS ABOUT THE CORPORATION

Finally, we come to the assumptions that concern the nature of the corporation. Of the eight models of the corporation discussed earlier, activist theorists make little use of the property and private contract models. They agree, of course, that property relations apply to the corporation in various ways, but they contend that this is not the principal corporate feature within which the questions of corporate responsibility must be raised. Much the same can be said of the private contract model. Although activists grant that executives are involved in a host of private agreements with other parties and that these agreements have at least *prima facie* authority, they typically reject the idea that any such agreement is entirely private in nature. All of these agreements come under the jurisdiction of the principles of common morality that require consideration of the interests of third parties. If the interest of these parties is significantly harmed, the constraints of the two-party agreements are usually taken to be less compelling. They also grant the negative side of this model, which emphasizes private conflict in corporations, but their theory typically seeks to lessen its impact upon corporate decision making.

We have seen that some activist theorists accept the social contract model of the corporation. For these theorists the implicit agreement that they believe is made between corporate executives and members of the public is a facet of the corporate structure playing a large role in the questions of corporate responsibility—much larger than the explicit two-party agreements emphasized by the private contract model. This version of activism typically views corporations as social inventions created to serve primarily a public purpose.

Activists also typically accept the public power model of the corporation. Not only do they believe that the corporate structure has enabled some firms to become enormously powerful, they also believe that the degree of responsibility of corporate executives is proportionate to the extent of this power. They maintain that executives should be compassionate in the use of their power and, at a minimum, work to relieve the distress of the unfortunate, even if they did nothing to cause this suffering in the first place. They further believe that the development of an appropriate corporate culture for social and moral activism is an important first step in meeting the demands of this theory.

As with stakeholder theorists, activists accept the enterprise model, but they typically conceive of it somewhat differently than do advocates of the stakeholder position. In the stakeholder theory, the corporation is conceived in large part to be the product of private purposes. The individual members of the firm participate in its common goals so that they might better achieve their own career and private objectives—so that they might grow both personally and professionally. Activist theorists agree with this view, but they usually emphasize a particular area of personal growth. They are less concerned with economic or career advancement; they focus instead upon character and upon the moral and professional growth of the members of the corporation. They emphasize the idea that the corporation, like other social institutions, is a moral enterprise for the development and building of virtue and character.

Of the remaining models of the corporation, only two have played a significant role in the presentation and defense of the activist position. The tool or machine model is typically not assumed by activists. While no contradiction is involved in presupposing this model, it is not a commonly held activist assumption. There is an air of paradox in assuming that the corporation is a nonmoral and mechanical instrument that is nevertheless designed to pursue moral purposes. Such a view seems to abstract out the human element from the corporate structure. It thus seems to remove (or to give secondary status to) the moral constraints placed upon the choices of the human members of this social institution. It is a model that usually endorses the values of standardization, productivity, and administrative efficiency—a model advocated by thinkers who believe that only outside pressure, such as that which comes from government agencies and consumer groups, is capable of altering corporate values or decision making, or of restructuring the corporate organization. It is a framework advanced by theorists who believe that a change in the nature or structure of this tool is usually sculpted by forces lying outside of itself and that any alteration in the use of this tool by corporate executives comes about primarily as a response to these forces. Activists, on the other hand, maintain that the corporation is a social institution or moral enterprise composed principally of a host of choices made daily by the members of this institution. They believe then that the corporation has an ineradicable normative, moral, and nonmechanistic dimension to it.

Finally, both the organic and mental or moral agent models have at times played an important role in the activist position. The organic model is assumed by some systems theorists, advocates of strategic management, and others who analyze the corporation in terms of its dependent and independent institutional or environmental relationships. They view corporations as distinct entities, with independent or quasi-independent goals, which nevertheless rely upon other social institutions for their own existence and direction. This is a position presupposed particularly by those activist thinkers who appeal to the consent or promise-keeping and impact models of accountability relations. Contractarian activists emphasize the need for executives to respond to the interests and goals of the wider society, while impact theorists defend activist programs by the usual or likely positive effects that they have upon the other institutions in society.

The mental agent model is assumed by many activist thinkers, who maintain that corporations are important centers for the gathering, processing, and generating of information. This forms part of the basis of their disclosure responsibilities. And like advocates of the other positions, they also grant that corporations can become psychic prisons of excessively bounded rationality, exaggerated conflict or inflexibility, and excessive egoism and materialism (or commercialism). But their theory seeks to overcome these real or potential features.

The moral agent or person model is accepted, at least by extension, by several activist theorists, especially those who emphasize the motive of corporate gratitude. They believe that corporations, insofar as they display the characteristics of self-correction, autonomy, and rational planning, are at a minimum to be treated as if they were unique moral agents or persons with their own distinct moral prerogatives and responsibilities. Those activists who endorse this model include the duty to respect these distinct agents and their goals as one of the added responsibilities of corporate executives and workers. But they do not believe that this responsibility supercedes the requirement of executives to relieve the distress of human agents and promote the social welfare generally. It is also assumed by those activist thinkers who apply a virtue ethic directly to corporations themselves.

We have now completed our review of the four theories of corporate responsibility, but several issues still need to be addressed. In the next two chapters we shall consider the question of the application of these theories, and in chapter 15 we shall examine the nature of individual and collective responsibility. This will help us to understand certain added assumptions that apply to the corporate responsibility debate and will introduce the last major question to be considered here—the responsibility of corporate subordinates, especially in cases of dissent with corporate superiors. This will indicate another dimension of the relationship between corporate responsibility and corporate legitimacy.

Before ending this chapter, however, a reminder and word of caution is in order. The organization of these last chapters from classical to social activist positions is for heuristic purposes. It is not meant to imply that social activism is the strongest theory of corporate responsibility. The debate on this issue is a continuous one.

THE CONTINUING NATURE OF THE DEBATE

Opponents of social activism contend that a significant weakness is its inability to agree upon a universally binding set of standards for corporate conduct. Not only are there major disagreements among deontological, consequentialist, and aretaic thinkers, but even within these camps there are important differences of opinion. Some of these were pointed out in chapter 7.

Social demandingness theorists suggest that these disagreements imply that the best and safest thing to be done in unresolved cases of normative dispute is to appeal to those standards most often urged in and by society. These are the ones most likely to be correct, or at least they are not likely to be wildly wrong. These theorists believe then that the uncertainty of this normative dispute should drive social activists back to their own theory of corporate responsibility.

Activists could quickly reply, however, by pointing out that this indicates that there is very little difference then between the social demandingness theory and activism. Both assume or endorse universal values. In the case of activism, there is a broad range of such values—even those over which there exists significant dispute. Social demandingness theorists, on the other hand, try to minimize or eliminate controversy by appealing to those ideas, standards, or demands that are most commonly accepted in society, which restricts the range of values urged by the theory that are likely to be the objects of dispute. But it also urges a theory in which the values of consent, respect for opinions (and perhaps respect for the persons who can hold these opinions), impartiality, fairness, and the like are given universal status. It seems then that the social demandingness position is simply a form of activism distinguished by its parsimony in recognizing universal values.

Classical theorists demur. They reject both of these theories because of their views on the nature of corporate responsibility in the context of controversy or dispute. They contend that the social demandingness theory is no better off than social activism; controversy abounds in both areas. The largely descriptive nature of the disagreements in the former area should not lead one to think that widespread controversy is thus absent. Classical theorists believe that in disputes that concern the question of what moral or social responsibilities executives have, managers have a metaresponsibility to choose in terms of the quality of their knowledge. They cannot risk the assets of the company in ventures whose necessity or value is still largely in dispute. What is not in dispute though is that executives have economic and legal responsibilities to fulfill. Thus, the presence of this type of controversy requires that managers be more stingy in their spending on social and moral projects. To the extent that conflict abounds on the nature of corporate responsibility, executives are most justified in spending on only those social or moral programs with proven economic or legal benefits for the firm. Beyond this, they are unduly risking the firm's assets.

This shows us something about the classical theory that we also encountered in chapter 8—its flexibility and integrative power. It need not deny that there are corporate responsibilities in the social or moral arenas. It can even treat these as justified, but only to the extent that they can be shown to be a means of obtaining or maintaining corporate wealth in a legally sanctioned manner. To the extent that either their legal compellingness or their wealth production is in dispute, such theorists would argue that they should be generally shunned by executives.

Stakeholder theorists are unconvinced by this reply. They believe that the classical theory is somewhat "schizophrenic" in its endorsing both economic and legal responsibilities. The latter bring the theory much closer to the social demandingness position insofar as it urges conformity to the legal standards and demands of society. They ask, "Why not admit additional standards, then—such as the law-like standards endorsed by professional groups?"

Basically, however, stakeholder theorists believe that they have the most compelling "second best" theory of the four. In the present situation of conflict, they reject the view of classical theorists that economic and legal responsibilities should determine corporate decision making. They urge instead a fuller examination of the nature of the controversy itself. From this metaperspective, it can be seen to be a conflict in which no one position dominates—no uniform first choice exists. But the stakeholder theory is one that all other parties could live with as the second best position. In fact, even the social activists could live with it. It seems that both classical and social demandingness theorists could live with the stakeholder position for, as usually conceived, it is the view that is closest to both. But there is some reason to believe that many social activist theorists would choose this theory as the second best alternative as well. It can be argued that they would prefer the stability and clarity of the stakeholder theory (particularly if it were accepted by almost all managers and other theorists as their second best alternative) to the vicissitudes and exaggerations of the social demandingness position. Activists are uncomfortable with the fact that the latter would demand or expect certain actions from businesses in the United States today and something else from those in Germany in the 1930s, or those in China since Mao, or even those in South Africa in the 1940s. These pronounced fluctuations are worrisome to thinkers who believe in universally valid values because they can lead to normative relativism and to much derision for the social activist theory itself. The failure of the social demandingness theory thus endangers social activism much more than does the success of the stakeholder position—a success that might be counted upon to produce a more socially and morally demanding minimum for corporations to meet in the future, a success that might make society more sympathetic to activism at a later time.

Social demandingness theorists are not about to quit the debate at this point, however. They could point out briefly that if this "critical" defense for the stakeholder theory were successful, it would prove too much; for the consensus or metaconsensus it is seeking to establish pushes the theory it is used to defend in the direction of the social demandingness position. The consensus that is alleged to exist empirically on this issue indicates the consent of theorists and managers to conform to the current ideas, conclusions, or standards of other theorists in this area. As a metalevel or consensus (or consent) position, this form of critical stakeholder theory makes significant concessions to the ideas and assumption of the social demandingness view.

Finally, activist theorists tell us that all of these points are academic, anyway. The problem with each of the other positions is that they can at best secure only a category three level of legitimacy for corporations. Social activism is capable of pushing corporations near or into category four. They believe it is the only appropriate position on corporate responsibility and legitimacy to defend; it thus deserves our serious study and commitment.

But is a higher level of legitimacy always good or needed? The debate goes on.

REFERENCES

Abt, C. C. 1972. "Managing to Save Money While Doing Good." *Innovation*, January, pp. 38–47.

Ackerman, Robert. 1973. "How Companies Respond to Social Demands." *Harvard Business Review*, July–August, pp. 88–98.

Ackerman, Robert, and Raymond Bauer. 1976. *Corporate Social Responsiveness: The Modern Dilemma*. Reston, Va.: Reston Publishing Company.

Almeder, Robert. 1980. "The Ethics of Profit: Reflections on Corporate Responsibility." *Business and Society Review*, Winter, pp. 7–14.

Bauer, Raymond, and D. H. Finn. 1972. *The Corporate Social Audit*. New York: Russell Sage Foundation.

Birdzell, L. E. 1975. "The Moral Basis of the Business System." *Journal of Contemporary Business*, Summer, pp. 75–87.

Blumenthal, W. Michael. 1976a. "Business Ethics: A Call for a Moral Approach." *Financial Executive*. January, pp. 32–34.

Blumenthal, W. Michael. 1976b. "Top Management's Role in Preventing Illegal Payments." *The Conference Board*, August, pp. 14–16.

Bowie, Norman. 1982. *Business Ethics*. Englewood Cliffs, N.J.: Prentice-Hall.

Camenish, Paul F. 1981. "Business Ethics: On Getting to the Heart of the Matter." *Business and Professional Ethics Journal*, Fall, pp. 59–69.

―――. 1978. "Linking Business Ethics to Behavior in Organizations." *S.A.M. Advanced Management Journal*, Summer, pp. 4–11.

Carroll, Archie, B. 1981. *Business and Society: Management Corporate Social Performance*. Boston: Little, Brown and Company.

Davis, Keith J. 1975. "Five Propositions for Social Responsibility." *Business Horizons*, June, pp. 19–24.

Fasching, Darrel J. 1981. "A Case for Corporate and Management Ethics." *California Management Review*, Summer, pp. 62–76.

Galbraith, John Kenneth. 1976. *The Affluent Society*. New York: Houghton-Mifflin.

Gewirth, Alan. 1979. "Starvation and Human Rights." In *Ethics and the Problems of the 21st Century*, edited by K. E. Goodpaster and K. M. Sayre, pp. 139–59. South Bend, Ind.: University of Notre Dame Press.

Goldman, Alan H. 1980. "Business Ethics: Profits, Utilities and Moral Rights." *Philosophy and Public Affairs*, vol. 9, no. 3, Spring, pp 260–86.

Goodpaster, Kenneth E. 1984. "The Concept of Corporate Responsibility." In *Just Business: New Introductory Essays in Business Ethics*, edited by Tom Regan, pp. 292–321. New York: Random House.

Hoffman, W. Michael, and Jennifer M. Moore. 1982. "What Is Business Ethics? A Reply to Peter Drucker." *Journal of Business Ethics*, November, pp. 293–300.

James, Gene G. 1982. "Crisis of American Ethics." *Journal of Business Ethics*, vol. 1, no. 4, November, pp. 285–91.

Jones, Thomas M. 1980. "Corporate Social Responsibility: Revisited, Redefined." *California Management Review*, Spring, pp. 59–67.

Knight, Frank. 1923. "The Ethics of Competition." *Quarterly Journal of Economics*, vol. 37, pp. 579–624.

McAdam, Terry W. 1973. "How To Put Corporate Responsibility into Practice." *Business and Society Review*, Summer, pp. 8–16.

MacIntyre, Alastair. 1984. *After Virtue: A Study in Moral Theory*, 2d ed. South Bend, Ind.: University of Notre Dame Press.

Murphy, P. E. 1978. "An Evolution: Corporate Social Responsiveness." *University of Michigan Business Review*, November, pp. 19–25.

Nader, Ralph, and Mark Green. 1976. *Taming the Giant Corporation*. New York: W. W. Norton.

Peters, Thomas J., and Robert H. Waterman. 1982. *In Search of Excellence*. New York: Warner Books.

Purchell, Theodore. 1975. "A Practical Guide to Ethics in Business." *Business and Society Review*, Spring, pp. 43–50.

————. 1978. "The Need for Corporate Ethical Specialists." *Review of Social Economy*, April, pp. 41–53.

————. 1980. "Institutionalizing Business Ethics." *New Catholic World*, November–December, pp. 260–63.

Raelin, Joseph A. 1987. "The Professional As the Executive's Aide-de-Camp." *The Academy of Management Executive*, August, pp. 171–82.

Rawls, John. 1971. *A Theory of Justice*. Cambridge, Mass.: Harvard University Press.

Sawyer, George C. 1979. *Business and Society: Managing Corporate Social Impact*. Boston: Houghton-Mifflin.

Sethi, S. Prakash. 1977. "Dimensions of Corporate Social Performance: An Analytical Framework." In *Managing Corporate Social Responsibility*, edited by Archie B. Carroll, pp. 69–75. Boston: Little, Brown and Company.

Singer, Peter. 1982. "Famine, Affluence and Morality." In *Social Ethics: Morality and Social Policy*, 2d ed., edited by Thomas Mappes and Jane Zembaty, pp. 359–65. New York: McGraw-Hill.

————. 1986. "Animal Liberation." In *People, Penguins and Plastic Trees*, edited by Donald VandeVeer and Christine Pierce, pp. 24–32. Belmont, Calif.: Wadsworth Publishing Company.

Solomon, Robert, and Kristine R. Hanson. 1983. *Above the Bottom Line: An Introduction to Business Ethics*. New York: Harcourt, Brace, Jovanovich.

Starling, Grover. 1980. *The Changing Environment of Business: A Managerial Approach*. Boston: Kent Publishing.

Steiner, John F. 1976. "The Prospect of Ethical Advisors for Business Corporations." *Business and Society*, Spring, pp. 5–10.

Sturdivant, Frederick. 1981. *Business and Society: A Managerial Approach*. Homewood, Ill.: Richard D. Irwin.

Trowbridge, Alexander. 1975. "*Watergating on Main Street*, Part I: Business." *Saturday Review*, November 1, pp. 18–20.

Wallace, James. 1978. *Virtues and Vices*. Ithaca, N.Y.: Cornell University Press.

Wilkins, Paul L. 1975. "The Case for Ethical Absolutes in Business." *Business and Society Review*, Spring, pp. 61–63.

Williams, Oliver F. 1982. "Business Ethics: A Trojan Horse." *California Management Review*, Summer, pp. 14–24.

13

THE QUESTION OF PLANT RELOCATION OR CLOSING—I

INTRODUCTION

We have thus far discussed the four dominant theories of corporate responsibility and have isolated various assumptions that play an important role in their statement and defense. It is now time to show the application of this analysis to a specific question of corporate responsibility—the question of the closing or relocation of corporate facilities. What positions advocates of the four theories of corporate responsibility take on this issue and how some of the assumptions discussed earlier play a role in this debate are the questions to be addressed in this and the next chapter.

I have selected the question of plant closing or relocation both for its significance and its timeliness. Other issues could have been considered, but the present question sufficiently illustrates the concepts and theories discussed here. And, in addition, it suggests how other specific or applied questions of corporate responsibility would be examined and considered using the present concepts and method of analysis.

Before we begin considering the particular arguments advanced in this debate, however, certain terms should first be clarified. Although I shall frequently use the phrase *plant closing* to refer to the type of decision or action contemplated or taken by corporate management here, it should be understood that this phrase is also meant to include the relocation of a firm or the large-scale layoff of its workers. In addition, it should be understood to include reference to any facility owned or controlled by a corporation; the facility need not be a plant carrying out a traditional manufacturing role. Thus, the releasing of office workers and others in the service sector is also included in the present discussion. Second, in addition to the more specific question of relocation, we shall also consider to some degree a few of the related responsibilities that firms are alleged to have, should they decide to shut down a plant. Stakeholder theorists, for example, propose such actions as (1) giving early notice of the closing; (2) offering transfer, counselling, and retraining programs; (3) making severance payments to the workers; (4) providing continued payment of the health insurance premiums of those former workers who are unemployed and, (5) making severance payments to the local community. We shall mention or discuss these matters, but still the basic question here concerns the actual decision to relocate or shut down a facility.

Finally, we shall see that two theories of corporate responsibility in particular have seemed to play a large role in the present debate because, as it has thus far been discussed in the literature, the basic issue usually concerns the interests or rights of stockholders versus those of stakeholders. It is to be expected then that most of the arguments would come from classical and stakeholder theorists. We shall also consider the last two theories of corporate responsibility. In fact, we shall provide an interpretation of the social demandingness position on plant closings that suggests that it has a more important bearing on the debate than has perhaps been previously supposed. And we shall consider certain relatively distinctive arguments advanced within the framework of the last two positions on corporate responsibility. But having said this, we shall nevertheless see that the brunt of the discussion is carried on by theorists who favor one of the first two approaches to corporate responsibility.

THE LEGAL RESPONSIBILITIES OF FIRMS IN PLANT RELOCATION

Of the four types of responsibility considered in this work, discussion of the present issue usually centers upon the nature and interconnections of the economic, moral, and social responsibilities of upper management in matters of plant relocation. Legal responsibilities are discussed naturally, but debates about these responsibilities generally concern the normative question of what legal responsibilities corporations should have in this matter. And this issue typically takes us back to the other types of responsibility. This is not to say that an examination of the current legal requirements of firms in this matter is unnecessary, however. Some general discussion of these responsibilities is in order, even if it must be admitted that it offers us only a momentary picture of an ongoing process of drafting, implementing, and adjudicating the law in this area, even if it must be admitted that it may be shortly outdated as changes in circumstance or philosophy occur.

For many years the approach of European countries differed rather markedly from that of the United States. In most states in this country a firm could relocate or close one of its facilities without having to meet early notice or severance pay requirements. By 1975, only Maine and Wisconsin had plant closing laws. The Maine law arose out of a crisis in the shoe and textile industries in New England in the late 1960s. The initial law applied to all firms with 100 or more employees that were considering closing or relocating their Maine facilities.

They were required to give a one month advance notice of the closing to the affected workers. If they failed to do so, they would be compelled to pay their employees of three years or more an amount equal to the latters' current weekly salary for every year they worked for the firm. Thus, a worker of ten years with the company would receive a payment of ten times his or her last-received weekly salary or wages. Subsequent amendments in 1973 and 1981 revised the law in various ways. For example, one amendment removed the early notification requirement for firms that chose to relocate in Maine (Rothstein, 1986, p. 26).

The Wisconsin law was also subsequently amended. Passed in 1975, it required sixty days advance notice of a closing or relocation for Wisconsin firms with 100 or more employees. Failure to notify employees properly made the firm liable to a fine of $50 for each of these employees. In 1983, the fine was removed and firms were urged to comply voluntarily with the advance notification requirement. By 1986, eight jurisdictions in the United States had passed some kind of plant closing legislation (Rothstein, 1986, p. 29). In 1988, Congress passed the first federal law requiring advance notice in certain cases of plant closing or relocation—the Worker Adjustment and Retraining Notification Act. In general, this law requires that firms of 100 or more employees give sixty days advance notice of a plant closing or mass layoff to the affected workers or their representatives. They are also required to give advance notice to certain governmental units or bodies. Failure to meet these requirements can lead to the payment of certain fines or penalties, such as providing back pay to the workers or continuing to contribute to their pension or health insurance plans. The enforcement of the law is to occur primarily through the civil court system rather than through the administration of a federal agency, such as the Department of Labor. There are added clarifications and exemptions to the bill, but these need not further concern us here.

It is clear that the new legislation brings the United States closer to certain European countries that have had laws concerning advance notice of a plant closing for many years now. For example, West Germany required its companies with more than twenty employees to give the workers council elected by the workers thirty days prior notice of layoffs. A plan of layoff, relocation, transfer, severance payments, and the like was then to be negotiated. Such a plan usually involved the giving of severance payments of some kind. Great Britain requires ninety days advance notice, depending upon the case, and typically requires firms to give some kind of severance payment to their workers. France requires advance notice of from two to fourteen weeks, depending upon the case, and like Great Britain, it includes reference to providing severance payments. Such payments are mandated by ministerial decree. All employees with at least two years of continuous service with the same employer are entitled to such payments. Finally, even Japan, although it lacks a comprehensive law on plant closings, does require notification of government and labor representatives in certain officially designated "depressed industries" (Tysse, 1986, p 13).

Naturally, classical theorists are in general dissatisfied with the recent direction of federal legislation in this area in the United States. They suggest that various problems can be expected to arise because of it. In contrast to this, stakeholder theorists believe that further worker and community protections are needed.

THE CLASSICAL APPROACH TOWARD PLANT RELOCATION: THE EFFICIENCY ARGUMENT

The classical theory of corporate responsibility is broad enough to accommodate various proposals or views on the plant relocation question. Much of the current literature of this position is aimed at lessening or eliminating legal restrictions on business mobility that now exist or are being proposed. But as we have suggested, within these discussions about legal matters can also be found positions that concern the nature and status of the economic, moral, and social responsibilities of management in this area.

We indicated in chapter 8 that the classical theory is distinguished from the other views of corporate responsibility in that its proponents believe that management's first responsibility is to the shareholders of the company. This principle is typically said to be the fundamental consideration in determining when to relocate or shut down a company's operations. Classical theorists also believe that management should have wide discretion in making and implementing such decisions. They should in general not be under any set of legal requirements to confer or negotiate with the affected workers, or to give them advance notice, or provide severance payments and the like to them. They believe that such restrictions are largely unjustified. Some classical theorists like Lunnie believe that management may have a moral obligation to take some of these additional steps, though he argues of course that this should not become the basis of a legally enforced duty (Lunnie, 1983, p. 7). However, others seem to believe that in many cases where management closes a facility without doing these things, companies have typically met all of the relevant economic, moral, and social responsibilities that apply to them. They have no overriding or general nonlegal responsibility to keep the facility open, or to do the additional actions just mentioned, if they choose to close it. As we would expect, they believe that the main factor making a decision on relocation unjustified is that it loses money for the firm and its stockholders.

We see then that several distinguishable views can be said to embody the classical approach to corporate responsibility in the plant closing issue. In one view, managers have only to meet their legal and economic responsibilities here; no other responsibilities apply to them. In another view, managers may have added responsibilities, but the latter always take a back seat to the economic and legal responsibilities that management have to the shareholders. These other responsibilities are thus rarely obligations. The classical approach is also at least partly involved in those views that accept the idea that management may have a responsibility to give some kind of advance notice to its workers but rejects the idea that it must meet the other proposals mentioned above. Finally, we can clearly see the classical approach in the work of many of those individuals who seek to remove those legal restrictions that currently apply to firms in this area.

The presentation of the classical and stakeholder approaches is made somewhat more difficult because there has been considerable response and counterresponse among the advocates of these positions. Therefore, it is difficult to discuss only one side of the issue, especially when much of what a theorist has to say involves responding to the earlier points and arguments of his or her opponents. Once again, as with the general question of corporate responsibility, the specific debate about the nature of corporate responsibilities in matters of plant relocation has thus far no clear winner. Realizing this, and appreciating the ongoing nature of the debate, we will first examine five positive arguments advanced by classical thinkers, after which, we shall turn our attention to the stakeholder position and its response to these arguments. In chapter 14, we shall discuss the classical counterresponse to the stakeholder position, and the social demandingness and social activist views.

The most frequently raised argument in behalf of the classical approach toward plant relocation is the efficiency argument. Classical theorists maintain that carrying out such responsibilities as giving advance notice, making severance payments, or choosing to operate unproductive plants in the first place is expensive and constitutes a tax upon the firm and its shareholders (McKenzie, 1982b, p. 140). They argue that management must have wide latitude in making decisions about capital mobility. Firms that lack such latitude, either because broad legal restrictions have been placed on their capital movement or because their management feels itself under the weight of other responsibilities it voluntarily imposes upon itself, will have greater difficulty surviving in the marketplace. They will, other things being equal, be involved in a disadvantageous market position relative to competitors who have no such restrictions or reservations (Sturdivant, 1981, p. 408). By functioning in this way, they not only lessen the return that is to be paid to the owners as the latter's reward for investing in the firm, but they also may be jeopardizing the jobs of all the workers of the company.

McKenzie, for example, tells us that the competitive market system continuously undergoes a process that Schumpeter called "creative destruction" (McKenzie, 1982c, p. 15). As a resource is used up or becomes too expensive to utilize, managers are responsible to move the firm into new areas where the firm can survive and flourish. These may involve new product, resource, or geographical areas. Such movement opens up productive possibilities for the firm and new opportunities for those in the selected area of development. Stern, Wood, and Hammer remind us that von Hayek's concept of catallaxy is frequently used by classical theorists in their analysis of the capital mobility issue (Stern, Wood, and Hammer, 1979, p. 83). Such theorists tell us that capital mobility is an important element in the market system's ability to improve itself.

Classical theorists do not, of course, ignore the costs associated with plant relocations and shutdown, but they believe that there are typically more winners than losers when a plant relocates for reasons of efficiency. The winners include most of those who participate in the market system for greater efficiency generally means stable or lower prices and perhaps even more jobs in the future. Largely or wholly unrestricted capital mobility thus improves the entire system, especially in the long run. Such mobility is currently to the detriment of many of the industrially developed countries because many jobs are being lost to workers in the less developed nations. But classical theorists maintain that this is the way the world market system adjusts or "corrects" itself as competitive firms pursue the least expensive resources and factors of production. It is, in fact, an important way for the market system and capitalism to extend itself to these areas of the world.

OTHER ARGUMENTS FOR THE CLASSICAL THEORY

In addition to the efficiency argument, classical theorists typically advance four other arguments in behalf of their position on plant relocation. A second argument centers around the need for management's freedom of choice in making business decisions. If legal, moral, or social restrictions are to be placed upon management, there must be very good reasons for doing so. Whether self-imposed or externally enforced, such restrictions interfere with a fundamental feature and condition of the market system—the freedom of producers, consumers, investors, and the like to make decisions in their own behalf. The presumption is in favor of this freedom rather than the restrictions urged by opponents.

Classical theorists further appeal to the property rights argument. Thus, McKenzie maintains that when individuals buy productive resources, they come into possession of the right to utilize and dispose of these assets as they see fit (McKenzie, 1982b, p. 131). They acquire the right to move these assets if better opportunities emerge elsewhere. For management this means that they must be loyal agents for the shareholders. To fail to seize the opportunities that exist elsewhere is to so something that interferes with the stockholders' rights for it compromises the present stock value of the corporation. Once again, only a very strong argument to the contrary can overcome the presumption in favor of the property rights of the owners.

Fourth, classical theorists contend that employees are not treated wrongly when they lose their jobs due to a plant closing for the conditions of employment are spelled out in their employment contracts. They are aware of the fact that their jobs are not guaranteed in perpetuity. Any number of factors may lead to layoffs or unemployment. Plant closing or relocation constitutes only one of these. Harrison mentions that management is under no legal obligation to bargain with the unions about a plant closing as long as it is partial—as long as it involves one of several plants or units in the company, rather than the entire firm (Harrison, 1984, p. 400). Matters such as early notice, severance payments, and retraining programs may be negotiated, but management is under no initial obligation to offer these to the workers. Management is bound only by the stipulations of the private contracts entered into in this area.

This leads us to the fifth argument for the classical position—the fairness argument. Advocates of this view maintain that lessening management's power to close or relocate a facility is unfair, first because such a move would give more power to the workers for they would still have the capacity to switch employers if they liked while the proposed restrictions would limit management's ability to transfer or fire employees. Second, it is unfair to consumers who must be asked to pay more for the goods or services of businesses than they would if firms could move with little or no restraints. Third, it is unfair to those areas of the country or world whose resources are presently less costly. Sufficiently high transfer costs caused by restrictions could lead to more outright closings of present facilities and fewer openings of newer facilities in other areas. McKenzie indicates that this is especially unfair to the populations of developing regions and countries (McKenzie, 1982a, pp. 130ff.). Last, it is unfair to future generations who will be expected to pay later for the present waste of resources and opportunities involved in restrictive plant closing or relocation policies, whether these are externally imposed or voluntarily acknowledged and accepted by management.

Stakeholder theorists and others question or reject these arguments. They maintain that companies have responsibilities to both workers and to certain members of the local communities in which the firms are located. They believe that management has a moral and social responsibility to consider the interests of these individuals to be on a par with the interests of stockholders in these matters.

THE STAKEHOLDER RESPONSE: THE COST ARGUMENT

As we have said, stakeholder theorists typically propose certain legal or moral restrictions upon management. They believe that some past closings or reloca-tions have been unwarranted and they suggest that such mistakes should be avoided in the future. They further contend that even if management is justified in deciding to shut down or move a facility in a particular case, it has the responsibility of giving appropriate early notice and offering some or all of the programs or payments mentioned earlier in the chapter.

We shall see that the arguments discussed here are sometimes advanced by social demandingness and social activist theorists as well. Which theory is being endorsed is based partly upon the focus of the argument under consideration (Is it a matter applying principally to the employees or to certain members of the local community, for example, or does it apply to a society or the world as a whole?) and partly upon the package of proposals and other arguments in which a certain consideration is bound. In the coming sections of this chapter we shall be concerned with those arguments that are relevant to the stakeholder position. This is so then even if some of the theorists mentioned here are not, strictly speaking, advocates of this view of corporate responsibility. It is, after all, the nature of the particular argument they raise that puts them in this discussion and not the nature of their overall position.

One of the most frequently raised arguments against the classical theory of plant relocation is the human and economic cost argument. Various studies have sought to show the impact that plant closings have had upon the workers or former workers of a company. Collins, for example, notes the large number of workers in this country who have been affected by plant closings and relocation. Between 1969 and 1976, 22 million jobs were lost in the United States; from 1976 to 1982, 16 million jobs were eliminated due to the closings of large firms (Collins, 1989, p. 67). The Bureau of Labor Statistics reports that from January 1981 to January 1986, nearly 11 million workers in this country were put out of work because of plant closings and permanent layoffs. The U.S. General Accounting Office reports in its study of plant closings that the median length of prenotification for these closings was seven days. Less than 20 percent of firms provided more than thirty days notice, and only one in seven employers offered these workers a comprehensive assistance package of income maintenance, continued health insurance coverage, job search assistance, and counseling. In another study, the Bureau of Labor Statistics found that in fact about two thirds of all laid-off workers in this country received no advanced general notice at all (Collins, 1989, p. 68).

Various studies have been conducted to determine the effect of job loss upon human health and well-being. Stakeholder theorists tell us that a general consensus seems to be emerging on this question. In their review of the research literature, however, Gordus, Jarley, and Ferman warn us of several things. First, they tell us that the full extensiveness of the problem of plant closings is not yet known. Relying upon the Dun and Bradstreet data on business openings, closings, and transfers has not been fully adequate for various forms of job loss are not considered in such data. For example, job loss due to successive business contraction is not considered in these data. Further, we do not know the full scope of the problem in terms of the regions of the country or world that have been affected by plant closings and relocations; nor do we know enough about the communities affected and the nature of the layoff phenomenon, whether it is permanent or cyclical in nature (Gordus, Jarley, and Ferman, 1981, p. 156). Second, they contend there is still much to be learned about the effects of job loss on psychological and physical health. They tell us that the problem of our lack of knowledge in this regard could be better addressed if we had more reliable studies, especially longitudinal ones with adequate control groups for comparison purposes. Still, as stakeholder theorists see it, most of the studies completed thus far point in the same direction—job loss is a stressful experience that is usually associated with a variety of physical and psychological dysfunctions. Since the literature of health studies is quite extensive, however, we must content ourselves with citing only a few of the studies.

We begin with two early studies. Brenner examined data from 1940 to the early 1970s. Focusing exclusively upon plant shutdowns, he correlated these closings with the increased incidence of various measures of personal or social problems in the communities in which the closings occurred. He found that a 1 percent increase in unemployment sustained over a six-year period was correlated with increases in the social indicators included in the table below (Brenner, 1976, pp. 1ff.).

Social Indicator	Percentage Increase*	Estimated Number for the Nation as a Whole*
General mortality	2.7	37,000 deaths
Suicides	5.7	920 suicides
Mental health admissions	4.7	4,000 admissions
State prison admissions	5.6	3,300 admissions
Homicides	8.0	650 deaths
Cirrhosis of the liver mortality	2.7	500 deaths
Cardiovascular mortality	2.7	20,000 deaths

*Correlated with a 1% increase in unemployment in a community sustained over a six-year period.

In a related study, Kasl and Cobb found high or increased blood pressure and abnormally high cholesterol and blood sugar levels in blue collar workers who lost their jobs because of a plant closing (Kasl and Cobb, 1970, pp. 106ff.). In another study they reported a significant correlation between job loss and increased incidences of ulcers and respiratory diseases. Finally, they found higher levels of serum glucose, serum pepsinogen, and serum uric acid in individuals experiencing job loss than in a control group of workers who had no such experience (Cobb and Kasl, 1977, p. 179). They also found that, when compared with individuals in a control group, persons experiencing job loss are more likely to be depressed, have low self-esteem, and be anxious, tense, and irritable. The suicide rate for such individuals is thirty times higher than the expected rate.

Similar findings are reported by Strange, who notes that after a plant closing in an Appalachian town, many of the people lost a central point of focus in the community. The plant loss led to a disruption in the usual social networks (Strange, 1977, p. 39). This disruption is also discussed by Kahn, who tells us that a Michigan study in which certain social indicators were examined after the unemployment rate increased between 1979 and 1980 found that the incidences of reported child abuse went up 37 percent, substance abuse cases increased by 10 percent, and the suicide rate grew by 27 percent (Kahn, 1981, pp. 78ff.).

Cobb and Kasl's work suggests that unemployment affects certain types of individuals more than others. According to them, it has the greatest impact on people in a situation of economic deprivation. And they tell us that the stress of job loss is experienced more acutely in the anticipation stage, but that most individuals adapt to their new situation, at least within the first twenty-four months after job loss. Urban workers are likely to experience greater stress than rural workers after such a loss (Cobb and Kasl, 1977, pp. 10ff.).

Their work is borne out by Buss and Redburn, who found that the coping behavior of unemployed workers in general became more effective as time went on, but the coping behavior of those individuals who remained unemployed (or who were laid off more than once) during the period of their study was less effective. They also found that blue collar workers coped less effectively than white collar workers and that minority workers had less success in coping with job loss than nonminorities (Buss and Redburn, 1983, pp. 68ff.). Several studies also suggest that such factors as family and community support can help buffer the individual from the severe effects of job loss.

Finally, Harris, Heller, and Braddock tell us that women report more stress and psychological health problems than do men after a layoff. These authors offer various factors that may be at work here, including the lower income of women initially, the age and educational status of women at the time of job loss, and the level of attachment of the worker to her job before the layoff (Harris, Heller, and Braddock, 1988, p. 393).

Some theorists have sought to quantify the economic costs involved in plant closings. They have estimated the dollar value of the jobs lost due to closing or relocation. One type of study estimates losses for the individual; another estimates it for a region or the nation as a whole. Frank and Freeman's work is of the latter sort. They tell us that U.S. firms spent about $10 billion in direct foreign investment in 1970. After making a series of calculations based upon different assumptions about international competitiveness and relative production costs, they calculated that the average domestic job loss resulting from this level of investment was 160,000 jobs. This suggests that for every $1 billion in investment transferred to other countries, 26,500 jobs are eliminated domestically (Frank and Freeman, 1978, p. 153). Multiplying this figure by the average annual income of domestic workers and the total amount of capital transferred to other countries in a single year yields an estimate of the aggregate national income otherwise lost by workers for that year.

Bluestone and Harrison further note that the impact of foreign investment on labor income within the Frank-Freeman scenario is such as to lower domestic wages by between 3 and 13 percent, depending upon the level of the premium on profits demanded by U.S. multinationals as a condition for investment. The lower the premium, the more jobs created outside the United States (Bluestone and Harrison, 1982, p. 46). The economic and personal loss involved here is felt both by the displaced workers and the local communities in which they live. It is also translated into lost revenue in income tax, which must be made up either by lessened government services or by higher taxes to be paid by others.

The second type of study concerns the financial loss to the individual worker, as illustrated by Jacobson's work. In his study of displaced workers in the steel industry in 1970, Jacobson estimated that the personal financial loss of displaced workers was about $1,000 in the year in which the job was lost and represented a life-time loss of about $9,500 per worker (Jacobson, 1975, Chapt. 5). Stern's study of workers who lost their jobs at an Armour plant suggests that their postdisplacement earnings after the fourth year of job loss were on average 20 percent below their prelayoff level (Stern, 1972, pp. 3ff.). He goes on to contend that such workers will have a lower level of income for the rest of their lives. Tolles's work on displaced carpet mill workers in a small community reveals a point also brought out by other studies: the hardship of job loss falls disproportionately upon women, older workers, and those with less education (Tolles, 1966, pp. 14ff.). Later studies add minorities to this list.

Another illustration of this type of research is the work of Dorsey, who sought to determine the success that displaced workers had in finding work elsewhere. Of 3,000 workers who had been laid off when Mack Truck closed a plant in 1966, 23 percent were still unemployed ten months later. He also found that the wages of reemployed workers fell about 33 percent (Dorsey, 1967, pp. 175ff.). Raines reports that *Fortune* magazine did a study of 4,100 workers who had lost their jobs when Youngstown Sheet and Tube closed in 1978. It found that 35 percent of the former workers had been forced into early retirement with an income half what it had been when they worked; another 15 percent were still unemployed two years later; and, 20 to 40 percent of the remainder had taken substantial pay cuts in their new line of work (Raines, 1982, p. 301).

Finally, in summarizing the data from several job loss studies, Holen tells us that plant closings lead to local labor force withdrawals of approximately 10 percent, while local unemployment rates reported in various studies typically cluster near 20 percent, and although the duration of the layoff period tends to be short (usually a matter of weeks), some studies report substantial numbers of individuals who were out of work for longer durations, up to and exceeding one year (Holen, 1976, p. 6). This extended unemployment is expensive for the country as a whole, not only in terms of lost productivity and lower tax revenues, but also in terms of the need to pay increased unemployment benefits to eligible recipients who, according to Mishel, constitute about two thirds of all displaced workers (Mishel, 1988, p. 59). Such a figure highlights the budgetary expense to society as a whole of extensive job loss. But it also reminds us once again of the significant personal expense to the displaced workers, especially the one third who are not covered by unemployment insurance.

THE INEFFICIENCY ARGUMENT

In addition to the cost argument as we have discussed it, it is also contended that certain forms of plant relocation undercut productivity, and thus end up wasting resources. Unlike the cost argument, though, the inefficiency argument is directed toward a certain type of plant closing. The cost argument is meant to apply to any plant closing or relocation that involves sustained unemployment and lost or lower wages for the workers' over time. The inefficiency argument applies to that class of plant closing that advocates believe are economically "unnecessary." Bluestone and Harrison have perhaps been more fully associated with this argument than any other theorists, so we shall discuss their view here even though there are elements in their overall position that are more akin to the social demandingness position (and even at times to social activism).

Bluestone, for example, tells us that a survey of the plant closings that was made between the years 1969 and 1976 revealed that very few of these shutdowns took, place because of bankruptcy. Most involved transfers of capital resources or employees to other facilities owned by a company. He suggests then that of the facilities that shut down, a good percentage could perhaps have stayed in operation (Bluestone, 1982, p. 45). These are the candidates for economically "unnecessary" closings. As these authors see it, bankruptcy is only one, relatively infrequent, reason for plant shutdowns. Other reasons or motives typically apply—from product cycle changes to lessened access to resources or markets, from the pursuit of lower taxes to the avoidance of unions. In pursuing some of these motives, firms at times close facilities that are otherwise profitable, or could be made profitable if managed by some other organization or set of individuals (including the workers or the local community). But instead of permitting the facility to be run autonomously, management chooses to close the plant down and transfer what capital or assets it can to another facility, one perceived to be less bothersome or costly to manage (Bluestone and Harrison, 1980, p. 7).

These authors go on to tell us that before relocation or shutdown, management may "milk" or "bleed" the facility. In both cases, management takes out more from the plant than it is willing to reinvest for the latter's maintenance, upkeep, or expansion. In "bleeding" the plant, however, management so affects the facility's ability to operate on its own that it virtually eliminates its chances of functioning as a separate unit. Such a policy may make a certain manager or firm look good in the short term, but Bluestone and Harrison contend that it encourages a management style that is unwarranted and wasteful in the long run (Bluestone and Harrison, 1980, p. 304). Stern, Wood, and Hammer indicate that such firms destroy productive capacity for which there may be an economic niche, (Stern, Wood, and Hammer, 1979, p. 13). These authors recommend that firms explore ways to keep such facilities open through employee or community ownership.

The general argument advanced here receives some initial support from Deily, who studied the investment policies of firms in the steel industry. She found that the management of these facilities, in the wake of strong competition from imports and mini-mills, first disinvested from their plants before they chose to close them down (Deily, 1988, p. 595). Unlike Bluestone and Harrison, however, she does not speculate upon the full intent of the managers. Nor does she contend that decisions could have been made by management in the predisinvestment period that would have saved the facility, a point that is at least implied in the Bluestone and Harrison analysis. But her work certainly indicates that the managers she studied had knowledge that they would close their facilities long before the workers were ever told of this.

THE DISRESPECT FOR WORKERS ARGUMENT

The inefficiency argument often leads to a third consideration urged against unrestricted capital mobility, though it is often implicit in the human cost argument as well. It is contended that eliminating plants in this way treats workers as mere things or instruments, or, as one displaced worker put it, ''like throwaway containers.'' Such treatment is said to ignore the human dignity of workers and is alleged to be born of an outmoded theory of work.

Bluestone and Harrison again, for example, contend that proponents of the classical theory of unrestricted capital mobility often argue as if they believe that the former workers of closed facilities are mere resources, like the physical plant or machines of a factory. They are said to be human capital to match the physical and financial capital needed for the operation of the firm (Bluestone and Harrison, 1980, p. 63). Such a view overlooks the vast difference between persons and things, though, a difference that inevitably affects the question of corporate responsibility. This so whether such dignity is seen as based upon Kant's idea of the value of the moral law within human reason, the Christian and Judaic views of the inherent spiritual worth of humans, the natural rights theory of humans as possessors of inherent or inalienable rights, the feminist view that grounds it upon interpersonal relationships of nurturance and mutual caring, Bowie's notion of the reciprocal respect that is due to persons who enter into explicit (employer-employee) contracts, or the Marxist view that workers create all the value of the firm in question. When workers lose their livelihood with no prior consultation and perhaps with little advance notice, when they may be given little or no chance of salvaging their jobs by finding a way to keep a plant in operation—all in the name of earning a more attractive level of profit elsewhere—they are being treated as little more than once productive resources or things that are now no longer useful to management.

A second phase of the disrespect argument challenges the view of work that the classical theory seems to assume. Advocates of the stakeholder view tell us that workers are not mere functionaries who carry out tasks merely for the sake of corporate profit or personal income. As we have seen, theorists such as Carroll, Fromm, and Maslow tell us that work is an activity that provides one with meaning, dignity, fulfillment, and self-definition. It is a way for individuals to make a social contribution and meet personal and professional challenges. It is not then just an activity done for pay (Carroll, 1981, p. 217; Fromm, 1982b, p. 25). Managers who eliminate jobs eliminate the worker's chance for self-development in the corporation or facility. To the extent that the worker fails to find a new job, or settles for one that less effectively meets his or her need for fulfillment and challenge, management has done something that negatively affects the worker's meaning in life. As Kavanagh puts it, managers have a responsibility to workers and their jobs because their actions can have such a significant adverse effect upon the latters' lives (Kavanagh, 1982, p. 25).

THE UNFAIRNESS ARGUMENT

Closely associated with the disrespect for workers argument is the argument from unfairness. Certain theorists contend that managers who relocate a facility in order to make a more attractive level of profit elsewhere treat their workers unjustly. This is particularly true when they make little or no attempt to save the jobs of their current workers, either by offering them retraining and placement services or by trying to keep the facility a going concern. The nature or basis of this alleged unfairness has been brought out in several ways. First, it can be said that such managers do something that would not pass the role-reversal test mentioned by Donaldson and Waller in chapter 10. Managers would not them-selves likely agree to be laid off or fired with little or no advance notice or with no chance for retaining or placement with a new employer. Nor would they likely consent to losing their jobs merely to help their employer make a more attractive level of profit in another state or country.

Fromm suggests that managers who lay off workers in the situations just sketched ignore the mutual interdependence that existed within the firm before the layoffs (Fromm, 1982b, p. 23). The firm was heavily dependent upon the worker's contribution before the closing. It counted on his or her loyalty. But where now is the reciprocal loyalty of the employer? Stein tells us that since the workers' efforts create value in the corporation, managers cannot ignore the proprietary claims of workers in a plant closing or relocation decision (Stein, 1978, p. 282). To do so is to treat them unfairly relative to the shareholders for the former have also invested something of themselves in the firm. This is an occasion for management to reciprocate something to the workers by acknowl-edging their place in the network of interdependent relations that exists and ultimately constitutes the corporation. It is also a chance to respond to the dependence that workers have developed on the managers in this type of situation. Or, as Kavanagh suggests, it is unfair for employers to expect the commitment of the workers in the daily operations of the business but to show little or no commitment to the workers when the latters' jobs are in jeopardy (Kavanagh, 1982, pp. 24ff.).

Finally, Fromm advances the fairness argument in another way. To those who point out that employees have the right and ability to leave the firm before or during a plant closing (so that managers are merely exercising a similar right when they choose to have a facility exit a community), he points out that the power of the managers and the impact of their decision in this case is decidedly greater than that of the individual worker. More equal in power and effect is the decision of a single shareholder to exit a firm in the search of greater dividends or capital gains (Fromm, 1982a, p. 37). Choosing to respond to the (dissatisfied) shareholder is thus no more fair than choosing to respect the needs and contributions of the workers.

THE PROPERTY RIGHTS ARGUMENT

A fourth argument for placing legal or moral restrictions upon plant closings is the property rights argument. Stakeholder theorists and others contend that workers gain a property entitlement to their jobs after they have worked productively or effectively for a business or organization for a certain period of time. There are usually additional conditions that must be met before the worker gains such title, but advocates of this argument believe that many workers who are displaced by plant closings meet these conditions. They are thus mistreated by managers in cases of job displacement, particularly if they were given little or no advance notice of the layoff or were offered no program to reestablish them in the work force.

The idea of a property right to a job is not a new one. Such a view has been held in Europe for many years. In the United States there are occupations, such as some appointed offices and college or university professorships, that involve tenure or extend throughout the individual's working life. Persons in such positions may still lose their jobs, of course, but if this occurs, it is typically for reasons of gross ineptitude or moral turpitude. Some managers have negotiated contracts that involve receiving substantial payments if they lose (or choose to leave) their jobs after a takeover or merger. In such "golden parachute" cases, the manager has something like a property right to his or her job; the job is not guaranteed for a lifetime, but the manager has a right to substantial payment if the job is lost or refused.

There are various bases that have been alleged to be the ground of an employment property right. We shall briefly discuss four such considerations here. The first we have already met with in Stein's work: workers can claim a property right to their jobs because through their efforts material value or wealth is created or enhanced in the firm (Stein, 1978, p. 282). As Biesinger points out, at least since the time of John Locke property rights have been associated with labor. He tells us that as an adequate reward for their efforts and achievements, workers deserve (1) an appropriate immediate compensation, (2) security in their means of production, (3) freedom to pursue their self-interest, and (4) conditions that allow them to identify with or take pride in the product of their labor (Biesinger, 1984, p. 140). Plant closings, particularly if they are otherwise avoidable, violate these principles. They ignore the past value-producing capacity of the workers as they helped to transform raw materials or concepts into finished goods or services. Thus, whether labor produces all material value or wealth, as Marxists believe, or whether it accounts for only some of this value, those who are sympathetic to a version of the labor theory of value believe that workers have as strong an ownership relation to the firm as do the stockholders of the company. They too have provided or invested something of personal value to enhance the wealth of the firm. Unannounced or avoidable plant closings violate these property rights.

Some stakeholder theorists base these property rights upon prior agreement. They thus stay within the private contract model of the corporation usually associated with the classical theory. Unions in the United States have rarely been successful in legally blocking plant closings, though they do have the legal right to negotiate about them. Unions elsewhere have been more successful in this regard. Unions in the United States have, however, sought certain concessions, should a plant closing occur. The property right agreed to in this type of case could call for such benefits as adequate advance notice, severance payments, continued health insurance, retraining services, and the like, even if the right is not capable of avoiding the closing of the facility in the first place. Rothstein tells us that about 15 percent of all collective bargaining agreements stipulate the need for advance notice of a week or more for a closing or significant layoff, while less than 40 percent involve some stipulation for severance payments (Rothstein, 1986, p. 16). Torrence provides slightly different numbers. From the 400 sample contracts he surveyed in 1983, he found that about 18 percent of the contracts had some stipulation about advance notice; this figure rose to 26 percent for the 400 sample contracts he examined in 1985 (Torrence, 1986, p. 463).

A third basis for the alleged property right to a job is past precedent. Sawyer, for example, tells us that present continuation in employment implies that this will go unabated in the future (Sawyer, 1985, p. 121). The principle here is something like that found in adverse possession. The continued use of something admitted initially to be another's property for a certain period of time legally (and perhaps morally) entitles one to its largely unobstructed use in the future. Past consistency in conduct creates at least a *prima facie* case for an obligation to continue acting in this way in the future.

Sometimes this argument is advanced in independence of the property argument. In this case, its utilitarian aspects are brought out more fully and it is seen to be a species of the impact model of accountability. It is said that the network of human relations is relatively fragile. Its success or effectiveness depends upon more than just the enforcement of law; it depends upon consistency in meeting human expectations. Past precedent generates these expectations, which then carry their own social or moral momentum. Plant closings run counter to this momentum and the human expectations upon which it is grounded. Such actions contravene the trust and consistency that had been a part of the worker-employer relationship. This effect has been noted in some of the studies done on worker reactions to a plant closing, such as that of Strange. They indicate that laid-off workers frequently feel a sense of helplessness and are more suspicious of others (Kavanagh, 1982, p. 28).

This argument, whether or not it is advanced in its utilitarian form, is typically used to defend the thesis that management has a responsibility at least to give sufficient early notice of a plant closing. It is generally not used to reject the decision to close a plant in the first place. It is admitted that past precedent grounds only a *prima facie* obligation to continued like behavior. Nevertheless, it does defend the idea that managers are obligated to explain ending a precedent in this regard. The presence of this obligation is to be contrasted with a recent General Accounting Office study done in 1983 and 1984 that found that one third of all firms involved in plant shutdowns provided neither prior explanation nor advance notice of the closing (reported in Mishel, 1988, p. 60).

Finally, we have the argument based upon collective ownership. It is contended that workers have collective property rights in their firms that are based upon their contribution to pension funds. Barber tells us that in the early 1980s 50 million workers contributed to pension funds that totaled $700 million dollars. They owned 40 percent of all bonds and 20 to 25 percent of all corporate stock. Classified legally as deferred wages, they are not the property of the employer (Barber, 1982, pp. 101ff.). Bluestone and Harrison suggest that since pension funds account for a significant percentage of all corporate stock owned in the United States, managers have as important a reason to respond to the workers' collective interests for meaningful and secure work as they do to respond to the collective interests of the other stockholders for higher stock values and more lucrative and secure returns on investment (Bluestone and Harrison, 1980, p. 128). Such collective ownership also generates responsibilities for the trustees of these funds, of course, as well as for the managers of the firms in which they are invested.

THE INCREASED REGULATION ARGUMENT

We end our discussion of the stakeholder arguments against the classical position with an argument that is often raised in the area of corporate social or moral responsibility. Taking their cue from the reverse-impact model of accountability relations, advocates of this argument contend that if managers ignore their social and moral responsibilities in plant closing matters, society will see to it that they are legally required to take some of the actions considered here. Sawyer, for example, indicates that if firms do not work to mitigate the negative effects of layoffs, the public may be induced or inflamed to pass more stringent government regulations in this area (Sawyer, 1985, p. 166). This point is seconded by Jarolem, especially as regards the negative impact of plant closings upon local communities (Jarolem, 1982, p. 34). And, of course, one could point to the legal situation in Europe as well as to the recent passage of the Worker Adjustment and Retraining Notification Act by the U.S. Congress as indications of the direction that industrialized nations may well take in the future toward government involvement in capital mobility.

REFERENCES

Barber, Randy. 1982. ''Gaining Control Over Our Economic Resources.'' In *Community and Capital in Conflict: Plant Closings and Job Loss*, edited by John C. Raines,

Lenora E. Berson, and David McI. Gracie, pp. 101–25. Philadelphia: Temple University Press.

Berry, Steve, Peter Gottschalk, and Doug Wissoker. 1988. "An Error Components Model of the Impact of Plant Closing on Earnings." *Review of Economics and Statistics*, November, pp. 701–7.

Biesinger, Gary. 1984. "Corporate Power and Employee Relations." *Journal of Business Ethics*, May, pp. 139–42.

Bluestone, Barry. 1982. "Deindustrialization and the Abandonment of Community." In *Community and Capital in Conflict: Plant Closings and Job Loss*, edited by John C. Raines, Lenora E. Berson, and David McI. Gracie, pp. 44–65. Philadelphia: Temple University Press.

Bluestone, Barry, and Bennett Harrison. 1980. *Capital and Communities: The Causes and Consequences of Private Disinvestment*. Washington, D.C.: The Progressive Alliance.

————. 1982. *The Deindustrialization of America*. New York: Basic Books.

Brenner, Harvey. 1976. "Estimating the Social Costs of National Economic Policy: Implications for Mental and Physical Health and Clinical Aggression." In *Report to the Joint Economic Committee, U.S. Congress*. Washington, D.C.: U.S. Government Printing Office.

Buss, Terry F., and F. Stevens Redburn. 1983. *Mass Unemployment: Plant Closings and Community Mental Health*. Beverly Hills, Calif.: Sage Publications.

Carroll, Archie B. 1981. *Business and Society: Managing Corporate Social Performance*. Boston: Little, Brown and Company.

Cobb, Sidney, and Stanislaw Kasl. 1977. "Termination: The Consequences of Job Loss." Public Health Service, Center for Disease Control, National Institute for Occupational Safety and Health, U.S. Department of Health, Education and Welfare. Washington, D.C.: U.S. Government Printing Office, June.

Collins, Denis. 1989. "Plant Closings: Establishing Legal Obligations." *Labor Law Journal*, February, pp. 67–80.

Deily, Mary. 1988. "Investment Activity and the Exit Decision." *Review of Economics and Statistics*, November, pp. 595–602.

Dorsey, John W. 1967. "The Mack Case: A Study in Unemployment." In *Studies in the Economics of Income Maintenance*, edited by Otto Eckstein, pp. 175–248. Washington, D.C.: The Brookings Institution.

Frank. Robert H., and Richard T. Freeman. 1978. "The Distributional Consequences of Direct Foreign Investment." In *The Impact of International Trade and Investment: A Conference of the U.S. Department of Labor*, edited by William G. Dewald, pp. 143–158. Washington, D.C.: U.S. Government Printing Office.

Fromm, W. E. 1982a. "Employee Participation in Decision-Making." In *The Ethical Factor in Business Decisions: Essays Toward Criteria*, edited by Arnold Berleant, pp. 35–40. Greenvale, N.Y.: C. W. Post Center, Long Island University.

Fromm, W. E. 1982b. "The Social Responsibility of Business to Employees." In *The Ethical Factor in Business Decisions: Essays Toward Criteria*, edited by Arnold Berleant, pp. 21–28. Greenvale, N.Y.: C. W. Post Center, Long Island University.

Gordus, Jeanne Prial, Paul Jarley, and Louis A. Ferman. 1981. *Plant Closings and Economic Dislocation*. Kalamazoo, Mich.: W. E. Upjohn Institute for Employment Research.

Harris, Michael M., Tamara Heller, and David Braddock. 1988. "Sex Differences in Psychological Well-Being During a Facility Closure." *Journal of Management*, vol. 14, no. 3, pp. 391–402.

Harrison, Bennett, 1984. "The International Movement for Prenotification of Plant Closures." *Industrial Relations*, Fall, pp. 387–409.

Holen, Arlene. 1976. *Losses to Workers Displaced by Plant Closure or Layoff: A Survey of the Literature*. Alexandria, Va.: Center for Naval Analyses.

Jacobson, Louis. 1975. "Estimating the Loss in Earnings for Displaced Workers in the Steel Industry." In *Removing Restrictions on Imports of Steel*. Arlington, Va.: Center for Naval Analyses.

Jarolem, Stanley. 1982. "The Community." In *The Ethical Factor in Business Decisions: Essays Toward Criteria*, edited by Arnold Berleant, pp. 29–34. Greenvale, N.Y.: C. W. Post Center, Long Island University.

Kahn, Robert L. 1981. *Work and Health*. New York: John Wiley and Sons.

Kasl, Stanislaw, and Sidney Cobb. 1970. "Blood Pressure Changes in Men Undergoing Job Loss." *Psychometric Medicine*, January–February, pp. 106–22.

Kavanagh, John P. 1982. "Ethical Issues in Plant Relocation." *Business and Professional Ethics Journal*. Winter, pp. 21–33.

Lunnie, F. M. 1983. "Statement of F. M. Lunnie, Jr., Assistant Vice President of Industrial Relations, National Association of Manufactures, on Plant Closings." Testimony before Subcommittee on Labor-Management Relations, House of Representatives, May 18.

McKenzie, Richard B. 1982a. "The Case for Business Mobility." In *Plant Closings: Public or Private Choices*, pp. 125–33. Washington, D.C.: The Cato Institute.

———. 1982b. "The Case for Plant Closures." In *Plant Closings: Public or Private Choices*, pp. 135–48. Washington, D.C.: The Cato Institute.

———. 1982c. *The Right to Close Down: The Political Battle Shifts to the States*. Los Angeles: Caroline House Publishers.

Mishel, Lawrence R. 1988. "Advance Notice: Benefits Outweigh the Costs." *Challenge*, July–August, 1982. pp. 58–61.

Raines, John C. 1982. "Economics and the Justification of Sorrows." In *Community and Capital in Conflict: Plant Closings and Job Loss*, edited by John C. Raines, Lenora E. Berson, and David McI. Gracie, pp. 282–311. Philadelphia: Temple University Press.

Rothstein, Lawrence E. 1986. *Plant Closings: Power, Politics and Workers*. Dover, Mass.: Auburn House Publishing Company.

Sawyer, George C. 1985. *Business and Its Environment: Managing Social Impact*. Englewood Cliffs, N.J.: Prentice-Hall.

Stein, Barry. 1978. "Who Owns Corporations: Implications for Social Responsibility." In *Proceedings of the Second National Conference on Business Ethics*, edited by W. Michael Hoffmann, pp. 278–82. Washington, D.C.: University Press of America.

Stern, James L. 1972. "Consequences of Plant Closure." *The Journal of Human Resources*, Winter, pp. 3–24.

Stern, Robert N., K. Haydn Wood, and Tove Helland Hammer. 1979. *Employee Ownership in Plant Shutdowns*. Kalamazoo, Mich.: W. E. Upjohn Institute for Employment Research.

Strange, Walter. 1977. "Job Loss: A Psychosocial Study of Worker Reactions to a Plant

Closing in a Company Town in Southern Appalachia." National Technical Information Service.

Sturdivant, Frederick D. 1981. *Business and Society: A Managerial Approach.* Homewood, Ill.: Richard D. Irwin.

Tolles, N. Arnold. 1966. "The Post-Layoff Experience of Displaced Carpet Mill Workers." In *Weathering Layoffs in a Small Community.* U.S. Bulletin of Labor Statistics No. 1516. Washington, D.C.: U.S. Government Printing Office.

Torrence, William D. 1986. "Plant Closing and Advance Notice: Another Look at the Numbers." *Labor Law Journal,* August, pp. 461–65.

Tysse, G. J. 1986. *Regulating Plant Closings and Mass Layoffs: A Summary of Foreign Requirements.* Washington, D.C.: National Center on Occupational Readjustment.

14

THE QUESTION OF PLANT RELOCATION
OR CLOSING—II

THE CLASSICAL RESPONSE TO THE STAKEHOLDER ARGUMENTS

Classical theorists have responded to the stakeholder challenge in various ways. And they have been particularly interested in arguments used to defend the placing or holding of legal restrictions on plant closings. In the present chapter we shall examine this response. We shall then go on to discuss the social demandingness and activists positions, and shall end the chapter by showing the applications of some of the assumptions of corporate responsibility to the present debate.

Against the human cost argument classical theorists contend that there are also human costs involved in the failure to transfer capital. These may not be as easy to detect and calculate perhaps, because individuals who would otherwise have gained by a capital transfer often are not aware of what they have missed, should a plant relocation not be completed. We cannot fully appreciate or measure the pain of missed opportunity. Displaced workers, on the other hand, are very much aware of what they have lost when a facility closes down. When dealing with those living in conditions of chronic poverty in other parts of the world, the human cost argument becomes then a forceful consideration for unrestricted capital mobility, say classical theorists.

In addition, they tell us not only is it the case that the problem of unemployed workers in typically greater in other parts of the world than it is here, but they also tell us that it is not as great in developed countries as it once was. In the United States, for example, there is a whole range of government programs that are meant to protect or buffer the worker from the more serious consequences of job loss. There is unemployment insurance, trade readjustment assistance, the job training partnership program, pension reassurance, aid to families with dependent children, food stamps, and the like. This leads them naturally to conclude that we do not need new government programs or regulations in this area. Some classical theorists add to this point the suggestion that some recent studies indicate the human and economic cost arguments of stakeholder and other theorists have thus far been exaggerated in any case.

Berry, Gottschalk, and Wissoker, for example, remind us that several studies indicate that although the displaced worker's income may fall substantially during and immediately after a layoff, over time the worker's income tends to return to its prelayoff level (Berry, Gottschalk, and Wissoker, 1988, p. 706). This suggests (at most) the need for short-term relief for these workers. It also suggests to classical theorists that when one compares the alleviation of suffering that a job would bring to people living in third world countries to the short-term pain its loss brings to workers in developed nations, the moral and social force of the invisible hand view of the marketplace becomes ever more evident.

McKenzie adds to these points the contention that legal restrictions or regulations on plant closings, including early notice provisions and the like, will likely hurt more workers in this country than they will help. They will add to the expense of hiring workers, contribute to more business failures, and lead to fewer jobs domestically or to lower wages for workers (McKenzie, 1982a, p. 126). Such restrictions will also likely decrease the perceived value of firms subject to them because the firms have lost one of their traditional rights (McKenzie, 1982a, p. 131). And communities or states that pass such regulations will ultimately put themselves at a comparative disadvantage in trying to attract capital investment. They will, in fact, unwittingly contribute to capital flight. Finally, as we have seen, classical theorists tell us that managers who voluntarily impose these restrictions upon their companies will simply make their firms less competitive. Such a policy may in the end jeopardize more jobs than it seeks to salvage.

There is some question in the literature, especially since the work of Cobb and Kasl, about what is cause and what effect in the health studies in this area. Since there are marked individual differences in reaction to job loss, the question arises whether such a loss causes stress, low self-esteem, distrust, and the like, or whether these factors help to bring on (extended) unemployment. Until these matters are clarified, classical theorists believe we should refrain from placing greater moral or legal restrictions upon management's ability to move capital quickly and efficiently.

Against the disrespect for workers argument, classical theorists remind us of the applicability of the employment-at-will doctrine. Such a doctrine recognizes the freedom of choice of both workers and managers. It emphasizes the voluntary nature of the employment contract—either party may void the contract, under the appropriate conditions, at will. Just as the government is not expected to examine and approve the worker's decision to seek employment elsewhere, it need not be called upon to approve management's decision to seek investment elsewhere, either. Since workers know that their effort is being purchased by the company for the time specified in the contract, they are unjustified in feeling betrayed when management indicates it no longer wishes to purchase this effort. If workers, through their own past agreement and acceptance, believe they have not been treated as mere tools while employed, it seems that they can hardly claim they are treated like things when the conditions of the contract are simply not renewed. This point also calls into question the compellingness of the past precedent argument of stakeholder theorists. The existence of renewable contracts itself sets a precedent that emphasizes the temporary quality of work in most occupations. So we need not focus upon the (continued) renewability of employment contracts to derive the precedent here; we should focus instead upon their being renewed *periodically*.

There are various ways for classical theorists to respond to the unfairness argument. First, it can be doubted whether mutual dependence entails the virtual perpetual duration of a human relationship. As we have seen, as long as workers have agreed to offer their services for a certain period of time for an agreed upon wage, they can hardly claim that unfair treatment has occurred if there is simply a break in the contract. And if they believe they were initially being treated unfairly in the contract, they could have rejected it and sought employment elsewhere. Further protections against layoff can be negotiated in employment contracts, but again these carry a price in terms of lower wages or fewer jobs. McKenzie suggests that individual workers can protect or insulate themselves from the pain of job loss by contributing to a personal fund that is designed to carry them through a period of unemployment (McKenzie, 1982b, p. 138). This suggestion is consistent with Cobb and Kasl's work, which indicates that the physical, psychological, and social costs of unemployment occur primarily or more dramatically in a context of economic deprivation. Removing this deprivation typically removes much of the stress, anxiety, social problems, and the like that often attend job loss. McKenzie suggests that if workers wished to build up a severance pay fund equal to that proposed in several state bills, they need only to save about 2 percent of their earnings (McKenzie, 1982b, p. 17). Economic security can thus be partially insured without the need for government mandates, and such a fund places the responsibility for providing economic security clearly where it belongs—on the shoulders of the individual worker.

Second, the unfairness argument as it is raised by stakeholder theorists concerns displaced workers, but there are versions of the argument that can be advanced that focus upon other groups of individuals. As we have seen, classical theorists believe that restrictions on capital mobility are unfair to shareholders and to citizens of third world countries. They are also unfair to future generations who may be expected to pay for the wastefulness that we show in not encouraging the most efficient or inexpensive use of resources.

Against the property rights argument, the classical theory again insists on the employment-at-will doctrine. We are reminded that courts in the United States have traditionally held that the property rights relevant to questions of closings are those of the stockholders; they have held that the decision to initiate a plant closing is a property right prerogative that is typically not subject to negotiation

(Rothstein, 1986, p. 18). (The situation is, as we have said, somewhat different from that in certain European countries.) The employment-at-will concept tells us that the existence of periodically negotiated and renewed employment agreements implies that workers do not have a property stake in their jobs. Thus, the authority, responsibilities, and benefits of employment functions stem in large part from the consent of management. Without this consent, under the usual circumstances there is virtually no secured entitlement to a job. In addition, though, even if the workers had property rights in this type of situation, there is no guarantee that these rights would take precedence over other considerations or rights.

Thus, the debate between these positions continues as stakeholder theorists respond to these points. We shall not follow this discussion any further for the present account, though incomplete and selective, illustrates some of the main considerations raised in behalf of these views.

THE SOCIAL DEMANDINGNESS POSITION

We noted in the last chapter that the question of plant relocation is frequently a matter discussed by classical and stakeholder theorists. However, we also noted in chapter 9 that the line between the stakeholder and the social demandingness theories is not always an easy or clear one to draw. We should thus expect considerable blurring or overlapping between these positions when applied to specific questions of corporate responsibility. In fact, what we find is that in some interpretations there is little difference between these views. And so we find little that is new here in the social demandingness position. There are, however, other interpretations that distinguish quite sharply between these theories in general. In some of these interpretations the social demandingness position brings to the present debate a number of new considerations and factors. In this and the next section, we shall seek to define the social demandingness position on plant closings by emphasizing the latter views; we shall then examine some of the arguments raised in behalf of one or other of these interpretations.

As I have said elsewhere, the social demandingness theory is noted for two theses that distinguish it from the stakeholder position. The first is that management must consider the likely indirect or secondary (as well as the likely direct) effects of its actions and decisions; the second is that management must respond to the actual interests, views, or expectations of the general community or public on business and moral matters. Social demandingness theorists may adhere to only one of these contentions, though it is not uncommon to see both entwined in a single work. When this happens, sometimes the first is given as (partial) defense for the second, while at other times the second is given as (part of) the rationale for the first.

Applying this to the plant shutdown question, there are two ways to advance the social demandingness theory. The first is to insist that management must also consider and respond to the needs of those who are only indirectly or secondarily affected by a plant closing decision; the second is that management must act according to what society presently wants or demands in this area. (There is also a version of this theory that insists that management must act in accordance with the interests of society or the public in general. But, as we have already noted, this version brings the present position very close to social activism.) We see the first version advanced by Drucker, who tells us that it is management's responsibility to lessen the (negative) impact of actions outside its own specific purpose and mission (Drucker, 1974, pp. 327–28). The second is urged by Carroll when he argues that the proposals about management action in the case of a plant shutdown that he advances are consistent with the (likely) social expectations and demands in this area (Carroll, 1984, p. 129).

The first thesis of the theory brings us to the question of what is a secondary or indirect effect of a management decision to close a facility. Such an effect is said to be one that is either outside the principal area of business of a firm or occurs through the mediation or intervention of the actions or decisions of those directly affected by the initial management action. In a plant shutdown, clearly the workers who lose their jobs are directly affected by the management decision. There are also certain members of the local community who are directly affected, such as those who did business with the facility before it closed. Both of these groups are definitely stakeholders. There is, however, some uncertainty about other members of the local community. What about other businesses and the taxpayers? Strictly speaking, it seems that they are only indirectly affected by the shutdown decision because they are affected through the decisions of others: the businesses suffer because former workers of the initial company choose not to spend money there any more; the taxpayers have their taxes increased or the level of government services reduced through the decisions of public officials. But from another point of view, because neither the unemployed workers nor the public officials have much choice in the matter (with little or no income or revenues, there is little else they can do), it might be argued that other businesses and taxpayers are stakeholders in this matter after all. The effects apply to them without the intervention of the (real or meaningful) choice of other stakeholders.

Clearly, however, there are members of the community and the public as a whole who are not directly affected here. There is, for example, some reluctance on the part of certain theorists to consider the children and the friends of former workers (who are not otherwise directly affected by the plant closing decision) as stakeholders. They seem to be affected by the decision, if at all, only through the actions of the former workers. Social demandingness theorists would say that management must respond to the interests of these individuals in any case, even if they are affected by the business decision solely through an increased incidence of divorce or child abuse, for example, or through having their friends (and former workers) move away from them physically or emotionally.

Another group that might be said to be nonstakeholders are those who run businesses affected by the loss of those enterprises that directly dealt with the closed facility. If a plant was quite large, there might be a secondary, or even a tertiary, wave of business failures some months or years after the closing of the initial facility. These extended business failures would also need to be considered by management in its initial decision. There are also those individuals who, and businesses and communities that, are affected by the plant closing decision in terms of the lesson or precedent it establishes (or is meant to set) for them. Since all of our actions can be said to be advertisements for a rule of responsibility when we act in its behalf (whether knowingly or not), our actions have the (secondary) effect of being examples or models to others of how to act in a particular situation. Social demandingness theory tells us that management must also consider this type of effect in its decision to close a plant. It goes without saying, of course, that classical and stakeholder theorists are also concerned with the precedents encouraged or established by corporate decision making. They too are interested in guaranteeing that the right lessons are learned, but they usually judge the adequacy of a lesson in terms of how it helps further the interests of stockholders or stakeholders and how it influences the public to support one of these groups. They do not typically or primarily judge it in terms of how it helps the public further its own expressed interests. Social demandingness theorists, on the other hand, do judge it in this way. The difference here is that the objects of concern for the first two theories are typically external to the public's interests, while the objects of concern for the social demandingness theory are largely internal to these interests. The difference is rather like the difference in deterrence effect between punishing one's own child and punishing a thief. In the latter case, the lesson is or can be exhausted in its deterrence effect upon persons other than the thief. In the former case, however, the lesson is primarily directed toward helping or improving the child, toward responding to the child's interest and need for direction.

What all this means for the present discussion is that we shall consider here the work of theorists who discuss the responsibilities of management to the wider community, even though some of this is also dealt with within the stakeholder framework. It also means that we shall consider a certain line of argument not met with in our discussion of the stakeholder position on plant closings. It is that form of argument that bases its view of management responsibility here upon what the public directly wants or expects from management.

Finally, before going on to examine some of the principal arguments for this position, we should consider by way of contrast from the other theories certain proposals endorsed by the social demandingness view. We shall focus our discussion on the work of Carroll, though it must be admitted that some of these proposals take him very close to social activism, at least as they are meant to apply to this country. Carroll tells us that a strong case can be made for believing that public opinion on this issue will eventually come on the side of certain views now expressed in the press, represented in legislative activity, or endorsed by the unions. Such views tell us that management should take the following steps when it is considering whether or not to close a plant.

First, management should study the proposed shutdown thoroughly to see whether it is necessary to close the plant in the first place. During this period it should have indepth discussions with community leaders and others affected by the decision. It should explore the possibility of new ownership, even community or employee ownership (Carroll, 1984, pp. 130ff.).

Next, if management chooses to close the facility, it should seek to mitigate the negative impact of the decision on the workers and the entire community. This involves conducting a community impact statement analyzing the main effects of the closing; providing sufficient advance notice to the workers and the public; offering transfer, relocation, outplacement services and severance payments; phasing out the business gradually and helping the community attract new business (Carroll, 1984, p. 132). Some of these proposals are also endorsed by stakeholder theorists, of course, though they tend to have a different basis than that typically advanced within the social demandingness position, and they are usually aimed at a smaller group of recipients.

ARGUMENTS FOR THE SOCIAL DEMANDINGNESS VIEW: IMPACT AND FAIRNESS

Several rather distinctive arguments have been raised for the social demandingness position on this issue. The first is consequentialistic in nature, emphasizing the impact that the decision to shut down has upon third parties. Advocates of the social demandingness view believe that this kind of decision is like any other; it is a decision in which one is expected by society to minimize its negative impact, just as one is expected to eliminate its otherwise avoidable negative consequences. And this principle is also meant to apply to those whose primary relation to the initial decision is indirect or derivative.

Two theorists who have advanced this point are Bluestone and Harrison. Although it is difficult to classify their overall view of corporate responsibility— they could almost as easily be categorized as stakeholder or social activist theorists—several of their arguments are social demandingness in nature, including the present one. They compare the present type of decision to those that concern or involve the environment (Bluestone and Harrison, 1980, p. 11). Society now demands that firms be accountable for decisions involving the handling and disposal of their wastes, and this is in large part because of the direct and indirect effects these choices have upon otherwise uninvolved third parties, living and to come. Bluestone and Harrison tell us that the logic here equally applies to the plant closing issue. Around the country people are beginning to appreciate this point.

Jarolem seconds this argument. He tells us that given the potential magnitude of both types of decision upon workers, members of the local community, and the public in general, management is expected to be careful and compassionate in its decision making (Jarolem, 1982, p. 32). This is especially so for plants in smaller communities where closings can destroy important social and emotional attachments in the community (Stern, Wood, and Hammer, 1979, pp. 86–87), and where employment loss at one of the better facilities can lead to the "bumping down" of jobs in the community. This is a situation in which those who were not former employees of the closed facility must settle for "lesser" jobs because the better employment opportunities are being taken by individuals who once worked at the closed plant (Stern, Wood, and Hammer, 1979, p. 127).

Lustig adds to this argument by telling us that in cases where a firm employs a significant portion of the local work force, the corporation becomes "in fact" the owner of community capital. Any shutdown destroys this capital. More than this, though, it also costs the larger community. He cites a U.S. Bureau of Economic Analysis report that estimates that for every percentage point of added unemployment, the larger community loses more than $68 million in foregone GNP, $20 billion in federal taxes, and $3.3 billion in various forms of public aid (Lustig, 1985, p. 132).

Chinitz appeals to these externalities in defending the proposal that certain firms may be responsible to make severance payments to the community. He tells us that after many years of operation, a firm may on balance have depleted the community's store of assets or aggravated its liabilities. It might have done this by affecting the quality of the labor force, subtracting from the supply of private physical capital, reducing the range and quality of services available to other enterprises, and the like (Chinitz, 1974, p. 270).

Jarolem indicates that implicit in management's decision to close a facility are certain views of community. One is a merely physical conception, where the local community is seen as simply the physical environment upon which a firm relies for its resources and ultimately for making its profit. Such a view is, other things being equal, likely to encourage plant closings. The second he refers to as the moral conception. Lustig calls it the active conception. In this view, the firm is seen to be interconnected with the community in a variety of ways— economic, social, political, and normative (Jarolem, 1982, p. 31; Lustig, 1985, p. 124). The web of these relations is destroyed when the facility is shut down or transferred. These authors urge that management conceive of the local community in these latter terms and strive more actively to find ways to keep a facility open.

Just as the equity or unfairness argument is developed by stakeholder theorists, so there is a version of it advanced by advocates of social demandingness, but now, of course, its focus is upon management's relationship to the wider community or the public.

Social demandingness theory tells us that there are at least five reasons why it is unfair for management to fail to consider and respond to the interests or wishes of those who are affected by its decisions in a secondary or indirect way. The first is that corporations have more than a mere economic relationship to members of the wider society. They are corporate "citizens" who are accountable to carry out the responsibilities appropriate to this status (Jarolem, 1982, p. 33). What this more precisely implies is somewhat unclear, however. For many of these theorists it at least implies setting a good example for further decisions made by firms in this area. Beyond this, it seems to cover such civic responsibilities as giving advance notice, so that the community may better explore various alternatives to save the facility or at least plan for its possible loss. It may also involve such actions as giving severance payments to the community, donating the facility to the workers or the community, or finding a new tenant for the facility.

An additional facet of the unfairness argument is brought out by those thinkers who believe that to fail to respond to the interests or wishes of the wider community is thus to ignore the mutually interdependent set of relations existing between the community and plant that permitted the business to be successful in the past (Davis, Frederick, and Blomstrom, 1980, p. 399). Such a firm ignores its teamwork responsibilities to the local area when it lets the community or public go along as if previous expectations and relations were yet intact. It is as if the company were abandoning the community in its hour of crisis, a crisis primarily brought about by the firm itself. Worse still is a situation in which the firm is content to leave the community in worse shape than when the company found it or than it would have been if the community had given its loyalty to some other firm or business.

To the extent that this mutual interdependence involves relations that are said to be based upon implicit or explicit consent, we have a contractarian view of fairness. Theorists contend that firms that ignore the community's needs or wishes are not keeping up with their part of the bargain (Davis, Frederick, and Blomstrom, p. 531; Jarolem, 1982, p. 32). This is especially true when they fail to give adequate advance notice of a closing. Their lack of regard in this matter suggests that they wish to be free riders in their relationship with the public. It also shows a lack of respect for the lives of those residing in the community.

It is also claimed that shutdown decisions are often irreversible. It is contended that management would typically not choose to have the community or its government initiate a new program of action that may have significant impact upon the firm without announcement, consultation, or input from management. Nor would it favor a public action involving no consideration of the interests of management. Thus, it is said that in some plant closing cases at least management has done something that it would not want done to itself.

Finally, there is the public agency view of fairness. Within this conception, firms are seen as recipients of past benefits from the community or its government (Harrison, 1984, p. 388). By accepting licenses, government-funded subsidies, and the like, the firm is accountable to the community for how it has used or disposed of these benefits. Bluestone and Harrison also mention the government-supported programs that may be necessary after a closing (Bluestone and Harrison, 1980, p. 14). And Stern, Wood, and Hammer include reference to the use of community talent, resources, and services (Stern, Wood, and Hammer, 1979, p. 9). Firms that ignore the benefits they receive from the community are less likely to be publicly accountable for their decisions in the case of a plant closing, and they are more likely to close a plant unnecessarily, leaving behind an unfilled economic niche. This has even lead some thinkers to conclude that it is then ultimately the community's responsibility to assure that this form of social or economic waste is prevented.

OTHER ARGUMENTS FOR THE SOCIAL DEMANDINGNESS POSITION

Closely connected to this latter point is another argument that we met with in the section on the stakeholder theory. It is said that unfair or unacceptable behavior toward the community will eventually incur its antagonism and lead to further intrusions by government into the affairs of the firm (Jarolem, 1982, p. 34). This reverse-impact consideration is itself sometimes said to be based upon an alternative conception of property from that endorsed by classical theorists.

In chapter 11 we mentioned the common property conception of Hoffman and Fisher and the view of property as a three-term relation advocated by Chaudhuri. Some theorists argue that since property, especially private property, is defined or determined socially, society may withhold its consent on the property rights of corporations in the case of a plant shutdown. An initial rationale for this view is expressed in *Munn v. Illinois* (94 U.S. 113, 1876). In this case the court ruled that when an owner uses his or her private property in a manner that has public consequences and affects the community as a whole, he or she in effect bestows on the public an interest in that use and may be legally controlled by the public. More recently, this position was expressed by a federal judge in a case brought against U.S. Steel for the shutdown of its Youngstown, Ohio, facility. The judge ruled that because of the long-term relationship that existed between the community and U.S. Steel workers, on the one hand, and the corporation, on the other, the community had a vested property relation in the company (cases cited in Lustig, 1985, pp. 140, 144). Lustig tells us the latter ruling implies that since large-scale industry is the community in its active, working aspect, those who control it impose "common burdens" on the community. Thus, it is in itself a vehicle of the public interest.

The "common burdens" view is also defended by Hoffman and Fisher. They tell us that the social determination of property, which makes it what they call "common property," is based in part upon the fact that the community can be expected to pay for an unwarranted or unfortunate management decision to close a facility. This it does by paying higher taxes, adapting to reduced community or government services, giving increased subsidies to other firms, accommodating itself to the underutilization of its local talent, and the like. Such a view may also be based upon the conception of property as a three-term relation. Thus, the agreement of society is now said to be needed in all cases of property holding, disposal, or abandonment. In addition, there is the view that simply because society has the power to intrude itself into company decisions (the reverse-impact concept), it is held that management must consider and respond to the needs of the community as a whole in decisions about work reduction or withdrawal from the community, whether or not society threatens to use that power immediately (Stein, 1978, p. 281; Carroll, 1984, p. 129). Stein and Baker add that society's input in these matters can be seen in the system of handling plant closings that has developed in various European countries (Baker, 1988, p. 317). In these countries the property rights of the shareholders do not always override those of the workers or the local community; a business facility is thus often seen as a social rather than a purely private holding.

Finally, there are two added arguments raised in behalf of the social demandingness position on plant closings. The first is also urged by social activists. Other rights are said to apply here. Adams, for example, mentions that the parties affected by the decision have an inherent right to know (Adams, 1982, p. 21). This implies an obligation by management to inform such parties in a timely manner of an impending facility relocation or closing. The impact argument discussed earlier may also be formulated within a rights perspective. But here the right involved could be said to be a general noninterference one or perhaps a right to avoid being unduly and negatively affected by the decisions of others. Such rights, as institutionally framed entitlements, can then be appealed to as the bases of some of the social demandingness proposals.

The last argument strategy to be discussed in this section has been met with earlier in partial form. It is that which is based directly upon social demands or expectations. Various writers have sought to show the diverse ways in which plant closings that occur without some or all of the programs or proposals mentioned earlier offend against present or likely public opinion or expectation. In some interpretations of the social demandingness theory, this is in itself sufficient to make such a plant shutdown unjustified. There are different vehicles for assessing public opinion on this issue, however, from opinion polls to the direction of legislative activity in a state, region, or country; from the number of editorials favoring greater restrictions on plant relocations to the type and number of court cases urging or requiring firms to consider both stakeholders and nonstakeholders in their decision making on facility reduction. Whatever the measure of actual social expectation or demand, however, theorists such as Carroll and Jarolem believe that firms are responsible to respond to community expectation in this area (Carroll, 1984, p. 129; Jarolem, 1982, p. 33).

SOCIAL ACTIVISM

The social activist theory of plant relocation is not an easy or univocal view to define or classify. Initially, there appears to be two distinguishable, and even at times inconsistent, facets to this position. The first is what might be called its regional aspects or interpretation. In this view, the focus is upon what management should do relative to those living in a specific region in which a business is presently located. The question is what can be done to protect the interests of both stakeholders and nonstakeholders residing in this region. This dimension of the position is typically based upon the assumption that a plant is already located in a certain area and the main question then becomes how to keep it there or, if it must go, how to reduce the negative impact of this decision.

The second dimension of social activism is more international or global in focus. Here the question is how to best organize and utilize the earth's resources. A predominate assumption within this interpretation is, as we have seen, that there are regions of the world that need or want capital investment from corporations and whose resources remain underutilized. In some cases this under-utilization translates into massive poverty, high unemployment, depressed expectations, and even malnutrition and starvation. Certain social activists question the fairness of this and urge a more equal sharing of the earth's resources and burdens.

The regional dimension of social activism illustrates the affinity it has to the stakeholder position, while with the global form, we seem to have extended certain features of the social demandingness view. And by an unexpected co-incidence, we seem also to have been brought back full circle to certain aspects of the classical theory. Naturally then these two versions of activism can at times be in conflict. This happens when the pull of the regional approach toward maintaining an employment and community status quo in a certain town or city runs headlong into the push of the global form for the further sharing and dispersal of resources and business facilities throughout the world.

Without wishing to ignore the affinities that this theory of plant relocation has with the other positions, it should be pointed out that it can also deviate from them in several important respects. We have seen that social activism in general differs from the other theories of corporate responsibility in that it holds that there is a normative standard for determining responsible corporate conduct that is specifically dependent neither upon the present interests of the stockholders or stakeholders of a company nor upon the actual demands or expectations of the public. And it is a standard that typically demands greater social or moral involvement from corporate leaders than either many of them have provided in the past or that is currently demanded of them by the other three theories. The regional form of this view as it applies to plant closings generally demands more from corporate leaders than is usually required by stakeholder or social de-mandingness theorists. As we have seen, these last positions typically demand such actions as conducting a thorough preliminary investigation of the need for a closing or relocation, giving adequate advance notice, providing severance payments and reemployment services, finding a suitable replacement, and the like. But social activism will in general demand that all (or most) of these actions be carried out with considerable vigor and conscientiousness. So, for example, while Carroll tells us that in the stage of preliminary investigation, management should consult with the parties most likely to be affected by a plant closing, a social activist might demand that all such parties be contacted, or perhaps that management should negotiate with these parties and abide by the determination that is reached. Beyond this, social activist thinkers in the United States might demand that firms make structural changes like those found in Europe, that they put interested stakeholders or members of the public on their boards of directors, or, as Bowie has proposed on another occasion to address the problem of job security for whistleblowers, the private sector should perhaps experiment with a system of tenure for some or all of its workers.

Lustig points out another facet of the regional form of social activism when he tells us that managers are responsible to conduct business affairs so that many plant closings can be avoided in the first place. He gives us a brief history of a few recent closings or relocations and contends that these disinvestment decisions were propagated upon questionable investment practices made many years earlier, for example, using revenues to acquire subsidiaries rather than investing in new equipment or upgrading facilities (Lustig, 1985, pp. 130ff.). Like Bluestone and Harrison, he believes that many plants that closed in the last twenty years were "milked" or even "bled" before they were laid to rest. The social activist position (or the activist aspect of Lustig's position) indicates that investment and resource questions must be diligently addressed now and continuously if we are to reduce the need for plant closings in the future.

Social activists may also make more sweeping and demanding social or legal proposals about such practices as early notice, retraining, and severance payments. Congressman William Ford's legal proposals in 1977 and 1979 illustrate this point. He proposed that the management of a plant of a certain size that closes (1) may need to give up to two years advance notice, (2) must in effect give its employees fifty-two weeks of severance payments, (3) must pay the community an amount equal to 85 percent of one year's taxes, (4) must offer the affected workers jobs at other plant locations with no cut in either their wages or fringe benefits and pay moving expenses for a period of three years, and (5) if management decides to relocate abroad, it must pay the federal government an amount equal to 300 percent of one year's total lost taxes (cited in McKenzie, 1982b, p. 135).

It is also possible for social activists to advocate proposals like those contained in Ford's bill but believe nevertheless that it is a social or moral, and not a legal, responsibility of management to carry them out. And it is generally a part of social activism that these responsibilities be carried out with an eye only partially focused upon profit.

Like the regional interpretation of social activism, the global form offers variations in the degree of vigor with which management is required to carry out the theory's proposals. As previously said, although the two forms of the position are at times compatible because of the scarcity of resources, they often imply specific responsibilities or actions that are conflicting in nature. And it should be noted that few social activists argue for unrestricted capital mobility in developing countries, as such. Like Bluestone and Harrison, they realize that multinational corporations can at times do more harm than good to nonindustrialized nations (Bluestone and Harrison, 1980, p. 299). Davis, Frederick, and Blomstrom list the disadvantages that can sometimes occur to a country hosting such corporations. Such disadvantages might include the loss of some control over its own economy; some loss of national sovereignty because the host nation cannot control what a multinational firm does in other countries; some reduction in political autonomy because the multinational firm may represent certain political interests found in its home country that are incompatible with views held in the host nation; possible dislocations in the host country's balance of payments; exploitation of its labor and natural resources; unwanted pollution problems; the introduction of values that may lead to fundamental challenges to and changes in the moral and social climate of the host country. These are counterbalanced by a host of advantages that Davis, and colleagues also mention (Davis, Frederick, and Blomstrom, 1980, pp. 18, 19). The social activist urges capital expansion into other countries only when management aims to insure the listed advantages, while it works to eliminate or mitigate the disadvantages.

As for the arguments for the social activist position on facility relocation, we shall briefly consider only a few points. We have already met with the activist strategies of argument in chapter 12. Basically the same strategies are used when treating the plant relocation question in both its regional and global applications. In addition, it should be noted that social activists often appeal to many of the same considerations already brought up in this and the last chapter. We see versions of the impact, unfairness, rights, and disrespect for persons arguments, for example, but now the point of reference is typically all humankind, including those living in the future. And social activists often contend that business must in its decision making actually improve the world rather than merely avoid or reduce the negative impact of its past or present decisions. Thus, their view of responsibility is frequently associated with moral and social perfectionism. They tell us that management should do the greatest good toward workers, the local community, and other regions of the world rather than acting merely to avoid or reduce the pain or suffering of these groups.

This is not to say, of course, that there is nothing new in their arguments. Within the framework of the impact argument, for example, some of these thinkers maintain that experiencing a significant but avoidable pain or injustice is worse than merely losing a present pleasure or benefit. We have also met with this view in discussing the classical theory. Because of this, Singer and other advocates of the global form argue that the immediate attention of firms should be to do what they can to improve the quality of life of unfortunate people around the world—not so much from the desire to make profit but more from a sense of moral or social responsibility. So there may be occasions when jobs and opportunities are lost in the developed countries in order that the people of the developing nations can relieve the distress of their lives. To allow these individuals to continue suffering when something can be done to reduce it is also to treat them unfairly and with disrespect. It is to treat them more like animals than human beings; it is to ignore their rights to life and liberty. It may even interfere with their property "rights." As an extension of the Marxist view of property, some activists argue that there exist regional and even "global" property rights rather than merely private ownership rights to particular things. Assuming this concept, one can see that the present pattern of ownership and investment appears to disregard such regional or global rights. Finally, Davis and colleagues tell us that failure to assist in the development of other countries may violate certain conditions of the social contract that exists among nations and between nations and other global enterprises (such as corporations, cartels, or industry or consortia groups). And it may leave certain countries more isolated and exploitable (Davis, Frederick, and Blomstrom, 1980, p. 532). Naturally, social activist theorists remind us that this kind of development should be done in such a way that multinational firms show that they respect the values and life-styles of the people of developing nations. It must be done without economic, political, and social exploitation.

PLANT RELOCATION AND THE MODELS OF THE CORPORATION

This concludes our discussion of the four theories of corporate responsibility as they apply to the question of plant closing or relocation. We can see from our review of the various arguments for these theories the presence of some of the assumptions we discussed earlier in the book. We can see for example, that one type of relation of accountability is more appropriate to a certain argument than is another or that a certain strategy of legitimization constitutes an important strategy of justification for one position on plant closing but not another. A complete account of the issue of closing or relocation would involve showing the application of all of these assumptions to the appropriate position and ar-gument. Rather than do this for every presupposition, we shall just consider the application of those assumptions involved in the models of the corporation. This will be sufficient to illustrate the next step in the analysis without having the presentation become unduly tedious. Besides, we shall examine the role of the relations of accountability to another applied question in a coming chapter.

I have selected the assumptions involved in the models of the corporation because one of the fundamental issues that arises in the plant closing question is the nature of the corporation itself. Are corporations organized in such a way that workers constitute an intrinsic part of the collective or are the workers merely discrete resources that are utilized externally by the shareholders and their immediate representatives in the firm? One who believes the latter is much more likely to advocate the classical position, for example. In addition to this point, however, the models of the corporation generally form an inherent and important part of the distinct strategy of legitimation advanced by an author. So, the better we understand the models, the more we will likely comprehend the strategies of legitimation used by a theorist.

The Private Property Model

The private property model is the predominant model of the corporation as-sumed by classical theorists of plant relocation. We have seen that they believe the corporation is the property of the shareholders. As upper management seeks to represent the interests of this group, it can choose to dispose of resources, physical or human, in whatever manner best serves the owners' interests. Since the workers and the community do not own the firm (at least in the usual case), any claim they may have in the matter is, at best, secondary in importance.

Stakeholder theorists usually either reject this model or try to show that workers have a property relation to the firm. They may, for example, assume the labor theory of value and productivity and argue that workers gain an ownership relation by adding value to the corporation. Supporters of the community's claim in this matter, whether they are stakeholder, social demandingness, or social activist theorists, have sometimes argued that the closeness and perhaps the duration of the relation between the local area and the facility, so that resources, services, and efforts have been inextricably bound together, gives the local community an ownership stake in the corporation. The property in question is now seen as being more communal in nature. We have also seen the direct denial or restriction of the private property model by those social activists who advance the idea of regional or global property in an effort to encourage the more equal sharing of the earth's resources. Finally, some stakeholder theorists who accept at least the legal authority of the private property model urge workers (or the community) to become the sole or principal shareholders of the company if they wish to have greater security from plant shutdowns.

The Private Contract Model

Classical theorists also assume the private contract model. Explicit agreement dictates the nature and direction of much of corporate responsibility for them. Thus, upper management is guided by its explicit agreements made with shareholders, workers, and the community. Such executives are directed by their own employment contracts to be fiduciaries for the shareholders. They are bound to the workers only in terms of what is explicitly negotiated in the employment contracts—the latters' continued employment depends upon management consent.

Those stakeholder theorists and others who accept much of the private contract model urge worker groups (or communities) to negotiate vigorously with management about the conditions of, or need for, job loss or plant shutdown. Workers need to make sure that provisions for adequate notification, discussion, retraining, and so on are clearly stipulated. Other stakeholder theorists reject this model when interpreted only in terms of explicit contract. They maintain that through years of mutual relationship and effort, workers and management become enmeshed in a web of implied responsibilities and understandings. Within this set of understandings, there is the tacit promise of continued job security for continued job service. Past precedent thus plays an important role in establishing this implicit promise.

The Enterprise Model

The enterprise model is most closely associated with the stakeholder theory. Within this model, the corporation is seen as a collection of individuals pursuing career and financial goals in a uniquely human institution. The business enterprise is thus a prime source of meaning, challenge, and value for its members. Stakeholder theorists contend that plant closings often destroy this meaning, or at least cause a substantial loss of value for the workers. Those that occur without adequate notice or compensation disregard the great personal and professional investments that the workers have provided for the firm. And closings that were preceded by the "milking" or "bleeding" of a facility, or that occur even though there is still an economic niche for the facility in question, are judged as most unwarranted from the standpoint of this model. They are the most ruinous to the fragile network of human pursuits and social commitments that ultimately constitute the firm.

Other theorists, such as social activists, may also assume this model and appeal to it as part of the reason why resources and enterprises must be shared more equally throughout the world. They suggest that those living in developing countries should also have an opportunity to participate in these shared projects of social and personal meaning.

The Social Contract Model

Social contract theorists are likely to oppose largely unrestricted capital mobility, though there are some exceptions. Because Buchanan, for example, has a different view of the social contract from many of these theorists, he believes in fewer government restrictions in this area. Other social contract theorists, however, contend that the corporation's permission to operate is based in large part on its willingness and ability to respond to the interests of those individuals who gave it this permission—members of the local community and the wider society. This tends to lead them to the social demandingness view or to social activism in its regional form. With the appropriate added presuppositions, it could even lead them to an "extended" form of the stakeholder theory that emphasizes the firm's relation and commitments to the local community or certain of its members.

The social contract is taken farther by some thinkers who support social activism in its global form. They view the firm as propagated upon an implied contract with nation-states and other international enterprises. This view tends to lead them to support capital mobility in a morally and socially active form for reasons of equity. Regional social activists, however, direct the contractarian model toward the community in a narrower sense. They thus often endorse proposals that lessen a firm's motive for relocating to a developing country.

The Public Power Model

Generally speaking, those who assume the public power model are quite skeptical about a firm's ability or willingness to use its power wisely. More than any other theorists, they are likely to call for greater legal restrictions on corporations in their quest for capital mobility. They are also likely to remind us of management's ability to "milk" and "bleed" before it dispatches a plant. So they draw our attention to management activity long before a closing is announced, which is sometimes also thought to need the firmer hand of government regulation.

Classical theorists and social activists also assume aspects of the public power model. The former largely reject the idea that corporations have excessive power. They are thus likely to emphasize the advantages of permitting these centers of power to move to areas with underutilized resources. It is here that the classical position sometimes meets social activism, though, as we have seen, activists generally urge capital mobility for other reasons.

The Machine Model

This model is most at home with the classical theory. If corporations are largely vehicles or tools of investment for the sake of carrying out efficient and productive economic functions, then support should be given management if it chooses to move a facility to a geographical region where it can fulfill these goals more effectively. Many other theorists question this model and the view of employees that it seems to imply. However, some social activist theorists, while not endorsing the model completely, do believe that as vehicles for productive effort, corporations should, other things being equal, try to "transport" themselves to the underdeveloped areas of the world.

The Organic Model

The last two models of the corporation do not by themselves appear to imply any one theory of corporate responsibility on the plant closing issue. Which theory is endorsed seems to depend upon the other assumptions of a theorist. Thus, for example, the organic model implies the teamwork relation of accountability. For stakeholder theorists this implies an obligation to retain the firm's workers as members of the team. But social demandingness theorists (and others) view the organic model as also applying to the firm's relation to the wider community. It is thus used to support setting certain moral, social, or even legal restrictions on capital mobility. Some activists, however, extend the teamwork relation and the organic model to the international context, which brings them into some conflict with the other applications of this model. Finally, even classical theorists may assume the organic model for they can use it to justify closing a specific subsidiary for the good of the entire corporation. Thus, some workers may need to be sacrificed for the economic well-being of the entire collective unit. Much depends upon how far and to what social units a theorist is willing to apply the organic model.

The Mental or Moral Agent Model

Like the organic model, this view of the nature of the corporation may also apply to each of the four theories of corporate responsibility. It depends upon whether it is taken strictly so that the corporation itself is viewed as the self-conscious entity, or more loosely where subsidiaries or individual plants are so conceived. And it depends upon whether the entire global network of states and enterprises is viewed as a megamental or megamoral agent. Quite frankly, it seems that these last models play a more prominent role in distinguishing between the four theories when applied to some of the other specific or applied questions of corporate responsibility.

The present discussion of the models of the corporation brings us to the question of how responsibility is divided or diffused within the corporation. This issue becomes particularly important when the position of subordinates differs from that of corporate superiors. This in turn applies to the question of the legitimacy of social institutions.

REFERENCES

Adams, Carolyn Teich. 1982. "The Flight of Jobs and Capital: Prospects for Grassroots Action." In *Community and Capital: Plant Closings and Job Loss*, edited by John C. Raines, Leonora E. Berson, and David McI. Gracie, pp. 11–25. Philadelphia: Temple University Press.

Baker, Andrew M. 1988. "Plant Closings: Lessons from the Maine Experience." *Human Resource Management*, Fall, pp. 315–28.

Berry, Steve, Peter Gottschalk, and Doug Wissoker. 1988. "An Error Components Model of the Impact of Plant Closings on Earnings." *Review of Economic and Statistics*, November, pp. 701–07.

Bluestone, Barry, and Bennett Harrison. 1980. *Capital and Communities: The Causes and Consequences of Private Disinvestment*. Washington, D.C.: The Progressive Alliance.

Carroll, Archie B. 1984. "When Business Closes Down: Social Responsibilities and Management Action." *California Management Review*, Winter, pp. 125–40.

Chinitz, Benjamin. 1974. "Regional Development." In *Social Responsibility and the Business Predicament*, edited by James McKie, pp. 247–73. Washington, D.C.: The Brookings Institution.

Davis, Keith, William Frederick, and Robert L. Blomstrom, 1980. *Business and Society: Concepts and Policy Issues*. New York: McGraw-Hall.

Drucker, Peter. 1974. *Management: Tasks, Responsibilities, Practices*. New York: Harper and Row.

Harrison, Bennett. 1984. "The International Movement for Prenotification of Plant Closures." *Industrial Relations*, Fall, pp. 387–409.

Jarolem, Stanley, 1982. "The Community." In *The Ethical Factor in Business Decisions: Essays Toward Criteria*, edited by Arnold Berleant, pp. 29–34. Greenvale, N.Y.: C. W. Post Center, Long Island University.

Lustig, R. Jeffrey. 1985. "The Politics of Shutdown: Community, Property, Corporatism." *Journal of Economic Issues*, March, pp. 123–52.

McKenzie, Richard R. 1982a. "The Case for Business Mobility." In *Plant Closings: Public or Private Choice*, pp. 125–33. Washington, D.C.: The Cato Institute.

McKenzie, Richard B. 1982b. "The Case for Plant Closures." In *Plant Closings: Public or Private Choices*, pp. 135–48. Washington, D.C.: The Cato Institute.

McKenzie, Richard B. 1982c. *The Right to Close Down: The Political Battle Shifts to the States*. Los Angeles: Caroline House Publishers.

Rothstein, Lawrence. E. 1986. *Plant Closings: Power, Politics and Workers*. Dover, Mass.: Auburn House Publishing Company.

Stein, Barry. 1978. "Who Owns Corporations: Implications for Social Responsibility." In *Proceedings of the Second National Conference on Business Ethics*, edited by W. Michael Hoffmann, pp. 278–83. Washington, D.C.: University Press of America.

Stern, Robert, N., K. Haydn Wood, and Tove Helland Hammer. 1979. *Employee Ownership in Plant Shutdowns*. Kalamazoo, Mich.: W. E. Upjohn Institute for Employment.

PART III

COLLECTIVE AND SUBORDINATE RESPONSIBILITY

15

INDIVIDUAL AND COLLECTIVE RESPONSIBILITY

INTRODUCTION

In the last seven chapters we have directed our attention to a discussion of the responsibilities of superiors as they seek to establish the direction that corporate decisions are to take for the other members of the firm. We are now prepared to consider the responsibilities of subordinates in corporate organizations. There are many questions that arise here, but the central question involves what responsibilities subordinates have in meeting the demands of the four theories just discussed.

In one sense, at least, the answer to this question seems perfectly straightforward: subordinates have, or are at least encouraged to have, the same general responsibilities that superiors do. Thus, classical theorists demand that subordinates protect the interests or wishes of stockholders; stakeholder theorists require them to respect the interests of fellow stakeholders; social demandingness theorists require respect for the public good, consistent with the actual expectations or demands of society; and social activists require response to the same group, consistent with certain values, rights, or interests taken to be universally or objectively valid in nature. But what happens if subordinates find themselves to be in disagreement with their superiors, if they believe their superiors are failing to meet their responsibilities? What are subordinates accountable to do then?

Unfortunately, we cannot answer this question in the present chapter; we must postpone our discussion of the literature that addresses it until the next. In this chapter, we will first examine a preliminary issue that has a direct bearing on the question of subordinate responsibility. The above way of formulating the question of subordinate accountability seems to assume that the collective responsibility of the corporation is to be evenly or completely distributed among all members of the firm. This presupposition is challenged by many theorists, however. They argue that the nature of responsibility at the collective level is not reducible or translatable into clear or equal responsibility claims or shares for all of the individual members, participants, or subordinates of the institution. This is so whether the collective is a single corporation (the subject of this chapter), an industry (where liability may be distributed by market share or some other means), or the entire market system (as, for example, happens in the "loss spreading" theory of compensation or liability, where every participant in the economy is expected to pay in some way for some of its detriments). About the single corporation, these theorists tell us that collective responsibility can become so diffused or otherwise transformed at the individual level that while some subordinates may be held responsible for corporate misconduct, others may not be so held. They also tell us that subordinates are often not to be held accountable for the same kinds of things for which superiors are held responsible. And they are often not to be held accountable in the same way as the latter.

We are thus brought to examine other assumption in the corporate responsibility debate, one that deals with how collective responsibility is shared within the corporation and when, if at all, it becomes filtered down to the level of the individual employee.

Theoretically speaking, there is a range of possibilities here. On one side, it might be thought collective and subordinate responsibility are two entirely different things; there is never any overlap between them. On the other, is the belief that the two are identical; subordinates are always accountable to do precisely what their organizations (or superiors) are required or expected to do, consistent with the usual excusing, extenuating, or exculpating conditions—circumstances that are meant to apply to any situation of assigning responsibility. These include insufficient knowledge or power, duress, being bound by a higher or more supervenient responsibility, and the like. The first position is called (moral) holism, while the second is referred to as (moral) individualism. When one surveys the recent literature of collective responsibility, however, one rarely finds advocates of the extreme version of holism defined above. What one sees instead are theorists who contend that collective and individual or subordinate responsibility should be treated as distinct concepts, even though they are capable of overlap, because the one does not always reduce to the other. There are even occasions when a collective will be blamed for something, while none of its members are blamed.

Between the two views of holism and individualism there exists a number of intermediate or hybrid positions (though it must be admitted that some of these hybrids do not take a clear position on the question of subordinate responsibility). And there are also metalevel theories that tell us that the disagreement arising among these various positions cannot be settled in specific cases without initially addressing certain substantial normative questions about the ideal of society and the purpose and legitimacy of blaming collectives or individuals in the first place. These views take us back to the four theories of corporate responsibility and to the strategies of legitimacy in order to address the question of subordinate and collective responsibility.

HOLISM AND RESPONSIBILITY

Some thinkers who are sympathetic to the organic or moral agent models of the corporation believe that on the issue of responsibility the whole is often greater than the sum of the parts—an organization may be guilty of misconduct, but none of its members are to be charged or otherwise held responsible for this misconduct. One theorist who develops this view is French. We have seen in chapter 6 that French advances the moral person model of the corporation. He views corporations as non-eliminitable subjects of moral evaluation that are capable not only of possessing but also of administering their rights (French, 1984, p. 38). Since they have a nature that is *sui generis*, their actions are not typically reducible to the actions of their members. Just as a hand or an arm of the body cannot be accused of an assault, so also individual members of a firm, especially those in subordinate positions, cannot be held accountable for such actions as joining a cartel or acquiring another firm. French realizes, of course, that corporations differ from human persons in that their members are also distinct moral agents. But he believes that this does not refute his basic point. It shows only that the lines of corporate and individual responsibility sometimes coincide for sometimes we blame subordinates for their roles in participating in corporate fraud or misconduct. But it does not show that they often or always do.

French bases his position in part upon the fact that there are certain actions that only the organization can perform. Only the firm can declare a dividend or be charged with predatory pricing (French, 1984, p. 75). Corporations are thus irreducible entities in their conduct. He also believes that they are irreducible in their identity. Because of its virtual perpetual duration, a corporation is not to be identified with the list of its current members. The list may change completely, while the corporation retains its identity (French, 1984, p. 27). Finally, he bases his position upon the nature of the corporate internal decision (CID) structure. He believes that this organizational center of intent (or rational responsiveness) is not reducible to the intent of the individual members who compose the organization. As we have seen, the CID structure is composed of such elements as the organizational flow chart, the procedural rules and indicators, and the policies that a corporation has initiated. It is this structure that organizes the individual thinking and effort of various members into a unified and coordinated action having the corporate stamp upon it. It is this feature that tells us when individuals are acting in their official or public capacities and when they are acting merely in their own behalf.

French suggests that one reason why the members of a firm may escape blame when a company is censured is that a corporate action may not be a reflection of anyone's specific intent. Each person's plans and actions can become so transformed by the CID structure that no one individual would be seen as the author of an organizational policy or even as an important agent of a corporate action. Combined with this is the fact that for particular actions there may be no subpar performance in the way in which members carry out their role functions. French feels it is unfair or otherwise unjustified to blame individuals when they act according to the organizational rules of the game (French, 1984, p. 15). We cannot automatically demand or expect them to try to protest or prevent the action in question. He does not deny that individuals within the organization may at times be blameworthy, but even here we cannot immediately infer this from the fact that the corporation itself is censurable. Both this and the reverse type of situation must be determined on a case-by-case basis. His account does, however, imply that there are situations of corporate misconduct in which even the top executives may escape blame.

Another theorist who contends that groups or organizations may be censured when no one within the organization is to be blamed is Cooper. We have considered his views on the nature of social responsibility in chapter 3. As we have seen, he provides us with several examples of nondivisible collective responsibility. The first involves the failure of a private tennis club. The failure of the collective is at least sometimes blameable because it involves a substandard performance. In these cases, however, this does not mean that the members themselves are also blameworthy or guilty of substandard performance. Given their other priorities and interests, they may not rank a tennis membership very highly. If a sufficient number of the members lose their *esprit de corps*, it may be nearly impossible for the managers of the club to avoid closing it (Cooper, 1968, pp. 264ff.). Cooper admits there may be little point to blaming the club for its failure, but its subpar performance may still admit of this type of criticism in any case.

Cooper provides a second example of indivisible collective responsibility when he imagines a town in the Wild West where vigilante justice is practiced. For thirty years it has followed a legal and social policy of favoring citizens' rights over those of strangers. This has led in a specific case to a citizen committee's acting in an official capacity to drive off an otherwise innocent nonresident cowboy for alleged misconduct (Cooper, 1972, pp. 87ff.). The newspaper of another town blames the committee for its unfair behavior. Cooper asks whether the members of the committee should be individually blamed as well. His answer is no. A collective can fall below a standard without its members falling below that standard. As long as they are following the well-established rules or customs of acceptable behavior in their community, we cannot expect them to challenge or reject the committee's decision. This is especially true if it would put them at substantial risk of losing the benefits of respectability or friendship in the town. This implies that in a corporate context, we cannot expect that subordinates should risk their jobs, friendships, or reputations by challenging the actions of a firm that are otherwise in accord with its accepted policies or practices. Only in very rare circumstances would subordinates actually be obligated to dissent or blow the whistle on their superiors.

Downie has criticized Cooper's theory. He believes that the central arena in which individual or subordinate responsibility is linked to collective responsibility is the moral one. Thus, to blame subordinates for their acts or omissions in a case of corporate misconduct is usually to blame them morally. But Downie tells us that in his illustration of the tennis club, Cooper has failed to show us that he is even discussing moral responsibility at all (Downie, 1969, p. 66). The case involves causal, legal, or even economic responsibility perhaps—areas of responsibility where collective need not reduce to individual accountability—but since a lack of *esprit de corps* is not a moral fault, the club's failure is not a moral one. Downie further contends that this conclusion is also suggested by the fact that Cooper grants that the outcome is otherwise unavoidable (i.e., given the general lack of interest of the members, the club's failure is all but inevitable). Downie responds, however, that since we do not morally blame individuals for unavoidable outcomes, this also shows the inapplicability of the concept of moral responsibility to Cooper's example. Moral criticism has no point, and may even be unfair, in cases where individuals can do nothing to alter or prevent a particular outcome (Downie, 1969, p. 67).

Cooper seems to grant these points. He responds that he was not necessarily speaking of moral responsibility in this example. The club may not have been morally responsible for the failure, but since some kind of blame or criticism is appropriate in this case, he proposes that the club had at least a social responsibility to avoid failing. He also suggests that none of the members had this kind of responsibility, however (Cooper, 1969, p. 154). There is some debate about the success of this response, though, for we can see from Downie's position that Downie is not interested in social responsibility as such. He is interested only in moral responsibility.

Cooper's second example has also been criticized in various ways. The point of both of his examples is to show that standards that apply to groups need not be applicable to individuals in the group. The vigilante committee may be blamed for its injustice, while its members are judged as otherwise acting appropriately. In this case, however, the issue is not avoidability for it is admitted that the committee's decision would have differed if a sufficient number of members had protested. The issue is one of determining the appropriate standard of responsibility. Cooper applies one standard to the group and another to its individual members.

Although she is sympathetic to Cooper's general thesis that collective responsibility does not always imply individual responsibility, Held disagrees with his treatment of this particular example. She believes that members of this committee are still under certain moral responsibilities, responsibilities that had they been fulfilled or discharged would have affected the outcome. As we have seen, she believes two conditions are necessary for moral evaluation: the agent has sufficient knowledge of the nature of the action (and its likely outcome), and the agent could do other than what he or she does (or omits to do) (Held, 1972, p. 106). As long as the members meet these conditions, they are morally responsible to exercise their choice to avoid the unjust outcome. They may then be judged responsible for abiding by group decisions and not protesting, for staying in the group (or even in the town) after the former has rendered unjust verdicts in the past, for supporting the committee in financial and in other ways, or even for joining the committee in the first place (Held, 1972, p. 109).

Held's position is close to Downie's when the latter appeals to the concepts of role acceptance and role enactment (Downie, 1972, p. 70). Downie tells us that we can apply moral standards to these concepts as well as to the role itself. Thus, moral criticism can be given for the role that the committee played in this case as well as for the acceptance of and participation in this role by its individual members. Insofar as they meet Held's two conditions, members are to be judged as irresponsible for their part in the committee's action. We can see then that both Held and Downie reject the idea that we judge the conduct of subordinates by their role functions solely or that we judge their behavior by the current standards of the group.

Consistent with these criticisms is the objection of Atkinson and Atkinson, who reject French's argument that because individual members do not themselves intend a certain outcome, the CID structure may be the only censurable party to blame for corporate misconduct. As these authors see it, this structure is still administered by individuals. Even if they do not believe they are the first-order authors or architects of a specific corporate policy, they reaffirm a policy whenever they choose not to protest it (Atkinson and Atkinson, 1980, p. 133). They are thus accountable for these acts of reaffirmation or metaconsent.

Cooper, however, disagrees with these objections. He believes that we may expect to encounter saints in heaven and heroes in folklore, but we cannot expect members of an organization to become saints or heroes in protesting the actions of the group (Cooper, 1972, p. 89). They are not responsible to risk friendships, careers, reputation, or safety in order to condemn the injustice of a social system or its conduct.

We can see from this discussion that the debate does not stay at the metaethical level only. The difference between these thinkers and their critics comes to hinge upon certain substantive normative and ethical matters as well. In fact, we shall see this same tendency at work in the theories of other thinkers to be discussed shortly. Thus, we are led to ask whether individuals should be held accountable for the acceptance and enactment of their social or public roles. Should the presence of role functions constitute an excusing or vindicating condition in morality? Should we judge individuals simply by the standards of their group? These are questions that bring us back to the concepts, theories, and assumptions already discussed in this book. Thus, for example, we can see that Cooper and French's position here treats subordinate decision making primarily within the context of the social demandingness theory and the strategies of conformity to law and conformity to current standards. And the role functions that they maintain are involved are framed primarily within the context of the first three and the last relations of accountability discussed in chapter 4. Downie and Held, on the other hand, view things differently.

THE PUBLIC ROLE POSITION

The social conformism and relativism implicit in the French and Cooper defense of holism has been advanced even more explicitly in the work of other thinkers, who also reject the idea that individual responsibility always goes along with collective responsibility—that subordinates are always or typically to be held accountable for the actions of their collectives. These theorists base their position upon what is called a public role defense.

One public role theorist is Ladd whose presentation of the machine model of the corporation we considered in chapter 6. We saw there that two theses are basic to this model: (1) Since corporations are social instruments designed to achieve certain ends, the logic of organizational discourse requires that they be evaluated simply in terms of their effectiveness in achieving these ends, and (2) both superiors and subordinates should be evaluated in terms of the efficiency and administrative impartiality with which they carry out their organizational roles or capacities. Ladd tells us that we make a category mistake if we attempt to apply other criteria to these roles (Ladd, 1979, p. 499). As he sees it, when viewed from the perspective of the formal structure of organizations, responsibility is an institutional concept: its meaning and authority are exhausted in the formal or institutionalized roles and functions that apply to members of the organization.

Walsh agrees with Ladd, at least with respect to the nature of individual responsibility in an organization. He tells us that public roles involve nonvoluntary actions. When individuals act in their private capacities, they have considerable discretionary power to act in one way rather than another. But this is not true of public roles. Such roles involve built-in criteria and responsibilities. Individuals occupying these roles have little or no leeway in their conduct. They either act in accordance with the externally imposed criteria or they will be replaced with someone who will. In either case, the nonvoluntary aspects of public roles make the public actions of individuals largely immune from moral or ethical criticism (Walsh, 1970, p. 7).

Finally, Jones has also advanced a public roles position. He tells us that private roles typically involve one-to-one relationships. The criteria used to evaluate these roles are much less clear than for public roles. As the former criteria evolve over time, individuals are expected to take responsibility for what they do and how they evaluate themselves in such capacities. Public roles, on the other hand, involve more standard expectations spelled out in advance. This is in large part to expedite what might otherwise become an unwieldly organizational task. Because public roles typically involve multi-party relationships, it is simpler and easier to specify their responsibilities before anyone occupies them. Since individuals holding public positions come and go, while the roles themselves remain largely unchanged, Jones tells us that particular people make little difference to the roles themselves (Jones, 1984, p. 607). Public roles apply to all levels of an organization and involve rewards and punishments given in strict adherence to impersonal standards. Such roles are expressly designed to help achieve the maintenance and growth of the organization. We cannot then automatically expect that individuals will compromise their role proficiency in an attempt to apply to these offices criteria that are more appropriate to their private roles or individual consciences. When such a conflict does occur, Jones tells us that there usually is no clear resolution (Jones, 1984, p. 613). This implies that individuals are sometimes justified in ignoring the moral reservations they may have with the public aspects of their institutional roles.

We see then that some of the same assumptions that play a role in the holism of French and Cooper also apply to the rolism of Ladd, Walsh, and Jones. Both views make heavy use of the regulation model of accountability and the conformity strategies of legitimacy, for example (though, of course, French appeals to these presuppositions within the moral agent or person model of the corporation, while Ladd assumes the machine or tool model).

INDIVIDUALISM AND RESPONSIBILITY

As we have said, holists and rolists believe that collective responsibility is in some sense a *sui generis* concept, typically admitting of its own unique criteria. However, some theorists are not even comfortable with the phrase *collective responsibility*. As they see it, responsibility is always an individual matter. Thus, the phrase is either misleading in nature or it is, at best, only a shorthand way of referring to the diverse responsibilities had by the separate members of a group. There are various ways in which individualists develop and defend this position.

Watkins, for example, advances this view in an attempt to tell us how social phenomena should be studied and explained. His form of individualism is thus methodological in character. We have briefly considered methodological individualism in chapter 8 in our discussion of the classical theory of corporate responsibility. Watkins believes that because the ultimate constituents of the social world are individual people who act in light of their dispositions and understanding of their situation, all rock-bottom explanations (and justifications, perhaps) of group phenomena involve statements about these individuals, their dispositions, situations, and beliefs, as well as the physical environment in which they act (Watkins, 1968, p. 271). He grants that few explanations in the social sciences actually reach this level, but he believes that they are in principle attainable, nonetheless. In fact, they constitute the only complete accounts of historical events or social phenomena. Thus, for example, a historian of the Civil War might explain the surrender of General Lee at Appomattox as in part due to the heavy losses sustained by the Confederate Army at the Battle of

Gettysburg—where this battle is not itself further described or explained by the historian. For Watkins, however, this battle, as a complex social event, admits of further explanation. It could itself be described in terms of the actions, decisions, and fortunes of the various participating combatants—right down to the level of the individual foot soldier. Such an account may be too exacting or cumbersome for a historian to actually attempt, but this does not entail the idea that the explanation is impossible or otherwise unimportant.

For Watkins, any account of social phenomena that appeals to interpersonal concepts or relations is incomplete. It admits of further explanation that would trace through the web of these relations in an effort to distinguish the separate contributions of the individuals participating in them. He holds this view because he believes that no social tendency or phenomenon exists that could not be altered if individuals wanted to change it and possessed the appropriate information to do so. Since all social or interpersonal phenomena are the product of human activities, no social phenomenon is entirely imposed from above upon individual humans (Watkins, 1968, p. 272). It seems then that when the question of responsibility arises, each member of a collective is to take responsibility for his or her part in collective conduct.

Friedman and Hessen specifically apply this idea of individual responsibility to the corporate context. Friedman rejects the idea that the corporation itself has responsibilities. What passes for corporate responsibility is really the responsibilities of the individual members of the firm, especially those who stand in policy-making positions (Friedman, 1970, p. 122). Hessen also advances the individualistic position in his analysis of the nature of the corporation. Since corporations arise as a result of a host of agreements made between individuals within and outside of the firm, he believes that corporations are akin to partnerships. All corporate responsibility is thus divisible and aggregative in nature. Corporations can be called responsible or irresponsible only because their members act or fail to act in certain ways (Hessen, 1979, p. 40). Ultimately, it is always individuals who are involved in the accountability relations discussed in chapter 4. Both of these theorists appeal to this form of individualism in their defense of the classical theory, but it should be added that it is possible for individualists to endorse one of the other theories of corporate responsibility as well.

Associated with the methodological version of the theory as just discussed is a form of individualism put forth in moral theory. Like Friedman and Hessen, the moral individualist believes that only particular human beings are moral agents; they are the sole subjects of such moral ascriptions as virtuous, praiseworthy, responsible, blameworthy, and censurable. Lewis, for example, puts forth this view as a necessary assumption of morality itself. From the moral point of view, an individual is to be praised or blamed only if his or her conduct or decisions contribute to an action or its outcome in some way (Lewis, 1972, p. 121). Thus, a person cannot be blamed for the misbehavior of another. Since Lewis thinks that the concept of collective responsibility involves blaming otherwise innocent individuals (especially subordinates in an organization) for the misdeeds of others (superiors), he thinks that the notion is incoherent if treated as an ultimate or unanalyzable moral concept.

Another theorist who appeals to an individualistic concept of moral responsibility is Velasquez. He believes that the concept is akin to that found in criminal law. Thus, two features are necessary to hold an agent morally responsible—a bodily component (*actus reus*) and a mental element (*mens rea*) (Velasquez, 1983, p. 2). The latter involves a specific intention to bring about a certain result, or it at least involves acting with sufficient knowledge that a particular outcome is likely to occur, and is quite risky, even if the outcome is not otherwise planned or desired by the agent. The former involves the bodily movements necessary to initiate or complete the action. If corporations are to be held morally responsible for their conduct, we must be able to isolate these elements. Velasquez tells us that corporations do not distinctly possess these elements, however. All bodily movements that help to accomplish an action are done by individual members of the firm. In addition, there is no irreducible *mens rea*. Whatever passes as corporate intent is actually the intent of particular human beings, especially those who occupy high-level positions in the firm (Velasquez, 1983, pp. 7ff.).

Against quasi rolists like French, who believe that the corporate internal decision structure organizes the efforts and ends of particular corporate members in such a way that a distinct organizational intention or response can be said to be formed, Velasquez points out that such a structure is merely a certain type of relationship found in the corporation, and relationships, as such, are not carriers of responsibility. So whether we identify this structure with the corporate charter, bylaws, flow chart, recognition rules, or some combination of all of these elements, we must realize that none of them are capable of forming an intent. This comes only from individual human beings. Hence, to blame a corporation from the moral point of view is ultimately to blame some or all of its members. Velasquez grants that in specific cases it may be difficult to determine which members share in this blame, but this does not imply that the moral responsibility applicable here is uniquely corporate in nature. Lacking the necessary synthesis of body and mind, corporations cannot be treated as irreducible moral agents (Velasquez, 1983, p. 8).

Keeley agrees with Velasquez that one cannot identify a unique corporate intention. He tells us that there are two collectivist concepts that are often confused with each other: these are the concepts of the goals *of* and the goals *for* an organization. The former phrase refers to the intentional outcomes of organizational activity, the latter to the preferences of individuals for certain organizational outcomes (Keeley, 1981, p. 150). The former concept is often identified with organizational intent. But Keeley contends that there is no independent way to establish the goals *of* a corporation without appealing to the actual preferences that members express *for* the corporation. Each internal constituent has his or her own vision for the firm. These become interrelated and blended in certain ways when combined with the expectations and visions of other members (in what we have called the enterprise model of the corporation); the connection between individual preference and collective intent is never severed. Keeley thinks that the CID structure mentioned by French or the formal institutional structure mentioned by Ladd are not immune to this analysis. Part of this structure, when it appears to involve intent or to express merely formal characteristics, actually reduces to the preferences of individuals *for* the corporation. Thus, such things as the goals expressed in the corporate charter and bylaws and the statements made by top executives at business meetings and in annual reports fit into this category. The rest of the formal (or CID) structure seems incapable of forming an intent as such. Thus, for example, the organizational procedures indicate *how* something should be done, but they do not indicate *what* should be done or *why* it should be done (Keeley, 1981, pp. 151ff.). It is thus unlikely that intentionality is a feature of corporations as such. When corporations act or produce outcomes, it is their members who are to be praised or blamed for preferring or intending, or at least for not preventing these outcomes.

Finally, Danley also rejects the idea that corporations are irreducible members of the moral community. As he sees it, they do not have responsibilities that are distinct from their members (Danley, 1984, p. 172). He too rejects the idea that corporations intend to act in certain ways. The concept of intent usually carries with it the notions of guilt, remorse, payment of compensation, the resolution to do better, and the like, when the intended action is injurious or otherwise substandard. Danley claims that none of these elements form part of French's view of corporate intent. What passes on his account as aspects of the corporate mind are really only the intentions and decisions of specific people— people who would themselves be blamed and punished for the misconduct of the organization. Danley thinks that in French's model then the members of firms would become scapegoats for corporations. They would become second-class citizens in the moral community, treated as a means to permit corporations to achieve their collective ends. We can see from this that he also rejects Ladd's idea of a formal structure for organizations. This structure has no greater authority than what is given to it by the preferences, decisions, and intentions of its members. In fact, it has no existence in separation from these psychological states.

As one might expect, the debate between individualists and those influenced by holism on the nature of collective responsibility has encouraged the development of intermediate positions. By an intermediate position, I mean one whose holder contends that responsibility claims apply in some way to both organizations and to their members. Thus, it rejects the idea that collective responsibility is *sui generis*, just as it rejects the opposite contention that collective responsibility as such does not exist. To refer to these views as intermediate on this issue is not, however, to imply that they endorse a moderate view of the demandingness of subordinate responsibility for one of the most demanding views on what subordinates are accountable to do is, as we shall see, an intermediate position on the nature of collective responsibility.

INTERMEDIATE POSITIONS

Agassi, following Popper, discusses an intermediate position that he calls "institutional individualism." Such a view seeks to incorporate elements from both individualism and holism (Agassi, 1960, p. 247). Like holism, it grants that social entities are real. They are not reducible simply to the activities or decisions of individual members. But, unlike holism, it rejects the idea that groups have their own distinct aims. Their goals always arise from the aims individuals have for the group. Against strict individualism (which he calls "psychologism"), Agassi tells us that the very existence of the group affects and conditions the decisions of the individuals in the group. The social or interpersonal relations existing here form part of the context of individual decision making. They must be considered by members of a group as the latter seek to plan their futures rationally. He refers to this, after Popper, as situational logic (Agassi, 1960, p. 247).

Methodological individualists like Watkins reject the idea that the interpersonal relations mentioned by Agassi form part of the given for collective decision making. As we have seen, Watkins believes they are capable of further explanation. Agassi insists upon their irreducible character, however, because he believes that the attempt to explain social dynamics solely in terms of psychological concepts and the material conditions of the situation is too cumbersome and complicated to be developed in very great detail. In specific situations of choice, individuals are forced to treat social relations as *sui generis*. This seems to imply that Agassi believes that there are times when individuals must accept the holistic or quasi-holistic goals that others in the group have imposed upon them. But he adds that this occurs only when it can be justified in terms of the pursuit of the rational ends of these individuals.

This suggests then that individual accountability claims do arise in some way in cases of corporate misconduct, even though subordinates may not be held directly responsible for this misconduct. For example, in this theory, while a particular corporation may be found guilty of excessive pollution, its individual employees need not be charged or blamed for this as such. They will, however, be held accountable for accepting the network of formal rules, procedures, and practices and the informal values and policies of the corporation that led to its acts of pollution in the first place. And subordinates will be held responsible for accepting the conclusion that their rational purposes are best served by following the procedures of the company and doing little or nothing to prevent this pollution. In this respect, his theory differs both from the holism of French and Cooper and from the individualism, or apparent individualism, of Velasquez, Keeley, and Danley.

Another theorist who offers an intermediate position on this question is Mandelbaum, who believes that sociological concepts are not reducible to psychological ones. He contends that societal facts form a relatively autonomous system of occurrences whose confirmation is only partially dependent upon statements made about the individuals who stand in social relationships (Mandelbaum, 1973, p. 115). Interpersonal relations offer a challenge to a strictly individualistic analysis because the individuals who occupy social positions are self-conscious of their roles. This means in part that there is an intentionalist opacity in any analysis that would seek to reduce social to psychological facts. This poses a problem to individualists because it refutes one of the alleged strengths of their theory, namely, that it can be verified along traditional empiricist lines. The referential or intentionalist opacity involved here indicates that statements about societal facts cannot be straightforwardly equated with statements about psychological facts. Mandelbaum uses the example of cashing a check (Mandelbaum, 1973, p. 108). As he sees it, individualists would seek to analyze this concept (or act) in terms of the dispositions, beliefs, and attitudes of the individuals functioning within the banking system. But because the individuals using this system have beliefs about their respective roles and relationships with other members in the system, and because some of these beliefs may be in error while these individuals are still successful in having their checks cashed, statements about the social phenomenon of cashing a check cannot be equated with the network of statements that concern or mention the actual attitudes or beliefs of individuals who use the checking system. The reason for this is that such an alleged reduction would yield an indefinitely large number of statements or equations, some of which would themselves be inconsistent.

Individualists might seek to restrict this reduction to only the true beliefs about the interpersonal aspects of the system, but it is unclear how a privileged set of beliefs could be determined without appealing to such concepts as deposit, withdrawal, certification, endorsement, and the like—the very social concepts that were alleged to be reduced. Mandelbaum suggests that there is no privileged conceptual system here. Both social and psychological concepts form relatively independent systems of thought.

Mandelbaum does not himself apply this perspective to the question of individual or subordinate responsibility, but from what he says about the two languages, it would seem that his position is somewhat more holistic than that of Agassi, for he believes that the language of corporate conduct or misconduct is not automatically translatable (or translatable in only one way) into the language of individual responsibility. Because these two types of ascriptions are parts of relatively independent conceptual or linguistic systems, evaluations at the group level need not entail or imply the same types of evaluation at the individual level. In fact, they need not imply any evaluation or ascription of responsibility at the latter level at all. Thus, for example, in the case mentioned above, one might criticize the corporation in question for its acts of excessive pollution, but this would not entail that any of the members would be criticized for this. Hence, the superiors might be blamed for negligence, mismanagement, or laxity, while the subordinates would not be held accountable for this at all. This is one type of translation of the collective into the individualistic language system, but others are also possible. Superiors could be censured for intentionally or knowingly causing the excessive pollution (even if they were not told about it by the subordinates), while most of the subordinates are held accountable for negligence, complicity, or cowardice. And a third alternative is one in which all employees of the company are held equally liable for the pollution. Mandelbaum's position permits each of these translations (and others). The variety of ways in which to express ascriptions of responsibility at these levels is, by the way, a chief point of the metatheories of collective responsibility to be discussed shortly.

Mandelbaum's account, while different from Agassi's position in important respects, does come to a similar conclusion about the relationship of individual to collective normative ascription. But he leaves it an open question to determine more specifically the types of decision or action for which subordinates in an organization are to be held individually accountable. This is to say that he leaves as an open question the presence or nature of the translation rules for connecting or equating the phrases of the one language system with those of the other. Agassi, on the other hand, suggests that subordinates are at least responsible for accepting the network of rules and practices embodied in the firm's standard operating procedures. Any translation of collective into individual ascriptions of responsibility that denies this point is incorrect for Agassi. He gives us at least this criterion from which to assess the translations of the one language into the other.

A third type of intermediate position is advanced by Downie, Held, and Flores and Johnson. Like holists, these theorists admit that responsibility claims can be made directly for collectives, but like individualists, they believe that individuals within an organization are always to be accountable as well. They admit, however, that the two types of responsibility claims need not be the same. We have already seen that Downie and Held hold subordinates responsible for the occupational decisions they make, decisions concerning their role acceptance and enactment. Thus, they reject many of the excuses or vindications offered by holists and rolists.

Flores and Johnson have also criticized these public role positions. In appealing to Downie's concepts of role acceptance and enactment, they point out that personal choice is not exempt from a subordinate's occupational or public roles. The individual chooses to accept the role in the first place. If it calls for improper or illegal conduct, the individual can resign and give his or her allegiance to less questionable public roles (Flores and Johnson, 1983, p. 542). Second, individuals generally have some latitude in their public roles, which enables them to bring to bear certain moral qualities to the exercise of their official functions (Flores and Johnson, 1983, p. 543). Downie also insists upon this point when he discusses the morality of role enactment. He believes there is no reason to think that one's public performance requires the suspension of individual moral thinking. Last, Flores and Johnson tell us that the public-private distinction advanced by many authors is not that clear in any case. Since there are usually private benefits that accompany the rewards for public role performance, the public decisions of officials cannot be said to be entirely impersonal. The individuals acting in these capacities may be deciding primarily for themselves. Even within the public role theory, such matters are open to normative or moral evaluation and possible criticism.

Another intermediate theorist who also believes that statements about group behavior are not redescribable merely as statements about the aggregate result of individual conduct is Werhane. She grounds her position on collective responsibility upon the distinction between primary and secondary action found in the agency model of accountability. This view is also discussed by Copp and is present in May's concept of vicarious agency (Copp, 1979, p. 177; May, 1983, p. 70). By a secondary action, Werhane means one that is performed on behalf of another party (Werhane, 1985, p. 52). The individual performs an act (primary action) that is then also attributable to the other party (secondary action). Werhane contends that individuals are the ultimate agents of primary actions, while corporations perform acts as secondary or dependent moral agents. To evaluate the actions of collectives is not then the same as evaluating the actions of its members, though some evaluation of the latters' primary actions is in order. As Werhane sees it, there are facets of secondary actions that make it more difficult to infer that statements about collective action are always translatable into certain kinds of statements about individual conduct. The collective roles in which secondary actions are often performed have a degree of the impersonal authority that is largely beyond the control of individual workers. Having said this, however, it should be added that she does not believe this relieves subordinates of the need to make personal decisions. They can be held responsible to dissent in certain situations—which situations will be discussed in the next chapter when we consider more specifically her theory of subordinate dissent. At this point, at least, we can see that she does at times hold subordinates responsible for failing to prevent or rectify acts of corporate misconduct.

Just as Copp, Werhane, and May appeal to the agency model or metaphor of collective action, the last intermediate theory of collective responsibility to be examined here appeals to the metaphor of conspiracy. It is put forth by Ellin and Nersoyan. Ellin grants that collectives, like a corporation, are distinct from their members. Like French and the other holists, he believes they have their own unique properties and aims, but, unlike these thinkers, he maintains that each member of a collective can be held accountable for the positive acts of the group, even if he or she is not personally at fault for this conduct (Ellin, 1981–82, p. 17). He compares the collective responsibility present in corporations to the type found in conspiracies. All members of a conspiracy are held accountable for the actions of the group, even if they do not themselves directly cause a certain negative outcome. Accountability is not grounded entirely upon personal causal agency or control. The very fact that members contribute in some way to a common purpose and outcome for which there is a division of labor indicates that they are responsible for the actions of the group. This is so even if they do not authorize, or even know of, the negative outcome in question. Thus, the actions of any one member of the collective in furtherance of group goals is attributed to every member of the group. The reasons for this are that each member initially chooses to belong to a group over which he or she does not exercise full control, and each is benefitted or rewarded in some way by the group's positive accomplishments (Ellin, 1981–82, p. 22). It follows then that each is also responsible for the negative outcomes (assuming that no other valid excusing conditions apply, such as acting under force, duress, and the like.)

Nersoyan tells us that corporations are strong collectivities. In a strong collectivity each member is a link in a chain and cannot be easily removed without changing the entire collective. Each member is conscious of a common purpose and his or her role in the group. Through this member consciousness, the group is said to be self-conscious and to exercise an autonomous will. The type of relations that exist between the members are said to be internal rather than external. This means that a relationship between one member and another affects other members: any change in the former alters the latter, and these latter changes reverberate back to affect the relationship between the initial members (Nersoyan, 1981–82, p. 90). And because members are conscious of their roles and relations, there is the possibility of a dual set of alterations (a part of Mandelbaum's referential opacity), one that applies to the relations themselves (the formal structure of the corporation, its rules, and policies, etc.) and one that applies to the members' interpretation of these relational changes. Each level is capable of reverberating throughout the organization, setting up what we have elsewhere called a turbulent field—one functioning primarily within a strategic or interdependent context where various members must consider how the others will think or act before they can determine what they themselves will or should do.

Thus far we have seen the holistic aspect of Nersoyan's theory. Although he believes that the conduct of strong collectivities is not reducible to the actions of the individual members, when taken in isolation, he nevertheless formulates a theory of responsibility in which individuals are still accountable for the actions of the group. This is particularly true when six conditions are present: (1) each member is in general aware of a common interest, (2) this interest is viewed as served by a certain project or action, (3) steps are taken to execute the project, (4) each member assumes some part in the project, (5) the success of the project results from the success of the various contributions, and (6) negativities or conflicts within the group are kept to a minimum (Nersoyan, 1981–82, p. 91). These six conditions are somewhat similar to the factors mentioned by Ellin for the presence of a conspiracy. When they are present, subordinates are responsible for the activities of the entire group, even when they do not agree with a specific action or policy of the group. And even if they do not know (or could not have known), or could not prevent the action in question, if they take no steps to explicitly protest the action, prevent its outcome, or sever their connection with the conspiracy, they are accountable for it. Hence, the conspiracy theory does not accept some of the usual excusing conditions mentioned earlier by Held and others, that is, insufficient knowledge or control, for example, are not usually granted as excuses. It is thus a more exacting theory of subordinate responsibility than the others we have thus far discussed.

Most of the theories examined here have been advanced with the assumption in mind that a more or less convincing theory of collective or subordinate responsibility exists—one that can be determined by appealing to evidence that is not itself normative or moral in nature. The last type of theory to be discussed here specifically rejects this assumption. We have referred to this type of view as a metatheory of collective and subordinate responsibility.

METATHEORIES

Theorists such as Donaldson, DeGeorge, and Feinberg tell us that no one theory of collective or subordinate responsibility suffices. They believe that while one model may be best for one type of situation, another may be more appropriate for a different situation. What determines the acceptability of any particular model are the values or normative concerns that we are trying to promote or preserve in initially appealing to these models, such as the general goal of blaming or punishing, the ideal of society, and the like. Thus, the accuracy or acceptability of the models is a normative rather than a purely factual or descriptive matter. In this section we shall consider the theories of DeGeorge and Feinberg that are representative of this type of position.

DeGeorge tells us that there are five ways to assign responsibility in a collective: two are individualistic, one holistic, and the remaining two involve a mixture of holism and individualism (DeGeorge, 1981–82, p. 10). The individualistic interpretations are (1) assigning responsibility to every member of an organization for every one of its actions or (2) assigning partial responsibility to every member of the firm for every action of the organization. The apportionment of responsibility in the second version may be based upon such factors as the amount of voting power a member has, for example. (DeGeorge also suggests variations of these two versions in which only the active members are assigned full or partial responsibility.) The holistic interpretation involves (3) assigning responsibility only to the collective, not to its members. The mixed models combine these interpretations in two ways. The first involves (4) holding both the collective and its individual members responsible, with every member (or every active member) being held accountable for every collective act. The last version involves (5) holding both the collective and its members responsible, with every member (or every active member) being assigned partial responsibility (perhaps in terms of voting power) for every collective act (DeGeorge, 1981–82, p. 10). DeGeorge tells us that no one version is the correct theory. Which theory we appeal to in a specific case is based upon the social purposes we are trying to serve. The accuracy or appropriateness of a theory is then contingent upon normative considerations rather than vice versa.

We can see from this schema that the holistic theories considered in this chapter endorse either versions three or five: the individualistic theories promote versions one or two (or variations thereof). The public role theories prefer models three, four, or five (with the exception of Ladd who would hold neither the organization nor its members morally responsible for its conduct). And the intermediate views are committed to the last two versions, though the conduct for which the collective is held accountable may not be the same as that for which individual members are held responsible.

Feinberg considers four models of collective responsibility (Feinberg, 1970, p. 233). The first involves holding an entire group responsible, while none of its members are held to be at fault. This is a form of vicarious liability in which otherwise innocent individuals are held accountable for the actions, or alleged actions, of the group. It applies to groups that already have great solidarity or are in need of forming it. Solidarity is based upon the sharing of a set of common interests, a bond of common and reciprocal feelings, or the facing of a common lot in such an integrated way that the interests of one member are the interests of another. To hurt one is to hurt all. This model of responsibility has been applied to tribes or clans, where an entire tribe is held accountable for some action, even though no member is blamed for having contributed to it. Because it strikes many as unfair, Feinberg concedes that it is not a commonly held position (Feinberg, 1970, p. 236). If advanced at all, however, it is likely to be put forth by holists. It is similar to DeGeorge's third model.

The second model involves holding a group collectively responsible through the contributory fault of only one or a few of its members. The rest may have been involved in similar actions in the past and so have the same fault as the person or persons who caused the negative outcome, but they may not have contributed to the outcome in the present case. An example of this model would be holding a private club responsible for an accident caused by the drunk driving of one of its members. All of the members may have driven home from meetings while intoxicated at other times, but they may not have been at fault in the case at hand. Another example would be a teacher's punishing an entire class for talking, even though only a few pupils were at fault. In the past, though, there may have been times when each member of the class spoke while not being given permission to do so. This model would likely be endorsed by some holists and by those advancing one of the intermediate positions on collective responsibility. It is similar to variations of DeGeorge's last two models. Feinberg thinks that one of its weaknesses is that it is impractical. This is because it is hard to determine when individuals are faultless and when they are guilty of the specific fault under consideration. The latter is especially difficult to determine if the group to which they belong is otherwise quite diverse (Feinberg, 1970, p. 242).

The third model involves holding the group responsible through the contributory fault of each and every member. This position is similar to the last two models proposed by DeGeorge and, in one form, is endorsed by the conspiracy model of Ellin and Nersoyan. Feinberg tells us, however, that it is a less convincing model in a case where a large number of people may be at fault but there is little communication between them. For example, in a situation in which 1,000 accomplished swimmers stand by and watch a person drown, Feinberg tells us it is difficult to hold each person morally responsible for the drowning, but he does add that from a legal point of view a surviving relative can sue any one of these individuals. Held argues that each can at least be held responsible for failing to develop a decision procedure to determine who should save the drowning person. In addition, Feinberg holds (against Ellin and Nersoyan) that this model is also less persuasive in cases where individuals play very diverse roles in a common project. Feinberg tells us that there are problems in assessing the degree of responsibility to be assigned to individuals in these cases, especially those who perform a subsidiary role in a project (Feinberg, 1970, p. 246).

The last model he examines involves holding a group collectively responsible through the collective but nondistributive fault of the group itself. In this model we may blame the group without blaming anyone in the group. This occurs when, as we have already considered, a group of individuals fail to stop a tragedy that could have been prevented by any one of them. As we have seen, unlike Held, Feinberg does not assign individual moral blame here. But it also occurs when an entire social system is criticized as being corrupt or vile, while no one person in the system is considered to be corrupt or vile. This position is like that proposed by Cooper and is similar to DeGeorge's third model. Feinberg tells us that we cannot blame particular individuals for failing to rebel against such a system. Individuals in this system are not to be faulted for failing to be heroic, though Feinberg does believe that the system itself may be additionally blamed for failing to produce a saint or hero when one is needed (Feinberg, 1970, p. 248).

Like DeGeorge, Feinberg tells us that the deciding factors revealing which of these models is to be preferred in particular situations depend upon the case at hand as well as upon the normative and social values we are trying to promote. As a consequence, no one theory of collective or subordinate responsibility is to be universally preferred to the others.

COLLECTIVE RESPONSIBILITY AND SUBORDINATE DISSENT

As we have said, one of the main reasons to discuss the question of the nature of collective and subordinate responsibility is to introduce the issue of the next chapter—the responsibility of subordinates for organizational dissent or whistleblowing. Therefore, we are not only interested in determining the general conditions of subordinate responsibility, we are also concerned with delineating the responsibility of subordinates in cases where superiors authorize corporate policies or actions that are viewed as illegitimate by one or other of the four theories of corporate responsibility. In these cases are subordinates responsible to express their dissent?

Without going into the specific arguments for or against subordinate dissent here, it can be seen that the theories discussed in this chapter can play a role in determining an answer to this question. Some of the theories or models of collective responsibility offer excusing or vindicating conditions for subordinates. They suggest that subordinates are not responsible for dissenting from their superiors, given the way in which collective responsibility is distributed within an organization. But we have also seen that other theories discussed here reject this conclusion, of course.

Theories offering excusing or vindicating conditions are proposed or discussed by holists, rolists, certain individualists, and by DeGeorge and Feinberg. In addition to the usual excusing conditions (insufficient knowledge or control, duress, and the like) that are admitted by most theorists (except conspiracy theorists and advocates of some of Feinberg's models), these theories advance additional reasons why subordinates should not be held accountable for expressing dissent. For rolists and some holists, following the accepted procedure in one's occupational role is always at least a *prima facie* vindicating condition for corporate responsibility. In terms of the concepts of this book such theorists believe that for subordinates the regulation, or perhaps the fiduciary, model usually "trumps" all the other relations of accountability. The logic of their position leaves open the possibility that subordinates may have other, possibly conflicting and overriding responsibilities, but they do not typically grant this point. They argue instead that dissent is rarely a subordinate responsibility in these cases. They seem to believe that when subordinates are not responsible for authorizing or causing a specific instance of corporate misconduct, they are not responsible for preventing it either.

Certain individualists like Hessen and Friedman also argue that dissent is usually outside the domain of responsibility for subordinates. Unlike holists, however, they do not argue that collective is often irreducible to individual responsibility, though they do believe in a two-track system of responsibility for superiors and for subordinates—a division of responsibility to match the division of labor that is said to contribute to corporate efficiency and effectiveness in meeting its institutional responsibilities. Superiors are said to be responsible to shareholders, subordinates directly responsible to superiors. Loyalty, obedience, and confidentiality are the principal virtues that compose the second track, not dissent or protest. (We see again their appeal to the performance, fiduciary, and representative models of accountability.)

It should be mentioned that it is compatible with the classical version of individualism to believe that subordinates may at times be accountable to dissent. This occurs either when superiors substantially ignore their responsibilities (to shareholders) or when superiors try to achieve their goals by serious violations of the law. In these kinds of circumstance, even holists and rolists who support the classical theory would grant that responsiveness to the shareholders could supercede the subordinates' responsibility to obey superiors. But it should also be mentioned that classical theorists rarely, if ever, actually argue this way. And they flatly reject the idea that dissent is a responsibility of subordinates in cases where superiors ignore only the social or moral (or noneconomic) responsibilities urged by other theorists. In fact, dissent in these cases is often viewed as irresponsible (i.e., an unjustified exercise of power outside the subordinate's legitimate domain of responsibility).

Other individualists advance more demanding theories of subordinate dissent, of course, depending upon whether they accept the stakeholder, social demandingness, or activist theories of corporate responsibility. But since we are concerned here only with theories of collective and subordinate responsibility that limit subordinate responsibility (to dissent), we need not detail their positions in the present context.

Finally, we have the models mentioned by DeGeorge and Feinberg, particularly the model that is completely holistic and rejects the idea of individual responsibility entirely. Within this model, a subordinate's responsibility to dissent simply does not arise.

Along with these views, there are theories of collective and subordinate responsibility that place considerably greater demands upon subordinates. Individualists and agency theorists who support the social activist position and conspiracy theorists come to mind immediately. And depending upon the activist theory in question, subordinates may even be required to dissent when corporate superiors ignore merely a social responsibility of the firm. But this depends upon the actual values supported within a particular activist theory and upon whether or not it holds that subordinates are merely *accountable* for expressing, or are actually *obligated* to express, dissent in these cases.

SUBORDINATE DISSENT AND THE RELATIONS OF ACCOUNTABILITY

A main thesis of the present work is that certain types of assumptions ground the various theories of corporate (or superior) responsibility. It can be seen that these same assumptions are also involved in the theories of collective and subordinate responsibility. Some of the strategies of legitimation concern a matter that also helps us to address one of the normative questions raised in the metatheories. They are meant to spell out the general features of those institutions thought to belong legitimately to one's ideal of society. The models of the corporation tell us about the particular features or functions of the specific type of institution under consideration, features or functions that have relevance to the responsibility debate. In telling us more about the organizational context of responsibility claims for subordinates, these models tell us how subordinates function in the corporation, how much knowledge, power, control, choice, or influence, for example, they are likely to have. And they tell us about the likely goals or ideals that the corporations themselves pursue.

Rounding off this account are the relations of accountability. Since they are meant to tell us about the specific features of the interpersonal context in which responsibility claims arise, they are the most direct and important factors involved in determining the responsibility of subordinates. Subordinates are expected or required to give a rendering of themselves whenever one of these relationships apply to them. This does not tell us when, if at all, subordinates are *obligated* to dissent, but it does tell us that the duty of dissent is likely to arise only cases where one or more of these relationships apply.

A brief comparison of two of the theories examined in this chapter reveals the crucial role that the relations of accountability play in the debate. Consider the holism of French and Cooper, on the one hand, and the conspiracy model of Ellin and Nersoyan, on the other. The holistic theories rely upon all but the ownership model; the conspiracy model can rely upon all of these models, though they are not all represented in the accounts of Ellin or Nersoyan just discussed. Some holists believe that subordinates are not responsible to dissent in cases where their input in the corporate misconduct is negligible, where they can be easily replaced were they to dissent, and where they have followed the accepted procedures of the company. They believe it is otherwise unfair to have them risk their jobs, careers, friendships, and so forth to dissent in cases such as these. We can see five types of relationship represented in the role functions brought up by these holists. The promise-keeping model applies because subordinates have typically given their consent to the general aspects of their occupational roles, though they need not have given their explicit consent to the specific requirements of the role in the action in question. They are thought to be constrained by the rules involved in their roles (the regulation model) as they act as agents for the stockholders and their superiors (the fiduciary model). They are viewed as agents who in some general sense represent their bosses and can be replaced by them (the representative or functionary model), so they must do their part to achieve the goals of the corporation (the teamwork model). When the actions of the subordinates play a negligible part in the corporate misconduct (the impact model), they should not typically be expected to risk the loss of friendships and security that would likely occur from being fired or demoted for expressing their dissent (the reverse-impact model).

The conspiracy model, on the other hand, holds every member of the conspiracy responsible both for their individual misconduct (the impact model) and for the wrongdoing of the group as a whole (the teamwork and impact models). Since they have given their consent to the goals, activities, and procedures that led to the misconduct in the first place (the promise-keeping model), they are to be viewed as agents or representatives of the other members of the conspiracy (the fiduciary and representative models) and are to be held equally liable with these other members, even if they do not approve of, or even know about, certain aspects or activities of the conspiracy. Without explicitly withdrawing from the conspiracy by dissenting, they indicate their continued stake in and title to the conspiracy (the latter involving a kind of possession or ownership of it). Because of these factors, all subordinates are to be held accountable for corporate wrong-doing, subject to those excusing conditions that apply only to conspiracies.

By explicitly appealing to the relations of accountability, as we shall be doing in the next two chapters, it will become clear that several general but significant implications follow from this. First, since the employment context always involves responsibilities of some type (typically these are responsibilities to be loyal or obedient members of the corporate team), dissent or whistleblowing is never a purely discretionary act of an employee. Second, given this initial set of employment responsibilities, the burden of proof rests upon the advocate of dissent to show why subordinates may be responsible or obligated to disrupt the usual practice. Last, it tells us that this is done by showing what relations of accountability ground the responsibility to dissent in light of the other strategies, theories, and models discussed in this book. We shall see these general points illustrated in the work of the theorists to be discussed in the next chapter. The issue for discussion will be the justification of a particular type of subordinate dissent—that found in whistleblowing. Since an anti-whistleblowing literature of considerable size has grown over the last two decades, we shall begin the next chapter with an examination of this literature. We shall also consider some responses to the arguments raised in this literature. This will help to determine if pro-whistleblowing theorists can meet the burden of proof just mentioned—whether they can show that this type of dissent is at times a responsibility of subordinates (just as obedience or loyalty are occupational responsibilities of subordinates).

REFERENCES

Agassi, Joseph. 1960. "Methodological Individualism." *British Journal of Sociology*, 11, pp. 244–70.

Atkinson, Christine, and Adrian Atkinson. 1980. "Corporate Social Responsibility: A Philosophical Appraisal." *Journal of Enterprise Management*, vol. 2, pp. 131–35.

Cooper, D. E. 1968. "Collective Responsibility." *Philosophy*, vol. 43, pp. 258–68.

———. 1969. "Collective Responsibility—Again." *Philosophy*, vol. 44, pp. 153–55.

———. 1972. "Responsibility and the System." In *Individual and Collective Responsibility: The Massacre at My Lai*, edited by Peter A. French, pp. 83–102. Cambridge, Mass.: Schenkman Publishing Company.

Copp, David. 1979. "Collective Actions and Secondary Actions." *American Philosophical Quarterly*, July, pp. 177–86.

Danley, John R. 1984. "Corporate Moral Agency: A Case for Anthropological Bigotry." In *Business Ethics: Readings and Cases in Corporate Morality*, edited by W. Michael Hoffman and Jennifer Moore, pp. 172–79. New York: McGraw-Hill.

DeGeorge, Richard. 1981–82. "Can Corporations Have Moral Responsibility?" *University of Dayton Review*, Winter, pp. 3–15.

Downie, R. S. 1969. "Collective Responsibility." *Philosophy*, vol. 44, pp. 66–69.

———. 1972. "Responsibility and Social Roles." In *Individual and Collective Respon-*

sibility: The Massacre at My Lai, edited by Peter A. French, pp. 65–82. Cambridge, Mass.: Schenckman Publishing Company.

Ellin, J. S. 1981–82. "The Justice of Collective Responsibility." *University of Dayton Review*, Winter, pp. 17–27.

Feinberg, Joel. 1970. *Doing and Deserving*. Princeton, N.J.: Princeton University Press.

Flores, Albert, and Deborah Johnson. 1983. "Collective Responsibility and Professional Roles." *Ethics*, April, pp. 537–46.

French, Peter A. 1984. *Collective and Corporate Responsibility*. New York: Columbia University Press.

Friedman, Milton. 1970. "The Social Responsibility of Business Is To Increase Its Profits." *The New York Times Magazine*, September 13, pp. 122–26.

Held, Virginia. 1972. "Moral Responsibility and Collective Action." In *Individual and Collective Responsibility: The Massacre at My Lai*, edited by Peter A. French, pp. 103–20. Cambridge, Mass.: Schenkman Publishing Company.

Hessen, Robert. 1979. *In Defense of the Corporation*. Stanford, Calif.: The Hoover Institution Press.

Jones, W. T. 1984. "Public Roles, Private Roles and Differential Moral Assessments of Role Performance." *Ethics*, July, pp. 603–19.

Keeley, Michael. 1981. "Organizations as Non-Persons." *Journal of Value Inquiry*, vol. 15, pp. 149–55.

Ladd, John. 1979. "Morality and the Ideal of Rationality in Formal Organizations." *Monist*, vol. 54, pp. 488–516.

Lewis, H. D. 1972. "The Non-Moral Notion of Collective Responsibility." In *Individual and Collective Responsibility: The Massacre at My Lai*, edited by Peter French, pp. 121–33. Cambridge, Mass.: Schenckman Publishing Company.

Mandelbaum, Maurice. 1973. "Societal Facts." In *The Philosophy of Social Explanation*, edited by Alan Ryan, pp. 106–18. Oxford: Oxford University Press.

May, Larry. 1983. "Vicarious Agency." *Philosophical Studies*, vol. 43, pp. 69–82.

Nersoyan, H. James. 1981–82. "An Analysis of Collectivity." *University of Dayton Review*, Winter, pp. 87–96.

Velasquez, Manuel. 1983. "Why Corporations Are Not Morally Responsible For Anything They Do." *Business and Professional Ethics Journal*, Spring, pp. 1–17.

Walsh, W. H. 1970. "Pride, Shame and Responsibility." *The Philosophical Quarterly*, January, pp. 1–13.

Watkins, J.W.N. 1958. "The Third Reply to Mr. Goldstein." *British Journal for the Philosophy of Science*, November, pp. 242–44.

———. 1968. "Methodological Individualism and Social Tendencies." In *Readings in the Philosophy of the Social Sciences*, edited by May Brodbeck, pp. 269–80. New York: Macmillan.

Werhane, Patricia. 1985. *Persons, Rights and Corporations*. Englewood Cliffs, N.J.: Prentice-Hall.

16

THE RESPONSIBILITY OF SUBORDINATES

INTRODUCTION

As we have said at the end of the last chapter, it is expected that the typical or primary responsibilities of employees as subordinates involve such activities as taking orders without complaint, carrying out their occupational tasks conscientiously, keeping confidential the trade secrets of the corporation and, in general, being loyal agents of the company. These responsibilities are implied to some extent by all eight relations of accountability and thereby by each of the theories of corporate responsibility discussed earlier. But what if a subordinate discovers that an authorized policy of his or her firm involves activities that are illegal or otherwise violate the accepted moral or social standards applicable to the corporation? What if a subordinate discovers that top-level executives of the corporation are defrauding the stockholders or are knowingly injuring the latters' financial interests in the firm? For what kinds of action (or omissions of action) are corporate subordinates accountable when they are asked or told to do something that they think is wrong or is viewed as illegitimate by one or other of the four theories? What responsibilities do subordinates have to express dissent in the corporation?

The question of employee dissent is a broad one involving different types and degrees of normative disagreement or protest. Initially, there is simple questioning, where a subordinate asks for further information about a project or further guidance in acting on its behalf. The issue of why he or she is being directed to do a certain action may arise. At this level we do not have dissent proper, however. Beyond this point there is (normative) disagreement. Here the employee is no longer seeking information but is indicating that he or she does not accept the action or policy in question. This type of disagreement may be expressed to superiors or to other subordinates. If an employee indicates a willingness to be removed from a certain project because of such a disagreement, we have individual protest or conscientious objection. (We should note here, however, that such protest or objection is also often involved in a more extreme form of employee dissent, namely, leaving the company.) If the employee stays within the firm and seeks to directly interfere with a questionable corporate policy or project, we have obstructionism. If the employee is successful in getting others to protest their involvement in the project, we have organized dissent or strike. Short of quitting, each of these forms of dissent involves using the internal channels of the company. When an employee uses outside sources to question or try to prevent a company policy or action, we have external disclosure. This can be done by informing a private organization, like a newspaper or television station which can make the issue a public one, or it can be done through a governmental agency or a professional group that may itself have the power to stop the company or its members from performing the action or instituting the policy in question.

In the present chapter we shall discuss the practice of whistleblowing. This form of dissent has been defined in various ways, but we shall see that it is closer to external disclosure than it is to the other forms of subordinate dissent. We shall be concerned with the justification or legitimacy of this form of disagreement as it is directed toward violations of the law, breaches of professional ethics, or infractions against the principles of common morality. In the next section we shall examine works that have offered definitions of the concept of whistleblowing, and then we shall consider some of the main arguments for and against whistleblowing as a general responsibility of subordinates.

Before we begin, a brief word on method and argument in this chapter is in order. Though we have said that the burden of proof initially rests upon the proponent of whistleblowing, we shall organize the present discussion around the arguments of the opponents to whistleblowing. We shall seek to determine if they are successful in showing that subordinates have no (overriding) responsibility in this regard. We do this in large part because, as we have defined the problem of dissent here, whistleblowing seems initially to be sponsored by at least three of the four theories of corporate responsibility discussed in this work (and is probably endorsed in certain versions of the fourth, as well).

In considering these arguments, however, it should be noted that most of them try to show that whistleblowing is usually or always unjustified. This is either because it carries no implication of accountability at all for them or because its slight degree of normative compellingness is (almost) always overridden by other subordinate responsibilities in specific cases. This means, though, that some of the proponents of whistleblowing who try to respond to these arguments seek to show merely the justified character of whistleblowing in certain situations. But justified acts need not be responsibilities or duties. We must realize that these proponents need not be defending the idea that whistleblowing is a responsibility or duty of subordinates. They may merely be trying to show that it involves discretionary or heroic acts, that is, that subordinates are as justified in blowing the whistle in a single case as they are in not blowing it—both are equally warranted. This tells us, though, that there are three relatively unique, yet interconnected, issues that arise here. Justifying cases of whistleblowing may involve showing its warrantedness as (1) a mere *discretionary act* or set of acts (where it and its opposite are not viewed as being unwarranted or wrong to perform), (2) a *responsibility* (where one of its opposites is a purely discretionary act) or, (3) a *duty* (where it is to be contrasted with an illegal or immoral act, an overruled responsibility, or an act of supererogation).

Given what was said in the last chapter, however, it can be seen that we have little interest in examining or justifying the discretionary nature or character of whistleblowing. In fact, from the perspective of this book, whistleblowing is never a discretionary act as such. Since it is always opposed to certain responsibilities, is sometimes sponsored by the relations of accountability and the four theories, and often arises in circumstances in which the interests of others are or can be significantly affected, whistleblowing does not belong in the arena of (merely) discretionary choice for agents. Hence, we shall interpret the arguments of the proponents of whistleblowing as trying to establish the conclusion that whistleblowing is, at a minimum, a responsibility of subordinates in certain occupational situations. Our prime concern in the coming sections will thus be with the latter two issues mentioned above. But it must finally also be admitted that not every author whom we shall discuss here clearly distinguishes between these latter matters. It is nevertheless important to do so, for certain excuses or vindications are appropriate for nondissenting subordinates if whistleblowing is being considered as only a general responsibility that are not appropriate if it is being considered as a duty.

THE CONCEPT OF WHISTLEBLOWING

The definitions of whistleblowing given in the literature focus on somewhat different features of the concept. Bok tells us that whistleblowing involves sounding an alarm within an organization that focuses upon neglect or abuses threatening the public interest (Bok, 1980, p. 2). For her, whistleblowing is an act that is performed within an organization and is aimed at disclosing practices that threaten the public good. Alarms that are sounded to protect the interests of the corporation, such as revealing employee theft, are not considered by her to be acts of whistleblowing. In a later work, she also grants, however, that alarms sounded by employees to outside agencies or to the public can be considered acts of whistleblowing (Bok, 1984, p. 211). Chalk and von Hippel agree with this latter point. They tell us that whistleblowing in the private sector is the unauthorized revelation of concerns about a corporation to individuals outside the organization (Chalk and von Hippel, 1979, p. 50).

More extensive definitions are given by Bowie, DeGeorge, and Elliston. Bowie maintains that whistleblowing is an act done by an employee of a public or private, profit or nonprofit organization, who has been ordered to perform acts, or knows that his or her organization is engaged in activities, that are believed to cause unnecessary harm to outside parties, violate human rights, or run counter to the defined purposes of the institution. The whistleblower is one who informs the public of his or her concerns in these areas (Bowie, 1982, p. 142). Bowie's definition indicates that whistleblowers can be found in both the public and private sectors of the economy. They make information public that concerns the violation of rights or the causing of harm to third parties. Unlike Bok, however, he believes that since whistleblowing can at times involve revealing information that indicates that members of the institution are not acting in conformity with the expressed purposes of the organization, it is not a practice that is necessarily aimed to protect the public interest directly.

DeGeorge agrees with Bowie in important respects, though his definition involves some differences in focus. For DeGeorge, the primary area of concern for whistleblowers is the safety and reliability of the products manufactured and sold by their firms. He tells us that the concept of whistleblowing can be further distinguished in three respects (DeGeorge, 1986, p. 223). There is internal versus external whistleblowing. The former involves staying within the organization to raise one's complaints; the latter refers to complaints that are voiced outside the institution. The second distinction concerns personal versus impersonal whistleblowing. A personal whistleblower is one who raises complaints against individual members of the organization but does not wish to protest the actions of the firm itself. An example of this form of dissent is an employee who maintains that he or she has been the victim of sexual harassment by a particular employee or supervisor. Last, DeGeorge distinguishes between governmental and nongovernmental whistleblowing. The former concerns complaints raised in public organizations and involves problems that are somewhat unique to the public sector. These include such factors as the recognized constitutional rights of workers in this sector, the lack of the presumption of employment at will by public agencies, and the expressed obligation of governmental organizations to serve the common rather than the private good. Nongovernmental whistleblowing concerns complaints that arise in private organizations, such as business corporations.

In his discussion of the issue, DeGeorge is particularly concerned with external, impersonal, and nongovernmental whistleblowing. It is this concept that he defines in terms of an employee's revealing of information concerning an unsafe or hazardous product of a company that can cause harm to the public or to its individual users.

The authors discussed thus far have somewhat different ideas about the object of the complaints raised by whistleblowers. Bok tells us whistleblowers sound alarms about negligence, abuses, or dangers; DeGeorge indicates the practice concerns the use or marketing of unsafe or hazardous products; Bowie contends that whistleblowers direct their attention to the causing of unnecessary harms to third parties, the violation of rights, or the failure to abide by the stated purposes of the organization.

After reviewing these definitions, Elliston proposes several criticisms of them. He tells us that the definitions of DeGeorge and Bok are too narrow. In addition to problems of safety, abuse, neglect, and danger, whistleblowers may raise concerns about mismanagement and inefficiency in their organizations (Elliston, 1982, p. 40). He criticizes the Bowie definition on several counts. First, he tells us that Bowie does not clearly define *unnecessary* harm. If a firm dumps toxins into a nearby river to reduce its pollution control costs, its executives may consider this harm to be necessary to preserve jobs at its plant or facility (Elliston, 1982, p. 41). Since many kinds of questionable activity may be viewed by managers as necessary to achieve corporate goals, Elliston proposes changing the concept of *unnecessary* harm to one that is at least quasi-normative in nature. He prefers to speak of *excessive* harm, where excessiveness is determined by a balancing test, comparing the expected or actual benefits of an action with its expected or actual harm. Second, he rejects the third condition in Bowie's definition of whistleblowing, at least to the extent that this is meant to apply to private organizations. Elliston believes that a direct concern for the public good is always involved in whistleblowing. Thus, if an act of dissent reveals that a policy or act sponsored by the superiors of an organization runs counter to the expressed purpose of that institution (as Bowie suggests), Elliston indicates that the institution in question must be either public or professional in nature for the expression of dissent to be properly considered as a possible act of whistleblowing. Only such institutions have as one of their explicit primary goals the end of serving the public interest. But since this is not the case for most private institutions, Elliston tells us that Bowie's third condition is not a necessary feature of whistleblowing. Last, Elliston questions those definitions that state or imply that whistleblowing is a single act. As he sees it, it is typically a *process* or *set of acts* that are involved in conveying information to external sources about organizational activities that produce a net harm to third parties (Elliston, 1982, p. 42).

Like Bok, Elliston believes that whistleblowing involves three elements: dissent, a real or apparent breach of loyalty, and an accusation (Bok, 1984, p. 214). By dissenting, the whistleblower indicates his or her disagreement with the superiors of a corporation, thus sounding an alarm to the public that its interests or rights are being jeopardized by a corporate action. A real or apparent breach of loyalty is involved because the whistleblower relies upon inside, sometimes even confidential, information to warn the public, and because the warning is often seen as opposing the interests of the corporation or its top executives. Finally it is an accusatory act or process because the warning usually names specific individuals, committees or departments in the organization that are said to be responsible for its illegal, unethical, or questionable acts or policies of action.

Keeping these points in mind, we shall use the term *whistleblowing* in this work in the following way. It will refer to an act or process of dissent in which a subordinate in a corporation provides information to parties outside the organization, warning stakeholders or the public that its interests or rights are being jeopardized by an action or policy of the corporation. Such a warning accuses certain individuals in the organization of mismanagement, neglect, lack of professionalism, or moral or legal wrongdoing; it accuses them of doing something that already has produced, or will likely produce, a net harm to other individuals. As used here, the concept involves what DeGeorge calls external, impersonal, and nongovernmental whistleblowing.

What then are the main arguments found in the literature for or against whistleblowing? We shall begin our discussion with four general lines of argument that have been raised against whistleblowing as a warranted responsibility of subordinates. As advocates of this view see it, if their arguments prove to be successful, they show that whistleblowing is, at a minimum, a nonresponsibility of subordinates. And since responsibilities override nonresponsibilities, they believe they have vindicated the institutional virtues of subordinate obedience and loyalty. Critics, of course, view the subject differently. The four arguments we shall discuss are those that raise concerns about (1) role responsibilities, (2) disloyalty, (3) disobedience and lack of confidentiality, and (4) harm. In the final section, we shall take up the question of whether whistleblowing is ever a duty. We shall thus approach this topic somewhat differently from the way we approached the question of plant relocation. For the latter issue we organized the main arguments around the four theories of corporate responsibility. In this chapter (as in the last), we shall first consider the arguments themselves and only afterward shall we show how they relate to the four theories.

WHISTLEBLOWING AND ROLE RESPONSIBILITIES

One argument that is used to deny that subordinates are accountable to blow the whistle against their organizations or superiors is advanced by rolists and some holists who contend that it is not within their responsibility to dissent in this way because it is not within their occupational roles. They suggest that when employees are hired by a corporation, they are expected to carry out the occupational roles specifically assigned to them. Thus, janitors are not accountable to check the financial records of the firms; nor are auditors expected to clean the company sinks or empty its garbage bins. Since no organization hires subordinates to be corporate gadflies or alarm sounders to the public, it is felt that such roles or activities lie beyond the legitimate domain of responsibility of subordinates.

As we have seen, advocates of this argument develop it in somewhat different ways. Walsh emphasizes the nonvoluntary aspects of occupational roles; Jones focuses upon their impersonal nature, one in which the individual employee is usually quite easily expendable or replaceable (Walsh, 1970, p. 7; Jones, 1984,

p. 607). French and Cooper rely upon the employee's standard of performance while acting in the role. They contend that if no one in the firm has acted in a substandard manner, then no one is responsible to dissent or blow the whistle against the company (French, 1984, p. 15; Cooper, 1972, pp. 87ff.).

This shows us then that the features of occupational roles discussed by Walsh and Jones are used by them as excusing conditions against whistleblowing, while the characteristics mentioned by French and Cooper are used as vindicating conditions. The difference here is that for Walsh and Jones whistleblowing is a nonresponsibility of subordinates; for French and Cooper, on the other hand, whistleblowing may involve a rendering, but employees are always vindicated by showing that they have followed accepted procedures in carrying out their roles. If whistleblowing is a responsibility, then it is never an overriding one in this type of situation.

The role responsibility argument has generated various responses and objections. One such response is advanced by Bowie and Werhane, who tell us that other responsibilities may override occupational roles. As they see it, even if the presence of these roles constitutes a basis for determining one's commitments or actions within a corporation, it need not provide the sole or most compelling basis (Bowie, 1982, p. 12; Werhane, 1985, p. 71). They remind us that there are other considerations that ground accountability claims. Following a particular role may interfere with a promise or with acting as an agent for another; it may have a serious impact on others, or cause significant harm to the agent; it may, in fact, conflict with a variety of other roles (and with the other relations of accountability). If one admits to there being conflicting roles and considerations of responsibility, the question of how to resolve these conflicts arises. Both Bowie and Werhane believe that the role responsibility theory offers us no guidance on this score.

Werhane addresses this question and provides the following list of rules to be followed when role responsibilities are in conflict. She puts them in lexical order:

1. The moral rights of the individuals involved take precedence over other, more utilitarian, benefits.

2. When there is a conflict between the basic rights of individuals, one should seek to honor all of these rights to the extent possible.

3. Only after weighing the rights of individuals should one choose that option which causes the least harm to the parties involved.

4. One should then weigh the benefits of each solution against its possible harms. (Werhane, 1985, pp. 72–73)

We can see from this list that Werhane endorses whistleblowing as a responsibility, if not an obligation, of subordinates in cases where the moral rights of third parties are jeopardized. She would not take as an excuse or vindication of subordinate inaction in these cases that the employee was only doing his or her job or was only following company policy. It is the company policy which is itself under attack. Nor would she accept the excuse or vindication that the employee might be risking his or her job by blowing the whistle. These considerations are secondary to the concern for moral rights. Hence, if one agrees with Werhane's rules, one must reject the adequacy of the role responsibility argument.

Another theorist who rejects this argument is Goldman, who tells us it would be more compelling if it could be shown that occupational roles are strongly role differentiated. To be strongly role differentiated means that the role in question is regulated by principles that are distinct from the principles of common morality. It also means that in cases of conflict the special principles that guide professional or occupational roles are not always of secondary importance relative to the principles of common morality (Goldman, 1980, pp. 260ff.). Ellin refers to this position as the parallel view, that is, the view that professional or occupational morality is parallel with, not subordinate to, ordinary morality (Ellin, 1982, p. 77).

If occupational roles are strongly role-differentiated ones, it could be argued that they involve responsibilities or obligations (such as loyalty, secrecy, or confidentiality) that override the subordinates' concern to protect the rights or interests of third parties or the public. Goldman does not, however, accept the idea that the roles found in business are strongly role-differentiated ones. A strongly role-differentiated role is founded upon certain rights of the individuals that it is meant to serve or protect. The role of physician, for instance, is meant to protect the health of patients. So if the occupational roles found in business were strongly role-differentiated ones, there must be a set of rights that these roles serve, rights that whistleblowers endanger by making public their accusations. The strongest candidate for such rights for Goldman is the alleged right of shareholders to receive a return on their investment. But we have seen that he rejects the idea that stockholders have a *right* to dividends. He tells us they are unlike creditors or bondholders in this regard (Goldman, 1980, p. 284). Thus, whistleblowers should not suppress sounding the alarm out of consideration for the alleged rights of shareholders. They are required or expected to give an accounting of themselves when their occupational roles conflict with the rights of third parties.

We have seen that one could argue against Goldman that while shareholders may not have a right to dividends, they have (among others) a property right in the corporation, and this right deserves to be respected by subordinates. But even if this is admitted, it does not justify subordinate inaction or obedience in cases where corporate superiors are themselves engaged in practices of mismanagement or fraud that violate the shareholders' property rights. And it could be further maintained that property is not a basic right in any case or, at least, that it is the type of right that is often overruled by third-party rights to such basics as health, safety, and freedom. Finally, it might also be added that otherwise justified cases of whistleblowing rarely jeopardize the property rights of shareholders of the company, in any case; few lead to definite and extended losses for the company.

Finally, I wish to mention again the responses of more individualistic thinkers like Held, Downie, and Flores and Johnson, whose positions we considered in the last chapter. Held, of course, tells us that responsibility is a function of knowledge and control, where control means, in part, the power to prevent (Held, 1972, p. 106). The impact model of accountability reaffirms this point. And since one is also held responsible for the impact of his or her omissions of actions, one may be accountable to try to prevent an act of corporate misconduct, even if one did little or nothing to bring it about in the first place. Held thus disagrees with what seems to be an important assumption of the role responsibility position—that responsibility is linked to causation. This assumption tells us that what one does not cause through one's employment role is not generally within one's domain of responsibility to prevent or protest.

For Held, the subordinate role does not commit one to blind obedience; nor does it exempt one from conforming to the usual conditions of morality or of responsibility. Downie concurs with this judgment. He believes, opposing Walsh, that since subordinates have chosen to accept their occupational roles, these roles do involve voluntary elements and thus workers are responsible for any corporate misconduct to which the roles contribute, either by their action or by their complicity (Downie, 1972, p. 70). Last, Flores and Johnson add that the public nature of occupational roles does not justify complete conformity to their dictates. Since every such role involves some private benefits, individuals occupying these roles cannot claim that they are entirely exempt from the standards of ordinary morality in their work life (Flores and Johnson, 1983, p. 543). Just as people are not justified in disregarding the canons of ordinary morality for personal gain in their private lives, so they are accountable for disregarding these canons for personal (and organizational) gain in their work lives.

THE DISLOYALTY ARGUMENT

In addition to the role responsibility argument, there are theorists who maintain that employees have special responsibilities or duties to employers. While these duties typically arise within the roles that employees are expected to perform in an organization, the focus of the special responsibility arguments is not so much upon the occupational roles themselves as it is upon their bases, or alleged bases. They tell us that because the occupational context of corporations implies the existence of these special duties, subordinates are not required to give a rendering of themselves for choosing to abide by the authorized directives of superiors. Thus, the failure to express dissent toward a company policy requires no rendering from subordinates—only the failure to obey does. One special duty that some opponents of whistleblowing maintain applies to subordinates and grounds their occupational performance is the duty of loyalty. Roche, for example, contends that the principal reason why whistleblowing is an unjustified action or practice lies in the disloyalty to the organization that it represents or expresses (Roche, 1971, p. 445). He compares it to corporate espionage and bemoans the conflict and suspicion it usually fosters within the organization.

There is, however, some ambiguity to the concept of loyalty. Two main approaches to its definition have arisen. Royce, for example, defines loyalty as thoroughgoing devotion to a *cause* (Royce, 1908, p. 16). In his view, the cause or purpose shares in the moral good to which loyalty applies (though loyalty is also conceived of as a supreme good in its own right). Ladd and Oldenquist, on the other hand, maintain that loyalty applies primarily in and to an *interpersonal* context. The object of loyalty is always a specific person or group of persons rather than an abstract cause (Ladd, 1967, p. 97). Oldenquist, for example, distinguishes between being loyal and having an ideal. He tells us that loyalty involves showing partiality toward another person or set of persons because they have some close relation to oneself. They are thus in some sense "mine." Hence, loyalty as such is directed toward people. Ideals, on the other hand, are aimed toward more abstract and impersonal causes (Oldenquist, 1982, p. 175). Oldenquist believes then that the devotion of which Royce has written may involve commitment, conscientiousness, fortitude, or character; but it does not involve or constitute loyalty.

From these definitions come two views of the nature of loyalty. In the first view, loyalty has both intrinsic and contributory value. It can heighten the value of an overall purpose to which it is directed (though it may be hard pressed to salvage the merit of an ill-conceived or harmful cause). In the second view, it is seen as a meritorious form of partiality or favoritism shown toward particular persons. Its opposite is not weakness, or lack of dedication, commitment, or motivation; its opposite is impartiality, impersonalness, or mere neutrality shown toward individuals with whom one closely identifies.

Advocates of the disloyalty argument criticize whistleblowing from both of these points of view. Whistleblowing is viewed as a breach of both trust and commitment within an organization—a breach of trust because it resembles tattling in making matters public that will likely embarrass the company or its members and a breach of commitment because it shows that one's purposes or loyalties ultimately lie elsewhere. A whistleblower is thus considered as a betrayer of the cause or causes to which the company is dedicated and is seen as showing little consideration for the other members of the firm who are likely to suffer from the revelations elicited. When this breach of trust and commitment is criticized for the climate of suspicion it tends to foster, we have a consequentialist argument against whistleblowing, which will be examined later in the chapter. When it is criticized for its failure to show partial or special consideration toward fellow workers, especially one's boss or bosses, and the organizational goals they pursue, we have the features brought out in the present argument. Thus, after studying and listening to managers of various companies, Jackall concludes that executives do not "feel comfortable" with whistleblowing.

This is largely because it violates the basic laws of fealty and teamwork that exist in a bureaucratic organization, such as (1) never go around your boss; (2) always tell your boss what he or she wants to hear, even when the boss asks for opposing views; (3) always drop something your boss wants dropped; (4) sensitive subordinates do not force their bosses to act as bosses; and (5) never report to your boss something he or she does not want reported; cover it up, if you can (Jackall 1988, pp. 109–10). Since whistleblowers do not adhere to these rules, they upset the fragile fealty relations that exist in the corporation and they make the already unstable positions and relationships of subordinates even more contingent and uncertain.

Various writers have criticized the breach of loyalty argument, however. One theorist who rejects the idea that loyalty to an organization constitutes an employee obligation is Duska. He defines loyalty as a special relationship binding individuals in a state of constancy and faithfulness for the purpose of mutual enrichment. It is a reciprocal relationship that is incompatible with the pursuit of simple self-interest (Duska, 1985, p. 297). He argues, however, that corporations are not entities capable of showing respect for their members. They are incapable of faithfulness and trust because they are not persons. If one seeks to respond to this objection by saying that even if corporations are incapable of trust, their members can form such relationships, Duska answers by saying that corporations are not teams, either. Members are not able to show *mutual* confidence and trust, nor can they act for *mutual* enrichment. As members of a profit-making enterprise, they act only from their own self-interest and from the one-way demands of their jobs. Since superiors must maximize profit for the shareholders, they are required to fire anyone, even a friend, who is perceived as harming the company. As Duska sees it, subordinates have the attitude that they only work at the firm; this is the extent of their "loyalty." What they owe to the company then is simply to abide by the contractual relations that ground their employment; loyalty, in the strict sense, is not an element of organizational existence. Thus, it need not be a consideration that enters into a potential whistleblower's calculations (though it must be admitted that the demands of the contractual relations would seem to be a consideration in such a calculation, one that makes it less likely that Duska's argument offers us an entirely successful defense for whistleblowing in general).

Even thinkers who do not share Duska's nonpersonal and noncollegial theory of the corporation agree with him in rejecting the breach of loyalty argument. Michalos, for example, maintains that the argument is inconsistent—at least in one of its formulations. As he sees it, a loyal subordinate or agent is expected to be fully altruistic in serving the interests of a principal or corporation, which in turn acts in a thoroughly egoistic way to protect its own interests. The agent is expected to be fully self-sacrificing in securing the thoroughly self-serving interests of the principal (Michalos, 1983, p. 248). Michalos asks how a loyal agent or subordinate can be directed by such exclusive, yet conflicting, motivations. Their attempts to be fully egoistic (for the principal) are constrained by their ultimate altruistic motives. Michalos recognizes that one might object to this apparent dilemma, as Duska has, by claiming that the agent or subordinate's ultimate motives are self-preservation and self-interest rather than altruism; but he responds to this point by suggesting that in this case the subordinate is not really being a loyal agent after all (Michalos, 1983, p. 251). Since the earlier dilemma was one of loyalty, the present objection does not apply.

Gulick rejects Michalos's formulation of the loyal agent argument in terms of motives, though. He tells us that subordinates are capable of being moved by mixed motives and can still be considered fully loyal agents of the corporation (Gulick, 1982, p. 35). Loyalty then is to be judged in terms of the performance of these individuals rather than by their motives. A loyal agent is one who vigorously promotes and protects the interests of the principal, whatever the nature of his or her own motives.

Both Gulick and Michalos agree, however, in stating a second factor that they take to be telling against the breach of loyalty argument. Subordinates or agents are not expected to give blind loyalty to their superiors. Agency law, for example, typically limits the loyalty of agents to the reasonable demands of the principal, where reasonable demands are those that do not violate the law, the moral standards of society, or the norms of professional ethics (Michalos, 1983, p. 252).

This point is also supported by Bowie, Baron, and Bok, who contend that even if loyalty imposes a duty upon subordinates, it is one that is at best only *conditional* in nature. Other considerations may take precedence in specific situations. Bowie and Baron, for example, contend that the rights of third parties may override the demands of loyalty to the organization (Bowie, 1982, p. 141; Baron, 1984, p. 14). Baron also contends that loyalty is a virtue conditioned by the value of its object. Loyalty to a harmful or injurious cause can constitute fanaticism (Baron, 1984, p. 23). Insofar as it possesses contributory worth, loyalty cannot be seen as a supreme value grounding an overriding duty. Since loyalty among thieves or thugs is no virtue, its existence in an organizational context is no more compelling than the value or validity of the purposes or projects to which the firm is committed.

Finally, Bok suggests that much of the plausibility of the disloyalty argument would be reduced if whistleblowing were used as the last resort by corporate dissenters (Bok, 1984, p. 221). She contends that disloyalty is greatest when subordinates sound a public alarm immediately or without sufficiently reliable knowledge. Assuming that the organization is not extensively corrupt, if the subordinate raises his or her informed criticism within the corporation initially and goes public only when the firm has ignored these concerns, it is far more difficult to contend that the employee is being disloyal (unless, of course, loyalty is simply equated with complete obedience). This observation suggests that another responsibility that corporate superiors have, in addition to those mentioned earlier, is that of setting up appropriate procedures to hear the occupational protests and complaints of subordinates without imposing harsh countermeasures against them.

THE ARGUMENTS FROM OBEDIENCE AND CONFIDENTIALITY

James tells us that agency law often specifies two added special obligations that employees have toward superiors. These are obedience and confidentiality (James, 1983, p. 289). Whistleblowing is sometimes thought to violate these obligations. It is seen as an act of at least indirect disobedience because the whistleblower indicates his or her willingness to disregard or reject a company directive and shows as well that he or she wishes to bring about a situation in which others in the firm will not be required to conform to this directive. In addition, the act of informing an outside agency about a specific issue may violate company procedures. It may be seen as a breach of confidentiality because it makes public matters that involve (or are conceived to involve) internal information, information that may have been taken in confidence by the subordinate. The duty of confidentiality in corporations is not identical to that found in the professions, of course, but there are still times when there is a need to protect certain types of internal information, such as trade or manufacturing processes, administrative procedures, financial plans and projects, and information on layoffs, hirings, plant relocation, mergers, and the like. Whistleblowers may not only reveal something about these matters, but their disclosures may expose other matters that the corporation or its members would wish to keep secret, such as the health status of the top executives, their sexual practices, past use of drugs, and so on.

Theorists have suggested that the special obligations of worker loyalty, obedience, and confidentiality have a fourfold basis. We shall consider each of these in turn.

Property Rights

In the first place, it is suggested that companies own the information that the worker is considering to disclose, and they are also said to possess the work effort of the employees themselves. For workers to appropriate this information elsewhere and for them to use part of their work effort against the firm is to violate the property rights of corporations—somewhat in the manner in which a trespasser violates the rights of a landholder.

Against this view, Bok has argued that even if corporations have property rights over their employees, these rights are not absolute (Bok, 1984, p. 119). Just as the legal property rights of private owners may be overridden for the public purpose of building a highway or constructing power lines, so it can be argued that the public (interest) has "eminent domain" over the legal and moral property rights of corporations or shareholders in certain cases. This is especially true when a company policy violates the basic rights of individuals or third parties (such as their rights to life, health, safety, or freedom).

Werhane tells us that the property rights argument is involved in a confusion when it treats the workers' productivity, labor, or effort as the property of the firm (Werhane, 1985, p. 88). It may be said that workers exchange the "fruits" of their labor for remuneration from the company. The corporation then comes to own these "fruits," but it does not, strictly speaking, own the workers' physical activity itself. This cannot be sold or transferred. Nor can the thinking activity of workers be entirely owned by the company. The knowledge that they possess about company activities and policies is their own. If they choose to reveal this knowledge to outsiders for the sake of protecting the public interest, they are not guilty of a kind of trespass. Even for trade secrets, the model to which courts sometimes appeal is that of joint ownership, and they have been unwilling recently to uphold the property rights of corporations over shared information when this conflicts in a significant way with the common good or with the basic rights of third parties. Werhane contends that to fail to grasp the distinction between labor as outcome (property) and labor as autonomous effort (employment) is to begin to treat persons as mere means (Werhane, 1985, p. 89).

Freedom or Autonomy

The breach of secrecy and obedience that typically occurs with whistleblowing is also said to impinge upon the freedom or autonomy of corporations, their superiors, or members. There are two ways to interpret the freedom argument, but in both versions it is maintained that important rights are violated by whistleblowing. Holists who advance this argument believe that, since the corporation is itself a kind of organism or person, whistleblowing typically violates the freedom rights of the corporation itself. While some individualistic thinkers, on the other hand, especially whose who accept the classical theory, believe this act or process violates the freedom rights of specific individuals within the corporation: the superiors, the shareholders, even one's fellow workers (though it must be admitted that respect for the latter group's rights more typically comes from individualists who are attracted to the stakeholder theory). Whistleblowing is said to interfere with the ability of these individuals to plan and impose upon themselves certain policies of action (especially those directly connected to the corporation) without interference from subordinates or outside sources.

As with the property rights argument, opponents believe the present argument has only *prima facie* compellingness. They maintain that other considerations may override the freedom rights of corporations (or their shareholders or top executives). One of these is the freedom rights of subordinates themselves. In summarizing recent court rulings, Blumberg and Walters, for example, tell us that courts in the United States are anxious to protect the free speech of subordinates on work-related matters when the exercise of this right has clear-cut public policy implications (Blumberg, 1983, p. 136; Walters, 1975, p. 27). The latter tells us that the recent rulings applicable to the public and private sectors indicate that the courts are, at a minimum, seeking to balance various corporate rights with the free speech rights of subordinates and the rights of third parties (Walters, 1987, p. 285).

From a moral point of view, Pollock and others have argued that the right to freedom of one party does not license the disregard of the right to freedom of others (Pollock, 1981, p. 14). Out of concern for consistency, breaches of corporate secrecy and obedience may be justified in cases where the freedom rights of individuals or third parties are significantly curtailed by a corporate policy or action. In these cases, subordinates are required to give a rendering of themselves if they fail to try to prevent the corporate action. It should also be noted that other opponents to the freedom argument take this position in *any* situation in which the basic (or moral) rights of individuals or third parties are jeopardized.

Contract or Promise

A third argument against breaches of corporate secrecy and obedience is that they usually violate conditions or facets of the employment contract. Some workers have stipulations within their employment contracts that commit them to observe the demands of their supervisors and keep confidential certain information that they gain from their jobs. For other workers, it can be argued that they have given their implied consent to abide by the orders of their superiors. They have offered their obedient services in exchange for the salaries or wages they receive from their employer. If they vigorously disagree with a company policy, they can always choose to leave the firm and seek employment elsewhere.

Various objections have been raised to this argument, however. In the first place, the legal duty of secrecy typically applies to a specific area of corporate behavior, namely, that area relative to competitors in the protection of trade secrets. Other facets of corporate activity are not usually covered by the confidentiality or secrecy clauses of an employment contract. And even in the area of trade secrets, the duty of secrecy does not always take precedence over other duties that the employee may have. In speaking about the legal duties of agents or employees, Blumberg tells us that the courts have limited an employee's duty of secrecy in cases where revealing information about manufacturing or trade practices has a substantial effect in safeguarding the public interest (Blumberg, 1983, p. 135). Similar principles apply to other areas of corporate conduct. Blumberg tells us that employees are not legally required to obey corporate policies that constitute violations of the law, breaches of professional ethics, or serious infractions against common morality (Blumberg, 1983, p. 135). This indicates that the *prima facie* duties of secrecy and obedience do not necessarily override other moral or legal considerations.

Another factor that opposes the present argument is the actual or potential promise that members of professions have made to their professional groups.

Physicians, accountants, and engineers, for example, typically have given their word that they will try to protect both the interests of the public and the needs of the specific professional group to which they belong. Peterson and Farrell remind us that professions are distinct from other occupations in that their members adhere to values that stress service to society. These values are usually embodied in codes of ethics or oaths that new members accept as part of the process of initiation into the profession (Peterson and Farrell, 1986, p. 8). Bowie adds that this commitment to a professional code of conduct entails special obligations that professionals have to protect or serve the common good (Bowie, 1982, p. 145). The power of such professions to regulate themselves without undue outside interference is in large part grounded upon society's confidence that members of professional groups will respect the conditions of such autonomous leadership. This indicates that, at times, the promises that certain subordinates have made to their professions will conflict with the explicit or implied promise they have made to their employers. In such a situation, it cannot be said that the latter commitment always or typically overrides the former. Some professions, in fact, specifically reject this idea.

James and Donaldson tell us that if an implied contract with the employer is thought to ground the subordinate's duties of secrecy and obedience in the work place, we cannot overlook the conditions and requirements of the implied promise between corporations and the public to protect the latter's interests (James, 1983, p. 292; Donaldson, 1982, pp. 42ff.). According to social contract theorists, the latter promise is the basis of the incorporation process itself, from which follows the distinctive corporate features of entity status, limited liability, and virtual perpetual duration. This point suggests that all members of the corporation (including subordinates) are under the constraints of this more general promise.

Last, we have Bowie's argument from chapter 10. He tells us that when employers enter into contractual relations with employees at all, this suggests certain facts about the nature of the parties to the contract. It implies that superiors must view subordinates as responsible and autonomous individuals, as moral agents who have rights that they can claim against others. Making contracts with other persons thus implies the duty to respect their rights (Bowie, 1982, pp. 46–47). Not only do employers have a duty to respect the rights of employees, they also have a duty to respect the rights of all of those with whom they have made explicit agreements, which includes customers, suppliers, creditors, government agencies, and the like. The failure to observe these duties by superiors offers a rationale for subordinates to blow the whistle. Hence, if the contract argument is thought to be authoritative in defending the *prima facie* duties of secrecy and obedience, it is also thought to carry authority in helping to defend the action or process of whistleblowing, at least in some cases.

The fourth argument for the duties of obedience and secrecy is also used as a general argument against the practice of whistleblowing itself. Because of its importance, we shall discuss it separately in the following section.

CONSEQUENTIALIST CONSIDERATIONS

The final argument against whistleblowing, and the last defense of the duties of obedience and secrecy, is based upon the negative consequences that would likely result from the act or practice of whistleblowing. Opponents to whistleblowing point to the climate of dissension and suspicion that would likely arise in the workplace if subordinate dissent and whistleblowing were to become more prevalent features of the corporation. Walters and Blumberg point out that courts have been concerned to protect the coherence of the workplace against certain real or alleged abuses of whistleblowers. They reason that without this coherence, efficiency and productivity would be markedly lessened (Walters, 1975, p. 32; Blumberg, 1971, p. 301). This could happen in a number of ways. If superiors believed that their orders would be questioned by subordinates and would be disclosed to outside agencies, they would become wary of sharing information beyond a few trusted associates, or they might become reluctant to develop a policy in any area that could cause offense. They might seek to avoid or postpone difficult decisions, such as those that concern issues of hiring and firing, the environment, or product quality. They might seek to cover themselves by disguising the true source of a directive, so that they would not be held personally responsible if someone were later to question the ethics of the directive. They might also try to shield themselves from hearing bad news from the lower ranks, so that they could plead ignorance of the existence of an illegal or unethical practice. While not treated as a virtue, such ignorance is usually perceived as preferable to active involvement in a questionable project, when it comes under fire. These latter strategies impede the clarity of the communication process in corporations and typically affect the vigor with which a directive is carried out. Not knowing the true source of an order often leads a subordinate to wonder how quickly and conscientiously he or she should execute it. And if whistleblowing became more widespread, superiors would likely spend more time and money examining the credentials and background of prospective employees, making sure they hired only the most loyal and obedient individuals. In such a climate, loyalty and obedience would likely become the reigning virtues for candidates aspiring to promotion within the firm. The one-dimensionality of middle and upper-level managers that would result from this could affect company planning in the long run, when greater flexibility or boldness might be needed from its top executives. James also mentions that a frequent consequentialist objection to whistleblowing, in addition to these detriments, is the economic cost of rectifying the situation that initially led to whistleblowing (James, 1983, p. 293). We might also add the costs of repairing the damage caused by hasty or inaccurate whistleblowing.

Further, were whistleblowing to become more widespread, it could affect worker morale. Obedient workers would be in conflict with dissenters. As second-guessing of the ethics or legality of company policy became more frequent, second-guessing of day-to-day business operations or decisions might also occur. In such an atmosphere of dissension, distrust, protest, and conflict, a company would be hard pressed to complete its usual work load, let alone expand into new projects or ventures.

Finally, we might mention certain abuses that could occur if whistleblowers were universally hailed as heroes. Westin and Bok, among others, remind us that disgruntled workers might portray themselves as whistleblowers, when in fact their motive is principally to embarrass or otherwise hurt the corporation or its executives (Westin, 1983, p. 271; Bok, 1984, p. 223). Even conscientious workers who have a sincere disagreement with management might not exercise sufficient care in obtaining information about corporate misconduct. Charges might be made that could ruin the careers of individual managers and seriously jeopardize the credibility of the firm with the public. In summarizing some of the actual or potential dangers of whistleblowing as a widespread practice, Drucker tells us that under such a system it is to be doubted whether mutual trust, productive interdependencies, and even ethics itself are possible (Drucker, 1981, p. 33).

Replies to the consequentialist argument focus around its two main features— the issues of cost and of potential abuse. Most respondents agree with the point made by James that there are financial, productive, and psychological costs associated with the practice of whistleblowing. They do not deny that it will cost the firm to correct a situation that initially prompted an act of whistleblowing or rectify the damage of an unwarranted accusation. Nor to they contest the claim that whistleblowing can at times foster dissension, disunity, and suspicion, and it can lower the productivity and efficiency of the workplace. They do, however, reject the idea that on balance the costs of whistleblowing to the company are always greater than the costs to society of failing to be informed about, or to have rectified, an instance of corporate abuse, mismanagement, neglect, or misconduct (James, 1983, p. 292). They argue that there are cases in which the danger to public health, safety, or freedom is so great that purely consequentialist considerations would justify some type of action to prevent or lessen this harm.

In addition, it might be mentioned that a society whose members are discouraged from ever protesting against or dissenting from an official policy or directive carries with it its own burdensome costs. The work of Milgram, for example, informs us of the social and psychological costs involved in an organizational atmosphere in which obedience reigns supreme (Milgram, 1974, pp. 6ff.). Finally, there is the hidden cost to firms when their methods of self-regulation and self-correction fail or are discouraged. When this occurs, a firm's level or degree of legitimacy may be questioned. This in turn may encourage the threat of increased regulation from government agencies to protect the public interest. Such a lessened degree of legitimacy may not only raise the financial and social costs to culprit corporations; it may also increase the cost to innocent companies as well.

Bok, Bowie, DeGeorge, and others address the second point. They suggest ways to mitigate the abuses that may be associated with whistleblowing. Some of these suggestions pertain to the actual or potential whistleblower, while others apply to the corporation. These authors suggest that whistleblowers should examine the situation carefully before disclosing information on corporate misconduct. They must balance the likely social harm of the corporate practice against the likely harm to the firm or its members that will result from the whistleblowing. Only when the social harm is serious, considerable, and imminent, should they consider sounding an alarm externally (Bok, 1984, p. 220; Bowie, 1982, p. 143; DeGeorge, 1986, p. 230; Peterson and Farrell, 1986, p. 14). Potential whistleblowers should also examine the accuracy of their allegations. The charges should be accurate enough to convince a reasonable person that a serious problem exists (Bok, 1984, p. 220; Bowie, 1982, p. 143; Peterson and Farrell, 1986, p. 14). Prospective whistleblowers should pursue internal channels before sounding an alarm outside the firm. Bok, Bowie, and DeGeorge tell us that in most cases whistleblowers should exhaust the internal channels. Bok recognizes three exceptions to this consideration, however. When there is not sufficient time to rectify a problem by going through internal channels, when these channels are not relevant to correcting the problem, or when the higher levels of the organization are themselves corrupt, coercive, or a part of the problem, then going outside the usual chain of command may be warranted (Bok, 1984, p. 221). Walters tells us that these exceptions are recognized by the courts as reasons for departing from the usual channels of communication within an organization (Walters, 1975, p. 30). Bowie suggests that potential whistleblowers should also determine their chances of success. Otherwise they may needlessly expose themselves to retaliation or subject the company to public suspicion and ill will (Bowie, 1982, p. 13). These considerations indicate that whistleblowers should consider external disclosure as a last resort—an option to be exercised only after careful thought has been given to it and other alternatives have proven to be ineffective.

These theorists also maintain that certain organizational changes may offset the abusive tendencies that whistleblowing can have. If the corporation has an "open-door" policy in hearing grievances from subordinates; if it has implemented an ombudsman program to communicate grievances and disagreements to higher management or the board of directors, while keeping the source of the grievance confidential; if management is concerned to explain to subordinates why it has initiated a particular program or policy of action, and if it indicates that it will not seek to retaliate against those who question or disagree with its conduct, then the incentive of corporate dissenters to go outside the firm (at least prematurely) will be much reduced. And the perception that other employees have of dissenters may be less antagonistic as well (Bok, 1984, pp. 225ff.). As we have said, these points suggest added responsibilities that corporate superiors may have in addition to those discussed in earlier chapters.

WHISTLEBLOWING AS AN OBLIGATION

We have thus far considered the question of whether there are strong arguments against the idea that whistleblowing is a warranted practice or general responsibility of corporate subordinates. We have seen that, in certain cases at least, it appears to be a general responsibility of subordinates to reveal corporate misconduct to outside sources, that is, if they fail to disclose such information, they are expected to give a rendering of themselves. The literature is in basic agreement in profiling the general circumstances in which whistleblowing is a responsibility in this sense of the term:

1. The subordinate has information about corporate mismanagement, neglect, or misconduct that is adequate enough to convince a reasonable person that something should be done to stop the corporation from doing the action in question, or at least that a full outside investigation of the alleged problem should be initiated.

2. The mismanagement, neglect, or misconduct involves serious and considerable harm to individuals or violates their basic rights without their consent.

3. The whistleblower has sought to go through the internal channels of the corporation and has either received no indication that the corporation would stop its action or has received no adequate justification of its conduct.

4. If the whistleblower does not go through inside channels, it is because he or she thinks that the organization is corrupt or part of the problem, there is not sufficient time, given the imminent harm produced or threatened by the corporate action, or the channels are not relevant to the problem at hand.

As we have seen, in addition to these four conditions, some authors add a fifth—the whistleblowing must have a good chance of success. This is a more controversial consideration that we shall discuss shortly.

From the standpoint of the concepts of this book, whistleblowing under such circumstances is a general responsibility of subordinates because one or more of the relations of accountability apply to actual or potential whistleblowers. From the standpoint of the literature of whistleblowing, however, its justification as a general responsibility of corporate subordinates under the above conditions is grounded in part upon the fact that there seem to be adequate responses to the arguments raised above against this practice. In addition, in positive support of the practice, Walters tells us that whistleblowing is an exercise of free speech that the courts feel should be protected when public policy issues are at stake (Walters, 1975, p. 27). Since it is a process or activity that can protect basic rights and promote important social values, subordinates are required to give a rendering of themselves when they do not dissent against corporate mismanagement, neglect, or misconduct in the above type of case. And there are only certain lines of defense that they can take to excuse or vindicate their inaction.

But when, if at all, is it an overriding responsibility or a morally obligatory set of actions? When is it the type of action that if not done would lead us to censure or punish a subordinate? There are three basic answers to this question.

The first view is that whistleblowing is virtually never a moral duty of subordinates, even in the *prima facie* sense of this term. This position is endorsed by French, Bowie, and Elliston, for example. Although they believe that whistleblowing can be a responsibility of subordinates, they reject the idea that it is an obligation. This means in part that although a subordinate is expected to give a rendering of some kind for his or her complicity, this rendering can refer to a number of different reasons or excuses. They are sufficient to warrant subordinate inaction. In the minds of these authors, various factors can override the call for whistleblowing. For Bowie and Elliston, these involve concern for self, career, and family; for French, these include certain features of the demands of role duties. Bowie and Elliston tell us that one cannot morally demand that individuals risk their jobs or careers and threaten their economic future and the financial security of their families to sound an alarm against their companies, even when the above four (or five) considerations are met (Bowie, 1982, p. 147; Elliston, 1982, p. 47). As we have seen, French maintains that since the role duties of subordinates rarely involve questioning corporate practices or policies, and because subordinates do not themselves initiate questionable practices, they are not responsible for corporate misconduct as long as they have not performed their assigned activities in a substandard manner as institutionally defined. They are not required to risk their jobs in order to sound an alarm against their company (French, 1984, p. 15). These authors view the whistleblower who observes the above conditions as a moral hero who goes beyond the call of duty. For them, a subordinate's complicity does not then merit moral blame or censure.

A second position on this issue is that whistleblowing may at times be a duty. DeGeorge, Bok, and Alpern seem to endorse this view. DeGeorge includes another condition, in addition to the five mentioned above, under which it is an obligation of subordinates to blow the whistle—the employee has documented evidence of corporate misconduct (DeGeorge, 1986, p. 234). Unlike Bowie, he believes that when sounding an alarm has a good chance of success, this action offsets or overrides the employee's need to protect his or her job, career, family, or financial future. And, unlike French, he believes that the values or rights protected by whistleblowing often take precedence over the good of conforming to role duties. Bok implies that whistleblowing is at times a moral duty by suggesting that one organizational or legal change that could be made to encourage this practice is to make it a legal duty for employees to blow the whistle under the general conditions listed above (Bok, 1984, p. 228). While legal duties are not identical to moral ones, a theorist's arguing for the former in cases involving the violation of basic rights or the promotion of significant harm to others offers us at least *prima facie* evidence for believing that she would argue for the latter as well. Alpern argues that certain subordinates, especially professionals such as engineers, are under a general rather than a special, obligation to blow the whistle in certain cases. The kind of duty that applies here is one of ordinary morality, namely, to avoid contributing to or promoting significant harms to people, other things being equal (Alpern, 1982, p. 41). He believes, opposing French and others, that whistleblowing by professionals does not necessarily involve acts of supererogation. It can, however, involve a different kind of moral heroism, one where professionals may be expected to show great fortitude and moral courage in persevering in their challenge or complaints (Alpern, 1982, p. 42).

The third view is that whistleblowing is usually or always an overriding obligation when the first four of the above conditions are met. Duska maintains that it is always an obligation when subordinates seek to avoid significant harm (Duska, 1985, p. 299). Some theorists add to these considerations another criterion that a whistleblower act from a good motive. Walters tells us a good motive is one in which the subordinate is primarily concerned with protecting the public interest (Walters, 1975, p. 28). Mankin, and Peterson and Farrell reject DeGeorge and Bowie's suggestion that the whistleblower should have a good chance of success. They believe that subordinates may be obligated to do what they can to prevent a serious harm, even when they are not sure that their actions will prove to be effective (Mankin, 1981, p. 15; Peterson and Farrell, 1986, p. 14). Since the costs borne by the subordinates in getting another job typically do not compare to the harm caused by a firm in violating the basic rights of third parties, the existence of personal risks or the reduced chances of success in whistleblowing do not excuse or vindicate those subordinates who remain compliant.

This ends our discussion of the main arguments for and against whistleblowing as a general responsibility and as a duty of subordinates in corporate organizations. As with our discussion of the responsibility of superiors, we have seen many arguments raised and several positions advanced here, but we see again that the proper evaluation of these arguments depends upon our understanding of the assumptions discussed earlier in the book. Both discussions are complicated by the inability of theorists to agree on these assumptions. The question of subordinate responsibility is further complicated by differences in assumptions about collective responsibility, differences that themselves can in part also be analyzed in terms of the concepts and assumptions discussed earlier. We shall pursue this theme more fully in the next chapter, where I shall seek to explain the relation of the assumptions of corporate responsibility to the present issue.

Before doing so, however, we should end this chapter with a matter that was mentioned earlier and then bracketed. I made reference to the positions on whistleblowing that have been advanced within the four theories of corporate responsibility. But, what would advocates of the four theories say in general about the responsibility or duty of subordinates to blow the whistle against their companies? Since we shall be making general observations, we shall speak only about the broad tendencies that these theories manifest.

Of the four theories, the classical position is the least likely to endorse whistleblowing as a responsibility or duty of corporate subordinates. Classical theorists who support this practice are likely to endorse it in cases where serious violations of the law have occurred or where upper management is engaged in practices that defraud or otherwise seriously jeopardize the financial interests or rights of the shareholders. This position is apt to view the labor of the workers as the property of the corporation and is less likely to advocate the idea that whistleblowing is ever a duty of subordinates. Moreover, the theory does not typically endorse the position that corporations should restructure themselves to encourage channels of internal dissent within the firm.

Since stakeholder theorists support the rights of stakeholder groups, they are more likely to defend the right of free speech of the workers. This is especially true when the interests or basic rights of (other) stakeholders are markedly threatened by a corporate policy. Because professional groups are stakeholders, these theorists are likely to appeal to professional codes of conduct (in addition to the law) to determine when internal and external dissent is justified. They may also suggest that professionals have a duty to blow the whistle in certain cases and that corporations should restructure themselves to accommodate the rights of speech and expression of their members.

Social demandingness theorists will tend to continue the arguments of stakeholder theorists. They will likely expand the list of individuals whose rights should be protected to include the general public and they will probably urge subordinates to blow the whistle, not only for violations of law or breaches of professional ethics, but also in cases where corporations ignore the standards of common morality. These theorists are also likely to expand the list of individuals for whom whistleblowing is a duty to include nonprofessionals as well. These general tendencies can, however, be counteracted in societies that do not demand much socially or morally from corporations or their workers.

Finally, social activist theorists are more likely than any of the other theorists to argue that in nearly every case where whistleblowing is justified, it is also a duty of corporate subordinates. They tend to be the strongest supporters of the practice in the widest of circumstances. They are also the most likely to argue that corporations must change their structures to facilitate, and even encourage, internal dissent without corporate retaliation or punishment.

REFERENCES

Alpern, Kenneth D. 1982. "Engineers as Moral Heroes." In *Beyond Whistleblowing: Defining Engineer's Responsibilities*, edited by Vivian Weil, pp. 40–51. Chicago: Illinois Institute of Technology.

Baron, Marcia. 1984. *The Moral Status of Loyalty*. Dubuque, Iowa: Kendall-Hunt Publishing Company.

Blumberg, Phillip I. 1971. "Corporate Responsibility and the Employee's Duty of Loyalty and Obedience: A Preliminary Inquiry." *Oklahoma Law Review*, vol. 24, no. 3, pp. 279–318.

———. 1983. "Corporate Responsibility and the Employee's Duty of Loyalty and Obedience." In *Ethical Theory and Business*, 2d ed., edited by Tom L. Beauchamp and Norman E. Bowie, pp. 132–38. Englewood Cliffs, N.J.: Prentice-Hall.

Bok, Sissela. 1980. "Whistleblowing and Professional Responsibility." *New York Education Quarterly*, vol. 2, Summer, pp. 2–10.

————. 1984. *Secrets: On the Ethics of Concealment and Revelation*. New York: Vintage Press.

Bowie, Norman. 1982. *Business Ethics*. Englewood Cliffs, N.J.: Prentice-Hall.

Chalk, Rosemary, and Frank von Hippel. 1979. "Due Process for the Bearers of Ill Tidings: Dealing with Technical Dissent in the Organization." *Technical Review*, June–July, pp. 50–56.

Cooper, D. E. 1972. "Responsibility and the System." In *Individual and Collective Responsibility: The Massacre at My Lai*, edited by Peter A. French, pp. 83–102. Cambridge, Mass.: Schenckman Publishing Company.

DeGeorge, Richard. 1986. *Business Ethics*. New York: Macmillan Company.

Donaldson, Thomas. 1982. *Corporations and Morality*. Englewood Cliffs, N.J.: Prentice-Hall.

Downie, R. S. 1972. "Responsibility and Social Roles." In *Individual and Collective Responsibility: The Massacre at My Lai*, edited by Peter A. French, pp. 65–82. Cambridge, Mass.: Schenckman Publishing Company.

Drucker, Peter. 1981. "What Is Business Ethics?" *The Public Interest*, October, pp. 18–36.

Duska, Ronald. 1985. "Whistleblowing and Employee Loyalty." In *Contemporary Issues in Business Ethics*, edited by Joseph R. DesJardin and John J. McCall, pp. 295–300. Belmont, Calif.: Wadsworth Publishing Company.

Ellin, Joseph. 1982. "Special Professional Morality and the Duty of Veracity." *Business and Professional Ethics Journal*, Winter, pp. 75–90.

Elliston, Frederick A. 1982. "Anonymous Whistleblowing." *Business and Professional Ethics Journal*, Winter, pp. 39–58.

Flores, Albert, and Deborah Johnson. 1983. "Collective Responsibility and Professional Roles." *Ethics*, April, pp. 537–46.

French, Peter A. 1984. *Collective and Corporate Responsibility*. New York: Columbia University Press.

Goldman, Alan H. 1980. "Business Ethics: Profits, Utilities and Moral Rights." *Philosophy and Public Affairs*, Spring, pp. 260–86.

Gulick, Walter. 1982. "Is It Ever Morally Justifiable for Corporate Officials to Break the Law?" *Business and Professional Ethics Journal*, Spring pp. 25–47.

Held, Virginia. 1972. "Moral Responsibility and Collective Action." In *Individual and Collective Responsibility: The Massacre at My Lai*, edited by Peter A. French, pp. 103–20. Cambridge, Mass.: Schenckman Publishing Company.

Jackall, Robert. 1988. *Moral Mazes: The World of Corporate Managers*. Oxford: Oxford University Press.

James, Gene G. 1983. "Whistleblowing: Its Nature and Justification." In *Business Ethics*, edited by Milton Snoeyenbos, Robert Almeder, and James Humber, pp. 287–302. Buffalo, N.Y.: Prometheus Books.

Jones, W. T. 1984. "Public Roles, Private Roles and Differential Moral Assessments of Role Performance." *Ethics*, July, pp 603–19.

Ladd, John. 1967. "Loyalty." In *Encyclopedia of Philosophy*, vol. 5, edited by Paul Edwards, pp. 97–98. New York: Macmillan Company.

Mankin, Hart T. 1981. "Commentary on 'Ethical Responsibilities of Engineers in Large Organizations: The Pinto Case.' " *Business and Professional Ethics Journal*, Fall, pp. 15–18.

Michalos, Alex C. 1983. "The Loyal Agents' Argument." In *Ethical Theory and Business*, edited by Tom L. Beauchamp and Norman E. Bowie, pp. 247–54. Englewood Cliffs, N.J.: Prentice-Hall.

Milgram, Stanley. 1974. *Obedience to Authority*. New York: Harper and Row.

Oldenquist, Andrew. 1982. "Loyalties." *Journal of Philosophy*, vol. 79, no. 4, pp. 179–93.

Peterson, James C., and Dan Farrell. 1986. *Whistleblowing: Ethical and Legal Issues in Expressing Dissent*. Dubuque, Iowa: Kendall-Hunt Publishing Company.

Pollock, Lansing. 1981. *The Freedom Principle*. Buffalo, N.Y.: Prometheus Book.

Roche, James M. 1971. "The Competitive System, To Work, To Preserve, and To Protect." *Vital Speeches of the Day*, May, pp. 443–46.

Royce, Josiah. 1908. *The Philosophy of Loyalty*. New York: Macmillan Company.

Walsh, W. H. 1970. "Pride, Shame and Responsibility." *The Philosophical Quarterly*, January, pp. 1–13.

Walters, Kenneth. 1975. "Your Employee's Right to Blow the Whistle." *Harvard Business Review*, July–August, pp. 26–34, 161–62.

———. 1987. "The Whistleblower and the Law." In *Business and Society: Dimensions of Conflict and Cooperation*, edited by S. Prakesh Sethi and Cecilia M. Falk, pp. 283–92. Lexington, Mass.: Lexington Books.

Werhane, Patricia. 1985. *Persons, Rights and Corporations*. Englewood Cliffs, N.J.: Prentice-Hall.

Westin, Alan F. 1983. "What Can and Should Be Done to Protect Whistleblowers in Industry." In *Ethical Theory and Business*, edited by Tom Beauchamp and Norman Bowie, pp. 270–75. Englewood Cliffs, N.J.: Prentice-Hall.

17

THE CORPORATE RESPONSIBILITY DEBATE

INTRODUCTION

It has been contended here that there is presently no clear resolution to the swirls of conflict that attend the corporate responsibility debate. Some positions appear to be more convincing than others, perhaps, but this still leaves several opposing answers available for the various questions raised in this book. Although I have not sought to resolve the disputes brought up here, I have tried to give the reader a better understanding of the conceptual ground upon which these theoretical skirmishes are being fought. And I have tried to show that a good part of the reason why no clear answers have yet emerged lies in the complicated nature of the debate. Not only are the various positions on corporate responsibility in dispute, but a host of accompanying assumptions and underlying models are involved in the disagreement as well. Until these are understood and addressed, it is doubtful that a convincing answer to the major question will emerge.

In a previous publication, I suggested that one way to begin the process of resolving some of the applied issues that arise in this area is to pair off considerations of the same sort and evaluate them with reference to each other (Brummer, 1985, p. 18). At that time, I was dealing with a specific moral issue and organized the pairs of arguments simply around deontological and consequentialist strategies of reasoning. In the present work, I have considerably expanded the matrix within which pairs of arguments are advanced. I have expanded the number of argument strategies to nine, made reference to eight models of accountability relationships, and considered eight ways of looking at the nature of corporations. I have also considered various positions on the nature of the diffusion or distribution of collective responsibility. This provides us with a debate matrix that is considerably more complicated than that of the earlier article. And I believe it has considerably more explanatory power as well. It permits us to evaluate the work of authors who write about the responsibilities of corporations, not only in terms of what they say and how they argue, but also in terms of what they overlook or do not express. The absence of argument is often as telling as the quality of the arguments an author actually presents.

We must then recognize that in this area a conceptual grid work of theories, models, arguments, and the like already exists. We must decipher and understand this grid work before we can begin the more arduous process of resolving various disputes and conflicts that arise here. Since the grid work, or system of matrices, discussed in this work is multi-dimensional, reference to its various dimensions will help us to appreciate both the depth and scope of the four theories of corporate responsibility and their applications. In this chapter I propose to illustrate briefly aspects of this multi-dimensionality, as well as to provide an example of the more expanded method of pairing. The method is supposed to be used for each of the assumptions: the relations, models, and strategies. But we shall apply it to only one matrix—the relations of accountability, using the arguments of the last chapter.

As a point of methodology, it should be mentioned that a fully adequate solution to the questions of corporate responsibility, such as the warrantedness of plant relocation or the compellingness of whistleblowing in certain types of situations, demands that a theorist show the strongest set of arguments in each of the paired groups; and he or she must do this for each of the matrices discussed in this book. If the strongest set of arguments uniformly points to the same conclusion, the applied problem is, of course, resolved. If they point to various conclusions, we must then develop additional strategies to determine what kinds of consideration take precedence in situations of conflict. Determining the nature of these latter strategies goes beyond the scope of the present book, however.

WHISTLEBLOWING AND THE RELATIONS OF ACCOUNTABILITY

Pairing the arguments for and against whistleblowing around the assumptional matrix of the relations of accountability yields the following account.

Promise Keeping

Various theorists who oppose whistleblowing do so because of the implicit or explicit promise made between employees and employers. They maintain that employment contracts often make reference to the *prima facie* duties of loyalty, confidentiality, and obedience, or they allege that workers give their implied consent to these duties by their continued employment with the firm. This implicit or explicit consent is often seen as grounding the role duties that subordinates have. And the presence of such duties disqualifies or overrides any alleged responsibility or duty to blow the whistle.

Proponents of whistleblowing point to the promise to serve the public interest that is typically given by individuals as a condition of their membership in professional groups. Social contract theorists contend that there is an implied promise between corporations and society to protect the latter's interests. They argue that all members of the corporation must respond to the demands of this promise. Last, some theorists maintain that the very presence of a contract or promise between subordinates and superiors or between corporations and external stakeholders demands that both parties respect the rationality and autonomy of each other. When corporate superiors fail to do this, subordinates may be responsible to dissent or to point out this omission.

The Fiduciary Model

Opponents of whistleblowing often defend their view by appealing to the fiduciary relationship that exists between managers and stockholders. The former are to oversee the financial interests of the latter and protect their investments in the firm. Derivatively, all employees are viewed as at least quasi agents for the shareholders. From a more general point of view, some opponents treat employees as agents of the corporation itself. In either view, the fiduciary model is seen as an important ground for the subordinates' duties of loyalty, obedience, and confidentiality.

While advocates of whistleblowing, on the other hand, do not usually argue that employees are unique stewards or agents for society who thus have special obligations to protect the public interest, there are two exceptions. Social contract theories treat corporate members as quasi fiduciaries for the public, but it should be mentioned that their position is in turn often based upon the implied promise between corporations and society (the promise-keeping model) and the power of society (through government) to replace corporations with other forms of business enterprise (the reverse-impact model). Much the same can be said for the second type of exception—those who emphasize the fiduciary aspects of professional responsibilities. In this case, however, the defense of professional duties is not entirely grounded upon one of the other models, though the responsibility is meant to apply only to professionals. Last, we should mention that some theorists challenge the allegedly altruistic aspects of the fiduciary model as it is endorsed by some opponents of whistleblowing. They argue that since self-serving motives are also at work in the role duties of employees, these roles are not entirely public or nonvoluntary in nature. Thus, the principles of common morality apply to them and may be used to justify whistleblowing in certain cases.

The Representative or Functionary Model

Critics of whistleblowing argue that since superiors have the power to replace subordinates, the latter must consider and respond to the formers' demands. They tell us that the employees' duties of loyalty and obedience in the private sector are founded largely upon the common law principle of employment at will. Employees are not encouraged to act upon their own discretion or prerogatives; they must act as the loyal representatives of those who can replace them. Furthermore, even those theorists who grant that whistleblowing is a legitimate responsibility of subordinates (but not a duty) argue that the power of replacement that superiors have over subordinates indicates that sounding an alarm against a company is too heroic an act to be considered as an obligatory feature of an employee's occupational role duties.

Advocates of whistleblowing sometimes point to other groups or constituencies that have the power of replacement or elimination. Professional groups can take away the licenses of those professionals whose failure to inform the public of the harmful consequences of a corporate policy leads to unnecessary deaths or injuries of innocent people. And social contract theorists remind us that government has the power to restrict or remove a corporate charter and even to abolish or significantly alter one of the traditional characteristics of the corporate form of business enterprise. That it has thus far chosen not to exercise this power is not a sufficient reason to believe it may not do so in the future. Finally, advocates contend that exceptions to the employment at will doctrine are now recognized by the courts. For reporting breaches of professional ethics, violations of the law, or corporate activities that significantly harm the public interest, employees may successfully sue to get their jobs back if the company has retaliated against them by firing them.

The Impact Model

One major strand in the argument against whistleblowing considers the negative consequences of the single act or general practice of external dissent. We have seen mention of inefficiency and lack of productivity brought on by dissension and discord in the workplace and by the second-guessing of orders that whistleblowing might foster. Opponents also maintain that corporate decision making might become risk aversive, slow to be made or implemented, and done by executives who are more one dimensional in their management style. All this translates into higher costs for firms and society. Finally, some theorists contend that their past obedience and loyalty binds subordinates to fulfill the expectation of continued obedience in the future.

Advocates charge that the economic and human costs to society in lives lost, injuries incurred, or rights violated are also great if acts of corporate misconduct or negligence go unchallenged from internal sources. Often these costs are greater than the costs of whistleblowing. In the longer run, society must bear the added economic and noneconomic costs of increased government regulation that will likely result if various strategies of self-regulation prove to be ineffective. Finally, they suggest that some of the burdens and costs of whistleblowing would be lessened if corporations changed their organizational structures and policies to permit expressions of subordinate dissent without retaliation and if the whistle-

blower would follow certain guidelines and precautions in the method of ex
pressing his or her challenge to superiors or outsiders.

Reverse-Impact Model

Opponents of whistleblowing point out that one of its costs is the retaliatio
that might occur if consumers, suppliers, lenders, government agencies, or othe
stakeholders decide to punish a corporation for an alleged wrongdoing brough
out prematurely by an employee. If safeguards against disclosure are not ob
served, the burden of this retaliation can be especially costly. Opponents of th
idea that whistleblowing is sometimes a duty argue that the retaliation (othe
than replacement) that corporate superiors can carry out against subordinate
gives additional weight to the conclusion that in the few cases in which it i
justified, it is a heroic act that is supererogatory or discretionary in nature.

Proponents of whistleblowing appeal to the reverse-impact model when the
point out that various groups may seek to retaliate against a firm if they believ
that they have been victimized by it, or if they believe that the degree of th
firm's legitimacy has been lowered. For example, the corporation must bear th
added burdens and costs of increased stakeholder suspicion, professional vigi
lance, and government regulation that might occur if methods of corporate self
regulation like whistleblowing remain dormant. And social contract theorist
mention the possibility that the corporate form of business enterprise might itsel
be altered.

The Teamwork or Collegial Model

Advocates of the disloyalty argument place particular emphasis upon the team
work model. The discord and dissension that whistleblowers can foster interfere
with the team spirit that superiors usually try to develop in the corporation. Thi
kind of discord is said to be unfair to those who are hurt by unwanted disclosure
or by the ensuing disruption in normal working operations and projects that ma
occur. Whistleblowing promotes an atmosphere in which not everyone is doing
his or her part in achieving company goals.

Proponents of whistleblowing sometimes appeal to what they take to be
higher standard of corporate loyalty, teamwork, and fair play. As they see it, i
superiors are demanding that subordinates break the law or infringe upon th
usual standards of common morality, they are not playing fair or being loyal t
the company. When this is eventually discovered, the entire corporation ma
suffer for the unwise decisions of a few individuals. This in turn may mean tha
otherwise innocent shareholders or workers in the company will suffer. Superior
would not order such actions if they were considering the long-term good of th
team. They have reciprocal duties to the other members of the team that the
are not fulfilling when they ask or demand that subordinates do such things
Moreover, advocates of whistleblowing maintain that concern for loyalty an

team spirit would likely lead prospective whistleblowers to use the safeguards mentioned in the previous chapter. And it would lead superiors to make organizational changes so that internal dissent would not be such a disruptive action or practice. Since the teamwork model also includes collegial relations, it is felt that whistleblowing is consistent with the collegial aspects of professional responsibility. Finally, proponents sometimes make use of a wider concept of teamwork, one in which an entire society is viewed as a kind of team, with corporations and other institutions being treated as its members. Within this scheme, corporations that significantly harm the public interest are seen as socially disruptive free riders that are willing to sacrifice the team's good in order to gain their own advantage.

The Ownership Model

The ownership or dominion model is used by some critics of whistleblowing to ground their thesis that subordinates have special obligations toward superiors or corporate stockholders. Since corporations own their assets, subordinates have a duty to respect their ownership rights to confidential information. Revealing this information is a kind of theft or trespass. In addition, some believe that the duty of obedience can in part be grounded upon the corporation's ownership or dominion over the work effort and activity of employees. And some theorists suggest that the ownership relation is the basis of the stockholders' right to have their investments protected. To the extent that whistleblowing interferes with this protection, it is unjustified.

Supporters of whistleblowing contest the idea that labor is to be treated as an asset on a par with the other pieces of property owned by the corporation. The corporation owns the results of labor, not the activity, expertise, and motivation that goes into it. Insofar as loyalty, obedience, and secrecy are connected to the motivation and work effort of the employee, they are within his or her power and prerogative. They are not entirely owned or controlled by the firm. Further, some theorists reject the idea that shareholders have a right to dividends. When the latter invest money in a corporation, the risk they willingly bear makes them more akin to gamblers than to property holders. Third, since all private property owned in this country is held under the condition and principle of eminent domain, it is recognized that concern for the common good sometimes supersedes concern for individual property rights. The same point applies in certain cases of whistleblowing. Finally, conspiracy theorists, who were discussed in chapter 15, believe that subordinates have some dominion over or ownership in the mismanagement or misconduct of the superiors if they follow the latters' orders without dissent or protest. This implies that they are part of a conspiracy-like relation if they fail to withdraw from it or blow the whistle. It is thus unjustified for them to try to assign responsibility elsewhere (or only to the superiors) in these cases.

The Regulation Model

Opponents of the idea that whistleblowing is a general responsibility of subordinates believe that corporate members should follow the implicit and explicit regulations of the company, regulations that are found in the codes of conduct and the corporate culture for subordinates, as well as in the functions of their occupational roles. These will for the most part reaffirm the virtues of subordinate loyalty, obedience, and confidentiality.

Advocates of whistleblowing, though, contend that following these regulations sometimes leads to whistleblowing. Moreover, they believe that there are other regulations that need to be consulted, such as the laws of the land and professional codes of conduct. Social activists would also contend that the universal laws of morality in which they believe constitute additional regulations to be considered. Each of these types of regulation gives some support for whistleblowing as a responsibility of subordinates.

MULTI-DIMENSIONALITY AND THE CORPORATE RESPONSIBILITY DEBATE

The present example of the method of pairing illustrates part of the intricacy of the corporate responsibility debate. We see that even within the various dimensions of a single matrix of assumptions, there are several arguments both for and against the warrantedness of a certain practice. The complexity here is further compounded when we extend the pairing process to the other assumptions and matrices. One can imagine the added intricacy of interpreting this set of pairings from the perspective of the private property model of the corporation when the strategy of legitimization is, first the performance strategy and, next the rights strategy, for example—and then using these same strategies from within the social contract model of the corporation, and so on.

It is not that consideration of the other assumptions yields entirely novel pairings or arguments, of course, though we would expect to see some new ones arise at times. Nor does such consideration immediately show how to select among or between a set of initial argument pairings. In fact, the relation between the pairings of various assumptional matrices is itself a rather complicated matter. Some of the unmentioned or newer argument pairings are relatively neutral with regard to the earlier pairings. They do not help to select a winner. For example, pairings for the formalist strategy of justifying claims to legitimacy do not always arbitrate between different elements or sides of the argument built upon the impact model. Furthermore, some of the pairings not considered here are neutral with respect to the components of the matrices themselves. They do not tell us which model or strategy should be included and which excluded. Thus, the formalist strategy again does not favor the impact model over the teamwork or fiduciary models. It applies equally well to all of these models. However, some of the newer dimensions of these matrices do support specific components of earlier matrices. The enterprise model of the corporation, for example, favors the teamwork model of accountability relations; the private property model of the corporation favors the ownership relation; the contract model of the corporation favors the promise-keeping model, and so on. This tells us that some of the grids or lines of argument that exist here naturally link up with others.

But even when one dimension of a matrix favors another, it does not always indicate how to resolve the paired arguments in the latter dimension. Thus, the consent form of the procedural strategy of argument favors the promise-keeping model of accountability relations, but this does not by itself tell us how to choose between or among the paired arguments that arise within the latter model for it does not tell us which promise or application of implied consent is to take precedence. Further, appeal to later matrices sometimes opposes an earlier dimension of a pairing. For example, Duska's specific appeal to the conflict version of the machine model of the corporation leads him to reject the application of the teamwork or collegial relation of accountability to the whistleblowing debate. And appeal to the strategy of respect for persons leads to a rejection of many of the arguments opposing whistleblowing from within the ownership model (because the latter seem to imply that certain internal aspects of the workers' lives are owned by the company). Sometimes appeal to a dimension of a later matrix favors a certain side in the pairing of arguments within an earlier dimension. But even here, additional interpretation may often be needed. Thus, we have seen in the whistleblowing debate that the organic and enterprise models of the corporation favor one side of the argument pairs within the fiduciary and teamwork models of accountability relations—the opponents' side—but when these models are broadened to apply to society as a whole (so society itself is viewed as an organism or an enterprise), they tend to favor the other side of these pairs and are used at times to support whistleblowing.

In general, it can be said that if one of these matrices becomes the focus around which an examination of the arguments on a specific question of corporate responsibility is performed, this will tend to yield a different mix or pairing of arguments and a somewhat different overall evaluation, than if another matrix is used. But greater uniformity, convergence, or congruity should occur as a theorist considers the other matrices. Given the overall complexity of the factors and assumptions that need to be considered, we can see the danger of coming to a conclusion on a particular question of corporate responsibility while building one's case around an examination of only a few dimensions of the assumptional matrices.

What general rules of methodology should be observed if we are to make headway in understanding the corporate responsibility debate? We must at a minimum follow these steps:

1. Consider and detail the main assumptions about corporate responsibility upon which a specific question is based (eg., accountability relations, the nature of the corporation,

strategies for justifying legitimacy claims, and collective and individual responsibility, etc.).

2. Isolate the various models or dimensions that belong to the assumptional matrices (eg., the promise-keeping, fiduciary, and impact models, etc.).

3. Rely upon the current literature and one's own analytical ability to state the various arguments for and against the issue in question.

4. Pair these arguments along one matrix. Fill in arguments, when appropriate, where there are gaps in the matrix.

5. Evaluate the arguments so paired. See if they converge to yield a uniform conclusion.

6. Pair the arguments along the other matrices. Fill in missing arguments, where appropriate.

7. Evaluate the arguments so paired.

If the latter process of evaluation converges to a uniform conclusion that is coherent with the conclusions reached by earlier evaluations of different pairings, one has good grounds for believing in the conclusion. But we can expect that this would in all probability occur very rarely. So, when the evaluation process yields diverse conclusions, additional steps are needed. These steps will take one into explorations of assumptions in theoretical ethics—assumptions such as how to evaluate normative issues and how to choose between conflicting evaluations (or theories of evaluation). This exploration is well beyond the content of the present volume, however. And it must be frankly admitted that, at this level, full consensus or adequacy of evaluation may not, perhaps, even be achieved. But whether or not this is so must be left for another work.

In conclusion, the present work has had as its aim to understand the theories of corporate responsibility and two important areas of their application. It has also sought to connect these matters to the question of corporate legitimacy. It ends with the somewhat expected conclusion that more work needs to be done for it to be said that we truly understand the issues involved here. We do know at least that we are studying an area whose conceptual gridwork has largely been in place before we have begun to think seriously about these matters. And we also know that it will pay us well to know or master this gridwork before we begin to speculate further on the nature of corporate legitimacy and responsibility. Beyond this, though, we must come to understand better the nature and resolution of conflict—especially the type of conflict of responsibility or duty brought up here. Gaining an understanding of this conflict is not the same as resolving it, of course, but the latter is perhaps presently the wiser or more prudent course to pursue. And it is certainly demanding enough to keep us busy.

REFERENCE

Brummer, James. 1985. "The Foreign Corrupt Practices Act and the Dilemma of Applied Ethics." *Business and Professional Ethics Journal*, Fall, pp. 17–42.

BIBLIOGRAPHIC ESSAY

THE THEORIES OF CORPORATE RESPONSIBILITY

There are several significant works in which the various theories of corporate responsibility are advocated. In addition to Milton Friedman's *Capitalism and Freedom* (Chicago: University of Chicago Press, 1968), and ''The Social Responsibility of Business Is to Increase Its Profits,'' *The New York Times Magazine*, September 13, 1970, pp. 32–33, 122–126, the classical theory is endorsed by F. A. Hayek in *Law, Legislation and Liberty: The Mirage of Social Justice* (Chicago: University of Chicago Press, 1976) and by James Buchanan in *The Limits of Liberty* (Chicago: University of Chicago Press, 1975). Finally, it can be seen in Robert Hessen's *In Defense of the Corporation* (Stanford, Calif.: The Hoover Institution Press, 1979).

The stakeholder theory is represented in the works of Douglas McGregor, *The Human Side of Enterprise* (New York: McGraw-Hill, 1960) and Thomas Peters and Robert Waterman, Jr., *In Search of Excellence: Lessons from America's Best Run Companies* (New York: Warner Books, 1982). It can also be seen in Russell Ackoff, *Creating the Corporate Future* (New York: John Wiley and Sons, 1981) and in David Ewing, *Freedom Inside the Organization* (New York: E. P. Dutton, 1977). And aspects of the stakeholder theory are present in the work of Patricia Werhane, *Persons, Rights and Corporations* (Englewood Cliffs, N.J.: Prentice-Hall, 1985) and Edward Freeman, *Strategic Management: A Stakeholder Approach* (Marshfield, Mass.: Pitman Books, 1984).

Books or articles that endorse the social demandingness theory include Melvin Anshen, *Corporate Strategies for Social Performance* (New York: Macmillan Publishing Co., 1980); George Cabot Lodge, ''Top Priority: Renovating Our Ideology,'' *Harvard Business Review* (September–October 1970), pp. 43–55; and, Darrell J. Fasching, ''A Case for Corporate and Management Ethics,'' *California Management Review* (Summer 1981), pp. 62–76. Aspects of the social demandingness theory can be found in Edward Freeman, *Strategic Management: A Stakeholder Approach* (Marshfield, Mass.: Pitman Books, 1984); and Robert Ackerman and Raymond Bauer, *Corporate Social Responsiveness: The Modern Dilemma* (Reston, Va.: Reston Publishing Co., 1976).

The social activist theory is represented in the work of Theodore Purchell, "A Practical Guide to Ethics in Business," *Business and Society Review* (Spring 1975), pp. 43–50; Norman Bowie, *Business Ethics*, (Englewood Cliffs, N.J.: Prentice-Hall, 1982); and Archie Carroll, *Business and Society: Managing Corporate Social Performance* (Boston: Little, Brown and Co., 1981). It can also be found in Peter Singer, "Famine, Affluence and Morality," in Thomas Mappes and Jane Zembaty, *Social Ethics: Morality and Social Policy*, 2d ed., (New York: McGraw-Hill, 1982), pp. 359–365, and in Alan Goldman, "Business Ethics: Profits, Utilities and Moral Rights," *Philosophy and Public Affairs* (Spring 1980), pp. 260–268.

PLANT RELOCATION AND WHISTLEBLOWING

The more specific problem of plant relocation is addressed in the following works: Richard McKenzie, *Plant Closings: Public or Private Choices* (Washington, D.C.: The Cato Institute, 1982); Barry Bluestone and Bennett Harrison, *Capital and Communities: The Causes and Consequences of Private Disinvestment* (Washington, D.C.: The Progressive Alliance, 1980); Arlene Holen, *Losses to Workers Displaced by Plant Closure or Layoff: A Survey of the Literature* (Alexandria, Va.: Center for Naval Analyses, 1976); and John P. Kavanagh, "Ethical Issues in Plant Relocation," *Business and Professional Ethics Journal* (Winter 1982), pp 21–33.

Books addressing the whistleblowing issue include: Marcia Baron, *The Moral Status of Loyalty* (Dubuque, Iowa: Kendall-Hunt Publishing Co., 1984); Sissela Bok, *Secrets: On the Ethics of Concealment and Revelation* (New York: Vintage Press, 1984); James C. Peterson and Dan Farrell, *Whistleblowing: Ethical and Legal Issues in Expressing Dissent* (Dubuque, Iowa: Kendall-Hunt Publishing Co., 1986). Articles on this question include Kenneth Walters, "Your Employees' Right to Blow the Whistle," *Harvard Business Review* (July–August 1975), pp. 26–34, 161–62; and Frederick Elliston, "Anonymous Whistleblowing," *Business and Professional Ethics Journal* (Winter 1982), pp. 39–58.

GENERAL TEXTS

There are many good general texts on the social responsibilities of business managers. These include: Robert Ackerman and Raymond Bauer, *Corporate Social Responsiveness: The Modern Dilemma* (Reston, Va.: Reston Publishing Co., 1976); Keith Davis and Robert L. Blomstrom, *Business and Society: Environment and Responsibility* (New York: McGraw-Hill, 1980); George Sawyer, *Business and Society: Managing Corporate Social Impact* (Boston: Houghton Mifflin Co., 1979); Grover Starling, *The Changing Environment of Business: A Managerial Approach* (Boston: Dent Publishing Co., 1980); and Frederick Sturdivant, *Business and Society: A Managerial Approach* (Homewood, Ill.: Richard D. Irwin Press, 1981).

Finally, there are several good general texts in business ethics. These include: Tom L. Beauchamp and Norman Bowie, *Ethical Theory and Business*, 2d ed. (Englewood Cliffs, N.J.: Prentice-Hall, 1983); Richard DeGeorge, *Business Ethics* (New York: Macmillan Publishing Co., 1986); Joseph DesJardin and John J. McCall, *Contemporary Issues in Business Ethics* (Belmont, Calif.: Wadsworth Publishing Co., 1985); and Milton Snoeyenbos, Robert Almeder, and James Humber, *Business Ethics* (Buffalo, N.Y.: Prometheus Books, 1983).

AUTHOR INDEX

SUBJECT INDEX

About the Author

JAMES J. BRUMMER is Associate Professor of Philosophy at the University of Wisconsin-Eau Claire. His articles have appeared in *Business and Professional Ethics Journal* and *Journal of Business Ethics*.